# TRUST NO ONE

———— ⚜ ————

# TRUST NO ONE

*The Glamorous Life and*
*Bizarre Death of*
*Doris Duke*

Ted Schwarz
*with Tom Rybak*

ST. MARTIN'S PRESS

NEW YORK

Design by Ellen R. Sasahara

Library of Congress Cataloging-in-Publication Data

Schwarz, Ted.
    Trust no one: the glamorous life and bizarre death of Doris
    Duke / by Ted Schwarz, with Tom Rybak.
        p.    cm.
    ISBN 0-312-14583-7
    1. Duke, Doris, 1912–1993.   2. United States—Biography.
3. Celebrities—United States—Biography.    I. Rybak, Tom.
II. Title.
CT275.D8769S38    1997
973.92'092—dc20
[B]                                                          96-44843
                                                                CIP

First Edition: April 1997

10  9  8  7  6  5  4  3  2  1

*For my parents, Mr. and Mrs. P. Rybak,*
*who taught me that you don't need*
*to be rich to be happy.*

# Acknowledgments

———— ⚜ ————

THE AUTHORS WISH to give special thanks to New York City researcher Brian Wimer for his extensive contributions to this book. Wimer was responsible for locating historical data, public information, and, at times, previously unpublished documents that helped shed a broader light on Doris Duke and her friends than had formerly been available.

# Contents

⸙

# Introduction

⚜

*T*HE MEN AND WOMEN who gathered by Doris Duke's bedside had been expected for seventy years. Her father, Buck Duke, had spoken of their coming in much the manner that parents try to frighten a child into good behavior with stories of the bogeyman. Had he lived long enough to know them, he probably would have considered them betrayers of Doris's trust. As it was, he would warn her of their deadliness without knowing what names they would use or in what occupations they would present themselves.

You are too tall, too rich, and too unattractive for any man ever to love you for yourself, Buck Duke had cautioned his daughter from the time she was entering puberty. The only men who will seek you out are those who want to use you, then break your heart by discarding you when they have enjoyed themselves at your expense.

Buck Duke's cynicism was born of a life spent amassing great wealth and defiling large numbers of virgins (as well as enjoying the favors of more experienced women). He had known the betrayal that great wealth can bring, even from supposedly loving bedmates. He was murdered as he lay ill by one of the few people he had trusted to coordinate his caregiving, his wife of eighteen years.

The fact that Nanaline Holt Inman Duke's deliberate hastening of her husband's death was never spoken of aloud had to do with the family's power and high society's desire to always protect its own. No one investigated whether the rumors of gradual poisoning were true. The servants remained publicly silent after Buck, suffering from pneumonia, was stripped of all covers and placed in a freezing room. Nanaline claimed it was an old Southern remedy for curing disease and one that the freezing, though unconscious Buck would have wanted if he could have requested it. Then she stayed by his side, wrapped in expensive fur coats to stay warm, until his body's immune system was so weakened that he died.

The less than grieving widow emerged from the bedroom to announce the tragic death of her supposedly beloved Buck. No one is known to have contradicted the charade. Only in the sanctity of the servants' quarters did anyone dare repeat the rumors. Only there did they whisper words that hinted of murder.

Ironically, Buck Duke's only child would inherit almost everything from her father, including what Doris might have considered to be his karma. The only difference was that Buck Duke was killed by an angry wife seeking vengeance for a will denying her first son by a previous marriage what she felt was the rightful inheritance from his stepfather. Doris Duke's untimely death had more to do with a self-destructive lifestyle in which the pursuit of pleasure would eventually be at the expense of her health.

<hr>

DORIS DUKE TRIED to follow her father's advice for most of her eighty years. Despite living on the edge of danger, she managed to survive a generation longer than her own father.

Buck Duke hoped to instill enough cynicism in his only child so that she would stay away from the users and betrayers. Instead, from the time she reached puberty, she spent her life feeling challenged to conquer, then discard, the men and, it was rumored, the occasional woman of the type her father had warned her against.

In the years before age, abusive lifestyle, and the ministrations of the medical profession brought her to her death bed, Doris Duke indulged her dangerous fantasies. She lusted after scoundrels and scalawags. She bedded pretentious men with the titles of royalty and the bank accounts of servants. She endured politically ambitious men in need of campaign financing and willing to sensually delight every inch of her anatomy in order to activate her checkbook.

Doris Duke came to desire the illusion of love without any loss of control. Sex alone could become a weapon to which both she and her lover had equal access. Doris never trusted an equal playing field. Marriage, handled correctly, allowed her to control a man until she tired of him. It was emotionally easier for her to commit adultery than to be victimized by it, and while husbands and lovers might wish to sneak around on Doris, her checkbook was a constant reminder of the benefits of monogamy. They learned to be faithful or, if they couldn't be faithful, so discreet that she could maintain the illusion of their steadfastness. Then, when she felt it was time to move on, she would be able to take the lead in ridding herself of a lover or husband. Rejection never hurt unless she was on the receiving end.

Doris Duke had to have control. Her drive for power was so great that she let down her guard only when she was old, ill, and heavily medicated.

Buck Duke's history and actions prior to his death indicated that what he wanted for Doris's successor was what he tried to create with Doris. This was a person trained in business, given an understanding of not only tobacco and power-generating stations, but business as it could be influenced by the vagaries of societal change.

Buck Duke originally wanted his nephew to handle the growing family fortune. When the nephew died at an early age, Buck gave his daughter a belated education in the world she would both be inheriting and, ideally, helping to grow.

Doris had learned well. The approximately three hundred million dollars she would ultimately inherit in cash, estate property, and trusts would be parlayed into a fortune she estimated between $6½ billion and $7½ billion. Although she trusted well-educated men with large sums of money at their disposal, Buck would have been outraged at the thought of a semiliterate butler's involvement.

Of the four who were present at her bedside or regularly visited her house when she passed from this life to the next (Doris Duke, like her father, believed in reincarnation and looked forward to returning to enjoy her wealth in a different body, a different period of history), none met Buck Duke's standards for education in business. Some said the caregivers included the most trusted people in her life. Others would later claim a dying old woman had been isolated from most of those who truly mattered to her, who telephoned or came to the gates, always to be turned away. Whatever the reality, even her late father, James Buchanan Duke, as ruthless a businessman as any of the nineteenth-century robber barons, could not have anticipated his daughter's death in the manner in which it occurred.

———— ❧ ————

IN THE END, the most financially successful of those who visited Doris Duke was too busy to come regularly. He also had been richly rewarded, having already received a check for a half-million dollars, which he said Doris told him was a gift of appreciation from one friend to another. He was the plastic surgeon whose scalpel, scissors, and sutures had lovingly caressed her face in recent months. Doris had been malnourished and dehydrated when he brought her into the operating room. She was seventy-nine years old, her body having shrunk from her full height of six foot one when young to the slightly more than five foot seven that would be noted on her death certificate. Her health had seemingly deteriorated, for she was no longer the robust woman she had been just a few months earlier. Despite this, and despite her advanced age, he agreed to perform one more procedure as part of her endless quest for the beauty that God had denied and the immortality she was certain she would have through reincarnation.

Perhaps the knife had become the heiress's ultimate lover. The pain it brought was deadened by anesthetic. And instead of the scars left by so many men and women in her life, the aftermath of its cuts seemed to restore her youth or at least revive her self-delusions. That was why she agreed to the face-lift, the lower right eyelid reconstruction, and the other techniques she endured on April 17, 1992.

What the heiress did not realize was that she had already been betrayed by her fantasies. The skin of her face had become so pale and taut that it looked almost translucent before she applied her makeup. Her jaw seemed to form almost a point: occasionally in photographs it looked as if you could open a bottle of Dom Perignon champagne by jabbing the cork with the tip of her chin.

Her eyes reflected the gentleness of a cat that, having tired of lightly slashing at a cornered, terrified mouse, was about to move in for the kill. Yet beauty is often in the eyes of the beholder, and so there had been one more surgery, one more attempt to fix the flaws that made her all too human, all too mortal.

Duke had been a woman of the world, yet the subconscious fears—of being unloved, of being kidnapped for ransom, of being deemed worthless except for her bank account—had caused her to withdraw from others. In the final year of her life, she had few friends, and the person who was apparently closest to her was her butler/personal assistant. After her death, he reportedly slept in her bed, wore her jewels, adorned himself with some of her clothing, and was chauffeured in her car.

But death had yet to occur. Through the last weeks of her life, Doris Duke lay helpless, her vast wealth no longer able to buy her the freedom for which she was once widely celebrated. Doris Duke, the richest woman in the world, could only remain in a drug-induced sleep, awaiting the moment when her healer would help her pass to what she felt would be the next stage of life.

# PART I

*The Fortune*

*Begins*

# I

## Tobacco Barons

*F*or Doris Duke and her father, life had always been about
sex, money, and agriculture. No matter what other pleasures they found in life—real estate, art, jewels, music, dance—ultimately they returned to the three basics. His love of agriculture
involved tobacco, and he was almost single-handedly responsible
for the American obsession with cigarette smoking that lasted
throughout the twentieth century. Her love was orchids, and she
became one of the world's great experts on their cultivation. She
also was a visionary in creating farm crop hybrids, and she would
amass some of the greatest collections of art, jewels, and other col-
lectibles to be seen anywhere in the world.

Money was a by-product of both their efforts. He amassed a
small fortune from his American Tobacco Company, the Southern
Power Company, and other ventures. She amassed a far greater fortune, both parlaying his holdings and making investments in everything from gold to Asian art just before their prices skyrocketed.
Buck Duke trained his daughter to be a master of his world, and
she taught herself to be a master of the world at large.

As for sex, each thought it was a delightful by-product of almost
any relationship. His preference was for women with large breasts
and red hair, though he was known to be courteous enough to dally
frequently with small-breasted blondes and brunettes when the
opportunities arose.

Her preference was for those men and women who lied about
their feelings. They declared their love for her, disclaiming any
thoughts about her money. They claimed that her being a multibil-
lionaire was of no greater interest to them than if she had been a

shopgirl. And for a few hours, she would help the illusion by focusing their attention and her own on the bedroom acrobatics that brought her fame among a favored few.

It was also sex that led to controversies preceding their deaths. Hers was because of allegations, later emphatically denied, of an affair with the young woman she eventually adopted and for whom she changed one of her wills. His was controversial because of a jealous wife who allegedly poisoned, then froze him to death when he refused to provide for a ne'er-do-well stepson, preferring his biological daughter on whom he doted.

———— ❧ ————

THE STORY OF Buck Duke's early childhood has become business legend. His father, Washington Duke, fought with the Confederates and came home, like so many other soldiers, a man without resources. His sole possessions were two army mules that had gone blind in the fighting and fifty cents in Yankee money. The latter was allegedly obtained from a Union soldier who wanted to purchase Duke's suddenly worthless Confederate paper money as a souvenir.

Life had been hard for Washington Duke. Two wives and two of his children died prior to the Civil War. His first wife succumbed to the difficult life of a tobacco farmer. His second wife and first son died in the typhoid epidemic of 1858. His oldest surviving child, Brodie Duke, would eventually become an alcoholic, frequently married ne'er-do-well—at least by Duke standards. Despite the opportunities that presented themselves to the family, Brodie lacked the ambition to rise above the status of a mere millionaire. By contrast, James Buchanan "Buck" Duke used those same opportunities to attain what some people would consider to be wealth beyond imagination.

The world of tobacco growers was an odd one prior to the Civil War. The farms were small, the growers independent, and the market quite limited. Men and some women chewed tobacco, smoked cigars, and frequently smoked pipes. Cigarettes, which had to be hand-rolled, were of little interest to the average person. They were small, expensive, and not particularly appealing.

The most popular tobacco was plug, meant for chewing, and

sold in the form of boxed loaves, a little like bread. A loaf weighed from ten to forty pounds and came with a free tobacco cutter that turned it into plugs—small chunks that could be popped into the mouth like bubble gum. Stores carried plug tobacco in barrels, but when the Civil War was over, some farmers developed brand names and elaborate packaging to create greater demand for their product. Buyers stopped asking for plug and started requesting brands such as Green Turtle.

The manufacture of plug tobacco did not utilize all of the leaves. There were always scraps and cuttings left over, and eventually these amounted to several tons of waste product per farm.

Among the dominant manufacturers of plug were the Bloch Brothers of Wheeling, West Virginia. They decided to make a new chewing tobacco that would be sold along with plug, utilizing the waste products and having a different taste. They experimented with additives, eventually combining the cuttings with licorice, sugar, water, brine, salt, and molasses. The mixture curled up in a way that they thought was appealing, and when someone took a small amount, placing it in his mouth for chewing, the taste was so enjoyable the company had a convert.

Chewing tobacco, unlike plug, was sold in paper bags with the Bloch Brothers' logo for the product, Mail Pouch Chew. The Bloch Brothers also created an advertising approach for their new "chew" that eventually affected the Dukes' tobacco business.

Back in the 1860s, when most of the nation was rural and most business districts served large farming communities, barns were natural billboards, readily seen from the dirt roads and paved highways coming into cities, towns, and villages across the nation. The Bloch Brothers' sales force would approach farmers, offering them free paint and a sum of money in exchange for being allowed to paint signs on their barns. Each sign was ten feet high and read CHEW MAIL POUCH TOBACCO, TREAT YOURSELF TO THE BEST.

Buck Duke was fascinated with the Bloch Brothers' approach as well as with advertising in general. But first he needed a unique product, and toward this end, he, his father, and his brother Ben began preparing a slightly different form of tobacco for sale. This was one developed by one of the slaves of Captain Abisha Slade. The leaf was a yellow variety that the slave accidentally cured too long. This change in the curing improved the taste and made it different enough so that those who tried it as plug or smoking tobacco wanted more.

Twice a widower, Buck's father Washington Duke decided to make his new tobacco business a family affair. Survival was more important than education, and though the Duke children received some schooling over the years, their focus was the business in which they would become the most successful family in America. However, this ultimate fortune would not prevent them from feeling inferior to those with college degrees, which was why they would later support what would become one of the finest universities in the South.

For most of the year, the boys worked in the tobacco fields, helping with the growing, harvesting, curing, and other preparations. The one daughter, Mary Elizabeth Duke, filled the bags and sewed new ones as needed.

The first load of tobacco the Dukes prepared was sold by wagon and paid for in gold. The money was enough for Washington and his sons—Ben, ten, and Buck, nine—to work full-time at their new business. They used the motto "Pro Bono Publico" for their trademark. They had seen it on a courthouse, did not know that it meant "In the public good," nor did they care. It sounded impressive, was Latin, a language for an educated man, and seemed the perfect logo for the new product.

Buck Duke loved the work he was doing. Although extremely bright and able to attend school, he was largely self-educated. He went to classes at the Durham Academy in Durham, North Carolina, where he lived, and eventually attended Guilford College. But he was traveling during many of his formative years, and his attendance at college was infrequent. He lost interest in the Guilford business program after just three months.

The Dukes had a difficult time with their new enterprise. The first crop was sold from a dilapidated wagon that would have been scrapped had the Civil War's destruction not made necessary the use of even the most broken-down equipment. The men slept by the side of the road because they had no money for any overnight accommodations. They subsisted on cornmeal and sweet potatoes, and they regularly worked twelve hours a day. Buck thrived in this atmosphere, delighting in the hardships as much as the success that gradually came to the family. Later he would travel by railroad caboose to get to the towns where he would be selling his crop. The caboose, actually a rolling office and sleeping quarters for the trainman on a freight, had no room for a passenger, and no one was supposed to ride in the car. Most people who could not afford fares would hop freights when they slowed for curves or were just leaving a station, sleeping in an empty or partially used boxcar. Buck must have bribed his way into the cabooses, where he slept sitting up, a habit that became so ingrained that years later, when he could afford to buy his own private railroad car in order to travel in style, he occasionally slept in chairs.

The Dukes might have done well staying with their core business, but thy decided to branch into cigarettes. At the time there was little market for the product. A typical hand-roller could produce just 1,500 cigarettes in the course of a day, which made them expensive. Most people were not interested in them, though Buck saw that they could be the growth product of the tobacco market.

Many of Buck's ideas for selling tobacco came from observing the changes in society in post–Civil War Durham, North Carolina, the city nearest the Duke land and eventually the city where they lived.

Durham had been declared a neutral area during the Civil War, and soldiers from both sides regularly passed through, always eager to make purchases from the shopkeepers. Their only other resource for nonessentials was the sutler who traveled with the military. Sutlers served as traveling post exchanges, although they charged much higher prices than in the cities and villages. They also extended credit, which a store could never do for a passing soldier. Many soldiers routinely had to turn over their whole pay envelopes to the sutler, a fact that built resentment and occasionally resulted in the sutler having his goods stolen.

Sutlers carried items such as writing materials for letters, canned meat and milk, and, when traveling with the Union army, even tobacco. (Soldiers in the Confederate army were issued an official tobacco ration.)

Buck Duke learned the tobacco business during one of the most unusual periods in American history. It would take less than fifty years following the end of the Civil War for Americans to know that cigarette smoking caused premature death from heart disease, lung disease, and cancer. As early as 1890, a cigarette was commonly called a "coffin nail," and Buck Duke warned those he loved against smoking them even as most tobacco companies experimented with adding addictive substances to the tobacco treatment process. However, when Buck first joined with his father, Ben, and Mary Elizabeth, doctors were convinced that the use of tobacco was critical for *good* health. The men who grew and sold tobacco were working to benefit the public, their crops considered a little like pharmaceuticals that had the advantage of being enjoyable to consume. The Confederate soldiers were all provided a tobacco ration not just because so many came from tobacco country but because of its health benefits.

According to the medical beliefs of the day, chewing and/or smoking tobacco reduced the rate of death from diarrhea and camp fever. It also was the natural antidote for Southern malaria. Some believed that tobacco also countered the deterioration caused by inadequate diets during long marches away from supplies.

Doctors in the North also were aware of the valuable health aid. Apparently the Union's failure to supply a ration of tobacco to each soldier to help keep him strong was a budget concern. Soldiers, their families, and their doctors regularly tried to get the Union leaders in Washington to authorize the funding so the soldiers would not have to rely on—and pay for—the sutler's supplies.

Tobacco was popular for other reasons, including the fact that it helped pass the time. Playing cards were the only other items the men could realistically carry with them. As a result, when tobacco was not available, the men would smoke or chew whatever they could find—coffee grains, dried tea leaves, and smoked white oak bark were among the more frequently used substitutes. But only tobacco was considered good for their health.

It was in Durham that the soldiers from both sides first experienced different-tasting leaves. The most common North Carolina tobacco before the Dukes became involved in the new type of leaf and curing process was Miksch, which had existed for over a century. Public tobacco warehouses had been established in the Southern cities of Richmond, Louisville, and Clarksville, and Miksch was the primary product being stored. It was also seen as a safe investment.

As the war was ending, several Northerners who had been trapped in the South when the fighting began knew that the Confederate currency they were using probably would be worthless. They had seen the demand for tobacco and decided that tobacco was the perfect way to launder their money. Therefore, they bought large quantities of tobacco perfect for plug and chewing, then had it shipped to Chattanooga, a city they felt would be captured by the federal forces. They assumed that the war would be ending and in the spirit of reconciliation, an effort would be made to protect the holdings of businessmen not connected with the war effort. Then, when conditions became stable, they would sell their tobacco to the Northerners in exchange for Union currency. Their worthless money would have been successfully laundered through the tobacco-buying process. Instead, however, the federal officers occupying Chattagoona, outraged over the prices their soldiers had been paying sutlers for a product essential for good health, seized the tobacco and declared that it was to be used for "Soldiers' Comfort."

The occupying forces served the Dukes' tobacco business better than they served the speculators. Soldiers who stole or purchased tobacco in the Durham area at the end of the war created a demand for the very different taste. With Reconstruction under way and North/South trade returning to normal, they sent for more of the tobacco to be shipped to their various home communities. However, while some growers saw the market as ideal for everyone, others felt that if they created a unique identity, they could sell more of their crops.

The most famous Durham tobacco company to benefit from the new concept of unique packaging and marketing was that of William T. Blackwell and Julian Shakespeare Carr. They wanted to connect their tobacco with the idea that its use was evidence of the user's manliness. Toward this end, they created a logo that featured a bull. The Durham bull became the symbol of Bull Durham Tobacco, and the company used the picture everywhere it could. Up to $150,000 a year was spent on advertising, including paying for testimonials from famous people and giving items such as clocks to loyal customers.

The Dukes had specialized in plug and chewing tobacco, but the Bull Durham competition was too strong. They saw no chance to increase their sales unless they tried a new product. (Ironically, Brodie Duke, Washington's surviving son by his first wife, had moved to Durham in 1869 and created the popular Duke of Durham brand of tobacco. But eventually he would be destroyed by his alcoholism. He did not have the strength of character in business of his two half brothers, Ben and Buck, which is why he made only a single million.) The logical answer was cigarettes, an underexploited market the high labor cost—80 cents per thousand cigarettes rolled—seemed to indicate would never be particularly large. The Dukes employed approximately 100 New York cigarette makers in 1881, but Buck Duke was not satisfied. He wanted to cut costs, then increase production and boost sales through aggressive marketing.

By this time the Duke tobacco interests were run by Buck, Ben, and a man named G. W. Watts, who bought into the company, as Washington Duke phased out of the active involvement. They were assisted by a mechanical genius named William T. O'Brien, who understood the benefits machinery could provide the production. Since Ben was in ill health, Buck became the dominant Duke family member of what had become Washington Duke & Sons.

In 1884 Buck Duke made the decision that would prove the start of establishing the fortune he would one day lavish on his only child. The Bonsack cigarette-rolling machine had been developed to replace workers who rolled an average of 1,500 cigarettes a day, with top workers able to produce 2,500 cigarettes. By contrast, the Bonsack was improved to the point where it produced 120,000 cigarettes a day, warranting the high expense for each machine. Most of the Dukes' hand-rollers would be dismissed, and with William O'Brien adding modifications, the Bonsack cut manufacturing costs to 30 cents per thousand cigarettes.

Other changes were taking place as well. Because of the growing demand for cigarettes and the expansion of the tobacco industry into both U.S. and European markets, what had been a seasonal business in Durham became a year-round operation. And because the area was racially segregated, the introduction of whites to what had been a business run with slaves providing the labor created a multitiered worker system that occasionally led to rioting.

Prior to the Civil War, most tobacco companies utilized slaves for nonmechanized production of tobacco and tobacco products. When mechanization began after the war, white men, who had long supervised the black workers, took over the handling of the new machinery. White single women and a few who were married also entered the workforce, handling some of the physically less demanding jobs. Black women also were hired, and though they were not forced into physically demanding positions, they were given the less pleasant tasks, such as stemming tobacco. Blacks and whites worked in separate rooms, and the average wage for all workers was just $101.25 *per year.*

The labor issues were rather simple ones. Given the post–Civil War economy, the Southern white males were pleased to be working at all, especially since areas outside the tobacco plants often offered only seasonal employment. Their primary complaint was that the wages barely covered their living expenses, that any emergency, including a death in the family, was beyond their finances.

Washington, Ben, and Buck Duke were sensitive to the bigotry in the industry. They had been destitute themselves. They had started with next to nothing. (One story, possibly true, possibly apocryphal but frequently quoted, says that the tobacco which Washington Duke and his sons sold as their first load was some they found stored but forgotten in the corner of an outhouse. The image of such a discovery implies the humblest of all possible beginnings.) They had experienced all facets of the tobacco business firsthand, learning exactly how hard everyone worked—whites and blacks, women and men. As a result, they developed a double standard for their lives: though ruthless in business, they made a point of helping those less fortunate than they were.

Washington Duke became interested in philanthropy, focusing on three causes: education, women, and blacks. Hiring practices and the giving of money to help the least respected members of American society all reflected this. He also financed Trinity College, giving it $50,000 and moving it to Durham. Another $2.1 million was added to the endowment during his lifetime, the only caveat being that the school had to admit women. The idea that women should receive a man's education was ridiculed in the state, but there was no alternative if the school wanted the money. Later, when Buck gave the school almost twenty times his father's endowment, he also had the college renamed in Washington's honor, calling it Duke University. Such philanthropy was an interest that would be continued by Washington's granddaughter, Doris, when she secretly began donating organs to black churches in the poorest sections of the South, among other charitable actions.

Buck Duke was less of a philanthropist than his father and daughter, but he put his father's principles into action within his companies. The employees had equal opportunity for jobs and fair wages for the times. Ironically, Buck's suppliers, all independent of the company, were kept in constant financial hardship through the tight-fisted buying practices of what became known as the tobacco trust.

Buck Duke moved the corporate headquarters to New York City in April of 1884, when he was just twenty-seven years old. He opened a loft factory on Rivington Street and took a two-dollar-a-week furnished room. From there he planned to make several moves, including going international with his products and utilizing new advertising ideas that would make Bull Durham and Mail Pouch Chew efforts seem amateurish. But first he destroyed the tobacco farmers whose crop prices did not meet his demands.

Buck Duke developed a network of warehouses and buyers of tobacco throughout the South. Their purchases were so massive, a grower's success or failure could be determined by whether this network purchased his tobacco or not. This also gave the network a buying monopoly that allowed it to pay whatever price it desired. Farmers had to accept the price offered or risk passing up what might be their only chance to sell that season's crops.

During what came to be known as the tobacco wars, the independent farmers organized a vigilante group of night riders. They would travel to towns dominated by the tobacco trust, as the Duke business practice was called, and destroy storage sheds filled with Duke tobacco. They traveled masked and would kidnap, beat, or kill anyone who either tried to stop them or represented the trust. Vigilantes owned the night, and local sympathies were so much in favor of the independent tobacco growers that even people with no connection with tobacco would alert the night riders when law enforcement was setting a trap for them. The night riders' movements were planned like military actions, and while they terrorized the tobacco-growing areas, they failed to break the trust. Yet Buck was determined to win, paying law enforcement officers and his own private security forces to stop those who would oppose his monopoly and price fixing.

Duke's other actions stepped up the pressure on his competitors. Buying from farmers eliminated the use of brokers and reduced costs. He obtained exclusive use of the Bonsack rolling machine, giving him the opportunity either to remain ahead of other cigarette companies in low-cost production potential or to license the technology to competitors, profiting from their profits.

Buck Duke also began buying older, established, smaller tobacco firms, receiving a signed a contract preventing the former owners from returning to the business as a condition of purchase. Many of the purchased companies were shut down. Those that stayed in business were melded into the Duke operations to ensure the greatest profit for them all.

With all the success, however, Buck Duke never stopped thinking like a low-income working man, even when he could afford to live a life of luxury. He understood what it was to be too poor for all but the simplest of pleasures. He knew that tobacco was something everyone could enjoy for no more than five or ten cents a package, depending on what they were purchasing. It was the same philosophy that would drive F. W. Woolworth, the inventor of the five-and-ten-cent store that catered to the needs and wants of the same buyer. And ironically, it would be Woolworth's heir, Barbara Hutton, who would vie with Buck's daughter for newspaper coverage of her outrageous antics.

During this same time, workers other than those involved with the Duke companies were protesting unfair labor practices and wages in the industry at large. Durham, as well as Richmond and Petersburg, saw the rise of the Knights of Labor and the National Tobacco Workers Union. Neither was very successful, though, because both represented all workers—both sexes and all races. Most white males in the laboring force at the time hated female and black workers. The new union members were almost as divided among themselves as they were divided from their bosses. Still, as a black Danville woman named Elviry Magee explained the life of the tobacco worker, there was no question of the need for change.

Magee, who stemmed and graded tobacco for sixty years, was quoted as saying:

"I tell you one thing, I knows tobacco. I knows all de grades an' blends. I knows bright tobacco an' burley tobacco an' Kaintucky tobacco an' all de rest. You 'members Old Man Hughes what built all dese here schools an' horspitals in town? Well, I learnt Mister John how to grade tobacco when he first come in de factory. Yes, Jesus, I give Mister John his start. I'm po' now an' I was po' den but he come to be a rich man. But it didn't do him no good. De Lawd called him away wi' Bright's misery. I believes one reason was 'cause he didn't pay niggers nothin'. I was his best hand—he say so hisse'f—an' he didn't never pay me no mo'n fifty to sebenty-five cents a day."[1]

Only the Dukes did better for their workers, and their positive attitude toward them, the oppression of their suppliers, and Buck's marketing strategies meant that by 1889, the Dukes were manufacturing half the cigarettes in the United States. At the same time, Buck was organizing the four major cigarette producers into the American Tobacco Company. He had already organized the plug tobacco manufacturers into the Continental Tobacco Company, then he took control of the entire industry with the formation of the American Snuff Company, the American Cigar Company, and the American Stogie Company. Finally, in 1901, he managed also to consolidate the major retail outlets under United Cigar Stores Company. Buck Duke had become the tobacco king of the United States, making himself and his family immensely wealthy.

Not all the success was due to the Dukes, though. In the late 1870s, George W. Watts sold his interest in the Duke company to Richard Harvey Wright. It was Wright who became the expert on establishing international sales and distribution of tobacco products, though his stake in the company was far less than that of the Dukes so he could never dominate business policy decisions. He was later bought out for approximately $90,000, leaving Buck to enter the twentieth century in complete charge of the Duke holdings. Ben also remained active, but ill health kept him from traveling and developing the company.

———— ✢ ————

THERE WERE TWO obsessions in Buck Duke's life as he gradually came to accept the fact that his business success allowed him to do anything he wanted. The first was advertising and the second was womanizing.

Duke saw New York City as a microcosm of the tobacco-buying potential in the North. He frequently walked the streets at night, looking at the discarded packages of cigarettes. He counted the empty wrappers of the different brands to see which type was being smoked the most. As a promotional stunt, he then offered $50 to the person who brought him the greatest number of empty packages from a Duke brand.

Other advertising was more elaborate. Buck Duke felt that beautiful women should be used to sell cigarettes. Proper women avoided cigarettes, though they often smoked pipes and chewed tobacco. However, women were appealing to men, and Buck understood that a man seeing a woman's face and body connected with his product might think that if he used the cigarettes being shown, such a woman would be sexually attracted to him.

The first woman to meet the standards for breast size and facial beauty that Buck established as the criteria for being hired to advertise cigarettes was a French actress who went by the name of Madame Rhea. She had become successful by always choosing stage roles that required her to appear sensuous and sexy. Her appeal was unique at the time and unique for an actress in dramatic roles. It would be matched a generation later in comedy by the American Mae West, but in her day, Madame Rhea was everything Buck could want in a product endorser appealing to men.

Madame Rhea understood that she would also benefit from the advertising exposure, a new idea at the time. She happily agreed to Buck's request that she pose for a poster and advertisement in the *Atlanta Constitution,* Georgia's largest newspaper.

The advertisement showed Madame Rhea holding a package of Duke Cigarettes. The caption read "Atlanta's Favorite," and the double message was deliberate.

Later, because of the success of the Duke approach, many companies would seek endorsements from the beautiful among the rich and famous. Debutante friends of Doris's frequently were selected and paid well to appear in advertising campaigns for a variety of products whose manufacturers wanted to emulate Buck Duke's success with cigarettes. The grande dames of established society were outraged by their daughters' actions, but the young women loved the attention and the money. Fees often reached $5,000 or more, exceeding the annual income of the average working man.

Duke also used pictures of less famous, but beautiful, well-endowed women on posters, billboards, and as inserts in the cigarettes. He developed a box that was the forerunner of the crushproof packaging used a half century later, giving a better product and protecting the advertising insert men carried in their wallets or tacked to the wall.

Many customers were outraged by the use of women as sex objects. Some sales were probably lost. However, Buck understood that the vast majority of his customers were men who would delight in the naughtiness. His advertising spawned numerous imitations, some more and some less flamboyant than his had been. These ranged from the "Harvey Girls," who worked for railroad station restaurants and handled guided tours at the Grand Canyon under the direction of restaurateur Fred Harvey, to the modern Virginia Slims cigarette model. Some were real women and others, such as Charles Dana Gibson's "Gibson Girls," were artists' illustrations.

Duke also was the first person to link cigarettes with sporting events. Always mindful of his working-class market, he first sponsored a polo team on roller skates. At least this is how the concept was presented to the public in order to ensure that both the wealthy and the working man might attend. In reality, the game was the roller derby, a sporting event in which teeth and blood flew almost as fast as the high-speed skaters.

Later Duke would also sponsor basketball and baseball teams. He had a number of opportunities to buy the clubs and become a professional owner, but he saw no point to it. Sporting events were vehicles for advertising and passing out samples of his cigarettes. He did not realize that they would one day become highly profitable businesses in their own right.

Just as Duke believed in sex for advertising, so his life was filled with affairs. He wanted to marry and have children. He was growing older, and many of his North Carolina contemporaries who had stayed to work the land were on their second or third wives. The work was so difficult and required so much help that a farmer often relied on children to assure the success of the family. Women were overburdened by pregnancy, child rearing, and farm chores, getting little sleep, their bodies not allowed to recover from pregnancy to pregnancy, and disease always being a risk. Many died, while their husbands remarried to get the additional help. Thus a widower in his late thirties or forties was not unusual, nor did it make him less desirable to young women.

Buck Duke had not found the woman to be his life's mate, but he did find plenty to share his bed. His favorite was Mrs. Lillian Nanette Fletcher McCredy, and she would prove to be the female equivalent of Doris Duke's first longtime lover, a Hawaiian sheriff named Duke Kahanamoku. Whether Doris would one day make the connection is unknown, but years later, when Buck was dead and she was a young woman, Doris would think fondly of Lillian, discussing her knowledge of her father's pleasures with friends.

Lillian McCredy liked sex. In an age when some women went to bed with their bodies covered, never fully removing their nightgowns when they made love, Lillian would do anything, anywhere, in any manner. Doris Duke later delighted in telling her cousin, Pony Duke, that she had overheard her father telling his brother, Ben, that Lillian would place strawberries in her various body openings for Buck to discover during sex. But whatever a man wanted, Lillian was eager to provide. As a result, her husband, William McCredy, armed with detective reports on at least a few of the men in her life, was able to obtain a divorce in what may have been one of the most publicized domestic cases of 1892.

Buck Duke met the scandalous Lillian shortly after the well-covered trial. He was ready for the experiences a woman like Lillian could provide, and she was thinking that monogamy might not be a bad idea. Unfortunately for the relationship, Lillian McCredy looked upon monogamy as something that involved limiting herself to just two regular lovers, only one of whom would be aware of the other.

When Duke became part of the Fifth Avenue social scene in New York City and began his affair with Lillian, he was both hated for his crude Southern ways and greatly in demand for his vast wealth. He started traveling the world, attending the opera, and learning about art. He was always self-taught, always sensitive to the value of what he was seeing rather than its history or social importance as he felt an educated man might be. He also began investing in real estate, sometimes for personal use, such as the stable he had built for his horses, and sometimes as a partial investment. He bought a suite of offices at 111 Fifth Avenue and spent $30,000 for a five-story mansion at 11 West 68th Street. He listed his personal address as the rooms he rented in the Hoffman House residential hotel, but when he moved Lillian into the house on West 68th Street, he never missed a night with her physical delights if he was in town. Many reformers, eager to break up the tobacco trust, saw only the coarseness of Buck Duke. They mistakenly thought his business empire was an aberration, that his ability to ruin any competitor was more a matter of luck than skill. Yet in truth, he was so brilliant that he frequently issued stock in the American Tobacco Company to politicians who could break up the trust he created, so they would have an incentive to let him continue.

The McCredy relationship was perfect for Buck. Lillian was a trained singer and the socially active ex-wife of a stockbroker, giving her at least a conversant knowledge of business. She was outgoing, extremely attractive, and could fit into any occasion where Buck needed an escort. He rewarded her not only with the mansion but also with jewels and stocks.

For six years Buck Duke used Lillian and she used him. He was forty-two years old when the affair started and forty-eight when his father, who had remained in Durham, first learned of what had been taking place. During that time Buck's devotion to work was so intense that Lillian had enough free time to indulge in any whim, ranging from shopping to a second lover, Frank T. Huntoon.

Huntoon was the ideal second man to service Lillian's brand of monogamy. He was from an old, respected family with little money, though enough to indulge his enjoyment of first-night Broadway openings and betting on horses. He lived in the Hotel Wolcott, ate in expensive restaurants, and understood discretion. Lillian's relationship with Duke was not well known to the press, and she was either not recognized when she went out with Huntoon or no one was concerned. They were not married, and she spent most of her evenings with Duke.

Washington Duke was outraged with Buck's behavior, in large measure because he had great hopes for his youngest son. Durham was a wild town, filled with popular houses of prostitution, gambling, and raucous night life. Men who had once been taught to utilize their slaves for sexual purposes rather than getting married young were paying for sex with any type of woman they desired. The drunken Brodie had overindulged himself in such matters, repeatedly marrying and divorcing, womanizing, and having limited business success. Ben was the opposite extreme, happily married, deeply religious, serious about the company, yet always in ill health, which prevented him from being as active as Buck.

Buck lived a life between the two extremes, loving his work, spending long hours building the business, yet finding time to enjoy the favors of the opposite sex with as much frequency as he desired. He was the key to the future of the Duke enterprises, one of the reasons Ben tolerated his personal life while respecting his business decisions.

Washington Duke had his own history of womanizing, but he wanted something more for his youngest son. If Buck was going to be involved in a long-term relationship, Washington wanted it to be with a woman who could produce an heir, not with a divorcée with loose morals. He encouraged his son to marry, so Buck decided to satisfy his libido and, he thought, please his father simultaneously. He married his mistress.

A man who built a business monopoly in the manner of Buck Duke expected to own his wife's affections or at least have exclusive rights to her ardor. Instead, he discovered that though Lillian still enjoyed bedroom acrobatics, she had developed other interests. She delighted in enjoying the New York couturiers, high-priced restaurants, and other indulgences in a manner possible only with unlimited money. She also found that she could not spend extensive time with her new husband without the two of them fighting.

Lillian and Buck were on their honeymoon when they realized that marriage had been a mistake. They were great lovers initially;

and since he simply spent his nights in town with her there was no stigma attached to their relationship. It was Buck's feelings of guilt about his father's wishes for his life that had caused him to propose. It was Lillian's wishes for greater access to the Duke money that caused her to accept. But ultimately she would have been happier in every way to continue as his mistress. And as at least one other woman involved in a long-term relationship with Buck could attest, being kept by Buck Duke meant the acquisition of great wealth through his generosity. He seems never to have had a dissatisfied lover. His wives, on the other hand, would always be left wanting.

The couple had been delighted with their quiet marriage in Camden, New Jersey, and both were looking forward to traveling to the French Riviera. However, the weather on the Riviera was cold, with rain and sleet a constant companion. Buck had long suffered from the gout and a variety of foot problems, all of which worsened in the inclement weather. By the time the couple returned to New York to settle into their home the second week of February 1905, he had developed blood poisoning and gangrene. He had to stay in the third-floor bedroom for six weeks in order to recover.

There was still enough life left in the marriage so that Lillian's ministrations stayed so physical in nature, Buck later joked that she helped keep him *off* his feet. But there were other problems, which Buck might have overlooked had it not been for the rapidly declining health of the eighty-five-year-old Washington Duke.

Washington, who had retired in Durham, was frequently light-headed. At one point he became so dizzy while in a Durham bank that he fell, breaking his right arm. A second fall in January left him with a broken hip. He died on May 8 with his sons by his bedside. With that death, Buck Duke was free to live his personal life in any manner he chose, and though neither he nor Lillian realized it at the time, the death marked the beginning of the end of their marriage.

# 2

## *Bloodlines*

$\mathcal{T}$HE SMALL TOWN OF Somerville, New Jersey, was as quiet a community as Manhattan was bustling. The land was used mostly for farming, the area sparsely populated. The roads were good, though, and a relatively large number of people passed through the community as they traveled from New York to the university town of Princeton. Because Somerville would be a convenient location, Buck decided to build himself a country place there. He fully expected to share it with Lillian, though she looked upon any location lacking skyscrapers, expensive restaurants, and designer clothing to be worse than the fires of Hell.

Buck bought what had been the Veghte family farm, a large working farm that had always been successful. There was a good-size farmhouse on the land, but Buck had no interest in the lifestyles of anyone who preceded him in owning a property. Once the deal was completed, he hired more than 300 workmen to transform the grounds.

The money spent was enormous for the day. The heated stables cost $10,000 more than his former mistress's New York mansion. They also had elaborately painted murals more appropriate for the walls of a civic building.

The house had every convenience, including electric lights, telephones, hot water heaters, a water purification system, new fireplaces, and other details each of which sometimes cost more than the price of the original farmhouse. The grounds were redesigned at a price of an estimated $10 million and included twenty-five miles of paved roads, artificial lakes, specially created fountains, lagoons, waterfalls, wooded areas, and even mountains. Each time something new was constructed, Buck would examine it in light of the whole, sometimes keeping it and sometimes having it ripped apart to be replaced by whatever he thought might be better. A mountain was created in one section of the estate, then leveled when Buck found it esthetically disappointing. A lake would be dredged, filled with water, filled back with dirt, landscaped, and then a new dredging effort would be made to find a better location for the lake.

The farm was meant to be worked, and would eventually be a profitable venture for Doris. But Buck Duke, who wanted minimum responsibility, bought only enough livestock to keep the place working, though far from what would be necessary to recover his investment. He purchased 250 purebred Jersey cows, for example, and his gardens supplied fruits and vegetables that more than met the needs of staff and family. Yet the property, three miles long and one mile wide, could have been one of the most successful farms in the region. Entire cities within the state often had less property.[1] He even had his own half-mile horse racetrack for a time.

Much of the furniture was handmade from heavy, dark, expensive woods. There were many sculptures of animals as well as a life-size statue of one of his idols, the late President McKinley. And when Duke was finished with the house, which ultimately had eleven bedrooms, a great hall for huge dinner parties, a drawing room, and other amenities, he planned to tear it down. It had only been interim living quarters while he built a *real* mansion on a hill overlooking the Raritan River. That project was never completed, though he spent well into six figures preparing the foundation and immediate grounds.

Duke also hired sisters Maggie and Mary Smith to be the year-round managers of what would become known as Duke Farms. Maggie acted as head of the business office, seeing to the housekeeping and disbursing money where necessary for the smooth operation of the estate. Mary acted in a similar capacity when Buck was out of town, but when he was in New Jersey, she tended to his physical desires.

Buck paid well but indirectly for the ministerings of the two women. He gave them tips on the stock market and large enough salaries to be able to invest. They became rich in their own right through his guidance.

Duke was always close to the land, having loved his childhood years in the tobacco fields and delighting in returning to the soil on his New Jersey estate. It was a love that would be passed on to his daughter, Doris. Both also enjoyed the animals, perhaps realizing that these were the only creatures they could love unconditionally and know they would not be betrayed.

What Buck loved about Somerville, Lillian hated. She was a city girl. She loved the fast pace, the museums, clubs, restaurants, shows, and all the other excitement. She also liked the ease of access to Huntoon as well as the knowledge that if she ever decided that her version of monogamy was too boring, it would not be hard to add another man or two to meet her needs.

The issue of adultery was an odd one for Buck and Lillian. It was several months into the marriage before Buck was certain that Lillian was cheating on him; he even hired detectives to document what was taking place in preparation for a court battle. Yet he felt little need to be discreet himself. Angry with Lillian and believing in a double standard, he openly flaunted some of his girlfriends— especially in Somerville, where many a night Lillian would go to bed while Buck and Mary Smith sat drinking, talking, and laughing together. They also often shared a bedroom, being careful, however, to make sure Lillian did not catch them.

There were times Buck would harass his wife by taking his wife, girlfriend, and girlfriend's sister, Maggie, on long drives in one of the three high-priced motor cars he kept on the land. It is not known if Mary was embarrassed, but Lillian knew she dared not stop her husband's pleasure if she wanted to continue enjoying his money. Her mistake was in thinking that he expected no greater faithfulness from her than he did from himself.

In July of 1905, having hired private detectives to follow Lillian, Buck went to London to see about a business deal. He made it clear that he would return on the steamer *Lucana,* which was docking in Manhattan on September 2. What she did not know was that he actually returned two days earlier, moving into Ben's Fifth Avenue mansion. From there he quietly brought in Lillian's servants one at a time, hiring them away from her or bribing those he could not hire. He took statements from each concerning Lillian's affairs with Huntoon, carefully documenting her adultery. Mary Smith, the mistress of Somerville, had joined him in Ben's home, soothing his fevered brow (and delighting the rest of his anatomy) while he plotted to rid himself of his wife.

The divorce was filed in New Jersey where Duke's new investments were so appreciated, the court was certain to be favorably disposed toward him.

The proceedings were upsetting for Lillian, who did not wish to lose the social position she had spent so much time in bed trying to achieve. She was angered when the *New York Times* ran the information on the front page of the September 3 edition. She also did not like Buck's deliberately going to a state that might be less favorable toward her.

Lillian wanted the divorce handled in New York where she could possibly persuade the court that she was the wronged woman. She named Mary Smith as his mistress in a countersuit, then accused him of mental cruelty beginning on their honeymoon. She claimed that she was frequently in pain, had insomnia, and was in delicate health, in large part because Buck had insisted that on their honeymoon they sightsee in open vehicles despite inclement weather.

Lillian discussed Buck's frequent beatings, which had left much of her body bruised. She said he drank too much and called her names such as "whore," "bitch," and "wench." The testimony about her own adultery was the result of bribes to servants, not a truthful telling of her devoted, virtuous life.

The fight became delightful theater. Buck Duke swore that most of the allegations against him were untrue, especially about the beatings. He never denied the name-calling, but explained that they were not derogatory terms, they were accurate representations of her character.

The strongest witness was Nellie Sands, Lillian's personal maid during the time Buck was courting her. Nellie knew where the family money came from and was not about to go against Duke. She detailed Lillian's relationship with Huntoon who, the public was delighted to learn, was twenty years older than Buck. Although almost seventy, he was handsome, powerful, and had a great body, which Lillian obviously enjoyed. He also had greater stamina than Buck, all facts that Lillian indiscreetly revealed to her trusted servant.

Nellie Sands gave testimony to the emotional stress Lillian underwent when she decided that marrying Buck would be more profitable than dating Huntoon. Nellie had witnessed a tearful lovers' farewell and learned that the couple communicated during Lillian's honeymoon with Buck by using the personal ads in the *Paris Herald*. The advertisements were partly in code, using the name "Octopus" instead of "Buck," for example. However, when the detectives located the advertisements, they clearly indicated an intense affair. Even the type of clothing that most aroused Huntoon—high-neck dresses—was mentioned in the personals listing.

Lillian was determined to not become poor without a fight. She attacked Buck where she thought she could hurt him most—with the government. She said that he had incorporated the American Tobacco Company in New Jersey to avoid New York's harsh tax laws. She claimed that the only reason he bought the Somerville property was because of business benefits, not because he ever wanted to live in the state.

The business revelations, if true, were meaningless because Buck Duke made certain that politicians were always on his side. He was also not embarrassed when Lillian revealed the living arrangements created with the house he purchased for her on 68th Street. His father, the only person he felt the scandal would hurt, was dead. Men of the old South frequently had mistresses when they were married, even if they had just used a convenient, favorite slave for sexual gratification. But Buck was a single man when he kept Lillian. He was only cheating on Mary Smith and a few less frequent trysting partners, all of whom were consenting adults. His intentions toward Lillian were honorable in that he never forced her to be his mistress, paid her well in the form of valuable gifts, and eventually married her.

Nellie Sands's testimony was the most damaging because she did not care for Buck Duke. She felt that Huntoon was the better catch, even though he was so much older. She watched sadly how unhappy Lillian was the night before her marriage when she had to leave Huntoon's arms in order to journey to Buck. She even admitted acting as a go-between, passing letters back and forth between Huntoon and Lillian whenever Buck was not nearby.

What happened next during the divorce battle has never been investigated fully. Buck Duke was a fighter engaged in the little-known war in the tobacco-growing fields. He was hated in the to-bacco regions, but in New York, no one really cared, not even the men who opposed him. The angry men of the country had neither the money nor the interest in going North for vengeance. They wanted to hurt Duke where he earned his money, not where he spent it.

At the same time, Lillian had betrayed Buck Duke's code of honor. It was all right for a man to cheat on his wife, but it was not all right for a wife to cheat on her husband. He understood her frustrations. He understood her loneliness when he traveled. He also understood that he had paid handsomely for exclusive use of her sexual favors. He determined to ruin her in a manner that would one day become a model for the actions his only daughter would take against her first spouse.

As the court battle raged, Buck Duke's private New York stables were set ablaze by a gasoline explosion; four horses died and carriages and a touring automobile were destroyed, along with the building. Although Lillian hated Somerville, she did have a fond-ness for the stables; and the loss hurt her more than her estranged husband. Since it was clearly the result of arson, presumably the fire was meant to send a warning message to either Buck (from the tobacco interests) or Lillian (from Buck regarding the divorce).

Did Buck Duke burn his own building to keep Lillian from get-ting it? Was he threatening his wife, hinting at the dangers to come if she did not stop contesting the divorce settlement? The truth will never be known. Buck was seduced by sex, held by sex, and ulti-mately angered by sex when he discovered he was not the only man enjoying his wife's favors. His reaction was as hostile as his lust had been great. Occasionally he even paid for false testimony, allegedly including the statements given by two women—Emma Morrison and Mrs. Louise Bail. They were Lillian's sisters, and Buck knew that even if they were not close, they each expected family loyalty from the others. Having them testify was a message to Lillian that she was truly alone.

Ultimately Duke won his divorce on May 7, 1906. The arson was officially listed as "unsolved," although Duke almost certainly arranged the torching, probably thinking that the arsonist would free the animals before setting the blaze.

Eight years later Buck paid Louise Bail an additional $7,500 after she sued him for failure to give her money she had been promised. The threatened court battle would have been potentially as interesting as the divorce. However, Duke settled out of court because Lillian had kept letters from him and his attorney sent during the earlier divorce battle. Those letters encouraged her to speak on his behalf and promised her an income for life as a reward.

Buck Duke wanted to destroy Lillian, leaving her penniless. His earlier generosity made that impossible, though. She was actually quite wealthy at the time of the divorce. The gifts Buck had given her in the almost dozen years they were together provided her with an estate that made her a millionaire. However, she spent and sold everything she had, then blackmailed Buck into giving her $3 million more when he was about to take a second bride. Lillian was going to claim they were still married; although she knew the claim would be proven false, she also knew it would delay or prevent the marriage.

By the time of the blackmail, Lillian had become determined to succeed in life through the pursuit of various schemes, and she found a willing partner for one of her ventures. The youth with whom she teamed swindled her out of her money, leaving her with no savings in old age. She lived in a boardinghouse with her pet Chihuahua Pom-Pom and supported herself, while she could, by giving music lessons. When even that source of work brought too little money to keep her alive, she starved to death. Her one satisfaction prior to losing all hope was that Buck Duke died before she did.

———— ✦ ————

BEN DUKE WAS embarrassed by what was taking place in the New Jersey divorce proceedings, although the business would not be hurt by scandal. People were going to smoke regardless of the Duke misfortunes, and Ben was religious enough to realize that his soul was not protected or damned by the actions of his brother. Still, he felt the need to intercede, and his solution was Nanaline Holt Inman. Twelve years younger than Buck, she was a widow— mature, sexually experienced—and desired a second marriage enough to engage in whatever kinky bedroom play Buck might need in order to feel he had found an adequate substitute for Lillian. What he did not realize was that her actions were calculated and that she had little interest in continuing such sexual frequency or variety once they were married.

Nanaline was also from a good Southern family, the Holts of Macon, Georgia, a sophisticated community of the old South. Like so many other daughters of the Confederacy, she went from a mansion to "genteel poverty" when she was thirteen, eight years after the Civil War.

Nanaline was a great beauty, extremely intelligent, and proficient in the social graces of prewar wealthy, white Southern living, and the survival skills needed in both occupied territory and war-ravaged land. Her father had been a Confederate cavalry officer who died when Nanaline and her sister were still quite young. Nanaline's mother took in boarders and did sewing for people whose lineage she would have looked upon with disdain before the war. The gowns and elaborate dresses she created were all for women who had gained prominence and money by taking advantage of Reconstruction opportunities. Some had been poor opportunists who got rich after their neighbors lost their wealth. Others were transplanted Northerners taking advantage of a devastated economy. They were newly rich from the same circumstances that had cost men like her father everything they had. She was angrily determined that Nanaline would be able to do at least as well as such despised young socialites.

The mansion was lost and the family frequently went hungry. But Nanaline was still sent to get a quality education, first at the Branham School and then at Wesleyan Female College. She also managed to acquire a new name in order to distinguish between the poor Southern belle who married in desperation and the traveled sophisticate who would draw the attentions of Buck Duke. Nannie Lane Holt became Nanaline, a name having a hint of European sophistication, a name that implied she came from the winning side of life. It was a pretension that would ultimately help turn her against the only child she and Buck Duke would have together.

For the daughters of Southerners who lost everything in the war, money was secondary to breeding when it came to garnering respect and the "right" husband. A man needed to show he was heading toward the restoration of the family wealth before he was given entrée to the new Southern elite. A woman just needed the breeding to show she would make a good companion when her husband earned back some or all of the lost family fortune.

Nanaline was the perfect catch by Southern standards, a fact not lost on both Ben and Buck Duke, who came to see her as the answer to Buck's need to settle down and produce an heir. She had known wealth, poverty, and genteel living. She had the education to assure she could be the proper wife for any man who appreciated the style, loyalty, and attitude of prewar Southern aristocrats. Thus it came as no surprise to anyone who knew her when she chose William Inman as her first husband. He was an Atlanta-based cotton merchant already earning large sums of money. Together they had two sons, one of whom died before his second birthday, the other of whom, Walker, was to prove an emotionally weak, alcoholic ne'er-do-well.

Today Walker might be seen differently than he was at the time. William Inman was an alcoholic who was financially successful despite his heavy drinking. He may have been abusive to his wife and sons. He may have been incapable of showing any of them the affection they needed. Whatever the case, he had to spend three months in a sanitarium before returning home to die on March 20, 1902. The official cause of death was diabetes, not an unusual health problem for an alcoholic, although the disease may have been listed to avoid revealing the truth.

Children of alcoholics are known to have difficulty with relationships. They are often insecure and desperate to please. The alcoholic parent frequently blames his or her child for anything that goes wrong, convincing the child that he or she can never be good enough. Some children become obsessed with success, working endless hours, determined to prove they can earn the love of the parent who may be long dead. Others give up, having problems with alcoholism and/or drug addiction, constantly seeing themselves as worthless. Such appears to be the situation with Walker Inman, whose mother never tried to help him change. She saw his weaknesses but also saw him as the scion of a once-proud family that should again be restored to wealth and position. She turned a blind eye to the fact that he was spending his life in a series of drunken binges and failed business ventures. Give him enough money and the Holt family would again prosper. And Buck, of course, had enough money.

The full story of Nanaline Duke has never been told. The people who knew her best are dead, and even Doris had little knowledge of the mother she came to dislike intensely.

Pony Duke, Doris's cousin, suspects that Nanaline may have been a child abuser. Certainly contemporary experts on child abuse would declare her to have emotionally abused Doris, whom she constantly berated for her lack of education, her height, and her lack of natural beauty.

Inman left Nanaline and young Walker financially well off when he died at age thirty-eight. She was able to travel and enjoy the type of life where she could encounter the very rich as she sought another husband and father for Walker.

There are many stories about Nanaline's attitude just prior to her becoming a Duke. She was said to have hated men, apparently blaming her father for abandoning her and her mother when he was lost at sea. Some say she was bisexual, using her body to please the men in her life but finding satisfaction only with at least one woman. Others say she was embittered by so many losses—of the home she loved, of a lifestyle she thought she would enjoy forever, of a young father, of a young husband, of a son she never knew how to handle—that she became a survivor. She acted from anger and fear, not from love. And if she eventually had the one known relationship with another woman, it was because she was seeking affection she had never fully realized, no longer caring about the source.

All that is certain is that Nanaline knew she needed a husband and found the opportunity in a chance meeting with Ben Duke while vacationing at the Lake Toxaway, North Carolina, health spa. Exactly what happened is uncertain. Different biographers tell different stories of the meeting. Some say that she decided to bed and wed Ben Duke, whom she either mistakenly thought was single or who was too happily married to consider an involvement. Others say that he found her beautiful, delightful, and potentially a mate for brother Buck. Whatever the case, when Nanaline and her mother, Florine, moved to New York's Hotel Webster, a hotel with suites for full-time residence, Ben and Sarah Duke hosted a party at the Waldorf to introduce Nanaline to Buck.

Ben had sent his younger brother a letter about Nanaline, calling her "the most beautiful woman in the world." But there was a coldness to Nanaline's beauty. She was small where Lillian had been large. She was withdrawn where Lillian was outgoing. And she had little interest in sex other than for catching a husband, where Lillian lived for sensual pleasure. But Nanaline seemed to have the sense to not cheat on Buck. She was tolerant of his less-than-handsome appearance, his growing potbelly, and his endless cigars. Like most Southern women of her generation, she had learned to indulge her man and endure his efforts at pleasure seeking, not expecting to feel pleasure herself.

The courtship followed what had become Buck Duke's pattern. Nanaline was given gifts of jewelry and even a limousine. A magnificent surrey with two perfectly matched black horses arrived for her at the hotel where she lived, and a pony cart drawn by a pair of equally flawless ponies came for twelve-year-old Walker. The average person could have sold the presents and lived comfortably in New York for several years. Nanaline, properly brought up and no fool when it came to money, demurely thanked her lover, knowing she was accumulating a substantial nest egg if matters did not work out well between them. She also had the sense to accept his invitations to Somerville, even though she, like Lillian before her, preferred the type of city life unlimited wealth can buy.

Buck Duke had another goal in his pursuit of Nanaline. He wanted to be accepted by New York society, especially the big-money entrepreneurial families whose success predated his own. Nanaline was both acceptable and accepted in this world.

THE MARRIAGE OF Nanaline and Buck Duke took place on July 23, 1907, in a private home in Brooklyn. It was a quiet affair attended by only a few family members and friends. Nanaline's mother and son were both there, though only the mother was pleased. Buck had reached out to Walker Inman, offering to adopt him, to make him a Duke. The young man was being given the opportunity to become a lineal heir, assuring his future success. Instead Walker, who both disliked his mother's choice in a new husband and was fool enough to have the ability to snatch defeat from the jaws of victory, arrogantly told Buck that he was too proud of being an Inman to consider becoming a Duke. That arrogance alone assured he would never be a part of the Duke money.

---

IT WAS FOR LOVE of Nanaline that Buck Duke made his presence in Manhattan known in a manner that impressed the Rockefellers, Vanderbilts, Astors, and other well-established Eastern millionaires. He bought several properties, including the former Henry H. Cook mansion at 1 East 78th Street (at Fifth Avenue) for which he paid somewhere between $1.2 million and $1.6 million. The mansion was not for living, though. He had other homes for his family. Instead he razed the Cook mansion and began building a massive estate on some of the most expensive real estate in the nation. This would be his gift to his bride, and the home was finished in 1912, just in time to discover that Nanaline was pregnant.

The Duke home had eight massive bedrooms and six marble baths for family use. These were all on the second floor; the third floor housed the quarters for a dozen of the servants. While other wealthy families provided cramped rooms and inadequate plumbing for the comfort of their live-in staff, Buck saw to it that the servants had quality quarters. The rooms were large and well built. The bathrooms more than adequate for their needs. The same was true for the chef's suite near the kitchen and the chauffeur's quarters near the garage.

Because of the surprise pregnancy, special quarters were designed for family use. Buck and Nanaline had separate bedrooms. His was simple but elegant, the windows overlooking the entrance to the house. Hers had a separate, two-story dressing room with mahogany closets, each designed to hold one of her gowns. The doors were carefully labeled so she would know which gown was inside. The system would also ensure she could plan her social outings so she would not wear the same outfit with the same people when entertaining or being entertained. A smaller room acted as a barrier between her quarters and what would soon be the nursery.

There were other rooms as well, including a massive main hall and staircase, library, ballroom with a balcony and room for a symphony orchestra to play, drawing room, elegant dining room and separate servants' dining room, kitchens, pantries, and other amenities. It was five floors in all, three aboveground to serve the family and their caretakers, and two belowground.

The total cost was $3 million *after* the expense of purchasing and tearing down the previous home. The design was French, an enlarged version of the Château Labottiere in Bordeaux. The plans were drawn up by Julian Abele, a black architect, and construction was handled by another architect, Horace Trumbauer, who was experienced in building some of the largest mansions owned by America's super rich.

Nanaline was not pleased to be pregnant, especially since she would be forty-three when the baby was born. Childbearing was for the young. Women did not wait until after they had experienced successful careers to consider getting pregnant. Having babies *was* their career, and depending on their backgrounds, a first child often was the product of a teen marriage. The wealthier usually waited until the woman reached adulthood, but even that might mean only twenty or twenty-one years of age. A woman of forty-three was likely to be a grandmother, and some physicians questioned the ability of someone that age to have a baby at all.

The pregnancy caused other stress on the couple as well. Buck Duke would be a first-time father at fifty-five, quite an old man for his day. And Walker Inman would be seventeen when his brother or sister was born. He should have been the heir apparent, his stepfather grooming him to take on the Duke family business. Or so thought Nanaline, who was interested solely in restoring the name and great wealth of the Holts.

Buck Duke had only one focus, the healthy birth of his biological child. He arranged to have Nanaline's bedroom turned into a hospital room complete with the latest designs of medical equipment used to handle a problem birthing. Although the doctors felt that mother and child would be fine, Duke made certain that if there was a chance to save the baby, all the instruments would be in place. Medical personnel were in the house twenty-four hours a day to assure they would be present the moment Nanaline started to go into labor. They had been privately told that, since there was a risk of death due to what was then considered Nanaline's advanced age, they were to save the baby, not the mother.

Prior to the pregnancy, Buck Duke expected to turn over the running of all Duke enterprises to Ben's son Angier. The youth was wild and rather careless. His right arm had been amputated at the elbow as a result of a hunting accident. Yet even the disability did not bother young women who eagerly pursued him and delighted in being wooed by him. However, despite the wildness, he was intelligent, and his father and uncle had trained him extensively about the world of tobacco. He also was a graduate of the family-supported Trinity College, giving him the first advanced education of anyone in the family. But the idea that there might be a natural heir, not just a nephew, albeit a trusted and respected one, delighted Buck.

As the time for labor approached, Duke arranged for the cleaning staff to begin regularly disinfecting Nanaline's bedroom. He wanted everything sterile to assure the baby's survival. He was not worried that his wife's past history of accidental or deliberate domestic violence might mean his child would be in danger. Child abuse would be prevented by having a proven, loving staff of child caretakers. Instead, he was most concerned with germs.

Medical science was still limited in those days; almost everything from colds and flu to diarrhea was untreatable and a possible cause of death. Buck Duke's son or daughter was going to be as protected as possible.

On November 22, 1912, many newspapers around the country carried the story of thirty Cleveland housemaids who joined together to demand fair working conditions from the wealthy families who hired them regularly. Their union would demand a work week not to exceed seventy hours, the chance to have two afternoons off each week, to stop working at 8 P.M. each night, and to be able to entertain a visitor once a week. They also wanted to have a minimum wage in exchange for this service—$4 per week.

The same day the cleaning ladies were fighting for a minimum wage of less than six cents per hour, Doris Duke was born. The moment the umbilical cord was severed and she was breathing on her own, she was worth a minimum of $100 million. It was the low point in her personal fortune, a time of relative poverty, for she would one day use her own business skills to parlay the inheritance into a net worth at least thirty times as great.

# 3

꒰꒱

## Open Season on the Rich

EWSPAPERS HAD changed by the time Doris Duke was born. No longer were they the staid chronicles of events thought-fully prepared by conservative printers/publishers/editors. A new breed of writer had been born at the turn of the century—the newspaper reporter. Prior to that time, the well-educated printers generally served as writers as well. But with increases in circulation, increases in the numbers of newspapers, and competition demand-ing new approaches to selling, poorly educated, sensationalistic voyeurs became the media stars. They needed to be impudent, dar-ing, and willing to go to any lengths, including fabrication, to cre-ate a product that would be popular with the public. They also needed a subject that would prove endlessly fascinating to readers throughout the nation, and that subject became the lives and ex-cesses of the very rich. Being wealthy was to be the subject of end-less speculation, gossip, and titillating feature articles throughout the second decade of the twentieth century, just as being a movie and television star would be in the last decade.

Part of the problem was that there was great disparity between the rich and the poor. Good times were coming for the nation as a whole, though not for large segments of the population. In 1910, the gross national product was $30.4 billion. It was $71.6 billion a decade later. Employment was high. Luxury goods such as auto-mobiles were being enjoyed by more and more people; 10 million autos were sold in the ten years from 1910 to 1920. But all of this had a price for working Americans. Some politicians fought child labor laws, believing that children should be free to work if they so chose. They ignored the fact that many of these children were six and seven years old and that quite a few were dying from injuries, were having partial sight loss from close work, and were having their future limited by a lack of education. Factory work required young women to work twelve or more hours a day for from $5 to $7 a week. Adults often were paid more than children for the same quantity and quality of goods. The elderly, who had no money for winter fuel, frequently died of exposure, hypothermia, or illness such as pneumonia. Articles about men and women starving to death, dropping on the streets while walking miles in search of work, and having to use soup kitchens and bread lines because their jobs paid too little to support their families were commonplace. These were counterpointed by stories of Fifth Avenue mansions in which the owners might pay $120,000 for a dinner set, $30,500 for a toilet set, and even $28,000 for a salt cellar.

For example, when New York's Mrs. Ralph Shainwald visited London, England, and lost the fur muff she used to keep her hands warm, the story was newsworthy. Such muffs were popular hand warmers for women and were sold inexpensively in many stores. Even Mrs. Shainwald was not concerned with the replacement price of her muff, though the sentimental value caused her to pursue the matter. To the amazement of both reporters and the public, the simple muff she lost had originally been purchased for $15,000.

New York City tried to keep everyone happy during Doris Duke's first decade, when the city's population increased more than 25 percent. A number of recreation areas were constructed on the waterfront, and a few of the piers employed kindergarten teachers to care for small children during the day. At night the same areas were used for band concerts and other adult diversions. Forty playgrounds were established throughout the city, as well as numerous small green areas meant to serve as miniparks.

Food was cheap for the drinking man since a free lunch was supplied when you bought gin, beer, or some other beverage in many saloons. Abstainers had fewer options, though they still could take advantage of the lunch wagons maintained by members of the Women's Auxiliary of the Church Temperance Society.

By contrast, the excesses of the rich became fodder for the traditional press as well as gossip publications such as *Town Topics,* the forerunner of *Spy, People,* and the *National Enquirer.* Party planner Harry Lehr worked with socialites such as Mrs. Stuyvesant Fish to put on parties such as the one supposedly honoring Prince del Drago. The food was served on a 300-piece gold service from Tiffany's. The guest of honor was not European royalty, as the invitations implied, but an elaborately dressed monkey accompanied by chorus girls and circus animals rented for the occasion from shows in the area.

At Fifth Avenue and 65th Street, Caroline Astor, her son John Jacob, and his wife, Ava Willing Astor, maintained a mansion with a ballroom capable of holding 1,000 people—guests and servants—as well as adequate kitchens to feed them all. Ava held her husband in disdain and was known to delight in counterculture art forms, frequent love affairs, and endless rounds of bridge.

The Astor money was relatively limitless because it was based on real estate holdings, not retailing or manufacturing. John Jacob Astor IV owned many of the most overcrowded tenements in New York City, and when he was not gouging tenants who lived two and three families to a single room, he was renting ground-floor space to sweatshops. His actions also contributed to epidemics in the city since his tenants frequently became seriously ill, then transferred the germs to the expensive clothing they made in the sweatshops. When the elaborately constructed dresses, blouses, skirts, suits, and other clothing, all carefully made by women and children, were sent to high-priced stores for sale, illness occasionally followed, the long-lived germs having become embedded in the clothing.

Reformers were regularly trying to change the anti-poor business practices of the Fifth Avenue families, usually without success. Just as Duke had bribed his way to exceptions in the antitrust actions against his tobacco companies, so the Fifth Avenue families distracted the legislators with their "gifts" to the city. John Jacob Astor IV was allowed to stay a slumlord because he also created the St. Regis and the Knickerbocker hotels. The former was for people so rich, no one dared ask their worth. The latter was for the "poor"— those whose millions could be counted in the single digits.

Buck Duke had avoided the worst excesses of the times until his daughter was born. Even then he had the good taste to be more subtle than most of his Fifth Avenue neighbors. He did not throw flamboyant parties. He did not try to get his name in the newspaper. And when he was bursting with a father's pride, his efforts to celebrate the newborn child were outrageous but not known outside his art dealer's office and the household staff.

The love for museum-quality art that Doris Duke would eventually acquire over her lifetime was nurtured literally from birth. Buck began buying art that depicted either scenes of children or scenes that would delight a child in order to hang them where his daughter could see and enjoy them. Price was no object; image was everything. Dealers would provide him with great masters, such as the work of seventeenth-century London portrait and landscape painter Thomas Gainsborough. Duke had no knowledge of what he was acquiring or the history of the artists, nor did he care except when he wanted to have someone such as Gainsborough commissioned to paint Doris. Only then did he learn that the painter was long dead.

Having a baby changed the lives of the Dukes in ways they never anticipated. Nanaline Duke still fantasized that her son Walker would be the heir to the Duke businesses and fortune. She overlooked the fact that Walker, jealous of his newborn sister and certain that his place in the family had just been made less secure, took to his room, drinking heavily. He was only seventeen, but already he was abusing alcohol as a buffer against the emotions he didn't want to experience.

Nanaline was relieved that her child was a girl. While she knew that the Dukes were activists in the movement to educate women and integrate them into the workplace, she did not understand that Buck's dream of an heir to run his business ventures could cross sex lines in an era when business changes almost always meant "and Son" added to the door. She felt that Walker had won by default. She did not want to have to raise Doris, but at least Walker was elevated to what she felt was his proper place. When she learned that there was no way her son would be favored, that Doris would become the primary heir to what she thought should have been the Holt/Inman family fortune, she was livid. While she kept Buck oblivious through more frequent sex, she felt betrayed by the man and wanted vengeance.

Ironically, Doris Duke may not even have been Buck's child. Her physical appearance was much closer to that of a Scandinavian employee with whom Nanaline was believed to have had an affair. She was delighted with tall, blond men, and Doris's build matched neither the Duke nor the Holt sides of the family.

Many years later, when Nanaline was in her late eighties, she told Doris that Buck was not her father. The information was meant to hurt her daughter, which it did, though only because Doris looked upon the man who nurtured, taught, and protected her over the years to be her father. Biology had nothing to do with the love she still felt intensely. Whether her mother's words were accurate has not been determined, although Doris's physical appearance certainly matches the "confession" her mother made. Doris did not want to investigate what had become ancient history. And even if Doris was the result of an adulterous fling, at the time of the birth, Nanaline had the good sense to remain silent.

There was no hint of scandal in the newspapers. Doris was viewed as the child of James "Buck" Duke, and as such she was the richest infant in the world. Newspapers were filled with accounts of her first days and weeks. And the fascinated public responded with letters. Some expressed delight in the birth. Some asked the newborn baby for money, as if with wealth came the instant ability to read, write, and handle a checkbook. And some threatened the baby with harm. Kidnapping, an act so rare in Europe that the French newspapers referred to it as "the American crime," was becoming an epidemic in the United States. And while twenty years later the story of the kidnapping of Charles Lindbergh's baby would make international headlines, the problem began around the turn of the century.

No one knew how serious the kidnap threats might be. Some families looked upon the letters as entertainers would when dealing with overly exuberant fans. While recognizing that there could be a danger, they did not feel they were ever at immediate risk.

Others were more cautious, turning their nurseries and often their homes into what could be seen as either fortresses or prisons. Barred windows, special glass, bodyguards, and other precautions were taken.

By 1920, when Doris Duke was eight, kidnapping was a crime regularly reported on the front page of American newspapers, and it was a problem that would continue another fifteen years. Bootleggers kidnapped their rivals or members of their rivals' families. Ku Klux Klan members, primarily in the Southern states, Oregon, and Indiana, were using kidnappings to terrorize and sometimes kill. Blacks were the obvious targets, but Klan members soon were kidnapping anyone they hated. Sometimes this meant Jewish business owners. Other times they would take bootleggers, laborers striking against businesses their leaders owned or supported, and even known adulterers.

The venerable *New York Times* would eventually keep a box score of the kidnappings that most affected their readers. They documented the problem going back to the 1899 kidnapping of Marion Clarke from the city's Central Park (recovered without ransom) to Edward Cudahy's kidnapping in Omaha, Nebraska, the following year (recovered after his parents paid $25,000 ransom) to the 282 kidnappings in twenty-eight states in 1932. New York experienced only seventeen of these compared with forty-nine cases in Illinois. But the latter were often related to rival gangs and the former frequently involved family members of the rich.

As Doris became old enough to understand, Buck warned her about possible kidnappings, kept her relatively isolated, and always had bodyguards to protect her. She accepted his fear and adopted it for herself. Later she would warn her servants to be cautious about saying where they worked for fear they would be kidnapped in order to extort money from her. She made clear to the staff members that if they were ever kidnapped, she would not pay a ransom. No matter what might happen to someone close to her, the act of paying a ransom would trigger dangerous copycat crimes that might otherwise not occur, Doris believed. She also traveled against type, preferring a battered farm pickup truck or other nondescript vehicle to the Rolls-Royce or other luxury car she easily could afford. Tom Rybak recalled one instance late in her life when he was her chef. The two of them, along with a woman named Chandi Heffner, whom Doris eventually adopted, left the Somerville, New Jersey, property to go swimming just as a tourist bus pulled up to the gate. Tom could hear the guide using the loudspeaker system to help the passengers see where Doris Duke might appear. No one suspected that the woman who passed them in the battered work vehicle was the wealthiest woman in the world.

The actual danger to Duke was never known. If anyone truly plotted against her, the incident never went far enough to become public knowledge. By contrast, Woolworth heiress Barbara Hutton would one day face a genuine threat when planning a well-publicized trip to Hawaii. Several men had read about what was supposedly her insatiable, rarely satisfied appetite for sex. Thinking of themselves as studs who could delight the "poor little rich girl," they developed an elaborate plan to kidnap her, then give her the best sex she had ever fantasized. They were caught before they could act it out, yet apparently they were sincere. There was no thought of ransom, no thought that what they were contemplating was rape, no idea that they would be hurting Hutton by their actions. She had become so familiar to them through the newspaper accounts, it was as if they fancied she would be delighted by the actions of her newfound friends.

The other fear Buck Duke had for his child was of disease. Colds and flu were for the poor. If he could have hired marksmen to shoot germs, he would have done so. Instead he paid the doctors and nurses who had helped with the delivery to stay in the house for the first year. He sterilized Doris's rooms both in New York and New Jersey. Ammonia was the disinfectant of choice, and the homes always smelled from it. Nanaline tried to counter the odor with perfume, but to little avail.

Another medical enemy was infantile paralysis—polio—which had reached epidemic proportion in New York and many other parts of the United States at about the same time that war broke out in Europe. Buck Duke wanted to do anything to be certain his baby Doris did not get sick. He arranged for the family to flee to England, where the illness apparently had not struck. He also had a private railroad car christened "Doris" constructed for travel in the United States, then carefully disinfected by a staff hired to do nothing else. He was determined to take his child anywhere in the world that would keep her safe from illness.

The trip was especially important to Nanaline, for she and Buck had the opportunity to be presented to the King and Queen of England. Although the event was not important to the American press, it was duly noted in the British papers.

The chance to appear at the Court of St. James meant different things for men and women. Women were allowed to show off their wealth. Nanaline wore ropes of valuable pearls, a velvet cape lined with gold tissues, and a gown that was white and gold brocade with pearls and diamonds embroidered on the corsage. Her husband, Buck, refused to attend.

The problem, according to Buck, was that he had had a fat stomach and skinny legs. Men all wore the same outfit—purple silk knee breeches with other traditional vestments. Buck later commented that had he gone, he would have looked like a "caricature of a brownie" or an elf. The U.S. Ambassador arranged for an escort for Nanaline while Buck stayed home.

The trip to London proved brief since the family had to return to Manhattan in order to avoid the violence that shortly was to overwhelm Europe.[1]

Not immediately related to concerns about Doris was another enemy with which Buck Duke had to contend: the new personal income tax. He was against anything that would deprive himself and his heirs of the money he had earned and was continuing to generate. Even worse, in order to be certain that the rich gave their fair share, the federal government was closely scrutinizing businesses. Duke decided to hide his wealth in ways that would avoid scrutiny or would be underappreciated by the investigators, assuring a much lower tax.

While Doris Duke would one day hide money in everything from art objects to precious gems used as part of the construction of one of her homes, Buck went back to basics—gold. He had a vault on Duke Farms, the Somerville, New Jersey, estate, in which he placed more than $11 million in gold. He deposited more millions of dollars in gold in Swiss bank vaults. No matter what happened with the economy or his businesses, no matter what the government might try to take from him, there would always be enough hidden gold to provide comfortably for several generations of his family, anywhere in the world. Eventually Doris would add to these holdings, with the volume of gold being valued by the *ton*; other wealthy Americans measured their holdings in large-denomination gold coins and 100-ounce gold bars.

The war to end all wars, as World War I would come to be known to the generation who fought it, temporarily prevented Buck Duke from engaging in the international tobacco business. This had been his specialty while Ben was overseeing the home front. Rather than redefine his corporate role, Buck decided to take advantage of the problem by becoming a stay-at-home father, doting on Nanaline and Doris.

This attitude was one of the great incongruities of Buck Duke. He liked to have long-term mistresses and brief affairs with women. He saw sex as a method for revitalizing his health and rejuvenating his spirit. He did not consider it to be the exclusive domain of marriage, though the more creative and aggressive the woman, the more likely he was to stay with her as his only lover.

Nanaline also seems to have had an occasional affair, which helped give rise to the rumors that Doris was fathered by someone other than Buck. And some of the house staff laughed when any Nordic-looking male wanting a job would be hired, regardless of his on-the-job skills.

Nanaline did not seem to have an intense sexual interest in Buck, though apparently she did not deny him. Part of this may have been her way of assuring that Buck would take more of an interest in his stepson as a major heir. Certainly she was much more sexually aggressive before their marriage than she was afterward.

Yet throughout most of the marriage, Buck adored Nanaline. His frustrations with her did not interfere with his wish to make her genuinely happy. And he was thrilled with any loving attention she gave him.

This is not to say that Buck did not spoil his daughter in ways that were undoubtedly upsetting for his wife, who wanted her firstborn child shown more respect, even though he was not Buck's progeny. For example, Buck knew that Nanaline loved fine clothes and thought Doris should have them as well. He purchased thousands of yards of fabrics and furs, carefully storing them so they could be utilized however long the war continued. He bought silk and white ermine, mink, leather for shoes, and other expensive material. Nanaline found a few former French designers working in the United States who had some sense of what few style changes were taking place during the war. But most of the clothing that

Buck had made for his wife and daughter had to be traditionally elegant rather than trendsetting. The international couturiers either were no longer working or had designs that could not be shipped to the United States.

Such shopping excesses were common among the very rich, who considered any change in their hedonistic lifestyles to be personal affronts. They were public enough in their actions that they became the subject of envy, ire, or derision when the press began reporting what was taking place. And such publishing increased when the new income tax allowed the federal government to release a listing of the wealthiest people in America.

James Duke was only Number 9 because John D. Rockefeller's oil, gas, and electric companies kept him in first place. However, the Rockefeller fortune would be dissipated quickly through bequests to family members. The Rockefeller heirs would become rich, but Doris would eventually become richer because James Duke had only one primary heir.

The publicity about the wealthy and especially their families, such as the newborn Doris Duke, who often was called the million-dollar baby, increased both the hate mail and the pleas for money. It also made the homes of the rich tourist attractions, just as the homes of the stars in Hollywood are tour bus attractions.

Buck Duke originally had not been overly concerned with security on the farmland surrounding his Somerville estate. He tolerated visitors to the property provided they stayed away from the house. But with the newspaper stories about Doris and the wealth of her father came an increase in sightseers.

Trash became a problem, as did the poaching of animals living on the land. Fire was a risk, as was the danger from a bullet from an improperly aimed hunter's rifle. There were even people who created Duke estate souvenirs, such as picture postcards, a popular collectible of the day, then sold them from the Duke land. Buck finally sealed off the estate, certain it was the only way to protect his daughter.

There would be nothing normal about Doris Duke's childhood, even by the standards of the very rich. She was raised in the manner of a wealthy grande dame, not a little child. There were nannies under the authority of a principal nanny. She had a personal maid

and a second maid whose only concern was clothing. There were
three bodyguards and four nurses. She had a laundress, and if she
needed to travel, a Rolls-Royce and chauffeur were reserved for her
personal use.

Clothing was an obsession with Buck Duke, and Doris had
more outfits designed for her in the first few years of her life than
Barbie would have in her first quarter century of toy doll existence.
One massive room of the Somerville estate was turned into a closet
for her. The clothing was carefully hung in an order that matched
the coding in a thick binder filled with page after page of designs
and fabrics. There would be a swatch from the material—usually
yellow, Doris's favorite color throughout her life—and the accom-
panying dress design sketch. Each morning she would be brought
the book, look at the designs, check the swatches, then decide what
she wanted to wear.

At the same time, whenever possible, Buck arranged for Doris's
toy dolls to have clothing created by the great fashion designers of
the day. Buck Duke delighted in telling a story about Doris and her
interest in one particular doll that was being sold at the F.A.O.
Schwarz toy store, then the nation's largest. The incident was later
related by Mrs. William Few, the wife of the former president of
Duke University to whom Buck first told the story.

"I think she was probably about seven years old. Her mother
took her into [F.A.O.] Schwarz's. And there was this doll, wonderful French doll, with a beautiful wardrobe, costumes, and it was in
the very earliest days of the talking doll. I think it had a record
playing in the back that you could turn on. It was a wonderful doll
but it was $300 or a big sum. Everything was beautiful. It had
French handmade clothes; it was the size of a two-year child. Doris
was crazy about it. 'Mother, may I have that doll?'

"She said, 'No Doris, that doll is just too expensive. You may
not have it. It's outrageous to pay that for a doll.'

"She couldn't get it out of her mind. The next time she went
down street [sic] she had her governess take her to Schwarz's, and
she wanted to see the doll again. It was still there. I think they had
only one of a kind at that price.

"She talked so much about the doll, but my impression is that
she was asked not to mention it to her father. So Mrs. Duke said,

'Well, you know now, you already have an allowance, and every month if you put aside some of the money, you will soon have enough. It will not be too long before you can buy that doll.' So one day—I think she had almost forgotten about the doll or stopped talking about it months later—Mrs. Duke called her and said, 'Doris, I've gone over your account and I found you have more than enough now to buy that doll. I had it put away. I made a deposit to keep it for you when you did get enough money to buy it. Now you can get it.'

"She said, 'Mother, I'm too old now. I don't want that doll.'

"Mr. Duke told Dr. Few that story with tears in his eyes. He said, 'I'll never forget that.'"[2]

# 4

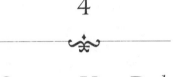

## Growing Up a Duke

THE SOMERVILLE ESTATE had ample grounds for Doris to explore, yet she had little chance for social interaction other than with adults. She saw cousins Anthony Drexel Duke and Angier Biddle Duke, but usually only for special occasions such as birthdays, when Buck would hire a circus to entertain. The same big-top arrangement would be set up on the farm as would be utilized when playing for an audience of hundreds in a large community. The only difference was that young Doris Duke was in charge, the audience limited to family and friends. Whatever acts she didn't enjoy were either cut short or eliminated for the day. And when she did find a performance to be particularly enjoyable, she could have it repeated immediately.

Doris Duke's education was haphazard but thorough. She was officially enrolled in the Brearley School in New York, a school whose program ran counter to that of most private girls' school programs of the day. She attended Brearley's classes when she was living in Manhattan, though with her travels among the family homes, the bulk of her education came from both her father and tutors.

The world in which Doris Duke spent her childhood was not one conducive to women becoming knowledgeable. The January 1926 *Harper's Magazine* carried an article by Bertrand Russell, a philosopher, mathematician, and author who would eventually win the Nobel Prize, in which he told the difference between a gentleman and a lady. He stated that the quality of a gentleman was determined by what he knew. The quality of a lady was determined by how little she knew. He believed that the highest attainments for a woman involved having little knowledge of the world around her. She was to be an ornament, an adornment, an attractive, empty-headed appendage who fulfilled whatever role her husband, lover, or employer desired within the social constraints of the day.

Private schools for girls of Doris Duke's generation did not fully ascribe to the Bertrand Russell idea, for they believed that exposure to certain areas of knowledge was critical for success. They focused on making a young lady conversant with the arts. She would learn history, including the history of art, English literature, biological sciences, and modern languages. She would become fluent enough to shop in any country whose stores and bazaars had merchandise that appealed to the elite.

The Brearley School was typical of the programs meant to send young women to college. In addition to the subjects mentioned, the students would be taught mathematics (including a minimum of algebra and geometry), physical sciences, Latin, French, chemistry and/or physics, as well as more history courses than were provided in finishing schools.

The Brearley School planned its educational program around the entrance examination for Harvard. Although Harvard was exclusively a men's school, Harvard was held in such high esteem that it was felt that if the Brearley girls could pass the entrance exam, they could succeed in any school they wished to attend. Most went on to attend Wellesley and Bryn Mawr.

Whether because of Brearley, her tutors, or both, Doris's intelligence and ability would become obvious when Buck Duke died shortly before his daughter's thirteenth birthday. He had provided for his child with a series of multimillion-dollar trust funds, the first in 1917 and the second in 1924. But no one, with the possible exception of Buck, expected Doris to challenge the decisions of the estate's trustees and caretakers. She insisted on taking control of her own life just as she reached the teenage years. To the surprise of those who fought her challenge to their control, she was successful.

⌘

DORIS DUKE WAS NOT always the heir apparent to the leadership of the various Duke enterprises. At first Angier Buchanan Duke,

Ben's son, seemed to represent the future success or failure of the businesses. Angier, a wild playboy who at first seemed likely to follow in the footsteps of his uncle Brodie, drank frequently and had lost his right hand in a shooting accident. Despite that, with no other heirs between them, Buck and Ben began training him in the businesses they ran. He graduated from Trinity College and briefly attended the same business college that Buck had tried before moving full-time into his father's tobacco business. And he was encouraged to experience all aspects of his father's and uncle's business world, the older men supplying constant tutoring.

Angier Buchanan Duke was already a young man when Doris was born, and Buck looked upon him as a potential guardian and guide for his first cousin, Doris. Although a playboy even after marriage, Angier Buchanan Duke was serious about business and family obligations. Since womanizing was a family sport, everyone overlooked that aspect of his character, including, it seems, the woman who agreed to be his wife.

Life changed radically for everyone on Thanksgiving day, 1914. Angier Buchanan was twenty-nine, his cousin Doris was a baby of two, and Cordelia Biddle was sixteen. Cordelia and Angier were at a party in New Jersey, and he was enchanted by the teenager.

Cordelia was the daughter of wealthy Philadelphia eccentric A. J. Drexel Biddle. Biddle had a rich inheritance and was a modestly successful author and amateur boxer who had the money to hire professionals to spar with him in his living room. His eccentricities were later captured in Cordelia's autobiography *My Philadelphia Father,* which was made into the movie *The Happiest Millionaire.* The girl's vivaciousness delighted Angier as much as her willingness to go to bed with him. Neither one seemed concerned with taking precautions or the potential consequences of their actions. Five months into her pregnancy, the couple had a large wedding, the bridal gown designed to downplay the evidence of the child who would be born on November 30, 1915. Doris, a toddler, was their flower girl, and the couple seemed as happy as if Angier did not have to make "an honest woman" of Cordelia.

Ben and Sarah Duke and Buck and Nanaline Duke were all delighted with the alliance with the Biddle family. They benefited in ways normally associated with arranged marriages, and they offered the newlyweds the type of help they thought the couple would need to get through their first year of marriage and early parenthood. Ben Duke gave his son $1 million to cover any help he might need around the 89th Street mansion he also bought the couple. And so the bride wouldn't think the elder Dukes considered only the practical side of life, they gave Cordelia a pearl necklace valued at $75,000. It was a nice accompaniment to the jewelry Angier gave his bride, which cost double the value of the pearls.

The Biddles had the social standing the Dukes lacked, and the Dukes had both the money and the potential for future income that the Biddles lacked. The brothers Duke and their wives decided to take advantage of their new society connections, a position that was enhanced the day of Angier's wedding when Ben announced that his other child, twenty-eight-year-old Mary, would marry Tony Biddle, a decade younger than herself and the brother of the bride. The arrangement was shocking by the standard of the day. Younger women could marry older men, but older women did not indulge themselves in high school boys. No one spoke too loudly, though. The Biddle/Duke alliance was respected, as were European alliances through arranged marriage between the heirs to two thrones.

Thrust into high society, the Duke brothers sought new homes where they could enjoy their new positions. Ben and Sarah turned to Great Neck, Long Island, formerly a haunt of Mrs. Cornelius Vanderbilt, where they rented a summer estate for entertaining. Buck and Nanaline selected Newport, Rhode Island, another haunt of the rich and prominent, for their party location. Once again it was a decision that eventually would affect Doris's lifestyle and special interests as an adult.

Newport was the popular summering place for the likes of the Vanderbilts and Astors. Social acceptance required renting for at least four seasons, then having the approval of whoever was considered the most prominent socialite in the area the year you arrived. Although these were summer homes, especially the ones along the rocky shoreline, they were the summer homes of people who had the money to be self-indulgent on a scale seen nowhere else in the world except among royalty. The Vanderbilt home had seventy rooms. At parties for friends, favors might be precious gems, and at parties for the pets of friends, animals were expected to be dressed as if they were humans going to a formal affair.

In 1922 the Dukes felt accepted enough in Newport to buy Rough Point, an estate built in 1886 by Frederick W. Vanderbilt, then subsequently owned by Greece's Princess Anastasia.

Prior to the Civil War, Rough Point was a drop point for ships loaded with human cargo. Some slave ship captains packed their human cargo in the hold approximately a third of a meter apart (roughly thirteen inches). The width was slightly more than a woman would need and slightly less than the average man's shoulders. Laid on pallets, chained to keep them from moving, large numbers of bodies could be jammed into the holds.

Due to lack of exercise, limited diet, and limited exposure to daylight, many became sick or died. Yet to slave ship owners, the survivors always assured profitable voyages. And some buyers may have felt proud to obtain the strongest among each new shipment.

On board, many captives died horribly. The lucky ones went quickly from disease. Many others died because they were suffocated by falling excrement from the men and women on the tiers above them. Because they were chained hand and foot, they could not shift to avoid the nightmare of falling waste and vomit.

Upon arriving in the waters off Newport, those slaves healthy enough to be sold were removed for shipment to the slave markets. The dead would be disposed of as swiftly as possible. In the interest of time and to avoid offending crew members' sensibilities, bodies were dismembered and tossed into the ocean. The callousness toward the dead almost matched the ship captains' attitudes toward the living.

Hundreds of men, women, and children were dumped into the water. Many people felt that you could sense the screams and moans of the terrified survivors coming in and out with the tide. Social critics did not miss the irony of Newport society homes being built on the captives' watery graves.

Nanaline saw the ownership of Rough Point as a way to become accepted by the New England moneyed class. Once she had the respect of the neighboring families, she could then move Walker into proper position to be the rightful Duke heir. He would be able to meet the daughters of the old-line aristocrats as well as the newly rich whose money had purchased their position. Regardless of what Buck might think of him, Walker, then twenty-seven, would become the obvious Duke heir.

Doris was not a consideration in her mind. The girl was ten, awkward, and already taller than her mother, who did not have any affection for her.

Walker Inman may have been his mother's favored child, but he lacked her social aspirations and the shrewdness to attain them. He had the poor judgment to fall in love with Garnet (her real name was Helene Patton Clarke), a young woman who was the daughter of a Kokomo, Indiana, minister and the ex-wife of a songwriter. Although he might have been able to enjoy her as a mistress—after all, affairs were a Duke tradition—he was too honorable. He married the woman despite the fact that the relationship was doomed from the start.

Walker was allegedly an alcoholic who liked to fight in bars and batter his wife at home. She apparently found solace in the arms of three men, a bootlegger known as Yip, a vaudeville entertainer, and a swindler who traveled the globe in order to bilk the gullible. The latter was known as Dapper Dan Collins, and his reputation was so notorious that when the Inmans divorced, the judges in Reno had compassion for Walker when they learned that his wife had been unfaithful with Collins. However, a woman usually was treated gently in divorce cases, even when she was the guilty party. Although she was given far less alimony than Walker could have afforded and would have had to pay had he been deemed the guilty party, the sum could have supported five families living modestly but comfortably in most cities. For the first three years following the divorce she was to receive $1,250 per month while she found work, education, or remarried. After that her allowance would be cut to $750 a month for life. Another $25,000 was provided for her attorney's fees, though whether this all went to pay lawyers is not known.

Eventually Walker did settle down, remarried, and became a trustee of both Duke University and the Duke Endowment. He also became the father of Walker Inman, Jr. However, in 1924, Walker's behavior led his mother to ban him from her Newport home, an action that pleased Buck but not the only child Doris, who longed for company, even if it was her older, ne'er-do-well half brother.

One theory about why Nanaline did not want Walker around was because when people learned his age, they would know she had lied about her own. Georgia census records listed her birth as 1869; however, any other documents requiring her age showed that she shaved off at least five years. Having Walker around the Newport area would have revealed Nanaline's lie and exposed her vanity.

At the same time, Angier Buchanan Duke and Tony Duke were experiencing their own scandals. Angier's problems were the worst. Both youths had their uncle's tendency toward womanizing, but Angier was a heavy drinker as well. Oblivious to caution, he had several serious accidents that earned press coverage, including killing a pedestrian after hitting a wall along a Bronx parkway.

Eventually the Biddle children had enough of the Duke siblings. Cordelia, the mother of two children by Angier, gained a divorce first. Then Tony, who also had two children, divorced his wife.

Buck's health was failing during this time, so he acquired a mansion in Charlotte, North Carolina, as a way of showing off his wealth back in his home state. Lavish dinner parties were held there, after which he frequently took his guests to the projection room, where he had his own movie theater. This was the latest fad of the very rich, and they were able to rent Hollywood's most popular silent movies. However, Buck went a step further, obtaining motion picture equipment so he could film Doris growing up, then show the movies along with the features.

Buck also arranged for an occasional mistress to stay in Charlotte, just as he had arranged for the Smith girl to stay on his Somerville estate. However, while Angier and Tony were happily exercising their libidos, Buck's health was such that he could satisfy neither the woman nor himself so often as he desired.

Nanaline turned a blind eye to all the Duke philandering. She knew how to use sex to get what she desired, but she never found great pleasure in the physical side of a relationship. She viewed sex as a tool in a woman's arsenal, not a sensual pleasure. As a result, she felt that the women Buck pursued served a useful purpose for herself as well, keeping him satisfied. As long as he did not begin to think about marrying one of the women. Nanaline was relieved to not have to deal with his sexual needs.

———————⟿———————

THE DECLINE IN Buck Duke's health seemed to be directly related to the stress of dealing with a moral crisis he faced in business in 1917. Over the years, market studies had been a major tool of his tobacco companies. He knew the sex and age groups of his buyers. He realized that cigarettes were mostly a man's product, so when he brought out Lucky Strike Cigarettes, a brand that would be enormously popular in the years to come, he used a pretty girl's face as part of the packaging.

However, he used another marketing innovation. Buck increased his sales by broadening the appeal to women. His ads showed the women smoking, not just holding a cigarette, as was standard for selling to men. The new ads were extremely successful. In 1917, however, Buck also saw research proof that cigarette smoking was killing his customers.

Three major studies on smoking and health were undertaken after cigarette smoking became popular. The first of the studies, in the 1890s, took place when there was really too little information about the long-term effects of cigarettes to make the study effective. The second study, in 1917, shocked Buck. It proved conclusively that anyone who smoked cigarettes, male or female, had a far greater than normal chance of dying from heart disease and cancer. (The third and best-known study, in the 1950s, triggered limitations on advertising and forced the manufacturers to add health warning labels.)

According to the second study, the problem was not caused by the tobacco but by some combination of paper and binder chemistry, perhaps enhanced when the cigarette was smoked. This meant that, theoretically, altering the method of production could eliminate the danger both to smokers and to those breathing what today is called secondhand smoke. The latter caused an increase in asthma and bronchial problems even when it failed to cause early death. Yet instead of paying for research to investigate safe alternatives, Buck ordered the study destroyed. He was able to purge most of his company's records, though word of the study was leaked to other companies whose executives were shaken by the news, recognizing the potential end of their business.

Buck Duke had a crisis of conscience, not wanting to lose a major source of his wealth yet not wanting to be the cause of others' deaths. He knew that burning the study was a delaying tactic, that too many copies had been leaked. Convinced that the public would learn about the dangers and be smart enough to stop smoking, he decided to stay in the business so long as money could be made, believing that the industry was doomed.

However, he warned family and friends not to smoke (he only smoked cigars), then kept his production equal to the demand resulting from his innovative advertising. Ironically, Nanaline secretly smoked and Doris developed the habit after her father's death.

———— ❧ ————

THE WORRIES OVER the future of the tobacco business were compounded when the plans Ben and Buck made for corporate leadership succession was shattered on Labor Day weekend, September 3, 1923. Angier Duke was the heir apparent for succeeding his father and uncle as the leader of the Duke corporations. He was also a playboy who owned a yacht named the *Althea,* which he regularly used for parties. Men and women would be invited on board for drinking and sex. The group would usually eat in the Indian Harbor Yacht Club in Greenwich, Connecticut, rather than have a chef prepare food on the seventy-six-foot yacht. Then they would return to the vessel for a night's frolic.

On the weekend of September 3, Angier and five friends—two men and three women—were in a small dinghy, traveling from the dock to where the yacht was moored. The dinghy capsized, something that startled them but did not seem to be a problem at first. They were mildly drunk, but they were strong swimmers in calm water. Angier, of course, had the use of only one arm, yet he had developed the strength and dexterity needed to use that arm to swim, row a boat, and otherwise handle himself as well as his able-bodied companions.

The friends saved themselves, laughing about the dunking and getting out of the wet clothes so they could pursue the rest of the night's planned activities. Only when they looked about did they realize Angier was not among them. He had swum into a piling, been knocked unconscious, and drowned before anyone knew he was missing.

Ben and Sarah Duke were devastated. Angier was their future, the company's future, a life that should have continued long after theirs was over. The idea that they would ever bury the vibrant, intelligent son they had raised was beyond comprehension. Nothing could have prepared them for his death. Nothing could make them understand it. They aged overnight, Ben becoming a sickly old man within a matter of weeks.

Buck was also devastated when the news was cabled to him. He was traveling abroad and could not be reached immediately. He grieved for the loss of his nephew and for the radical change in corporate plans. With the changes in the tobacco industry he was anticipating, Angier was to be his gift to Doris. Angier would know how to diversify the business, what to fold, what to exploit, and how to assure the stability of the family wealth. Angier would also be able to care for Doris as she matured into womanhood. He would be her guide and he would not steal from her wealth as others might do. Without Angier there was only Nanaline and her son, Walker Inman, neither of whom Buck trusted.

Buck made several decisions. He did not feel he could quickly find someone trustworthy to teach his business to; therefore, he would have to work with his daughter, educating her about the business she would inherit as well as the world of investment, entrepreneurship, and related matters. He would work with her as much as possible while he still had his health, hoping that she would master the essentials, learning whatever else she needed on her own after he was gone.

Buck Duke began to rid himself of much of his tobacco stock.

Fuel and power became the primary Duke investments of choice. He acquired extensive holdings in Texaco, and the growing aluminum industry drew his attention.

# 5

## *Learning to Be Independent*

*A*PART FROM BUCK's teachings about business, there was another important influence in Doris's young life—Jenny Renaud, a French-born governess. Jenny was perhaps the most important person to Doris besides her father in her early years.

Probably Jenny would not have been hired had Nanaline realized how much influence the woman would have on Doris. Jenny was young, attractive, and a part of the post–World War I swinging generation. She smoked and drank in public, attended nightclubs, danced the latest steps, and generally had a good time. She was rumored to be bisexual and to delight in sensual pleasures of all types.

Exactly what Doris's childhood had been like before Jenny Renaud is uncertain. Most biographers create an image of a wealthy, spoiled, isolated child filled with great loneliness and longing for friends. Pony Duke, Doris's cousin, has stated that prior to Renaud's hiring, the servants were ordered to behave in the formal manner common with the British. This meant that they did not speak unless spoken to. Nanaline was a social climber who adopted the image she felt a Northern woman of her means should have.

Yet when a much older Doris spoke with friends, such as the Reverend Lawrence Roberts who was close to her for the last twenty-five years of her life, she gave the impression that the early years of her life were happy. While Jenny may have given her more attention than the other staff members, apparently Doris never felt isolated when growing up.

Jenny Renaud was unimpressed with Doris's wealth. She genuinely liked the girl she was hired to teach and guide. She also liked broadening Doris's awareness of the world at large, whether this meant telling her about the nightclubs of France she had frequented or having the chauffeur take them into entertainment areas of whatever city they were in.

Jenny Renaud didn't introduce Doris Duke to piano playing, but Jenny did offer the first encouragement. She imbued in Doris the belief that she had the skill and talent to be an accomplished musician. And it was at the piano that Doris Duke always came alive.

Over the years, Doris's musical skills were the subject of jokes and derision by those who knew her only superficially or who worked on her estates. The complaints generally centered around her singing. She would, however, eventually become an adequate singer for a professional choir so long as she kept her alto voice soft, blending with the others.

The Reverend Roberts, for many years the pastor of First Baptist Church in Nutley, New Jersey, saw this side of Doris Duke. She had the ear and understanding of a professional musician. She was gifted in the field, a natural improviser as well as being grounded in proper technique.

Piano playing, for rich women, was a requisite social skill meant to entice a young man into marriage. It was also part of the expected skills of a society mother who let other people raise her children. A tutor would be hired for the young, and the child would learn that tutor's style. Often it was possible to identify the students of different society piano teachers by listening to their style of play.

Doris wanted to learn all that there was to know about playing the type of piano music she enjoyed. She did not want to play like anyone but herself. And because her father indulged her, she, not her mother, was responsible for hiring her piano teachers.

Doris would take her regular noon lesson, learning all she felt that particular tutor could teach. Then she would fire that person and hire someone else, usually someone no better than the first, but one who had a different approach to playing. Doris would master that skill, then move on again and again, each time blending what she was learning so she had the background needed from which to begin improvising.

Although it is uncertain where and when she first began hearing jazz music or its forerunners such as gospel and blues, Doris was dedicated to the form from early childhood. She also mastered music theory, arranging, and, eventually, composing. Although barely competent as a singer, she was a gifted piano player capable of holding her own with many professionals.

Nanaline and Buck did not encourage Doris's musical ability. The girl was given lessons because that was what good parents were expected to provide. But Nanaline hated listening to the endless wrong notes that are a part of practicing and learning. And Buck was too focused on business to be much of an audience. Only Jenny Renaud applauded her skills, paid attention to her progress, and regularly encouraged Doris by being able to cite specific areas of improvement.

When Doris was nine, Jenny Renaud was in full charge of her daily life. She even shared the girl's bedroom at times, taking one of the two twin beds there when Doris was young. There was also a sitting room for Doris's use and to separate her rooms from her mother's quarters. She and Jenny would sit there and talk, Jenny behaving like a naughty older sister who had traveled the world, then returned to tell her convent-educated younger sibling what life was really like.

To further frustrate Nanaline, Doris and Jenny spent most of their time speaking in French. Doris wanted to master the language and have privacy from her mother and the other servants. Jenny was bilingual, French being her native tongue, and liked helping Doris learn it.

The fact that Doris Duke was not a total recluse in her later years probably was due to Jenny Renaud's influence. Although Duke would always be a private person, she wanted to live life to the fullest. There was nothing she would not try. And all of this seemed to stem from the encouragement she received from her governess.

It was also Renaud who took her frequently from whichever estate they were living into the community at large. And it has been alleged that it was Renaud who shared Nanaline's bed from time to time, which is why she did not encourage Doris to fire the woman who was so unlike the servants she preferred. In fact, while Nanaline frequently did not talk with the rest of the staff or made minimal comments necessary to give orders, she, Jenny, and Doris often had lunch in Doris's second-floor rooms. Those were more spacious than many apartments. There was a fireplace and a sofa on which they would sit. There was a crystal chandelier overhead, and Doris's grand piano in the corner.

———————— ᦰᢀᢣ ————————

BUCK DUKE GREW close to his daughter during the time they shared. He delighted in talking with her, in discussing his business and the world he knew. She, in turn, adored him to the point of writing him love notes from the time she first learned to write.

Buck and Doris also had spiritual discussions. She was raised a Methodist, though no one, including her closest spiritual friends at the time of her death, knew how her religious upbringing was actually handled. The Reverend Roberts found that Doris had an in-depth knowledge of the Methodist church, its theology and structure. She also was strongly interested in other faiths, including his own Baptist beliefs as well as those of the Catholic church. But one of the few stories concerning Buck's interest in providing his daughter with a grounding in religion was told by Robert F. Durden in his book *The Dukes of Durham*.

According to Durden, when Buck Duke was visiting an engineer friend, A. Carl Lee, he mentioned that he had been telling Doris, who was then around six or seven years old, that he was a Methodist, as his father had been before him. Buck and Doris were in North Carolina at the time, and Buck was mentioning his family's religious affiliation in hopes that she would one day follow what he felt was the family tradition.

Doris was supposed to have said to him, "Daddy, what's the difference between a Methodist and a Presbyterian?"

Buck, uncertain how to answer, told his daughter that it was her bedtime and that they would discuss the matter the next day. Then, before he could talk with her, he located a Presbyterian minister in order to learn the church's history and basis for theological differences. So armed, he returned home to answer his daughter's questions.

Doris also learned that her father believed in reincarnation and did not find the idea incompatible with the teachings of the church. He felt that he might be able to return and enjoy some of his own estate, an idea that eventually became a part of his daughter's thinking.

Religious issues aside, Buck continued spending money for the family's enjoyment. His original Pullman car was replaced by a new private car he bought in 1917 and again named *The Doris.* This one was eighty feet long, longer than the oceangoing yacht Angier purchased for sailing and holding elaborate parties. Ten people could sleep comfortably on *The Doris* as it was pulled across the country. There was a waiter and chef always in attendance, expensive linens and china, and a humidor for the cigars Buck smoked endlessly. He also bought the Piedmont and Northern Railroad, which traveled the Carolinas; a small railroad, it was profitable and provided easy travel within those states.

In those days, having a private railroad car of the size and quality owned by Buck Duke was comparable to owning a private jet equipped for international travel today. Buck Duke played one-upmanship with the other private rail car owners by keeping his car stocked with expensive liquor, wine, and champagne. Cigars were always in abundance, for he smoked as many as thirty a day, and the men who attended parties or other gatherings on the car were encouraged to indulge themselves as well. Nanaline hated it, but the memory of the odors of the car, especially the cigar smoke, would forever remind Doris Duke of her father.

Buck also understood Doris's need for independence despite its risks. As she grew older, he let her walk from their Manhattan home to the Brearley School on her own or with a friend. No adults were obvious. However, a careful check of the traffic would have revealed the chauffeur driving the Rolls-Royce far enough back to blend in with the other cars (as much as a Rolls-Royce can blend with anything other than another Rolls). There were also at least two private detectives on foot, also following at a discreet distance. Doris may or may not have known about all the protection she received, but it was planned so as to give her the illusion of complete freedom. She could talk with people, meet other children, look in store windows, and otherwise enjoy herself. There was almost no chance that she would be kidnapped.

As the years passed, the Charlotte mansion was expanded. A

live-in staff of sixteen had quarters designed on the third floor. There were formal gardens and elaborate fountains, including one that sent water streaming 150 feet into the air. The estate was opened in winter to allow area children to ice skate in those same fountains once they froze over.

Buck also became a part of the Charlotte community as much as he could, hoping that Nanaline and Doris would decide to live there (after he removed the mistress of the moment) as their primary residence. Charlotte seemed the perfect location for Doris to meet and fall in love with a Southern boy when she grew older. He also found it an ideal place to relax, where he could walk the streets and talk with the neighbors about flower gardens, growing seasons, and the nurturing of plants.

Nanaline never liked Charlotte. She might have been happier had Buck left the property small and unchanged, but the community was not one that fit her style. Also she was always afraid of financial loss, and she hated the amount of money Buck spent, even though his shifting of investments and diversification of holdings meant that there was no way Nanaline or Doris could ever want for anything, no matter how much he spent on his mansions.

Doris Duke loved the performing arts, and Buck indulged her interests. He let Doris use his projection room, arranging for her and her friends to see the latest Charlie Chaplin films and other comedies. He also arranged for Doris to have dance lessons in a school that was a training ground for dancers who eventually went on to Broadway careers. She was serious about learning and exercised to stay limber throughout her life. As often as possible, she would take lessons in both classical and modern techniques. She tried to become competent in ballet, tap, jazz, Middle Eastern traditional dance (belly dancing), and others, never letting her advancing years interfere with her lessons.

Ben Duke was the man who exposed Doris to what would become the most important arts focus of the last twenty-five years of her life—black and Southern regional music, from gospel to Stephen Foster. The music was found most readily in the bars and clubs of Harlem, New York, and Ben took his niece to experience them.

Although not yet a teenager, Doris had enough experience with

music to understand the blending of harmonies and voices required for the music she was hearing. She delighted in the songs
with their different rhythms and phrasing, frequently singing them
to her mother, who hated what she was learning. The music reminded Nanaline of Buck's "white trash" roots in post–Civil War
poverty. Even worse, Doris's singing voice was not particularly
good, and only Jenny Renaud seemed to notice that she was more
skillfully adapting the newly discovered styles of music into her piano playing.

It was also during this period that Buck Duke, no longer able to
ignore health problems, began to put his affairs in order. His leg,
always a problem, had become so painful that frequently he could
not walk unaided. He felt that his life was coming to an end,
though not before he seduced one more woman, or so Nanaline
believed.

Buck Duke felt that his deteriorating health would improve if
he were involved with a woman who would focus most of her time
on sexually stimulating him. He had never forgotten his first wife's
sexual dexterity and thought he should seek someone with similar
abilities. After all, he had enjoyed better health with Lillian than he
had with Nanaline. And Nanaline seemed to have sensed that she
might become the next *former* Mrs. Buck Duke.

According to Mrs. Edward C. Marshall, wife of one of the
trustees for the $40 million endowment Buck left to Trinity College
on December 8, 1924, when the school was to be renamed Duke
University:

> Now, Mr. Duke never bothered about buying new clothes or
> new shoes. Like his wife would go buy a new coat, a new dress,
> a hat, and make her happy, but he would buy about every three
> or four years a new suit or if she told him to.
>
> She had a big influence over him; he would take her letter
> from his pocket and he would kiss it and put it back in his
> pocket. Then he would do that two or three times and take it
> out and read it all over and kiss it and put it back in his pocket.
> He really adored her.
>
> My husband and I saw it happen every day. The mail would
> come early, and that letter would come and that would happen
> every day. And many times we walked down to breakfast and

he would be kissing her and loving her, and I said, "Go as far as you like. Don't bother about us." But he really was devoted to her. And he admired her mind; but she said that she got that mind from him. She admired him; she said she learned so much from him. She could sit every evening and not go anywhere and enjoy him as much as she enjoyed any party or anything in the world.

She told him all the things that happened and he just loved that. You see, he hadn't had any of that life. He hadn't had any real home life, and she made such a beautiful home for him. And Doris—he just adored Doris.[1]

That he adored Doris was without question. That he worshipped Nanaline is less certain, at least at the end of his life.

Whatever the case, Buck Duke was convinced he would not have long to live. He wanted to distribute his wealth in a manner that protected everyone. He wanted a new mistress. And he wanted to be free of pain.

The money for Duke University was in some ways an odd bequest. Buck was focused on the business world, convinced that the education a man needed in business would not come from any college or university. Spending time in an institution of higher learning was valuable only for future preachers, teachers, lawyers, chemists and engineers, and doctors. The time spent in school was frivolous for anyone else.

Duke University would overnight become one of the richest schools in the country. The city of Durham was instantly transformed from a party town to a university center concerned with intellectual pursuits.

The school's name change, meant to honor Washington Duke, may have been Buck's idea or it may have come from the president, William Few, who had spent several years cultivating Buck. There is also an indication that the money, actually connected with the tobacco and power industries he ran, was meant to influence the state legislature. Overnight Trinity/Duke had become the Harvard of the South in its financial potential. With the money tied to the tobacco and power companies, the legislators might be nervous about corporate tax and business laws that could reduce the financial potential of the gift.

Buck was right. Stock in his tobacco, utilities, and power companies were included in the Duke Trust Endowment. The money was designated for education and health care, areas that had been of poor quality in North and South Carolina. The legislators knew North Carolina would profit by ignoring Duke's business improprieties. The Duke holdings' success assured desperately needed money for the state. The legislature buckled under the pressure, and Buck's businesses were given special protection they otherwise would not have received. No one wanted to see their value decrease.

More important, and often overlooked in the seemingly self-serving bequest, was the result for the poor. Some interesting requirements were attached to the $40 million in securities that were turned over to the Duke Endowment trustees. The basic endowment would be untouched, only the income used for the charities and other purposes Buck designated. The two Carolinas were to receive 46 percent of the money spent on educational institutions, with 32 percent going to Duke University. A Presbyterian school called Davidson College and Baptist Furman University were each to receive 5 percent, and 4 percent more was given to Johnson C. Smith University, a Charlotte school exclusively used by blacks.

The 32 percent earmarked for health care had some interesting twists. At the time of the trust, hospitalization cost an average of $3 per day. Some hospitals provided free care to the indigent and/or low-income minorities, either as part of their mandate or by area law. Buck Duke wanted to increase the care that was given free as well as reduce the burden on the hospitals of such patients. He authorized a portion of the funds designated for health care to be used to offset the cost of paying for the indigent. Each hospital would receive $1 for every $3 spent on indigent care. While he did not eliminate the cost of such treatment to the institutions, he expanded their resources by a third. The only stipulation was that the hospitals had to be nonprofit and admit all minorities along with whites.

The gift is remarkable in part because of its timing. In 1925, segregation was normal in the South and in many cities in the North. Lynchings of black men were commonplace. In some communities, if a white person ate in what were then known as colored-only restaurants, the black restaurant owner had to destroy the dishes the white person used. By law, the dish could not be further "contaminated" by black use. Night riders and the Ku Klux Klan often terrorized black families for imagined slights or just for not being born white.

The Methodist churches in North Carolina were given 12 percent of the money, 2 percent specifically earmarked for supplementing pension funds for retired ministers and financial aid for their widows or orphans. Another 10 percent went to the institutions that served both black and white orphans in the two Carolinas.

Buck's will made clear that racial and sexual discrimination would not be tolerated. His bequests would change no one's attitude, but they would forever alter the institutions benefiting from him. This meant that the students who attended would also change, if only by nature of a type of interracial contact formerly foreign to their experience. Later this concept was discussed by another Southerner, newspaper publisher Daisy Bates of Little Rock, Arkansas, who, after the 1954 desegregation of the school system (*Brown* v. *Board of Education*) commented that no one can legislate morality. However, you can legislate changes that cause people to act in a moral and ethical way. This was what Buck succeeded in doing.

Among the personal bequests, the will gave Doris the New Jersey farm, although apparently she would have to bid for it at public auction. Buck was going to have it sold, the proceeds paid to Doris. Nanaline would receive the three other homes Buck owned in the form of a lifetime lease, with Doris inheriting them when Nanaline died. All other property Nanaline was allowed to use would also eventually revert to Doris.

Nanaline was granted $100,000 per year for whatever purposes she desired. Doris, in addition to her three-part financial bequest, was given the Doris Duke Trust, which controlled vast quantities of stocks in Buck's businesses, far more than Duke University would receive. The interest and dividends alone totaled $57 million by the time Doris was twenty-eight years old. However, for twenty-one years after the death of the last living direct beneficiary, a third of the money was to be divided among Doris's first cousins and their offspring. Then all the money earned by the trust reverted to Doris.

The list of executors indicates how much Buck cared for Nanaline and trusted her, at least several months before his death when he put his affairs in order. There were three in all, Nanaline being one of them.

Another $100 million trust fund was established in 1924, this one for his daughter, Doris. She would receive the money in three installments—at ages twenty-one, twenty-five, and thirty. In addition, Walker was banned from the Duke homes because he repeatedly came in drunk, rowdy, and occasionally vomited on staff members. He was also left a relative pauper, as his ultimate total combined inheritances from his mother and stepfather came to "only" $30 million. By Duke standards, such a "small" sum was an insult, though one Walker bravely managed to endure.

Buck Duke was also faced with another problem. His first wife, Lillian, who had lost her money to a confidence man, was trying to prove that Buck had not legally divorced her. If she could make a believable case, she felt she could extort more money from him.

Lillian's claim was that the New Jersey divorce was invalid because the Somerville residence was not their primary home. If that was true, Buck's second marriage would be invalid, because Buck would still legally be married to her.

Nanaline was humiliated by the false charges reported in the press. Buck didn't care about the publicity, nor would he pay hush money. He fought and won the case. However, at that time Nanaline also turned against Buck, as if she hated him for the unexpected action taken against their marriage by his ex-wife.

Buck was a big man—six foot two inches tall—who loved to eat. Over the years, he had gained a lot of weight, and Nanaline suddenly decided that this would have to change. No one was certain if she was worried about his health, wanted to deprive him of the sensual pleasure he gained from his food, or wanted him to be more appealing. All that is known is that he agreed to go on the strict diet of her creation.

It was the diet more than anything else that seemed to prove the truth of Mrs. Edward Marshall's words concerning his love for Nanaline. Buck agreed to follow what she ordered, despite the fact that the diet appears to have been without any foundation in the nutrition beliefs of the day. Nanaline had her own ideas, and they were dangerous ones. Very likely Buck received far less nourishment than he needed, based on his body size and activity level. He also was malnourished because of her choice of foods.

There was more to Nanaline's plans than weight loss. It is now believed that she may have added her own special touch to the food he ingested—poison. Buck Duke became seriously ill during the time he was on the diet. He was exhausted from work. He was worried about Lillian's lawsuit. The doctors felt he might be anemic, and his improper diet could have been causing the problem.

To be fair to Nanaline, his poor health could have been caused by several other problems besides poor diet and poison. He had been having fainting spells, severe stomach pains, and other problems for several months. Blood transfusions caused him to rally for a short time, yet each time Nanaline took exclusive control of feeding him, his health rapidly deteriorated.

Three diagnoses were made after his death. The first was that he had either aplastic or aregeneratory anemia. The second was that he had undiagnosed leukemia. Both of these would likely have been affected by the improper diet Nanaline was feeding him.

But the third possibility, one that is quite likely given the way he ultimately died, was that she was slowly poisoning him. What poison may have been used is not known. However, many poisons were readily available in that era, all of which either would have not caused death themselves in very small quantities (e.g. arsenic) or would have caused slow deterioration and death.

The motive for the murder was a simple one—anger and, perhaps, greed. Nanaline had some hope of controlling the Duke holdings, at least for a few years, if Buck died while Doris was still very young. (She was only twelve when he died.) This would enable Nanaline to increase the Holt family wealth and benefit Walker Inman. Buck's survival might have meant that she would be cut off from the Duke money altogether.

The second reason was anger. Nanaline may have had a brief affair or occasional sexual relationship with Jenny Renaud. She also did not want to have sex with her husband. However, his affairs were blatant slaps in her face. She could not tolerate his apparent ability to separate sex acts from love. Assuming the comments of Mrs. Marshall reflect an ongoing situation, not an aberration in

Buck and Nanaline's relationship, he certainly separated the two experiences. But this did not mean that Nanaline was able to tolerate such abuse of the marriage vows.

Whatever the reasons, Nanaline Duke most certainly gave her husband a deliberate premature death.

---

Doris's cousin, Pony Duke, would later claim that Buck's last words to his daughter were "Be careful who you trust. You cannot always trust the people who say they love you."[2]

Buck was already in frail health when he developed pneumonia. There were no antibiotics at the time, no effective medical treatment for the illness. Previously healthy individuals often survived. Those who were elderly, weak, or already sick frequently died. In every case, it was critical to get bed rest, stay warm, and avoid stressful situations that made breathing more difficult.

Besides having a doctor see Buck regularly in their New York City residence, Nanaline took control of Buck's medical treatment. She informed the staff that there were to be no visitors. Doris had managed to slip into her father's bedroom when he was coughing and lucid. But when he fell asleep after a few moments of holding her hand, her mother came in and forced their daughter to leave. Then she told the butler that even Doris could not come back inside.

Next, Nanaline Duke ordered that all the windows be opened and all heat in the room be turned off. It was October, unusually cold, with near-zero temperatures, and the chill was dangerous for Buck. Cold air is more difficult to breathe than air warmed to normal room temperature, even for healthy people. The fluid in Buck's lungs made breathing difficult for him even when the room was still heated. With the windows open and the heat turned off, he fought for each breath.

Nanaline also took all covers from Buck, leaving him only in his nightshirt. She told the maid that they were from the South and that in the South it was believed that a man needed fresh air. No one dared challenge the statement, although the staff knew there was a difference between getting some fresh air and lying in a room chilled to below freezing.

Nanaline Duke then had her maid bring several sable coats to the room. She positioned these on her chair and around her body so she would be warm no matter how long she had to wait.

Buck Duke quickly went from fitful sleep into a coma. There was snow blowing in the room, and his labored breathing became more and more shallow. Finally, at 6 P.M., October 10, 1925, approximately six weeks short of Doris's thirteenth birthday, Nanaline Duke left the room to tell her daughter that Buck was dead. Then she ordered the staff to turn on the heat and close the windows.

Later it would be revealed that Nanaline had had black widow's clothing designed and made for her several weeks earlier. She may have made preparations simply because Buck was trying to prepare for the end. Or she may have plotted the murder far longer than anyone knew, which is a strong argument for the idea that she was slowly poisoning him. Ironically, Buck's first wife, Lillian, would live only two weeks longer than her ex-husband, starving to death in her rented room.

Nanaline Duke had Buck's body moved into the drawing room. Ben, one of the few people in Buck's life who genuinely mourned his passing, sent a ten-foot-high arrangement of orchids. Years later Doris would say that it was the beauty of the orchids in so emotional a moment that influenced her later interest in cultivating them. Overwhelmed by grief, unwilling to talk with the business associates and her mother's friends, Doris began studying the orchids intensely. They brought solace to her and a sense of beauty in the midst of the horror of her father's death. She would later develop hundreds of new varieties, all of which were named for her.

⌘

THREE DAYS AFTER the death, Buck's body was loaded onto his private railroad car and transported to Durham for the funeral. Schools were closed for the day, and many offices let their employees have the time to attend. Mourners numbered in the thousands. The football team of Duke University served as pallbearers, and 1,400 students acted as honor guards. It was the largest funeral in the history of Durham. And Ben, probably with input from young Doris, made certain that Buck never had to be with Nanaline again.

The corpse was buried with the bodies of Washington and Brodie Duke in a crypt in Maplewood Cemetery. Nanaline would be buried elsewhere.

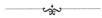

On October 11, 1925, the *New York Times* headlined the story that

> James Buchanan Duke, formerly President of the American Tobacco Company, who was probably the greatest figure in the American tobacco industry and one of the nation's leading philanthropists, died at 6 o'clock last night at his residence, Fifth Avenue and Seventy-eighth Street. He had been ill for several weeks with bronchial pneumonia, but hope was held for his recovery until a relapse set in three days ago. From that time he sank rapidly.
>
> Those present at the bedside last night were the widow, Mrs. Nannie Lee Holt Duke, their 12-year-old daughter, Doris, and the family physician, Dr. Robert H. Wylie . . .

The lengthy article quoted Buck's appraisal of himself and the success that resulted in a fortune the paper estimated at $150 million. "I have succeeded in business, not because I have more natural ability than many people who have not success led, but because I have applied myself harder and stuck to it longer. I know plenty of people who have failed to succeed in anything who have more brains than I had, but they lacked application and determination.

"I had confidence in myself. I said to myself, 'If John D. Rockefeller can do what he is doing in oil, why should I not do it in tobacco?' I resolved from the time I was a mere lad to do a big business. I loved business better than anything else. I worked from early morning to late at night. I was sorry to leave off at night and glad when morning came so that I could get at it again. Any young man with common intelligence can succeed, if he is willing to apply himself. Superior brains are not necessary."

The newspaper credited Duke with three innovations that made his tobacco business a success. "The first of these strokes was the placing of the firm's cigarettes in little, sliding pasteboard boxes. In the early days cigarettes were packed in loose, fragile paper packages, which, with their contents, broke easily while carried in the pocket. Duke was the first manufacturer to see the value of the boxes and his prompt ordering of 50,000 of them was followed a year later by an order for 1,000,000." The second innovation was the taking advantage of the drop in the cigarette tax so that he could cut the standard cost of ten cigarettes for a dime to ten cigarettes for a nickel and still make a profit. And the third was the introduction of the automatic roller.

---

DORIS DUKE'S CHILDHOOD ended the day her father died. Over the years there would be those who looked upon her as a pleasure-seeking heiress with too much money and too few brains. They would point to her lack of formal education and scorn her abilities. They would see her as a spoiled rich kid who grew up to be a thorn in the side of everyone who knew her. They would gossip about her sexual exploits. They would ridicule her lack of charity. And in every instance, they would underestimate her.

Doris Duke was her father's daughter. He and her uncle had been forced to build a world from the ashes of their Confederate homeland when their father had come home from war almost broke. They had been children who had to act like adults; while it made Buck strong, the work adversely affected Ben's physical health.

Doris knew she had to listen to her mother in many ways. Nanaline could rule on issues of school and society, especially since Doris's was an era of debutantes and society balls. But when it came to the Duke estate, Doris had learned her lessons well.

Nanaline Duke delighted in being a widow on Fifth Avenue. She was feted by the rich and powerful. She attended parties and loved to shop the luxury establishments catering to the carriage trade. She anticipated being able to aid Walker in some manner that would not have occurred had Doris been older.

The one mistake Nanaline made was in thinking that Doris would go along.

Doris hated the Fifth Avenue mansion because it was where her father had died, though she did not want anyone else controlling it. He had loved the farm in Somerville, and she had come to love the

land and the animals. The estate was the one that gave her pleasure, the one where she planned to live. However, her mother agreed
to the auction of Duke Farms, the railroad car, and other assets.
Stocks and other holdings were carefully controlled, but the will
seemed to be less clear as to whether Nanaline could sell the real
estate. Since she could gain millions for herself by unloading the
property she didn't enjoy, she put it up for sale.

Doris sued her mother. Buck had trained her well. To everyone's
surprise, she had paid attention to his lessons and knew which attorneys would be on her side. She was thirteen years old, planning
her action initially without advice of counsel, and Nanaline would
soon find that her daughter was more formidable than the most
high-powered attorneys who might be thrown against her.

Doris Duke's first suit was for the New York property at 1 East
78th Street. The value, as of February 11, 1927, when the story was
reported in the press, was $1,600,000 (there was a $615,000 mortgage remaining to be paid). There was a minimum estimate value
of $600,000 for the art objects and other contents and an unnamed
additional sum connected with extremely valuable tapestries currently in storage, the four automobiles for use in New York, and
the private railroad car meant to take family members from Manhattan to their other homes.

The executors of the estate, including Nanaline, claimed that
the Duke will authorized the auctioning of the property. Doris said
that if the estate was put up for sale, she would outbid everyone
else, a fact no one could dispute. She also said that the sale through
auction would reduce the value of the property to the estate since
there would likely be damage from curiosity seekers and bidders
walking through the property, handling all the valuables.

The judge agreed to give her all the property requested. The
only request she was denied was the chance to have the mortgage
paid off. He said that she would have to be responsible for what
was still owed to the bank.

On September 25, 1927, Doris Duke filed suit to take control of
the Somerville, New Jersey, estate and to have the sole right to operate the $2,500,000 property. This action assured her claim to the
property and also gave her control of both Rough Point in Newport and the Duke estate at Myers Park in Charlotte, North Car-

olina. Buck's daughter's determination was inadvertently shown at the end of the *New York Times* report of the event when the writer noted, "It will be several years before she is old enough to be presented to society."

⸎

DORIS DUKE'S BOLDNESS in taking control of her father's estate was matched by her shyness in other parts of her life. She wanted no publicity, no adoration, no speculation on what she was doing. Yet the press found her endlessly fascinating, and reporters often fantasized about her daily activities. Even worse, bags of mail regularly arrived at her New York home, as they had since birth. The mail was always screened by the staff, and when Doris's father died, she discovered that she was not seeing most of what was sent to her. Outraged, she demanded that she be allowed to see everything. Only then did she discover how much she was hated for being rich. Many of the letters were death threats. Others were verbally abusive in ways that were terrifying, including threatening rape and torture. She immediately ordered the continued screening of the letters. The reporters' fascination with her both continued and increased the volume of mail.

Doris Duke, Heiress, was portrayed by the press as a fantasy figure from a fairy tale. She slept on expensive silk sheets with lace trim, according to the false reports, then had them shipped to Europe for washing. The sheets had to be cleaned in a precise, consistent manner unknown to American laundresses. That was why the expense was necessary.

Doris had a sensitive sense of smell, according to the stories. No unpleasant aroma dared disturb her. Servants were forced constantly to press fresh flowers in order for her to have a nonoffending scent forever near her nostrils.

Supposedly an ancient Italian fountain had been carefully disassembled, shipped to America, then reassembled in her bathroom. The water was colored and scented to please her mood.

Gold fixtures were said to be everywhere. Even the plates on which she dined were alleged to be solid gold. The alleged value of the serving pieces for every meal was more than most elderly people had earned in their lifetimes.

Depending on the newspaper, Doris might be engaged to be married each time she was seen dancing with a boy. And if she wasn't seen, a sighting would be created in order to show the readers the exciting life she was living.

The real Doris Duke was someone quite different. The press considered her to be beautiful because anyone rich was automatically called by that adjective. She considered herself too tall, too thin, and too unattractive to have any male friends, an evaluation shared by her late father.

Tourists made regular visits to the Duke homes, and buses would stop at the gates so the passengers could catch a glimpse of the heiress. As she would do in her later years, Doris routinely walked unnoticed past the gawking sightseers who never connected the tall, shy blonde in casual clothes with their fantasy of the way the richest girl in the world should appear.

Duke Farms in Somerville had to become a guarded estate when Doris was present. There were gates, armed guards, and off-duty police officers on patrol, the police usually from the nearest city's motorcycle squad. The protection was due to a combination of fear and a desire to be left alone, especially by reporters, who regularly tried to crash the gates of one or another of the Duke residences.

Buck Duke wanted his daughter educated in the ways of the world. Nanaline wanted her daughter graduated from a proper finishing school. She chose Fermata in Aiken, South Carolina. Besides teaching the elite among young Southern women, it was a boarding school. Nanaline could have some relief from her daughter while pretending she was doing what was best for the child.

There were just under one hundred students, slightly less than a third of them day students, in the school, which was founded in 1919. The uniforms the girls wore included bloomers, gray stockings, and bright green tunics. And the subjects being taught were important ones for the newly rich girls of the twentieth-century South—how to pour tea, how to manage a household staff, and how to set a table. (Though God forbid the young ladies would ever set the table themselves. They simply had to know how to be a proper executive of the estates they would gain through marriage.)

The girls attending Fermata did not have an easy life by the standards of the carefree childhoods they had enjoyed prior to arriving. Sports practice could start before sunrise, and the girls were expected to make their own beds. Still, some servants were usually present. In Doris's case, for example, the detectives guarding her were disguised as gardeners who were readily noticeable by the fact that they never worked with the dirt.

Money was the standard by which each girl was judged. The ideal was to have enough money to be respected and not so much as to arouse jealousy. Ten to twenty million dollars might be a nice figure for a family. Ten times that amount meant social isolation. And if the money was the girl's, not the family's . . .

The school was also the preferred educational institution for the granddaughters of former slaveowners. This was one of the last bastions of the bigoted old South, a world Doris wanted no part of. However, despite her wealth and hostility, she went along with Nanaline's wishes. Doris stayed two years in Fermata, though her mother visited her only once. Approximately a decade later, when a fire destroyed the school, Doris held a party in celebration.

Doris Duke's early goal was to get a college education, and one lifelong regret was that she never did. She was a woman who loved learning, who would teach herself botany and other subjects in a manner that would provide her with greater expertise than most formally trained scholars. But her mother discouraged her from gaining a formal education and friends discouraged her from pursuing her dream. Years later she would scorn Duke University because she felt that she was never shown respect for her accomplishments since she did not have a degree. She also was aware that other wealthy people who had donated lesser sums to other colleges than her family had received honorary degrees. Yet she was never so honored or encouraged to take classes.

The one moment of honor came on June 5, 1928, when Doris Duke helped lay the cornerstone of the new buildings for the Duke University campus being established in Durham with her father's bequest. However, even that event took place under a cloud. The new university was in trouble. The money provided was generous but inadequate for the plans the president had developed when working with Buck. Ultimately much of the landscaping had to be abandoned in favor of seeking the finest faculty money could buy.

It was felt that with a solid core of professors, the students would come. The number of degree programs offered were reduced to ensure that the students could be educated. But the instant big-league school had no credibility with the greater academic world, and its connection with the old tobacco trust caused it to be held in disdain by many newspaper writers.

The new medical school had the greatest potential for success. The area desperately needed such a facility, and the physician chosen to head it was the highly respected Dr. Wilbur Cornell Davison, a former Rhodes scholar, excellent administrator, and skilled teacher. It was his selection that helped the school gain a grant of $300,000 from the General Education Board, a Rockefeller-funded grant that supplemented the Duke money shortfall.

The Duke Endowment established offices at 535 Fifth Avenue in Manhattan. The location allowed Nanaline, the only female trustee, to involve herself with its activities. Despite the opposition from her daughter, Nanaline was considered to have both sound business judgment and an awareness of what she did not know. She understood when to defer to expert consultants and when to trust her own skills.

But Nanaline's primary interest was in getting her daughter married, and toward this end she began planning Doris's debut.

# 6

## *Coming Out*

$\mathcal{T}$HE ESTEEM WITH WHICH debutantes were held cannot be underestimated in the circles in which Nanaline Duke and her daughter, Doris, moved. There were several criteria to be met, and a great many young woman failed to meet one or more of them. Having large sums of money was critical, of course. But there also was a series of events—specific dances and subdebutante events—in the years preceding the coming out that ensured that the girl under consideration was afforded due respect. The guest list for each was scrutinized by the Junior Assembly committee at its annual April meeting.

In the 1920s, the Junior Assembly in New York also held two dances each winter that the girls serious about making their debut had to attend. The cost was high—between $50 and $75 each—easily two weeks' pay or more for the average worker. In addition, parents had to pay a minimum of $10,000 in fees, for clothing, flowers, and numerous other essentials, for each debutante during the season in which she made her debut.

Technically, according to the rules of the day, Doris Duke should not have had a debut. According to her friend Dorothy Mahana, as quoted by Stephanie Mansfield, she and Doris crashed a coming-out party in Newport when they were fifteen years old.[1]

The girls knew some of the boys going to the party, though how they got an invitation is uncertain. Mahana did say that Mrs. Duke ultimately approved, although she was not happy about what they were doing.

According to Mansfield, the girls sent themselves corsages from a local florist. Then, when they got to the dance, none of the boys wanted anything to do with them. The girls supposedly spent the evening sitting on the ballroom stairs, with everyone ignoring them. They went home rather miserable, but apparently word did not get out to the New York committee. Any girl who attended such a party before she herself came out would be denied the chance to be a debutante.

Debutante parties were considered important moneymakers for the providers of services ranging from gowns to ballroom rental to the caterers. For such businesses, the season when debutantes came out was as critical for their success as the Christmas selling season was for retail department stores. Thus there was a relief when, following the stock market crash in October 1929, those families who had their money better protected, such as the Dukes, still found the party critical for their social season.

To give a sense of the money that could be spent, approximately 250 debutantes per year came out in New York state and Rhode Island. Their parties were held in exclusive country and yacht clubs or in hotel ballrooms. The cost for the private clubs was seldom reported, but rental of the ballroom in New York's Pierre Hotel cost $1,500 (with food, decorations, staff, and so on all being extra) and could handle 750 guests. Catering prices started at $3 per person and could go much higher. Sauterne and champagne were the drinks of choice; about forty cases were used for the event, each case averaging $65. The money easily exceeded two weeks' pay for many financially comfortable working men with families.

Various men were hired for the event. First was the announcer, who read each girl's name as she entered the ball where the debutante was coming out. His pay for the evening was $50. Generally his job went to only one man because, upon being found acceptable to the socialites, the same person usually was hired from party to party. Often announcers were needed only when events overlapped.

A social secretary also was hired, but her work brought in money and she received a percentage, usually no less than 10 percent nor more than 20 percent, for her efforts. Among the sources of income was the stag line that she would prepare.

The typical debutante might know a maximum of forty boys she could invite to the party—too few to fill the dance cards of all the

girls who would be in attendance. However, the boys selected had
to be from the right families, with the proper educational background and the right amount of money. Not only would they assure
a pleasant evening for the debutante, but they were potential husbands. It was expected that a debutante would at least meet her future husband at her coming-out party. She might already know
him, or she might be introduced to him at the time. But when the
couple began seriously dating, they could look back to the coming-
out party and share the memory of what that evening had been like.

Stag lines were purchased. The list of the highest-quality men
went for $500. The lowest quality, though still acceptable, went for
$150. In between was the $300 list. And it was the parents of the
debutante who had to buy the boys' tickets. The social secretary's
arrangement was a little like that of a travel agent taking a percentage of the hotels, airlines, resorts, and other bookings made for the
customer.

The girls did not have to know the boys, nor did the boys have
to be familiar to the specific family in whose name an invitation was
sent. What mattered was the boy's father's standing, whether the
boy was good-looking, and if he had proven himself to be a gentleman. Earlier in the century, when liquor was provided in too great
an abundance, the parties degenerated into high-priced versions of
contemporary fraternity beer busts. Society leaders had squelched
the problem, but drinking was still a rite at the events.

The debutante coming-out party that set the standard for Doris
Duke and all the others who followed was that of Barbara Hutton
at the Ritz-Carlton Hotel in 1929, the year before Doris's debut.
Hutton was the heiress to the F. W. Woolworth fortune, an inheritance greater than that of anyone other than Doris Duke. The Huttons hired Joseph Urban to coordinate the transformation of the
Crystal Room, the grand staircase, the oval restaurant, and the big
and small ballrooms. For approximately sixty hours a crew of
workmen brought in birch trees, wreaths, and other greenery to re-
make the opulent rooms. The trees were $100 each, all of them
shipped from Florida or California, and 10,000 American Beauty
roses were utilized throughout the redecoration, with the Huttons
paying a dollar *each* for the roses. (The flowers were sent to hospitals the following day since they were still in perfect condition. Al-

though florists wanted to resell them, the Huttons felt that they had already been paid for and should not provide a second profit.) Outside the ballroom, a grove of silver birch trees was created to be the receiving area for Barbara Hutton and her stepmother, Mrs. Franklyn Hutton. Candelabras were placed along the stairway and in the ballrooms. Blue gauze was used between the lighting and the dance floors to give the impression of being outdoors. A large yellow moon was suspended in the sky, then electrified to look as if it were reflecting the sun's rays.

Other foliage included scarlet poinsettias, tropical greens, and mountain heather. There were also 20,000 white violets.

Two hundred waiters served a thousand guests. A hundred musicians staffed four complete orchestras to ensure continuous music throughout the night. Rudy Vallee, the most popular singer in America, was present to entertain the debutante. The midnight supper consisted of five courses. The guests also stayed to partake of an elaborate breakfast. At a minimum, the party cost $50,000.

Doris Duke's coming-out party was held in Newport at the Rough Point estate, whose history fit the mood of the times. There were only 600 guests present, the result both of Nanaline Duke's frugality and because it was held in 1930, the year after the stock market crash.

Doris had been allowed to return to New York from Fermata in December of 1929, her education effectively ended. It was time to get her married, and the debut was important.

The stock market crash gave Doris Duke her first awareness of the instant reversal of fortunes that can happen in real life. Many of the young women with whom she had been raised were suddenly without funds. Overnight their social status changed and they were no longer eligible debutantes.

Buck Duke, ever a realist, understood what was happening in the stock market, the potential for disaster, and how to invest to avoid such a problem. Some of his stock holdings dipped slightly in value, but there was never a meaningful loss of income or long-term problem. Ironically, much of this was Nanaline's doing. Her management skills, when combined with those of the other trustees, led her to triple Doris's net worth in a few short years following Buck's death. Yet Nanaline was so anxious to benefit her son, Walker Inman, that she placed her own money in rather spec-ulative ventures. To her dismay, her fortune, earmarked solely for her son, was reduced. While she was not in serious trouble, she could not continue with her plans to improve her son's inheritance from her.

Doris Duke was the logical person to whom less fortunate friends might turn during this period. Her holdings were worth a mini-mum of $250 million and the figure was climbing. Her wealth was so diversified that the failure of any one source of income would be offset by either another source or the sale of a rare collectible. The Great Depression might be raging for most Americans, but there were always people who would spend large sums of money on museum-quality gems, paintings, and the like. She could sell some of the items acquired over the years and still do extremely well for herself. As a result, Doris began quietly slipping money to her friends. Anyone in need who did not actually scheme to get hold of some of the Duke money might find that she, and perhaps her fam-ily, had a place to live and enough money not to feel disgraced. These were not loans. They never had to be paid back.

By contrast, those who came to her seeking loans were in-evitably denied. Some would approach Doris with grandiose in-vestment schemes that would clearly fail, but the borrower would assure Doris that she would make millions. Those girls and their family members were always turned down.

And so Doris's debut was discreet compared with Barbara Hut-ton's. It was also less dramatic than it might have been had she held it before the crash. Still, the lighting was magnificent, due to assis-tance provided by experts from the Duke power companies, and the revelers dined and danced in a beautiful area overlooking the water.

More important for Nanaline Duke, attending the party was Jimmy Cromwell, the man who seemed to fit her dreams for Doris's future perfectly.

# PART II

---

## Till Debts
## Do Us Part

# 7

⤜⋆⤛

## *First Marriage*

ANALINE DUKE had reason to worry about Doris's coming of age. Her daughter had an interest in men that seemed to match her father's interest in women, and like the late Buck Duke, Doris could afford to rent or buy any thrill she desired. She also no longer tolerated being chaperoned, flaunting her independence.

Doris was naive about sex. She understood the biological urgings and the general mechanics, and it was doubtful that Doris was a virgin when she became serious about the man who was to become her first husband. There were rumors that at some time before her twenty-first birthday she was "deflowered" by New York Senator Elmer F. Quinn or by one or another young men in her immediate social circle. However, if the rumors were false and she remained a virgin, she looked upon the condition as a curse. And because the relationships among debutantes and their dates were carefully chaperoned and scrutinized, most of the men Doris could meet for an illicit rendezvous were those of the "lower classes." Servants, jazz and blues music buffs in the Harlem clubs she visited, and similar "undesirables" were readily available. Nanaline worried that since Doris was color blind when it came to her friends, there was a chance she might seduce, perhaps even marry, a black man.

There was little Nanaline dared do about the problem of her daughter's aggressive adolescence. She had tried the usual activities. Doris had been sent to Europe, a standard trip for a debutante in waiting. She had also been one of the privileged American debutantes introduced to the King and Queen of England prior to her coming-out party. But neither going to England nor coming out

87

had left the impression on Doris that Nanaline hoped it would. Instead of recognizing that the world of high society, with all its traditions and responsibilities, was to be honored and preserved, Doris had seen it as something to be endured as briefly as possible.

The British visit, which received little press coverage compared with her coming-out party, occurred on May 14, 1930, approximately three months before the Newport event. Although many daughters of the wealthy sought the honor, Doris Duke was one of only nine American debutantes presented to the royal couple on that date.

The American ambassador to the Court of St. James was forced to make the final selection. The pressure was enormous, mothers lobbying the ambassador, offering bribes of money, sex, and anything else they thought might work. As a result, most American ambassadors hated the approach, and Joe Kennedy would eventually end it a decade after Doris's experience—though only after his own daughters were presented.

Despite the fantasies of the debutantes and the public reading about the event, the king and queen rarely paid attention to the women. The royal couple could not recall names or faces, nor were the women allowed any special access in the years that followed. It was just another ritual that happened to be modified to please the wealthy and influential parents who might sway a president or members of Congress to provide needed economic and/or political support for England.

Doris had no illusions about the ritual, which involved little more than curtsying for the king and queen, yet the idea of going to the court did excite her. She was seventeen years old, and this was the most romantic experience of her young life, more so than her coming out at eighteen. Money could buy a mansion but normally it could not gain you entrance to a castle.

The history of American debutantes going to England was quite different from the romantic image of Doris's fantasies. It began after the Civil War when the British government was making a strong effort to be closer to the United States. Transatlantic travel was becoming popular, steamships were increasingly comfortable for long voyages, and the wealthy American leisure class was growing. However, after World War I, the number of wealthy American girls becoming involved with titled British men of far more modest financial circumstances began to increase. The bride prospered because, having great wealth, she already owned everything anyone else could envy except a title. And the groom, who knew how meaningless the title had become with the reversal of family fortunes, needed the bride's money to ensure the lifestyle that had been or was in danger of being lost.

The men in such marriages were much like the heroines in melodramas where a young woman agrees to marry the wrong man in order to save the family homestead from foreclosure. The aristocratic men were selling their sexual favors in order to restore their family fortunes. The women were never considered quite proper, though some men perceived them to be a curiosity, excitingly different. Still, if the men had retained their wealth, these were not the women to whom they would have been drawn.

Lady Randolph Churchill has been quoted as saying, "In England, as on the Continent, the American woman was looked upon as a strange and abnormal creature, with habits and manners something between a Red Indian and a Gaiety Girl. Anything of an outlandish nature might be expected of her . . .

"As a rule, people looked upon her as a disagreeable and even dangerous person, to be viewed with suspicion, if not avoided altogether. Her dollars were her only recommendation, and each was credited with the possession of them, otherwise what was her raison d'être?"

The appeal of American women to the British was such that they were almost invariably described as beautiful, popular, generous, pleasant, amusing, a good figure. Frequently they were described as having an artistic temperament and/or being fond of athletics. The only negatives mentioned in print were their dress, usually an exaggerated style, and their slang speech.

To be presented at court was a tremendous boost to a girl's value on the British marriage market, even though the titled young men recognized the meaninglessness of the event. What interested the potential suitors was the fact that these were the wealthiest, most politically connected of eligible American women, and thus the best catches.

Doris Duke did not go to Europe to seek a husband, though.

Like her mother, she had no desire to marry a man who had no money, even if he was royalty. There was no one she had to impress in her life, not even King George and Queen Mary, although their lifestyle was one of the few that could leave her awestruck.

The British society girls and most of the American debutantes being presented the same day as Doris had gone to curtsy school. The schools—the Vacani School of Dancing being the most popular—taught young women the proper way to comport themselves when meeting the royal couple.

The ceremony began at a set hour, the girls being presented already lined up in the order in which they arrived at the palace. Doris arrived earlier than anyone else; her chauffeur reached the palace at five in the afternoon. The police were not ready for anyone at that hour so Doris's chauffeur was ordered to keep driving. He wanted to leave. She refused. Instead, he drove as slowly as possible along the Mall for the next hour, at which time she was allowed to get out.

Doris was impatient with the length of the ceremony. The last society woman to be presented would have waited approximately two hours for her audience. She would have had to remain standing in an elaborate gown with no chance to rest. Although Doris eventually waited just as long to be first, she felt that the stress was less.

Once the king and queen were seated on their thrones in the ballroom, the debutantes were checked by the court usher. Then the lord chamberlain announced their entrance at the Throne Room.

The Throne Room had place markers similar to those used for stage productions in theaters. Instead of the masking tape or chalk marks used by theaters, however, the red carpeting was embedded with small gold crowns. When the girls were at the proper mark (crown), they would smile, give a quick back kick to free their lengthy gowns (the trains were so long, they were carried over the arm and still trailed eighteen inches on the floor), and curtsy. Then they would take three steps to the right in a gliding movement, curtsying again. Finally they would continue in a rightward movement to the door, never turning their backs to the royal couple. By being first, Doris did not have to endure the endlessly repetitious spectacle that frequently caused the king to fall asleep on his throne.

Nanaline was more impressed than Doris. She was seeking a potential husband for her daughter, and among those under consideration was Albania's King Zog, whom Doris thought to be a joke. She had already met her future husband and had even put him on the guest list for her coming-out party.

———— ⚜ ————

Jimmy Cromwell targeted Doris Duke as a possible wife when she was sixteen, visiting his mother's fifty-room summer home, Wingwood, in Bar Harbor. The house was cozy by the family's standards; their primary residence on their Philadelphia estate had 150 rooms. Although not so wealthy as the Dukes, Jimmy was expected to inherit in excess of $100 million in his own right. He was not a fortune hunter.

The merger of the two families was encouraged by family friend Evalyn McLean. Evalyn was a multimillionaire who, with her husband, Ned Stotesbury, gave elaborate parties. Their children, Vinson and Evalyn, were indulged to the point where the Ringling Brothers Circus made special appearances on their grounds just to entertain the family. She delighted in spending money and thought that the only way for the rich to have fun was eventually to die broke after indulging themselves. However, at the time that Jimmy first met Doris, when he was thirty-two, the Stotesbury money still seemed plentiful.

The problem was the Depression and the way in which Jimmy Cromwell's family held their sources of income. Jimmy's father was Washington, D.C., financier Oliver Cromwell, a man who made enough money to keep his wife, Eva, in great demand on the party circuit. Politicians wanted his money. Businesspeople wanted his backing and influence. And everyone knew that the way to Oliver was through his wife.

Oliver Cromwell died of a stroke in 1909, leaving Eva with three children and enough money to stay in the right social circles until she could land a second husband at least as wealthy as her first. This she did three years later, becoming Mrs. Ned Stotesbury. Stotesbury was a financier who dominated Philadelphia business and society and had even better Washington connections than the late Oliver. As a result, when the couple married, President William Howard Taft was among the guests.

Jimmy was not a very bright man; he mistook his growing popularity in business and politics as due to his innovative ideas for social change. He did not realize that he was seen as a tanned, muscular, rather undereducated man with little common sense but enough money to finance the careers of anyone he supported for office. Still, he was fun to be around. He was a serious amateur boxer, and during World War I he felt patriotic enough to leave the Wharton School of Business to enlist in the navy and then the marines. He used his family's money to outfit his own submarine chaser, gaining a command post that might otherwise have been denied him.[1] And when he finally chose to marry, he united two great fortunes, that of the Cromwell/Stotesbury families and the Dodge automobile heirs.

Delphine Dodge was a spoiled child who respected the world of business. As one of their wedding presents, the couple was given the use of the family yacht, named *The Delphine,* to cruise the world. The vessel was approximately 250 feet long, and though it had a crew of sixty, Delphine could easily handle it. She was a champion speedboat racer who loved engines almost as much as her inventor father.

Delphine and her family trusted Jimmy's business sense. He had first been rewarded with the vice-presidency of the Cleveland-based Peerless Motor Car Company. From that position he was highly successful selling Dodge cars, a fact that impressed his new in-laws.

The couple was sailing in Hong Kong when Horace Dodge, Delphine's father, died unexpectedly, forcing them to return to the United States. Jimmy's mother-in-law, Anna Dodge, was too emotionally devastated to think clearly. She chose to trust Jimmy because his mother, Eva Stotesbury, understanding how her son's mother-in-law felt, took Anna Dodge into her home for several months. She wanted Anna be able to begin to adjust to the loss without having to worry about her own household or the community where she was always in demand because of her wealth and image.

Oddly, Philadelphia society shunned the very wealthy Anna

Dodge during her stay with Eva because Anna's background was quite modest and her husband was an inventor. By Philadelphia standards, making money in the automobile business did not ensure respect. If anything, it made it harder to be considered part of society, even if you could afford to buy prestige with the right donations to the right causes.

Because of Eva, Jimmy was asked to sell the Dodge family's holdings in the car company Horace founded. In what was considered a highly successful deal, Jimmy brought somewhere between $146 million and $160 million (the figures vary in a number of different sources) to the family fortune. The money came from the sale of Anna Dodge's stock, and it enabled her to live a wild life of spending with her second husband, Hugh Dillman, before she felt he was using her and divorced him. Jimmy also felt that such success entitled him to business backing, something both Delphine and her friends agreed with. They believed that Jimmy was a brilliant negotiator as seen by his success with the car company.

Cromwell could have lived a leisurely life if he and Delphine had been capable of frugality. They had access to income of $200,000 per year, far more money than the heads of most major corporations were earning. But when you are used to spending family money in the range of eight figures annually, it is hard to give up the fruits of a lifetime of hedonistic pleasures. Thus Jimmy was forced to generate additional spending money through his entrepreneurial spirit.

Jimmy attempted several business deals, including an effort to develop a winter haven for wealthy Northerners interested in wintering in Florida. The state was in its infancy for major development, with areas such as Palm Beach just beginning to become famous as escapist locations for the rich. Many other areas had earned bad reputations because of land fraud schemes, including the selling of worthless swampland and the multiple selling of the same acreage to unsuspecting buyers who lost millions of dollars.

Jimmy was serious about his concept, but what he failed to realize was that the appeal of anything other than Palm Beach and similar locations already in use by the wealthy was nonexistent. To make his error even more serious, the Stotesbury family had a modest forty-room house called El Mirasol. (The limited number of rooms was compensated for by the garage they built to house their motor cars. The building could park as many cars as the mansion had rooms.) He was quite capable of learning the attitude of the potential customers toward his new development idea.

The second mistake Jimmy made was in not recognizing the worthless nature of much of the land he acquired for housing development. He purchased a 3,600-acre parcel located between the cities of Miami and Palm Beach, both so popular that the idea of living in between them was ridiculous. Even worse was the fact that the acreage, though beautiful, was swamp. The cost of making it usable to support housing was prohibitive. He lost $6 million (including $1 million his mother invested) and the love of Delphine even before he completed the deal.

Delphine divorced him in 1928. Eva was more forgiving, putting her son on a six-figure allowance until he could find himself another business venture or, preferably, another heiress.

Jimmy thought that Doris Duke might be the best person to serve as his next wife. She was younger than Delphine, less experienced, and perhaps more willing to work with him on his schemes. She also already had possession of her inheritance, when so many other debutantes were waiting for someone to die before they could truly call the money they were spending their own. Doris could become his personal banker, and with her money, he was certain he would succeed. And if he decided to involve himself in politics, the couple could call upon two fortunes to sustain them through the rigors of the campaign.

The stock market crash changed everything for the Stotesbury family. Ned's money had come from banking, stocks, and investments, all a part of his Drexel & Company, and it was dependent on the vagaries of the businesses affected by the stock market. At the time of the crash, Ned Stotesbury had an unknown number of millions of dollars in his Drexel account. The family survived without touching this money until 1933, at which time Ned Stotesbury began withdrawing just enough cash to cover his normal cost of living—more than $900,000 *per month,* or approximately $10 million per year. This continued until his death on May 21, 1938, when he was eighty-nine years old. He had spent $50 million from the account, leaving only $5 million. Anyone else would have been rich.

The Stotesburys, however, were poor because they had never cut their expenses. In only six months servants would have to be let go, one or more houses sold, and numerous other compromises made. Even worse, Eva's inheritance was reduced because Ned's two daughters from his first marriage were each given a one-third share. This meant that the three women had to "make do" with just $1.6 million apiece.

Eva also received the Philadelphia mansion and its contents, none of which she could afford to maintain. The house had to be put up for sale, a lost cause because of the Depression. It finally changed hands in 1943, during World War II, and the highest bidder offered approximately $167,000.

As for the interior furnishings, there was a strong resale market for the art objects, but at substantially lower prices than Horace Dodge had paid. In some cases this was because of a depressed collectible buying period. In other instances it was because he had overpaid in the first place. And the third reason was that what he had purchased was based on what he thought was fashionable rather than on what had shown long-term investment value. When fashion changed, demand plummeted.

Following Ned's death, Eva Stotesbury quickly decided to live less pretentiously. The transition was made easier with the help of Anna Dodge, who came to her rescue as she had done for her son's former mother-in-law.

Nanaline Duke understood what might be happening with Jimmy's family immediately after the stock market crash. She lost money herself, having used aggressive investment practices to bolster her personal wealth. She made sure she acted conservatively with Doris's trust, ensuring that her daughter would have no problems during bad economic times. The women despised each other, living together only because society expected that of a young single woman. But Nanaline took seriously the responsibility to protect Doris's financial interests. She worried that Jimmy might become a fortune hunter, bringing nothing to a marriage with Doris but a lust for her money. She had no idea that her fears were well founded because of the good front his father put up before the older man's death.

Where previously Nanaline had delighted in the tall, handsome

man who was almost twice her daughter's age, now she began crit-
icizing him. As a result, Doris sought him out for special attention
the night of her coming-out party. No one is certain if she was emotionally and physically aroused by him or if she was determined to
desire any man her mother did not want for her. They did everything but go to bed together, although apparently she made it clear
to Jimmy that such intimacy was in their immediate future if he
wanted it.

The problem for Nanaline Duke, Barbara Hutton's parents,
and the parents of all the other wealthy socialites headstrong
enough to make impractical decisions was that the times had
changed. Previously women had led sheltered lives, living with
their parents until marriage, carefully chaperoned, and banned
from nightclubs, bars, and similar locations unless accompanied by
men. Sex before marriage was not accepted. Women were never
openly the aggressors in a relationship.

The end of the Victorian era, the rise of the movie industry, the
backlash against Prohibition, and the entry of women into bars, the
workplace, and other previously forbidden locations had changed
Doris Duke's generation. Frequently both men and women were
sexually promiscuous. Many drank heavily. They experimented with
drugs such as cocaine. They delighted in violating the old taboos
even when, in some instances, the actions were self-destructive.

The socialite parents of Doris's generation worried about the
immorality of their children, and they feared for the stability of the
family fortunes.

There was also the problem of generational backlash. The first
families to gain great wealth—sometimes called the Old Guard—
developed standards for living that were rigidly followed. Philanthropy was expected among the Old Guard. The Carnegies built
libraries, the Severances funded symphony halls, and the Rockefellers established a foundation funding all manner of arts-related
projects.

Some of the older generation deliberately gave away the vast
majority of their wealth. John L. Severance, for example, lived his
last years on the charity of friends while being hailed for the millions of dollars he donated for the benefit of others. However, that
was an extreme example. Most combined philanthropy with en-

suring that their children and grandchildren gained excellent educations, were exposed to a broad range of cultural experiences, traveled, and otherwise led rich, full lives.

The New Guard, usually the children of the first families of money or those who became rich at the same time that the Old Guard children were coming of age, followed a different attitude. They lived to spend money on opulent self-indulgences. They liked being famous for being able to buy anything, go anywhere, do anything, and own anyone. They were imperious to their staffs, often creating an inviolable hierarchy that protected them from having to speak directly to a servant, and often prevented a servant from speaking to anyone other than his or her immediate superior in a chain of command that often involved thirty or more people. The private secretary was the only person accessible to both an underling and the master or mistress of the household.

Social position was critical. The parties attended, the people you dated, and where you lived all helped determine your status. In Newport, for example, only the older rich were comfortable living in mansions that did not overlook the water. This had nothing to do with personal taste in lifestyle and scenery. The space overlooking the water was finite and therefore so limited as to become a status location. Ostentation was never for one's own pleasure, though it was to be hoped that conspicuous consumption of life's indulgences could be fun. Rather, to overindulge in a highly public and visible way assured the envy and respect of others.

Breeding had been important in the past, although that did not always assure that the children and grandchildren of brilliant entrepreneurs would be of more than average intelligence. Members of the new money were likely to have flings with anyone interacting with their social set, from other millionaires to a tennis or golf instructor. And always possessions meant more than anything else. These were the people who were the forerunners of the Beverly Hills joke that the rich person who dies with the most toys wins.

Doris Duke was caught between the two worlds. Nanaline believed in the administrative philosophy of Edith Rockefeller McCormick, heir to a Cleveland and New York fortune who married into Chicago wealth. As mistress of her family's estate and arbiter of social propriety among the very rich, she bragged that she never learned the names of her servants. No one in her employ was allowed to speak to her, nor would she acknowledge their presence directly. Instead she had a chain of command; only her closest personal assistant was favored with the orders that might be meant for a lower-level servant standing right next to them.

Doris found such pretentiousness and condescension outrageous. At the same time, she had numerous personal philanthropies that would have delighted the Old Guard, had they been aware of them. The Old Guard's standards were split, requiring them to help those far less fortunate than themselves provided they never had to speak to them.

Jimmy Cromwell liked spending money. He wanted to show off his wealth, be in the public eye, and buy his way into political power. He was part of the New Guard, a situation that both appealed to Doris Duke and repelled her.

Nanaline had a different problem. She suspected that Jimmy Cromwell, once the perfect catch, was actually less rich than he seemed. The problem was that the Stotesbury family was able to maintain the image of wealth. Even worse, other rich young men in Doris's social circle were in the same situation.

Nanaline also realized that although Doris would not see herself as being independent of her mother until her twenty-first birthday, her daughter's sexual appetite was not to be denied. Nanaline felt that there was a chance that Doris would make an inappropriate match based on the first person to please her in bed. Given her daughter's rebellious ways, that could be someone from a lower socioeconomic bracket. Such a marriage would be a disgrace and a financial disaster for everyone except the man.

Walker had already made that mistake with Helene Clark, though Nanaline had been too much the interfering mother in that regard. Her constant harping on Helene's unsuitability for an Inman was partially responsible for the divorce. Helene's revenge resulted in a lawsuit against her ex–mother-in-law, a lawsuit she might have been able to win. Rather than experience the publicity a court trial would generate, not to mention the possibility of the judge ruling in Helene's favor, Nanaline paid Walker's ex-wife $75,000 and guaranteed double that amount annually for life if she did not remarry. It was a low enough sum that Nanaline could feel relieved that she was not seriously depleting her own funds. It was also large enough that Helene would not risk the loss of future income just to say spiteful things to newspaper reporters.

Nanaline was also worried about Doris's interest in gospel, jazz, blues, and other forms of music most readily heard in the black areas of New York. Doris routinely visited clubs in Harlem, befriending both the men and women who played there and the regulars among the listeners. She had much to learn about the music, and she found she shared many interests with the musicians who only knew that she was a serious student of what they were playing.

Given all the concerns of the times, Nanaline probably saw Jimmy Cromwell as the best of a bad lot when he and Doris Duke decided to get married. Doris was becoming increasingly limited in her options, as press attention forced her into a less public existence. When she turned twenty-one, reporters turned out in force around her home on 78th and Fifth Avenue. As reported in *News-Week* for December 23, 1933: "Behind the smoke exhaled by millions of cigarette fiends who have made her America's premier heiress, burns an intense, slightly embarrassed, and seldom satisfied curiosity about all that concerns Doris Duke. Last week, on her twenty-first birthday, she received another $10,000,000 or more of her inheritance, and the legend she embodies was retold with all its glamorous inaccuracies multiplied."

The article continued with a discussion of Buck Duke's successes, then mentioned her birthday. "Last week, when the tumult of curious interviewers became a little too pressing, she fled from that house to the broad acres of Duke Farms near Somerville, New Jersey. There she was sought by the sheriff (who received a 'not at home') intent upon serving her with papers for Mr. and Mrs. Raffaela Gimillo, local residents. Mrs. Cimino desires to be paid $25,000, maintaining that Miss Duke's four Great Danes attacked her a year ago to that extent."

The *New York Times* for November 22, 1933, headlined Doris's birthday, giving it an added importance because of the conservative image of the paper. The only mistake it made was in grossly underestimating her wealth, in part because the writer did not know about the trusts and in part because it was conjecture based on what had happened with other fortunes.

The *Times'* writer, along with many other observers of the rich, did not realize that Buck was one of the few wealthy entrepreneurs who had recognized the need to diversify his holdings and investments. Such men did not anticipate the stock market crash, but they did understand that relying too much on any narrow area for earning money could result in serious losses.

The story was otherwise accurate, though. And even with the mistake in Doris's wealth, the public would be amazed since a dollar an hour was considered enough to feed, clothe, and nicely house a family with several children.

The article stated in part:

> Miss Doris Duke came of age last midnight and on the last stroke of the clock, was automatically the richest girl in the world.
>
> The extent of her wealth is not definitely known. When her father, James Buchanan Duke, died in 1925 he left an estate appraised at more than $101,000,000. In 1927, Miss Duke's share was appraised at $53,000,000. The shrinking process begun in 1929 is believed to have cut that to about $30,000,000.
>
> Miss Duke inherits a third of her estate today. She will receive half of the remainder on her twenty-fifth birthday and the balance when she is 30.
>
> She celebrated her twenty-first birthday—if it can be called a celebration—by dining quietly last night at the home of friends.

The article continued,

> Miss Duke's coming of age celebration was unostentatious, simple and a trifle mysterious. . . .
>
> Various stories have sprung up about her. One is that she is another member of the "poor little rich girl" class. Another is that she cannot move outside her door without a bodyguard or detectives. A third, suggested by the frequency of reports concerning her engagement, is that she has been forbidden to see any young, or eligible man, a second time.
>
> All three reports are erroneous, it was disclosed last night; Miss Duke goes to parties and, as a general rule, with whomsoever she pleases. She is a frequent visitor at the leading social clubs and any one of a half-dozen midtown restaurants. There

is no rule against her going out, for a second, third or tenth time, with any one escort. She travels with a maternal body-guard—Mrs. James B. Duke—or with a fraternal one, her half-brother, Walker Patterson Inman.

Having no vocation and little expectations of ever having to follow one, she has taken up the study of what are generally known as "cultural arts." She devotes a definite fraction of each day to the piano, to French and Italian. According to one member of the household, at least, she speaks both languages "more fluently than she does English."

She is interested in the theatre and is a frequent patron of local movie houses. To neither the theatre nor the cinema will she go on a "first night," however. Again the explanation is her desire to escape public attention.

The menace of the public magnifying glass is always present, never to be ignored. As inevitably as the seasons, there come times when the volume of letters begging or threatening, when the numbers of "crank" callers, when the telephoned messages, increase to such a degree that flight is the only alternative. . . .

"Everywhere we go it is the same," Mr. Inman once said. "She gets to see a few of the sights, goes out to dinner a few times and then her identity becomes known and we have to rush off somewhere else."

But Miss Duke has rarely made the same complaint. A few years ago in Paris she publicly expressed the wish that she could change places with a poor girl. The exchange would have been merely for a few hours, while she went shopping. Being rich, she explained, meant that the prices usually went up twice as high to start with.

There is one thing more that Miss Duke gains by reaching the age of 21. She will fall heir, also, to a trusteeship of Duke University, which received a $40,000,000 endowment from Mr. Duke before his death.


Doris attempted to avoid newspaper coverage after she came into her money, but this did not make her a recluse. She simply was more discreet than some of the other daughters of the wealthy. She also began to gain the independence she craved from her mother.

Nanaline seemed alternately to want Doris married to the "right man" and to want her to remain a spinster. A single Doris would be better for Walker's fortunes. At the same time, being married would get the two women out of each other's way.

Doris could never forgive her mother for causing her father's death. Nanaline was said never to have had pangs of conscience over her action and was concerned with Doris's happiness more than her daughter realized. When Nanaline became convinced that Doris had no friends, she tried to encourage other New York socialites to spend time with her daughter. By contrast, the press created stories of Doris leading a life of glamour and excitement with other rich and beautiful youths.

The truth of Doris's life was somewhere in between her mother's fears and the press's fantasies. She traveled frequently, although usually quietly and with misinformation being spread concerning where she would really be visiting. Her supposed rival, Barbara Hutton, wanted her life and loves captured by the press, including when she spent $25,000 for a well-publicized twenty-second birthday party. But Doris just wanted to travel and be independent, seeing Europe, visiting Mexico, and generally experiencing the world. When she spent large sums of money, such as buying a Bellanca Skyrocket prop plane to travel more readily between her estates and throughout the country, the purchase was generally a practical one.

Although legally free from her mother's control, Doris knew she needed to be married to escape the constant pressure Nanaline exerted over her life. She had desires, including flirting with the idea of becoming a Hollywood actress, but Nanaline always seemed to mock or discourage anything Doris wanted to do except spend her money.

The one way Doris did seem to thwart her mother was with her charity work. She utilized the foundations as they were intended, but she also began donating money personally, looking to causes similar to those that would have interested her father and grandfather. She created Independent Aid, Inc., which provided money anywhere she desired, from the First Methodist Church in Charlotte to a New York home for unwed mothers. There was no publicity involved, no special staff other than Marian Paschal, her secretary who, over time, became a combination of employee and longtime confidante/friend. It would begin the pattern of giving she would follow all her life, the only public donations coming from the Duke Endowment and similar charitable arrangements.

Jimmy Cromwell's courtship of Doris Duke began in earnest in 1934 when they exchanged visits during the summer months. He went to Rough Point, and she attended a dinner dance in her honor at Whitemarsh Hall. It was the perfect place to impress an heiress for, among other amenities, it had a dozen elevators, forty-five bathrooms, and even its own ice-making plant, barber shop, tailor shop, movie theater, and bakery. The location was like a small town, and forty-five servants lived on the premises, with numerous others commuting each day and for special events. When Ned Stotesbury was constantly withdrawing money from his firm, there were no obvious changes in the family fortune. Only Eva knew how critical finding a fortune was for her son, and only Nanaline had any suspicions about what was taking place.

Jimmy Cromwell, nervous about being discovered, was old enough to understand the subtler ways of courtship. After impressing Doris Duke with his family's money, proving that he could not possibly be a fortune hunter, he also showed he knew how to touch her heart.

Doris Duke used a portion of the Somerville estate to raise orchids. While still in her adolescence she began growing hundreds of the flowers. She also kept animals of all types. While Jimmy knew he could not impress her with his love of the orchids, he could win her heart through the animals.

Doris loved all creatures. Over the years her pets would include camels, but at age twenty-two, her pets were primarily dogs. Three Great Danes were her favorites, the animals serving as both bodyguards and companions. They were never attack trained, but Doris made clear to all visitors that they would become dangerously aggressive if they felt their mistress threatened.

What Duke did not have were cats, natural farm and house animals. Therefore, Jimmy gave Doris a pair of Siamese kittens for her twenty-second birthday, the most intimate gift she had ever received. He used her love for cats to prove his sensitivity to her desires, something no one else had ever done. The fact that it would eventually prove one of the only sensitive gestures he would make toward Doris was unknown at that time. He made the right impression.

The Stotesburys' financial problems created an unusual relationship between stepfather and stepson. Jimmy Cromwell became convinced that when the banks were closed at the start of the Great Depression, Franklin Roosevelt was the one man who had saved the country. Cromwell believed that the American people were close to revolution against the government. He believed that Roosevelt's actions had averted a national uprising.

Ned Stotesbury, by contrast, blamed Roosevelt and the New Deal for all the problems both the world and his own funds were facing. He told his stepson that he was determined to spend all the money he had left the way he wanted. He was quoted as telling Jimmy, "Your deity, Franklin D. Roosevelt, is ruining free enterprise. He's destroying my firm. I made all this myself. FDR is not going to waste it for me. I am." Whether the quote is apocryphal or accurate, Stotesbury did spend himself almost into bankruptcy before he died.

Pragmatic Jimmy not only genuinely liked Roosevelt, he also saw the Democratic Party as the key to his future. He wanted to enter politics, and the simplest approach was the most direct one—to buy his way in. This required money such as he once had and that Doris Duke would seemingly have forever.

There are many stories about the six-year courtship of Doris Duke. Stephanie Mansfield tells of Jimmy Cromwell's first sexual attempt with Doris occurring when she was sixteen.[2] He allegedly slipped naked into her bed and attempted to seduce her. The incident was unsuccessful, and he later called her "my Frigidairess." Others dispute the truth of this account, though there seems to be no question that the two tried to enjoy each other's company in more intimate ways than their families would have felt proper.

Some reports indicate that Jimmy Cromwell's abilities were apparently limited, yet he chose to blame his failings on the woman of the moment. If he could not perform, or if he performed too quickly, then the woman was at fault. He would be the first source of rumors that Doris Duke was not interested in men at all, only women.

Other men did not suffer from Cromwell's failings. Doris Duke had no intention of being a virgin when she married, and though she was not exposed to great lovers (in her estimation) until several years later, she did find men who apparently satisfied her. She also seemed to keep them interested in her, even though it would be only after one of her affairs that she mastered a sexual repertory that would have pleased the most creative lovers.

Jimmy had successfully fathered a child, a daughter, Christine, born on September 10, 1922, to Delphine, but that may have been the high point of his sex life. Prior to Jimmy's marriage to Doris, Nanaline arranged for private detectives to investigate Cromwell's personal life. Their report indicated that he might be gay. From what they could learn, if he was not homosexual, then he had an extremely low sex drive toward women. No matter how aroused Doris might have been by the man, no matter how much "heavy petting" they might do, her sex drive was almost certainly far in excess of his own. Even if she had known of Jimmy's apparent ardor when Doris was sixteen, Nanaline would not have been overly worried. It was doubtful the two would go beyond a point that left Nanaline's daughter quite frustrated.

With the Stotesbury fortune on the wane, Jimmy and his family pursued Nanaline and Doris to Cannes where they were vacationing. Jimmy and Doris alternated between reviving their former romance and fighting. Jimmy thought Doris was self-centered, always demanding her own way. Doris felt she had a right to do what she wanted since she seemed to always be paying for the privilege.

It was during this trip that they both met thirty-seven-year-old Alec "Bobbie" Cunningham-Reid, a Conservative member of Parliament and a war hero who eventually would try to sit out World War II anywhere but in England. He was known for his friendship with the Duke of Windsor, for whom he occasionally acted as a pilot. But he was infamous for pursuing heiresses from whom he would take as much money as possible.

Cunningham-Reid was generally successful with women and hated by men. Frequently he tried to buy his way into men's organizations, where the idea of offering money in exchange for a membership was considered improper. But extremely wealthy women adored him, even though he ultimately cheated on them. For example, he married the very wealthy twenty-one-year-old Rush Ashley, whom he first began courting when she was eighteen. He felt that he had spent £36,000 during their courtship, so after their marriage, besides using her funds to pay for the honeymoon, he withdrew the courtship money from her account to replenish his own. By comparison to such a man, with whom, Nanaline could see, Doris was infatuated, Jimmy Cromwell seemed a reasonable catch.

The other love of Jimmy's life, second only to his desire to ensure fresh money in the family, was unusual political thinking that went beyond his efforts on behalf of Franklin Roosevelt. He was also a supporter of some of the beliefs of Father Charles Coughlin.

The brief Coughlin connection was an odd one and showed how little Jimmy Cromwell knew of the world at large. Catholic priest Father Charles E. Coughlin broadcast his beliefs from the Shrine of the Little Flower in Royal Oak, Michigan. From there he also started a political movement called the National Union for Social Justice, which registered 5 million members the first two months, all of them listeners to his radio program. Neither Coughlin's beliefs nor his political sentiments reflected Catholic church policy, nor was it sanctioned by his bishop. But it was enormously popular in the Depression-era 1930s.

"In politics I am neither Republican, Democrat, nor Socialist. I glory in the fact that I am a simple Catholic priest endeavoring to inject Christianity into the fabric of an economic system woven upon the loom of greed by the cunning fingers of those who manipulate the shuttles of human lives for their own selfish purposes," Coughlin explained.

The truth was quite different, and eventually Coughlin was shown to be a man filled with hate and bigotry. He was probably a Nazi sympathizer and eventually would become dangerously anti-Roosevelt. Criticism of Coughlin was tempered at first because he was supposed to be a man of God, and many people feared he might truly be speaking for the Lord.

Jimmy Cromwell seemingly did not have religious concerns. He liked many of the Coughlin economic theories. Had he been more politically astute, he would not have stayed with the priest while trying to win favor with the Roosevelt administration. The only sense he showed was to stop being so openly respectful of Coughlin's theories after a September 1936 broadcast, when Roosevelt was running for reelection, during which Coughlin said, in part: "When any upstart dictator in the U.S. succeeds in making this a one-party form of government, when the ballot is useless, I shall have the courage to stand up and advocate the use of bullets." Coughlin continued, becoming dangerously personal as he stated, "Mr. Roosevelt is a radical. The Bible commands 'increase and multiply,' but Mr. Roosevelt says to destroy and devastate. Therefore I call him anti-God."

Over the years Jimmy's ideas filled several books, but the most important one was *The Voice of Young America,* published in 1933 by Charles Scribner's Sons. Birth control and sterilization programs would deal with the issue of hunger during the Depression, limiting the population and thereby reducing the demand on our resources. Hot dogs seemed to be the food of choice for nourishing the poor. Jimmy apparently felt they were tasty, assumed they were popular with the masses, and liked the fact that they were cheap at a time when people needed to stretch their food budgets. In addition, utilities and the nation's rail and bus lines would be nationalized.

Eventually he also came to believe that the Soviet Union needed to be recognized, Hitler needed to be attacked, and an international organization had to be established to ensure peace after the war. He wrote several other volumes, including *Pax Americana, In Defense of Capitalism,* and *Sound Money.* None were major sellers, though they did upset his stepfather's friends. Since Jimmy never lived by his own ideas, preferring the rich life of champagne, caviar, and the world's exotic delicacies that Doris Duke would be able to give him, it was hard to believe he was seriously committed to his cause.

The Roosevelt people recognized him as a man who was little more than Doris Duke's "bimbo." What they did not consider was that although Jimmy Cromwell may have been self-centered, not particularly bright, and a cad, he was not going to go away. He wanted a political career mentored by Franklin Roosevelt that just might eventually put him into the White House. That he expected Doris Duke to help bankroll such a run for office seemed perfectly logical to him.

Despite all this, many people courted Jimmy Cromwell. Doris Duke was fascinated by him because he was older, well connected, and seemingly far more interesting than the men of her age. She thought he would be fun. She thought he would provide her with sexual adventures. And she knew he would be the key to getting away from Nanaline forever.

Franklin Roosevelt, hated by the wealthy conservative Republicans who made up the Stotesburys' social set, saw in this rather comical liberal Democrat someone who could gain him entrée to the very rich. If nothing else, likely pragmatic Republicans would quietly give large sums of money to the man they perceived as their enemy if they felt they needed political leverage while Roosevelt was in office. In addition, Cromwell was a potential source for substantial financial support the president would soon need for hotly contested reelection campaigns.

There are many stories of other pressures on Doris to marry, including the alleged rivalry with heiress Barbara Hutton. Some biographers feel that Doris felt competitive with Barbara. Others felt that the press created a rivalry that did not exist. Assuming family members were familiar with the truth, her cousin, Pony Duke, believes that when Barbara married first, selecting the allegedly gay but importantly titled Prince Alexis Mdivani, Doris wanted her own husband. The Mdivani/Hutton marriage celebration was as extravagant and well publicized as her debut had been, and though Doris claimed to not care, the idea of being a celebrity was important to her. Doris quietly maintained a thick scrapbook of clippings relating to every aspect of her own life. She hated the problems publicity could bring, from the kidnapping threats to the lack of privacy, yet she delighted in being the center of attention, in knowing that people felt she was special and wanted to read about her.

She even made her first trip to Hollywood, a fact that so frightened Nanaline, she decided that Doris's marrying Jimmy was a reasonable solution. A tall blonde with money, ego, and naïveté could be hurt far more in Hollywood than by a bad marriage.

On February 13, 1935, Doris Duke and Jimmy Cromwell were married in a manner designed to upset Nanaline. There would be no rented hall, no taking over of one of the grand hotel ballrooms still favored by those who had weathered the Depression. She would not even use one of the grander rooms in the Newport or Duke Farms estates. Instead, the wedding was held in the library of the Fifth Avenue mansion, a room that still smelled of Buck's cigars, that still reflected his decorating taste. Had Doris not had the legal right to block all her actions, Nanaline would have changed the room after she killed her husband. Instead, it was a room Doris loved and her mother hated; thus it was the perfect place for a marriage that assured her independence from maternal control.

Doris also ignored the traditional wedding dress, preferring a clinging blue crepe. Beyond the fact that the color, material, and design upset her mother, the dress made her feel sensual for one of the few times in her life. Jimmy, the amateur boxer, had not yet lost his trim, muscular physique to the excesses of food and drink he would enjoy with his new wife. With Jimmy in formal striped pants and morning coat, taller than his bride's six foot one, Doris undoubtedly felt feminine and beautiful perhaps for the first time in her life.

Supreme Court Justice Burt Jay Humphrey was present to perform the civil ceremony from which Doris had stricken the word "obey." Hers would be a marriage of equals—a merger of what she thought were great fortunes and equally great passions.

There had been no advance publicity. Doris's friend Dr. Richard Hoffmann had arranged for the license to be issued at the Municipal Building without her presence, as was normally required by law. He claimed she suffered from a nervous condition that would be aggravated by any publicity. The excuse was accepted and no one alerted the press.

The ceremony did include a few traditions, the most important being the giving away of the bride. In yet another effort to thumb her nose at Nanaline, Doris sent for Walker Inman to escort her in place of her late father. He was honored by the invitation. His mother was not. She knew that Doris saw Walker's presence as symbolizing her stepbrother's loss of the vast fortune Nanaline hoped he would acquire. It was one last hostile gesture, adding to the tension of the day.

Those present, with the exception of Marian Paschal, represented the business side of the marriage. There was a much relieved Eva Stotesbury, of course, decked out in her finery, and a frustrated Nanaline wearing a conservative navy blue outfit. But the rest seemed more appropriate to a corporate meeting, such as William Perkins, the Dukes' attorney, and Norman S. Dike, another Supreme Court Justice. (Unlike Justice Humphrey, who had never met the couple but could be hired if the price was right, Justice Dike was long familiar with the Dukes.)

The honeymoon was to be on board the ocean liner *Conti di Savoia*. Trunks had been loaded the day before, but Doris and Jimmy's last-minute essentials—a dozen suitcases and Doris's maid, Catherine Walsh—followed the couple's Rolls-Royce to Pier 19 from which the liner set sail that noon.

Jimmy Cromwell's ego was too great to allow the couple the privacy Doris had worked so hard to ensure. There had been no pictures of the ceremony, no reporters flocking outside the Fifth Avenue mansion. Rut Jimmy had tipped off Roy Howard, publisher of the Scripps-Howard newspaper chain, who made certain he was on the ship in time to capture the arrival of the newlyweds. Unfortunately, knowing the importance of the images and his ability to sell them throughout the world, he made certain that numerous photos were taken. Doris became annoyed and went to the cabin. Jimmy stayed behind to talk about the overnight love affair that brought them to the memorable moment, ignoring the six years of plotting that actually preceded their "love at first sight."

Once Jimmy finished being immortalized, he sent a telegram to Washington senator Robert Owen, his associate, along with Father Coughlin, in The Sound Money League. He wanted his friend and partner in rather unconventional politics to be certain he had not forgotten what really mattered to him—fame, power, and money. And the newspapers confirmed that Jimmy Cromwell would have the attention he needed to build the political career that was building rapidly in his imagination.

Had Jimmy Cromwell had any sense, he would have spent the first afternoon and night of his honeymoon working to give Doris the sexual delights she sought. She was ready to try any sensual pleasure. There was nothing she would not do that day, and had her new husband had the sense to pursue her in the manner she desired, his future and their life together might have been very different. Unfortunately, Jimmy was a fool, a fact his mother well understood. She warned him to not mention money to his bride, even though money was at the center of both their thoughts. She did not think it necessary to talk to him about sex.

Doris was radiant that evening. They had delayed sex to enjoy the ship, but they retired early. She slipped on a negligee. Jimmy asked his bride what he could expect in the way of an annual income.

Whatever future Doris Duke might have had, whatever her relationships with men might have become, everything changed at that moment. She understood the nature of fortune hunters. She had been to England to be presented. She had made her debut. She had friends who married to gain European titles. She had friends who bought the men of their dreams. And she had friends who lost everything in the Depression, then married men whose financial circumstances were all that made them desirable. She was not naive. Her father had certainly warned her about the cads and fortune hunters. But Jimmy Cromwell was supposed to be different. The Cromwells had money and the Stotesburys had even more. There was no way she could have anticipated the question he asked, no way she could have anticipated the depth of the pain.

Jimmy Cromwell was the type of man who could never take personal responsibility for his actions, never see himself as he truly was. His new bride evicted him from the Honeymoon Suite on their wedding night, forcing him to spend the time in the bar. Obviously there was something wrong with her, not him. After several drinks, he decided she was frigid. After several more, he began to think she might be a lesbian. Ultimately he would be the source for rumors that Doris Duke Cromwell preferred women to men when the reality was that she wanted an uninhibited romp in bed with the man she previously thought she might even love.

Jimmy Cromwell's fate was sealed the next day. He had earlier told Doris that he was going to pay for the honeymoon. He had gone to the Cook's Travel and worked with them to plan a tour of the Middle East and Far East. The newlyweds were going to travel from Egypt and the Mediterranean to China, Japan, and the Philippines—among the most romantic tourist spots on earth.

But the check Jimmy wrote to Cook's was bad. He didn't have enough money in his account to back it; obviously he'd hoped to have a transfer of funds from his new wife before the first payment came due. The next day he compounded his wedding-night mistake when he had to confess to Doris. She wired her business manager, and from then on, Doris Duke Cromwell was paying for the honeymoon she had thought was a gift from her husband.

Ironically, if Jimmy had not felt compelled to confess exactly what occurred between his bank and Cook's Travel, Doris might have blamed the bank. She had no idea what it meant to write a bad check. She assumed that if you wrote a check, the bank always honored it. She had no sense of the finite nature of checking accounts because she had unlimited credit. She would become an astute businessperson in the years ahead, including understanding the limitations of people who were normal wage earners. But at the time of her honeymoon, she had no idea how different her life was from others'. And since Jimmy was supposedly from wealth almost as great as her own, she assumed that his experiences would always match her own.

What actually happened on the honeymoon is uncertain. There were attempts at lovemaking, but for years later, Doris would ridicule Jimmy's small penis and inability to sustain an erection. At the same time, Cromwell would leave the ship at every stop, then return to the ship's bar a few hours later and brag about his sexual conquests while away.

Probably the marriage went unconsummated during the honeymoon. If Jimmy was able to perform, it is probable that he had premature orgasm quite possibly exacerbated by Doris's anger. She had gone from an aggressively willing partner to one who had lost all respect for the fortune hunter she realized she had married.

Whatever the situation, Jimmy's asking about his allowance assured the end to the future they might have had. The marriage was a failure, something to which Jimmy alerted his mother. At the same time, Doris indicated to friends that she intended to make the best of matters. Marriage might not be forever, but she was not going to seek a divorce within days of the ceremony.

Jimmy Cromwell was as mean-spirited as he was a fool. He

could not admit that his verbal indiscretion led his bride to hate him for being the opportunist he was. He could not admit that he was less than brilliant in bed, given a naturally handsome physique made even better looking by his training as a boxer. Instead he felt compelled to make matters worse by implying that he was a flawless stud hampered by a lesbian bride.

The issue of Doris Duke's sexuality would haunt her throughout her life. It would be exploited by others seeking her wealth. And it would define the way she pursued the hedonistic side of life.

Without question Doris Duke preferred men to women. Without question Doris Duke was open to every type of sexual experience she learned about. And the idea that Doris Duke may have tried to see what sex with a woman was like, perhaps going only so far as to let a woman touch her in an intimate way, is quite likely. But Jimmy Cromwell wanted to hurt Doris in the manner considered most horrendous by the society of the time. He implied that Doris and Jenny Renaud had enjoyed a sexual relationship that destroyed Doris for any man.

The accusation, made when the couple was first estranged, was ironic since it is doubtful that Jenny ever considered Doris as anything more than a little sister. Jenny's relationship with Nanaline may have been sexual as rumored. If Jenny was drawn to women, she was not drawn to children. However, Jenny was French at a time when French women were perceived to be morally different from Americans. They were viewed as loose-moraled, sexual libertines who might be comfortable in relationships that would shock nice people in the United States. A French nanny seducing her young ward seemed a safe fantasy to weave. It was both shocking and could bring sympathy for poor Jimmy.

Compounding the issue was the public attitude toward lesbians and homosexuals at the time. The idea that a new husband might hint at such a charge was enough to make it have the ring of truth. After that no one considered that Cromwell might be the one with a problem.

As to the question of Cromwell's infidelities, there is every indication that they occurred. The women with whom he may have dallied included at least one former girlfriend who was a professional actress in Naples, where the honeymoon couple had one of their stops. However, it is likely that the sex was little more than Jimmy's angrily acting out against Doris.

Later Jimmy would claim that his actions had resulted from a desperate desire for sex. He wanted the image of the super-aroused male anxiously waiting to "perform" with his bride only to be thwarted by the "Frigidairess."

As bad as things were going for the marriage, Jimmy Cromwell made certain that the honeymoon tantalized the public. Using friends in journalism, Jimmy and Doris's conspicuous spending was reported by wireless to American papers:

Dateline February 20, 1935—Cannes, France—"James Cromwell and his bride, the former Doris Duke, spent a few hours today visiting the French Riviera on their honeymoon tour.

"They landed from the liner Conte di Savola here this afternoon and motored along the coast to Beaulieu, where they dined with friends. They rejoined the liner at Monte Carlo, whence it is sailing for Haifa tomorrow.

*"Most of their visit in Cannes was spent in trying to dodge a throng of reporters and camera men."* [Emphasis added.] *New York Times,* February 21, 1935

Dateline Monte Carlo, Monaco, February 21, 1935—"James H.R. Cromwell and his bride, the former Doris Duke, left Monte Carlo today without patronizing its famous gambling casino.

"They came ashore from the liner Conte di Savola wearing berets and sports clothes, which would have prevented them from entering the Casino Sporting Club anyway, as formal dress is compulsory.

"They passed yesterday afternoon admiring the natural beauties in this vicinity. In the evening they dined, sipped champagne and danced in a night club . . ." *New York Times,* February 22, 1935

Dateline Lahore, India, April 6, 1935—James H.R. Cromwell and his bride, the former Doris Duke, heiress to American tobacco millions, have been suffering from ptomaine poisoning contracted at Agra, it was revealed today. The illness was not serious enough to interfere with their tour of India.

"Recovering from temporary disability, they were engaged in combined research work and sightseeing. Mr. Cromwell was collecting material, which led to the belief he intended to turn author and write about this country when he returned home.

"The Cromwells learned what his period of silence meant to Mahatma Gandhi. They wanted to talk with him again while they were at Wardha, but they found him in the midst of a month's self-imposed silence to permit him to catch up on his correspondence. As the next best thing they submitted a list of nine comprehensive questions concerning his doctrines of the simple life and passive resistance. They expressed the hope he would write out the answers for them . . ." *New York Times,* April 17, 1935

Dateline Calcutta, India, April 19, 1935—"Mrs. Doris Duke Cromwell, frequently called the 'richest girl in the world,' has yet to satisfy her ambition for an audience with the Mahatma Gandhi.

"He recently refused to grant Mrs. Cromwell's request for an interview at Wardha. Since that time, it was learned today, she has been writing him repeatedly in an attempt to learn something of his philosophy of life.

"Her correspondence has been fruitless, however, forcing the tobacco fortune heiress to turn to lesser known mystics in Northern India for knowledge of their teachings. She and her husband have been spending their honeymoon in India." *New York Times,* April 20, 1935

Dateline Calcutta, April 23, 1935—"Mrs. Doris Duke Cromwell plans to rebuild a wing of her Florida mansion after the style of the famous Taj Mahal, the three-century-old marble mausoleum at Agra.

"It was learned today that the glories of the ancient memorial to a Mogul emperor's wife so impressed Mrs. Cromwell that she ordered an architect in Delhi to prepare the plans for the remodeling. She especially wants tessellated windows and doors. Their construction of Indian marble has already begun, and they will be transported to the United States. . . ." [Note:

Each door took six men three months to make as they were in-laid with agate, jade, lapis lazuli, malachite, and mother-of-pearl.]

". . . They [Doris and Jimmy] have run a gamut of experiences, including touches of ptomaine poisoning and talks about the supernatural with Indian mystics along a meandering route from Bombay. They plan to go north again, heading for the foothills of the Himalayas, touring the famous scenic district of Darjeeling and the native Indian State of Kuch Behar.

" 'We are enjoying every minute of our honeymoon,' said Mr. Cromwell on his arrival, after being delayed at Kashmir by the rains. 'Although this is anything but a progressive country, our tour made us sympathize with the Indians' desire for freedom, the same as we Americans wanted our freedom centuries ago.'

"He said Mrs. Cromwell was in wonderful health despite the intense heat and that she regarded Mahatma Gandhi as the greatest religious teacher of the century. . . ." *New York Times,* April 24, 1935

Dateline Calcutta, India, May 4, 1935—"James H.R. Cromwell and his wife, the former Doris Duke, left for Bangkok, Siam, today on the regular airline plane, continuing their honeymoon tour. The flight included a sight of the sunrise over Mount Everest. . . ." *New York Times,* May 5, 1935

Dateline Bangkok, Siam, May 5, 1935—"Carrying $20,000 worth of ancient rugs, which a valet described as 'not fit for hanging over my telephone booth,' Mr. and Mrs. James H.R. Cromwell arrived today by airplane on their honeymoon.

"Engine trouble forced Mr. Cromwell and his bride, the former Doris Duke, to spend the night at Rangoon. . . ." *New York Times,* May 6, 1935

Dateline Singapore, May 29, 1935—"After having spent five days in a hospital, resting from the fatigue of her travels, Mrs. James R. Cromwell spent $5,000 in Singapore shops before departing with her husband for Batavia, Java, yesterday.

"The former Doris Duke took with her $3,000 worth of clothing, Chinese-style pajamas, lingerie and jewelry, and ordered merchandise worth an additional $2,000 delivered to her in Hongkong [*sic*].

"Among her most valuable purchases were four Shanghai costumes of Chinese satin brocade and a two-centuries-old Chinese ivory carving." *New York Times,* May 30, 1935

Dateline Hongkong [*sic*], July 19, 1935—"James Cromwell of New York brought his bride, the former Doris Duke, to Hongkong today on their honeymoon, but said he must return to the United States in the Fall.

" 'We must be back by October,' said the economist-bridegroom. 'There are a lot of things needing our attention, particularly the Roosevelt regime. Something has to be done about it, and people with money are the only ones who can check the present collapse into chaos.'" *New York Times,* July 20, 1935

Dateline Shanghai, July 28, 1935—"Unperturbed by a wave of recent kidnappings here, James H.R. Cromwell, honeymooning with his bride, the former Doris Duke, called 'the richest girl in the world,' said today he would not hire bodyguards in the fashion of wealthy Chinese residents.

"Mr. Cromwell denied reports of lavish expenditures on curios and art objects in South China and said he and his wife had spent *only $30,000* on purchases [Emphasis added. This was in the depths of the American Depression, which had affected the economies of the world. For many people, this was ten years' pay.] since leaving the United States on their round-the-world tour.

"He said his wife would view the devastation of the Chinese floods from the air in a specially chartered plane." *New York Times,* July 29, 1935

Dateline Honolulu, August 30, 1935—"James H.R. Cromwell and his bride, the former Doris Duke, found Hawaii so restful on their first day here that they decided to spend a whole month in the islands. They arrived from Yokohama late yesterday and took a suite at the Waikiki Hotel, but after deciding to extend their visit went house-hunting and selected a cottage in the Black Point residential section." *New York Times,* August 31, 1935

The honeymoon had been a time of conspicuous consumption of what would prove, in several instances, to be priceless antiquities and art objects. It had also been, for Doris, a bitter lesson in men. But Hawaii would prove quite different. In Hawaii, Doris Duke would come alive, discovering both sex and love for the first time in her life.

# 8

※

# A Fool and His Wife
## Are Soon Parted

*I*F THERE WAS any chance of saving the marriage of Doris Duke and Jimmy Cromwell, it had been shattered in India. Despite the difficulties so carefully reported in the *New York Times,* the Cromwells were able to meet with Mohandas Gandhi, the highly eccentric Hindu nationalist and spiritual leader. Gandhi was a highly visible proponent of passive resistance against the British who controlled India. Through his nonviolent encounters, he united the people in a manner that ultimately led to the nation's independence. It was a concept that ultimately influenced other social protesters, the most famous in the United States being the Reverend Dr. Martin Luther King, Jr.

The British government hated Gandhi, jailing him and attempting to undermine his influence, but he was a man respected by the world. He spoke of his religious philosophy, of his concerns for justice, of the dignity of all persons. His words made him more powerful against the British government than armed militancy ever would have been. Eventually Gandhi was silenced by violence, but his assassination took place more than ten years after Doris's audience with him. At the time she arrived, Gandhi was that rare individual—a celebrity with humility whose cause was others, not himself.

Gandhi, who usually dressed in a loincloth, met the Cromwells in a small, unfurnished room. The simpleness of his lifestyle, his focus on the spiritual, and his use of what he felt was the divine in the struggle for human freedom made a lasting impression on Doris. It was her first encounter with someone who could be considered selfless, whose life reflected inner peace without the need for outward trappings of wealth and conspicuous consumption. Although Doris would never be able to curb her spending or give the bulk of her wealth to others during her lifetime, she saw in Gandhi a source of power and inner peace she had never before witnessed.

Gandhi wanted to speak with the Cromwells about human existence, about the meaning of life. Jimmy wanted to explain to Gandhi all his economic theories. At the time India was considered a backward nation, a country with a vast population and great economic potential. Jimmy Cromwell was certain that his theories could help the nation achieve the greatness it deserved, regardless of what Gandhi wished to share with them. He wanted to explain capitalism and how industrialization would change lives.

Being the self-centered fool that he was, Jimmy ignored the opportunity to hear one of the great leaders of contemporary history. Instead he dominated the conversation, ignoring the information Doris was seeking in what would become her own spiritual quest for peace. Even worse, either by chance or design—Doris seemed to suspect the latter—Gandhi was called away rather suddenly. His aides knew that he could not waste his time trying to speak to a man who had not come to listen.

Jimmy's arrogant stupidity, the failure to have what Doris expected as normal marital relations, and the question of an allowance caused her to turn away from marriage and develop other interests. (Eventually Doris settled $10,000 per month on Cromwell so he would never be caught wanting when he was away from his bride. The purchasing power of that allowance in 1935, still a time considered to be the depths of the Depression, was more than twelve times what it would be today.) Instead, she concentrated on learning about and acquiring the art of the Muslim world as well as developing her home/museum dream house in Hawaii.

———— ⚜ ————

DORIS BEGAN THE Hawaiian mansion in her mind while still on her honeymoon. There were three motivating factors in her planning. The first was a genuine love for the art she was discovering in her travels, art that would be used in the home. The second was the belief that not only had she experienced reincarnation, she had once been a fish who still needed to return to the water in order to be complete. And the third was the fact that Jimmy Cromwell hated Hawaii, a perfect reason to plan her special home in what was then an American territory.

Because Doris was reticent to talk about the construction of Shangri-La while it was taking place, and because reporters did not try to observe the property, little was known at the time about how she had it constructed. Ten years after its completion in 1937, the story was revealed by Doris herself, who was then working as a freelance writer. One of her assignments was for the August 1947 issue of *Town & Country* magazine, a lifestyle publication for the rich. She was asked to describe her Hawaiian home on Black Point, two miles east of Waikiki. It was on a hillside, the ground partly covered with outcroppings of black lava. Nearby was a private yacht harbor so she could go quickly from her patio into the Pacific Ocean if the mood struck her.

The mansion was created in a series of L shapes so that every wing had both a view of the ocean and a view of Diamond Head, Doris revealed. Patios and gardens ran throughout. And the furnishing were original Near Eastern pieces, though not necessarily used as originally intended. Duke wrote:

> . . . in my Indian bedroom the carved, cut-out marble jalis, or screens, which were formerly used by Indian princes to keep their wives from other eyes, have a new purpose: they are not only decorations, but a means of security, for they can be locked without shutting off the air, and when not wanted can be pushed hack into the wall.[1]

Doris Duke understood tax and estate laws, and the way she furnished the house showed a sophistication not evident until after her death. She bought priceless items of museum quality and historic value, then used them as furnishings. They were treated so casually that, although they were placed where they would not be damaged, they were not displayed as their value might warrant. There were no special cases, no sophisticated alarms. As a result, they were easy to overlook, a fact that ultimately fooled the estate appraisers following her death, who assumed that furnishings, though undoubtedly expensive, did not need a close examination if they were casually displayed. By this reasoning, the *jalis* could be dismissed as a room divider when removing them for sale would result in their being taken for the historic treasure they were. It was a classic example of the idea of something being hidden in plain sight; for Shangri-La alone, the estate valuation was underestimated by hundreds of millions of dollars.

The mansion had a Persian-style patio, but used tile pieces dating to the eleventh century. Then Doris used thirteenth-century luster tile to build a *mihrab,* the portion of a wall that always faces Mecca. And as Doris well knew, there were collectors who would pay handsomely for each tile; again, it was a way to hide her wealth.

The entrance hall utilized sixteenth-century Rhodian tiles. Also from the sixteenth century was a Clienca carpet around which the living room was designed.

Some of the design was done to resemble a particular period, Doris wrote. What she called the "playhouse" was a "reduced version of a Persian palace, the Chihil Sutun in Isfahan. The main room and the two dressing-rooms have been done in a later, rococo period of Persian art, known as Kajar, which reflects the deteriorating effect of European influence."[2] That "playhouse" was used as both a tea room and a swimming pool bathhouse.

The house and grounds were magnificently finished, with a series of waterfalls adjacent to the stairs from the main house to the pool. The architecture was a conscious mix of Egyptian, Moroccan, Persian, Syrian, and Turkish, all in the midst of Hawaiian vegetation. At the same time, even all this was created in a manner that was meant to be reminiscent of the Mogul gardens of Lahore.

Some details, such as many of the columns, were copies. Others, like the tiles and the rug, were originals. The dining room table, for example, used a slab that had formerly been an Indian bed. The wall was lined with Persian flagons, plates, and ewers, all of which were functional, and all of which had enormous collector value on their own. The house was a case of the whole being worth far less than the sum of its parts.

Doris Duke essentially created a museum, then set up house-keeping within its walls. When she traveled, she sought the finest-quality arts and antiquities from countries just beginning to be appreciated by art lovers and museums, and she did it at a time when laws protecting such items had yet to be passed.

Doris Duke's actions would not be possible today. The loss of pre-Columbian art, Middle East artifacts, Greek antiquities, Roman treasures, and the like that occurred during and after World War II caused governments around the world to tighten their laws. Today, though looting from excavations and archaeological digs still takes place, the items cannot be legally removed from the country where they were found. When such removal is discovered after the fact, some governments will buy back the items, matching or exceeding the current market value. Others simply outlaw the sale and/or removal of antiquities from their nations, prosecuting owners who fail to return what was taken.

Doris Duke began her collecting of Near Eastern and Middle Eastern treasures before other art buyers were interested. Her actions might he compared with someone who travels from Europe to America buying art treasures five years before they are desired by the Smithsonian, the Metropolitan Museum of Art, and other major repositories. Later, she established trusts to make her collections available to the public and to scholars doing research.

Doris was not content with mere excess, though. In her writing she explained that she was already having a "Mogul-inspired bedroom and bathroom, planned for another house" being completed for her in India. She decided to ship it to Hawaii "and build a house around it."

In later years, Duke frequently talked about her love for the Muslim countries and her obsession with Hawaii. What she did not mention was that the reason she loved the water so much was because she believed she had once been a fish. In her search for spiritual understanding, Doris Duke came to believe in reincarnation, something supported by a number of Eastern religions. She took matters to what some of her friends considered an extreme, however, by convincing herself that she traced her existence back to a time when she lived in the water. Eventually it would be the reason she occasionally talked of having her body tossed back in the ocean, perhaps to be eaten by sharks. She would simply be letting her corpse return to its physical roots, her spirit already inhabiting the next life it was to experience.

None of this mattered to Jimmy Cromwell, though. He was frustrated with Doris and had few interests other than tennis and a political career that remained real only in his own imagination. He decided to return East early, traveling back in September even though Doris would not leave for the mainland until close to Christmas. She wanted to enjoy the visual pleasures of local, dark-skinned, heavily muscled Waikiki beachboy divers. She took up surfing with the young men, at the same time attempting to learn the culture of the native Hawaiians. She was fascinated by their history, their songs, their dances, and their food.

The young men were, in turn, fascinated by Doris Duke Cromwell, a woman they liked for herself, not her money. It wasn't that they were pure of heart, uninterested in something so crass as net worth. Rather, they were from a race of people whose lives rarely crossed paths with tall blond women. She was strikingly different, exciting, and daring enough to wear a two-piece yellow swimsuit at a time when "nice" girls wore one-piece bathing suits. This was, after all, a decade before the introduction of the only slightly smaller bikini. The men found the tall, lean, fair-skinned woman in a two-piece suit to be extremely exciting, a fact Doris recognized and delighted in knowing.

Although Doris and Jimmy shunned guards, Honolulu's sheriff, Duke Kahanamoku, felt that he should keep a close eye on the heiress. He did not want her to get into trouble, and so he began spending time with her. His desire to protect her soon became something more.

Duke Kahanamoku was something of a local legend. He had been a medalist in swimming in both the 1912 and 1920 Olympics. He was also quite tall, at least two inches taller than Doris, broad-shouldered, and with a manner affected by the minor acting roles he had had in Hollywood films, where authentic-looking Polynesians were in short supply

At first Duke maintained a professional distance from Doris, although later they would admit they had been drawn to each other from the start. However, it was strictly hands-off in those early days of their relationship; only his brother Sam became involved with Doris, because she wanted him to teach her to surf.

The sensual nature of the island and the closeness of Sam and Doris soon led to an affair revolving around Cromwell's fitness regimen. Whenever Jimmy and Doris were in Hawaii together, Jimmy would go to the courts to play tennis. Sam would go to the bedroom to play with Doris.

There was an intensity to Doris Duke's sex life with Sam Kahanamoku that, in hindsight, seemed to be the result of her troubled past. She enjoyed the physical pleasure, but she acted driven, as if determined to prove her husband wrong in his assessment of her. She had undoubtedly heard his comments about her supposed inability to enjoy sex with a man. She also knew that he was cheating on her. She wanted to prove to herself that she was a fully heterosexual, highly desirable woman.

---

DORIS QUIETLY RENTED a small, private house near the beach in Honolulu to serve as her trysting place for illicit rendezvous. She stocked it with champagne, caviar, and other fine food. It was there she began partying with some of the handsomer beachboys, allegedly with sex as part of her pleasures.

Apparently Jimmy Cromwell was aware that Doris was being as unfaithful to him as he had claimed to have been to her. He probably did not know the details, nor did he want to know them. His concern was avoiding a public scandal by getting her back to the mainland where she was likely to be more discreet. He may have hoped his leaving would prompt her to follow. Whatever his reasoning, 1935 ended with Jimmy learning just how independent Doris could be.

---

THE YEAR 1936 was not a good one for Jimmy to face a sex scandal. His ex-wife, Delphine, was in the midst of a lawsuit, and Jimmy Cromwell's name occasionally appeared in the papers. He knew that while reporters were reluctant to reveal the personal side of the lives of politicians in office; they would be quite willing to smear the name of a potential contender. He had to avoid scandal with Doris, letting all criticism remain focused on his ex-wife.

As much as Jimmy Cromwell's position was precarious, the Democrats saw his wife as someone to be cultivated. The cost of political campaigns in the 1930s was so low that she could easily finance the campaigns of every candidate running from both parties and spend less than she earned from her investments in a year. Equally important, with war talk building in Europe, politicians were keenly aware that Doris owned power plants in both North and South Carolina that served major military posts.

Jimmy wanted Doris to finance his own dreams and to spend extensive time at Duke University, which was gaining an international reputation thanks to the changes financed by Buck Duke's endowment. Jimmy felt that with Doris present, he would be placed on the board. Such an image would give him credibility since it would imply that he was both a scholar and a business leader.

The problem was that every time Doris went to Duke she was reminded of the limits of her education. She had a stronger business sense than most corporate CEOs. She was gaining a knowledge of horticulture and botany that would make her one of the world's greatest authorities on the orchids she loved, grew, and sold from her greenhouses. She had mastered the different centuries of Middle Eastern and some Far Eastern art. She knew how to look at the work of a modern sculptor or painter and know which items were the best. She understood the value of different Old Masters, having the eye of an appraiser from the time she was a young woman. But the proper woman of Doris's day, whether educated in a finishing school or respected public institution, also had a solid grounding in classic literature that Doris lacked.

Doris always felt inadequate with women who, though less intelligent than she, had a "proper" education. She was an avid reader of information that related to her interests. But each time she spent a day or two at the university, she was reminded of the gaps in her education. Jimmy thought only of impressing Franklin Roosevelt and having a political career. And Doris lacked the courage to tell him why she wanted to avoid the world of Duke University as much as possible.

———— ❧ ————

DORIS AND JIMMY traveled to Somerville during the summer of 1936, so that she could begin designing her planned home in Diamond Head and he could host a series of parties to boost his political image. She would pay the bills, of course. Her staff would handle all the preparations. He would just make speeches about the need to reform the banking system and somehow get the rich to change their ways.

Franklin Roosevelt had no sense of the tension between the Cromwells. He needed Doris's money and thought that if he humored Jimmy, he might get a check. He had his aides begin discussing the idea of making Jimmy governor of the territory of Hawaii. However, Doris made clear that she was not in favor of the idea. She was extremely protective of Hawaii and the home she would always consider her primary residence. Jimmy Cromwell was not to intrude.

Doris returned to the island in December of 1936. She owned what was supposedly the best property in Diamond Head, land that cost her the staggering sum of $100,000, twice what the president felt he would need to assure his reelection in every state in the union. Jimmy was not with her, but Sam Kahanamoku met her in San Francisco so she would not be bored when she sailed back to her home.

Doris planned to call the house she was building Hale Kapu, according to her cousin, Pony Duke. The meaning implied her state of mind at the time, for *Hale Kapu* was Hawaiian for "keep out of this house." Instead she changed the name to Shangri-La, the mythical kingdom from the novel and movie *Lost Horizon*. The story told of people living high in the Himalayas who never get old, an idea that would appeal to the heiress throughout her life.

(Research by author Stephanie Mansfield indicates that the name may have been a play on words as well. A man named Ali Kapu, pronounced the same as *Hale Kapu,* lived in a mansion in Isfahan, Persia. Doris was familiar with its beauty and may have found humor in the Hawaiian translation of the sounds of the name.)

Eva Stotesbury was more nervous than the Democrats over Doris and Jimmy's estrangement. She needed him to stay with his bride in order to help his family's finances. Instead he was openly courting women in New York and Palm Beach. He knew word would get back to Doris, which it did. However, she no longer cared. She knew he could not perform, and she was more than satisfied with her lover.

At his mother's insistence, however, Jimmy returned to Doris. Eva was the one person who had strong influence over him. Yet both realized that the marriage could not last when Doris insisted that Jimmy use not only a separate bedroom in the home she was renting during the construction of Shangri-La, but one that was located on a different floor from her own.

Jimmy's economic concepts were contained in his latest book *In Defense of Capitalism,* which showed how to redistribute the nation's money. The work was not impressive, but after its publication Jimmy was given an opportunity normally reserved for men of greater sophistication. He was asked to lecture before the U.S. Senate's Agriculture Committee, whose members greeted him enthusiastically. They were certain that support for Jimmy could be translated into campaign contributions from Doris.

Jimmy's idea was a negative interest plan, perhaps the most ridiculous concept he had devised to date. First there would be a law requiring the rich to give one-third of their money to orphanages, schools, and colleges. He determined this amount based on the Duke Trusts his late father-in-law had established. One third of Buck Duke's money was already being spent in this manner; if Jimmy's ideas were enacted into law, his own standard of living would in no way be altered.

Jimmy's plan called for an incentive to the wealthy to spend their money. Investors in major businesses would be loaned money to make more investments. Then they would also be paid 6 percent *by the government* for their efforts. They would have to repay the loans, but instead of paying interest, they would profit by a minimum of 6 percent.

Next, Jimmy arranged a trip to Russia. At the time, Joseph Stalin was at the peak of his power and proving himself to be one of the deadliest dictators in history. Joseph Davies was ambassador to Moscow, a position requiring great diplomatic skills and extensive personal wealth. The latter was brought by his wife Marjorie Merriweather Post Davies, Barbara Hutton's aunt. They invited the Cromwells to visit them and arranged for Jimmy to have a brief meeting with Stalin. However, before that appointment, Jimmy felt the need to record the experience of being in Moscow photographically.

The Leica camera Jimmy owned was the most expensive miniature camera in the world. Originally created as a light meter for the motion picture industry, it became the world standard for construction and precision optics. It was made in Germany and imported in limited numbers into the United States. Military versions served as spy cameras. The civilian models were owned by professionals experimenting with what was then a tiny negative (news cameras of the day used film twenty times the area of the Leica) and by the very rich, who carried them in the same manner as they wore diamonds and other jewelry. Carrying such a camera to Russia made him appear to be the embodiment of the arrogant capitalist oppressor.

While Doris waited in the car, Jimmy insisted on either stopping to get out and take pictures or photographing through the window. Given the Soviet Union's tensions with Germany alone, it was natural that he would get arrested, a fact that delighted Doris. She later joked that she hoped the Soviets would keep him.

Jimmy Cromwell was taken to the National Hotel, the headquarters of the local plainclothes police. He probably would have been sent to prison had not Ambassador Davies intervened. As it was he was detained for only a few hours.

The meeting with Stalin that followed Jimmy's release was both brief and anticlimactic. The dictator had no interest in Cromwell other than the possibility of some positive connection with Roosevelt.

───────── ✦ ─────────

DORIS, BEMUSED BY her husband, did support Roosevelt and gave him a $50,000 contribution prior to the 1936 election, ensuring his victory. In his future dealings with politicians, Jimmy always made subtle reference to this money, implying that there would be more if he was properly rewarded. He convinced politicians that he controlled Doris Duke's purse strings. What he did not say was that though he could suggest places for her to contribute money, she sent a check only if she too believed in the cause. This was the case when Doris, at Jimmy's suggestion, gave $1 million to the Birth Control League.

During this same period, Jimmy announced—without consulting with Doris—that the couple would build a swimming pool on their Somerville estate exclusively for the use of poor children. He never discussed how they would get the children to the pool or whether the children had other needs that were more important. The plan generated publicity, however, something important for Jimmy. The fact that the pool was never built went unnoticed by the papers.

Jimmy did succeed in gaining a higher profile because of his wife's wealth. Duke University wanted him to conduct seminars on his economic theories, not because anyone agreed with him but to bring Doris back with more money. While this did not happen, she did supply a donation to Princeton University to underwrite a study of the state tax system that affected both Cromwells.

Cromwell was soon on the board of directors of a number of community organizations and businesses. He was on the Somerset Hospital board, where he took his duties more seriously than the other board members. He was on the board of the Raritan Savings Bank. He became an honorary member of the Hillsborough Fire Company after arranging for equipment to be given to the local rescue squad. And he donated as generously as he could get Doris to write a check to various local charities and concerns.

The high point of 1937 for Jimmy came when former New Jersey senator Harry Moore was elected governor and said that Jimmy was on the short list of possible successors to his previous position. As governor, he had the right to appoint the new senator because he had left midterm and no election had to be held. The announcement was Jimmy's payback for having Doris give Moore a $5,000 campaign contribution. It was all the payback he would receive, though. Jersey City mayor Frank Hague controlled the state's corrupt politics, and Hague despised Roosevelt. At best, he saw Cromwell as a fool; at worse, he saw him as being in the enemy camp. Either way, Jimmy was too naive or too blinded by ego to recognize the hopelessness of his fantasy so long as Hague was firmly in control of the state.

———————— ❦ ————————

ALTHOUGH JIMMY CROMWELL did not recognize the fact, there were two sides to Doris Duke. One was the quiet, determined woman who could sue her own mother, take a lover when her husband failed to satisfy her desires, and manage her own business affairs. The other was a woman of intense compassion, someone who would give money to anyone in genuine need if their plight came to her attention. She had aided ramshackle churches serving the most disenfranchised members of Southern society so that there could be beauty, joy, and hope in their worship services. She was a genuine admirer of Franklin Roosevelt, truly moved by his compassion for the people enduring the greatest suffering during the Depression.

Doris frequently looked for ways to quietly help others in need, and the work in Appalachia of Eleanor and Franklin Roosevelt seemed ideal to her. Eleanor Roosevelt, also estranged from a husband who obviously had long ago stopped caring for her, busied herself with working for the most disenfranchised of America's poor. She searched out small communities in Appalachia, finding at least one that was so isolated from society that the people still spoke the Elizabethan English of the earliest white settlers. She met with coalminers whose lives seldom lasted more than thirty or thirty-five years, as well as with the widows who had to raise several children with inadequate food, limited water, and no outside support. She found that most people, all of them white, were illiterate, a fact that would come to haunt the nation at the start of World War II when the draft revealed a shortage of white men who could read and write. She fought for social programs that would assure a better quality of life for the poorest of Americans. And she did all this despite coming from a background of power, social prestige, and lifelong privilege

At the same time, Jimmy Cromwell expected Doris to contribute heavily enough to the Democrats that he would be backed for senator from New Jersey. (Frank Hague was led to believe that

Jimmy would pay $300,000 to gain the Democratic Party's nomination for the Senate.) Jimmy felt he would serve several terms without meaningful opposition, both because he fancied himself to be brilliant and because he believed that his wife could buy the state.

After serving in the Senate, Jimmy felt he would be named vice-president, from which he would launch a campaign that, in either four or eight years, would move him into the White House. He would be president. Doris would be first lady. The only problem with the scenario was that Doris Duke Cromwell didn't share her husband's ambitions, and she may even have wanted to deliberately hurt his future. If he was sufficiently damaged, he might see an uncontested divorce as the only way to salvage what little potential for success might remain for him.

Jimmy wanted to mount a campaign that would put both Cromwells in the spotlight as the friends of the poor. He felt that favorable publicity in this area was just what he needed to receive the New Jersey Senate appointment.

Doris, Jimmy insisted, would travel with Eleanor Roosevelt during one of her regular visits to the West Virginia communities that were suffering as much or more than any other locations in the nation. At the same time, he gave a radio address discussing the ways in which the Depression had changed America's rich. He said that no one wanted to engage in conspicuous spending anymore. The construction of mansions that were nothing more than monuments to money was an idea of the past whose time was over. Instead, the rich were attempting to upgrade the lives of the average citizen. The fact that he made the statement as Shangri-La, his wife's mansion, was still under construction went unnoted by the press.

It was Doris who decided to undermine her husband's relationship with the Roosevelts and to do it during the West Virginia trip. It is important to note that Doris Duke was only twenty-five years old when all of this was taking place. She was brilliant and tough, had seen parts of the world most people did not know existed. Yet she was a very young woman who sometimes thought like a rebellious teenager. Certainly that seemed to be the case during the West Virginia visit.

Doris arranged to travel to the poorest known section of white America wearing custom-made English walking shoes and a coat made from perfectly matched Russian mink. She adorned herself like a glamorous movie star at the world premiere of a publicity-hungry film.

Eleanor and an imperious Doris were driven from the White House to the Tygart Valley, West Virginia, Cooperative where five hundred miners and their families were gathered. They had barely enough food to stay alive, lived in shacks, and were fortunate when their children stayed healthy enough to grow to adulthood.

Doris signed autographs for the children who thought she had come from Hollywood. They did not recognize her name, but they also could rarely afford to see a movie. They assumed she was special, an image reinforced that night when the First Lady and Doris attended a square dance, and Doris feigned boredom.

The trip back to Washington was made in relative silence. Eleanor Roosevelt wanted nothing more to do with either Cromwell. Franklin would face the toughest fight of his career when he ran for a third term in 1940. Among the Democrats seeking to take him from office was Joseph Kennedy, a man with enough money to undermine an incumbent president. Jimmy Cromwell lost all chance of going to the Senate.

Cromwell was livid with Doris when he learned what had happened. She never told him the truth. She also never revealed to either Jimmy or the Roosevelts that she was more deeply moved by what she had seen than by anything she had previously encountered. The wood-and-tin shacks in which the people survived were of a quality she would have considered inferior for a household pet. The idea that families had to live in them was appalling to her. She arranged to give money privately to the community to help them raise their standard of living. No one ever knew the source of the funds. She sought no publicity. And she acted in a manner that would have pleased Eleanor, since the money helped underwrite self-help projects the people were developing. She also never returned.

Jimmy Cromwell was not yet ready to abandon his young bride, although he knew the marriage was over. He also knew that Doris was good for a settlement that would assure his having at least a few million dollars while searching for his next wife. The money would continue to make him desirable to the Democrats, and he might be able to revive his career if he waited until she decided to get rid of him.

Doris, by contrast, was determined to see that Jimmy was left with little or nothing of the Duke wealth. She wanted to make him feel that she was such a liability in his life, it was better to walk away from her without a financial settlement than to stay with her and see his desires destroyed one after the other.

In 1939, when the Roosevelt administration decided to thank Jimmy quietly for his campaign contribution, Cromwell was awarded the position of ambassador to Canada. Roosevelt awarded ambassadorships to nuisances several times, most notably with Joe Kennedy, who was sent to England. Jimmy was sent to Canada. And Doris saw the political machinations as a way to cause Jimmy to want to break with her once and for all.

In 1938, in addition to her political actions, Doris switched her Hawaiian affections from Sam to his brother Duke, the sheriff. There was no animosity between the brothers. Sam and Doris had enjoyed an affair involving sex but not friendship. Doris and Duke were close friends who gradually fell into bed together. He was a lover in a sense that exceeded the physical. The sex came naturally from the deeper relationship. He did not want to marry her, which meant that he had no designs on her money.

Doris also spent time in Hollywood, where she briefly enjoyed a fling with Errol Flynn.

While in Hollywood, Doris also explored the possibility of doing some acting. It was an ambition that made Jimmy nervous. The Hollywood image was the wrong one for his wife.

Ned Stotesbury died that same year, and true to his word, Jimmy was not in the will, although even the family chauffeur was given $1,000. There was somewhere between $4 million and $5 million after the inheritance taxes, as well as the value of the possessions in the three homes he shared with Eva. More than ever, Jimmy realized that, like it or not, Doris was his key to everything he desired.

Jimmy attempted to make himself more appealing by getting a face-lift from the highly respected Gloria Bristol Limited at 745 Fifth Avenue. However, the change did not alter the couple's relationship in any way.

Doris also took a third lover during this period, an odd man for her to choose since he was so much like Jimmy Cromwell. This was the infamous London Conservative member of Parliament, Alec Cunningham-Reid, whom she first met prior to her marriage. She had had made contact with him again when she and Jimmy were passing through England on their way to Russia. Doris spent 1938 traveling among her husband and three lovers, using rail, boat, and the unusually daring new form of mass transportation—airplane.

Cunningham-Reid would later be criticized in the British press when, during the bombing of London, he agreed to arrange for the placement of a number of British children in temporary homes in the United States. Children were evacuated routinely during the early months of the war, but Cunningham-Reid, a captain in the military, traveled with them and made certain his visit was extended by stays with Doris in Somerville and Hawaii. He was considered a coward for leaving England when he was both a government official and a military officer. It is not known if Doris was bothered by his action, but she certainly enjoyed the idea that one of her lovers would go to such extremes to be in her arms.

Doris was reluctant to travel with Jimmy to his new ambassador's post in Ottawa. She explained to him that she was going only to maintain appearances. A married couple was expected, so a married couple was what the Canadians would see. He should just not expect to share a bed with her.

Doris also informed Jimmy that she would not meet most of the embassy expenses, as was expected of the ambassador, which is why the post always went to a wealthy individual. She did pay for flowers, wine, and liquor used for entertaining, but nothing more. What his salary could not cover would be out of his pocket from the allowance Doris provided for him.

Doris further protected herself from Jimmy by replacing the embassy servants with people who worked for her at Duke Farms. However, even with a staff she liked, she lasted only ten days during her first Canadian visit following Jimmy's appointment. Then she traveled to New York for a vacation with Cunningham-Reid.

Eventually Jimmy convinced Doris to return north and attend the dogsled races in Val d'Or, a Canadian mining town. The ambassador needed to maintain an image of friendliness, and that image frequently meant engaging in popular local social functions, such as the race. The community meant little in terms of American foreign policy, but it was the type of event where the public expected to see the ambassador. More important, Jimmy promised that Doris, far more popular than himself, would crown the winner. This she did, but using the approach she had used when traveling with Eleanor Roosevelt, she deliberately made a remark meant to upset the locals. She stepped up to the microphone and said, "Hi, Ma. It was a great fight but we won."

It was on the day of the presentation that Doris told Jimmy she was going to seek a divorce. But the estrangement was not what marked the end of his political career; it was Cromwell's misguided thinking that eliminated any support from Washington.

Franklin Roosevelt desperately wanted to enter the war then raging in Europe. He wanted to do more for the Allies, both to stop Hitler and to keep the violence overseas. At the same time, he was facing isolationist members of Congress. Roosevelt was working behind the scenes on a one-to-one basis to convert enough isolationists so that he could provide any and all support the Allies needed. Deals were being made that could not be revealed. Extreme tact had to he used, and Roosevelt wanted no one connected with his administration to publicly chastise the isolationists for fear they would turn back against him.

Most of Roosevelt's ambassadorial appointments understood this, but not Jimmy Cromwell. In an effort to win favor from the Canadians, he attacked his own government for not doing more to help the Allies. He embarrassed Roosevelt, risked the ending of the negotiations with the isolationists, and lost all chance for political support for any campaign.

———————⚜———————

WHILE JIMMY WAS shooting himself in the foot, Doris was undergoing a far more profound experience that led to a moral crisis from which she would never fully recover. The incident would always be in the back of her mind, ultimately affecting her relationship with the young woman she would one day decide to adopt as her daughter.

Birth control was not as accessible in the 1930s as it is today. There were condoms, but they were not sold openly. Buying them was embarrassing for some men. And the failure rate was such that they carried a risk of pregnancy, although far less of a risk than unprotected sex.

Doris Duke became pregnant in 1939 and went to a New York hospital where, according to her cousin, Pony Duke, she had an abortion.[3] He later speculated that the child was Duke Kahanamoku's because she felt that the treatment she received from the staff indicated the baby was interracial. The abortion itself was against the law, and though she could buy the finest care, as well as the silence of the staff performing the procedure, she could not buy their respect. A brown-skinned baby born to a blond woman would have earned their disdain.

Apparently the only man Doris told about the abortion was her lover, Cunningham-Reid, who was outraged. He may have been a cad toward women, but he wanted any children he sired. Since he knew that Doris had long ago given up sex with Jimmy, he assumed the child must have been his. He had no idea that Doris was not faithful to her lovers.

How the abortion affected Doris is unknown. What matters is that she became pregnant by her Hawaiian lover a second time. She learned about the pregnancy during her divorce from Cromwell, and the news shocked her. Doris would not talk about it to reporters, and Jimmy Cromwell found it best to remain silent. Everyone would assume that he was the father, and such a position would help his political campaign.

Doris's concerns with the second pregnancy all revolved around money. Her child would be rich based on trust fund arrangements already in existence. Her child's legal guardian would have access to the money while the child was growing up. And because Doris had cheated on Jimmy, the law was very clear that he could gain custody, could be declared the legal father even if the child did not look like him. The idea of biological responsibility did not exist as a strict point of law. The act of being married gave the husband custodial rights even to the wife's children by other men.

Attorneys warned Doris that custody could become an issue in the divorce, which it did. Jimmy refused to give up custodial rights to the unborn child because he felt he could receive a large sum of money to stop his protests. Doris even offered to pay for Jimmy's political campaign if he would get out of her life and not claim the child. But Jimmy never knew when to quit a battle; he always took matters one step too far.

Finally Doris had enough. She could not stand being manipulated. She was not about to give Jimmy custody of the baby. She was not even certain she wanted a child, since its presence would radically change her life. However, she also felt that another abortion was out of the question.

The answer was to get rid of the baby in one of two ways that were reasonably common among women seeking to end their pregnancies in the 1930s and 1940s. The first, which Doris shunned, was the self-abortion, utilizing an instrument such as a coat hanger. This was the method of total desperation—painful, crude, frequently ineffective, and always life threatening. The woman who had bought the silence of a major New York hospital would not stoop to such an approach.

The second method was based on myth. This was the idea that if you were physically active enough, the baby would spontaneously abort. Women choosing this route would engage in intense athletic activities, such as calisthenics and gymnastics, the end-result rarely being what they anticipated. The womb is a wonderfully protective shell for the baby growing inside and intense activity usually does not cause problems. If anything, it often strengthens the mother and makes the birthing process easier.

Doris Duke did not know how hard it is to use athletics to end a pregnancy, but she did choose the best possible exercise to assure a spontaneous abortion. She went surfing in Hawaii.

Doris traveled from Canada to Hawaii, alerting Duke Kahanamoku to what was happening. It is not known if he wanted her to keep his child, though he understood that she would not.

On July 11, 1940, Doris took her surfboard into the ocean and began riding the waves. She took the biggest, most dangerous waves she could find. She was concerned only with how much violence she could do to her own body as she went back into the ocean again and again. Only when she reached a level of exhaustion where her own life would be threatened did she stop abusing herself.

Duke took the physically and emotionally drained Doris back to Shangri-La only to find that she had begun to go into labor. She was rushed to Queen's Hospital where she gave birth to a daughter.

There was no chance for the infant to survive. It is doubtful that she would have lived with access to modern technology, but at the time, death was certain. Despite these facts, Doris named the newborn Arden. In the twenty-four hours before the baby died, Doris Duke Cromwell changed.

This was her first real accomplishment. Doris Duke had never created anything herself before. She had only had what money could buy.

Doris was able to see her daughter only briefly. She was weak herself, physically and emotionally drained. Normally she probably would have been denied access to her daughter, but no one was going to stop Doris Duke from pursuing her desires.

Friends and family members would later claim that in those few hours Doris fell in love with Arden. It is certain that the birth and death of her only child profoundly changed her life. Although it is also not known when Doris Duke's intense interest in religions began, her daughter's death led to her becoming firmly convinced that there was reincarnation. As the years passed, Doris would search for her dead daughter in strangers. She knew that she was destined to meet her child again, just as her father Buck was certain he too would return one day.

Doris refused to allow Jimmy to be with her, in part because her grief left no room for a fool she did not love and in part because his absence would look bad. If the press learned she lost her child and her husband was not at her side, he would look like a cad. Since the Democratic National Convention was to be held two weeks later, and Jimmy wanted to use it as a starting point for a Senate race, there was nothing she could do that could hurt him more in the eyes of the public.

Cromwell's hopes were kept alive when he attended the convention on his own and was allowed to stand onstage with President Roosevelt. The moment was Franklin's, though, for he won an unprecedented third term against strong opposition within the party. The press and power-broker attention was focused on the president. No one cared about Jimmy Cromwell.

Cromwell was bitter toward Doris, and his anger increased when he discovered that Cunningham-Reid was living for a time in Hawaii, just when travel from England was restricted. The scandal was increased because most of those close to Doris felt that Cunningham-Reid was more interested in avoiding German attacks and protecting his sons by moving them out of London during the war than he was in serving his country.

To defuse public relations, Doris returned to her New Jersey estate in September and Cunningham-Reid flew to New York to work. But Doris continued to visit him, and the two dined at the very public restaurants where the gossip columnists either hung out or had maître d's or other restaurant employees on their payroll.

The impending divorce was obvious to everyone, including Mayor Frank Hague and his New Jersey machine. They withdrew all support from Cromwell, knowing that he was no longer in a position to help them.

Desperate, Jimmy went to Roosevelt, who ignored him. With the election soon to take place, Roosevelt needed the New Jersey Democratic Party machine far more than he needed Jimmy Cromwell, especially since it was almost certain there would be no more Duke contributions.

Newspaper gossip columnist Walter Winchell learned of the impending Duke/Cromwell divorce the first week of October, presumably from Doris or someone acting on her behalf. Winchell reported that the divorce would take place after the November 5 election. Given the conservative nature of the times, Winchell's columns assured his readers that Cromwell could not win the Senate race.[4]

Naturally Doris Duke was interviewed about the race. She explained that she was permanently separated from her husband. She also said it was a shame that he had lost the Senate seat when he had worked so hard to take it.

The remark made Jimmy bitter. Both he and his estranged wife knew that she failed to buy him the seat he coveted, and he was outraged with her for not admitting her complicity in his defeat.

Jimmy Cromwell made one last attempt to see Franklin Roosevelt in Washington. The effort was futile. As a result, he moved to Palm Beach with his mother to lick his wounds and see what he could obtain from Doris as they prepared to go their separate ways.

---

CROMWELL'S PASSIVITY WENT only so far; he refused to be divorced without a fight. What began in 1942 ended with Doris going to Reno, Nevada, the following year, establishing residency, and declaring that Jimmy was guilty of extreme cruelty as well as having made numerous demands for money. She revealed his $10,000 monthly allowance, his lavish lifestyle, and his foolish criticism in Canada of U.S. policy on the war in Europe.

Jimmy countered by publicly discussing Doris's adultery with an unnamed British man. He also stated that she had done all this to prevent him from gaining the U.S. Senate position he sought.

Ironically, Jimmy Cromwell's experience and the divorce Cunningham-Reid received in 1939 when he sued the extremely wealthy Ruth Mary Clarisse Cunningham-Reid for half her money were in some ways similar. Cunningham-Reid said that any decent woman would share equally with her husband at the time of their parting. And in England, the incident in no way affected his political career.

The Reno divorce was granted immediately. The court cut Cromwell off without a cent. He then claimed it was invalid, saying that they lived in New Jersey and the case should be decided there. Jimmy assumed he would receive more favorable treatment, apparently forgetting that any support he might receive from political cronies depended on the availability of Doris's money. The war was not over, but Jimmy had lost this battle.

# 9

❧

# *Playgirl, Spy, and Writer*

*D*ORIS DUKE WAS twenty-eight years old when she ended her marriage to Jimmy Cromwell. In a sense there were two divorces, the first from Nanaline, the second from Jimmy. Inheritances and money from investments gave Doris a net worth conservatively placed at $300 million. She could do anything she wanted.

For a brief period of time, "anything" meant using Hawaii as her base. Doris loved Shangri-La, loved the parties she could have there, the way her guests were shocked by her pet birds and monkeys. She was being aggressively wooed by actor Errol Flynn, who was openly interested in her money and willing to perform whatever sexual antics Doris desired in order to earn it. She was being sought after to invest in Hollywood films. She was the host to such international figures as Clare Booth Luce, the well-known journalist and wife of the man who owned *Time, Life,* and *Fortune* magazines. And she continued her relationship with Duke Kahanamoku, who had the good grace not to be jealous of any of Doris's other affairs. Then, on December 7, 1941, Japan attacked Pearl Harbor.

Doris's home was unharmed—the Japanese were concerned with destroying military targets, not civilian property. However, she could not return because no one knew if there would be another attack.

Desperate for water craft, the navy began requisitioning private yachts from the wealthy Americans living in Hawaii. These were to be used to patrol the coastal waters, and though the program was theoretically voluntary, with the Maritime Commission paying for the vessels' use, it was obvious no one could refuse. The nation was at war, and the government was going to be doing everything necessary to ensure there were no further surprise attacks.

Doris Duke was oblivious to the issue of patriotism. Business was business. She did not want the *Kailani Lahi Lahi* used unless she was paid $35,000. Equipment on the boat would be extra. However, she was told that the boat would be taken regardless of her desires.

The house was a different matter. Shangri-La was an expensive home to run if she wasn't there to enjoy it. She decided to offer the house without charge to the navy so the government could have a base of operations. She was certain that only the officers and high-ranking officials would be there, and she could trust them to keep it in good repair. They would also secure the location from attack. Doris felt it was the easiest way to keep her property safe.

The government rejected the house, however, recognizing the same problem of maintenance costs that Doris faced. They could not afford the upkeep. However, they did use her swimming pool as a place for recreation for the officers.

To add to her problems, Jimmy Cromwell was contesting her Reno divorce. Cromwell had moved to Washington, D.C., but had arranged for a long-term lease on a hotel room in New Jersey, to maintain a residence there. At the same time, Jimmy bribed the doorman at Nanaline's New York apartment to claim that Doris had visited while she was supposedly residing in Reno, to satisfy the six-week residency law in Nevada.

On May 10, 1944, the New Jersey court held that the Reno divorce was not legal. Doris's lawyers filed an immediate appeal.

During the same month that Doris found herself frustrated in her court battle, she arranged with the War Department to become a trainee with the United Seaman Service (USS). It was the only way she could get around her boredom.

Doris Duke's reaction to the war was no different from that of many other wealthy people who had no immediate family on active duty. For them, the war was a nuisance. Travel was impossible due to gas rationing and because use of public transportation was restricted. New clothes and other nonessential items could be purchased only in stores near her East Coast homes. She was cut off from lovers in Hawaii and London. Public service seemed the ideal way to pass the time.

It would be wrong to say that working with the volunteers helping the USS changed Doris or made her sensitive to the hardships of life. However, the organization maintained hotels and rest areas for merchant seamen. The wife of Kermit Roosevelt, the president's son, gave up her Long Island estate so that the USS would have a training center, and it was to that Oyster Bay address that Doris was assigned. She would learn new business skills and become intimate with the problems of men experiencing the horrors of war.

At first Doris did little more than play cards and go boating with the sailors. Her job was to keep them relaxed and entertained, just as volunteers with the United Service Organization (USO) did. The difference was that merchant seamen often faced the greatest risks of all noncombatants. They traveled on unarmed or lightly armed vessels, transporting supplies throughout the world. They were targeted by enemy planes and vessels because they helped the Allies' cause and could be sunk with limited risk even when traveling with an armed escort. The USS provided a genuine service to these men.

By running the club, Doris learned how to operate a small business. She learned how to order supplies, prepare programs for the seamen, and manage personnel. Once properly trained, she was transferred to Egypt, where she was assigned to a USS club in Alexandria.

The work at the Egyptian club delighted Doris because no one cared about her money, her homes, or her experiences. They needed an accepting friend and nothing more. For perhaps the first time in her life, she became sensitive to the concerns of others.

The problem was that Doris Duke still wanted a man, and nearby Cairo was teeming with British royalty, military officers, and soldiers. It was a place away from the war where the rich could relax in the splendor to which they were accustomed.

There are several stories about this time in Doris's life. The first is that she was determined to find Cunningham-Reid in Cairo, where they could continue their love affair despite the fact that he had grown more serious about his responsibilities. He was a member of Parliament and a military veteran. After initially running away from the Blitz, he came to understand the seriousness of the military situation. He matured in his sense of duty and leadership. He no longer wanted to hide out with a wealthy American woman.

This is not to say that Cunningham-Reid was celibate or a saint. On October 27, 1944, he married the daughter of a British naval officer. She had become pregnant by the MP, a man almost twice her age, back in June.

Doris was not notified in advance of the marriage, and whether she cared is unknown. Neither Cunningham-Reid nor Doris Duke Cromwell were known for their fidelity to anything other than their libidos. Cunningham-Reid was now concerned about his reputation and the war. All Doris knew was that she wanted to be with him.

Doris Duke Cromwell's original plan to join Cunningham-Reid had been obvious to some leaders of the USS volunteer group to which she belonged. He had been rumored to be in Cairo, and that was why she wanted to go to Egypt.

Just prior to Cunningham-Reid's marriage, Doris determined that the best way to pursue him was to create the rumor of a new affair, a new love. The man she chose to be the recipient of her ardor was a Captain Henderson. He was, according to Doris, a member of the British Armed Forces assigned to the desert war. He was based in Cairo at the moment, where Doris met him.

Henderson was perfect for Doris. He was a gentle man with no interest in her wealth. He was a great lover. He was a brave leader of the British soldiers. He put honor and country before sex, but when he wanted to be with a woman, his heart was solely with Doris. She talked of Henderson ceaselessly, like a teenager in love for the first time.

The only problem, according to Pony Duke in whom she confided years later, was that Henderson did not exist. Doris understood that the only way she would have the freedom to travel during wartime was to seem to be in love with someone other than Cunningham-Reid. In that way there was a chance she could return to England without her superiors fearing she would create a scandal.

Once Cunningham-Reid married, life at the club in Alexandria and in the shops and night spots of Cairo held no joy for her. She decided to go to Italy, basing her desire on the "fact" that Henderson was being transferred there. No one had met Henderson. No one had seen him. But unlike her beloved member of Parliament, the relationship with Henderson would never cause scandal. He was "safe," so trying to appease Doris seemed a valid action to take.

Doris began meeting with the members of the Office of Strategic Services (OSS), the spy organization that would later become the Central Intelligence Agency. Many wealthy individuals had become part of the OSS as a way to participate in the war, travel, and help stop the enemy while mostly avoiding the risk of being on the front lines. Most of the men involved at the top were stationed in the command posts in China, Burma, the Mediterranean, and northern Europe. However, there was also a place for "action junkies" when OSS teams worked with Burmese tribesmen waging war against the Japanese, parachuted into France and Norway on special assignment, and went to the Balkans to destroy bridges. The men spied against the Japanese and, most important, provided intelligence analyses for the American commanders in Europe and Asia. The OSS men who were part of often-secret battle missions worked with existing special units such as the Ranger and Raider units of the army and marines.

Because Doris traveled in the same social circles as some of the leaders' families, most of the men at the top of the OSS were comfortable with her, especially the founder, General William J. "Wild Bill" Donovan. Thus her application to join the OSS was taken seriously at the top, perhaps to encourage her financial support of the Democratic leadership in the White House.

Assuming Doris Duke met the standards needed to join the OSS, which most critics say she did not, she would have had to undergo a security check. The security issue was a minor one. Doris had been to the White House and was a Democrat. She also owned power companies critical to the war effort. No one thought that she might be a risk, but the routine should have been followed. Then she would have been sent back to the United States for training. The Washington headquarters would have indoctrinated her in the philosophy of the fledgling spy organization, instructed her in how to handle assignments, given her rudimentary weapons and unarmed self-defense techniques, and otherwise trained her for duty. Instead, she was assigned the code name "Daisy" and sent by B-25 bomber to Italy on January 6, 1945.

The code name came from Daisy Mae, a curvaceous blond cartoon character from the Al Capp cartoon who lived in the ultra-poor community of Dogpatch. This sexy blonde whose appearance challenged the conservative nature of the newspaper industry of the day was man-hungry. She was constantly chasing Li'l Abner Yokum, especially on Sadie Hawkins Day, the one day a year when all the single women in Dogpatch chased all the single men. They would set traps, use lassos, and do anything else necessary to catch the men, who ran desperately from marriage. The successful women would drag their future husbands back to "Marryin' Sam," the local justice of the peace.

The comic strip was so popular that many social groups had annual Sadie Hawkins Day dances where the women were expected to invite the men. Thus the nickname "Daisy" was not only complimentary—Daisy Mae was far more beautiful than Doris Duke—it also recognized her man-hungry nature.

Many Americans connected with the OSS work were livid that "Daisy" was sent to Caserta in Italy. The organization was being used, they felt, to help the heiress in her scheme to get back to England and her lover. The British had refused Doris a visa, not wanting further scandals. By going to Italy with the OSS, there was a good chance she would have to be on official business in London. Annoyed at being manipulated, the State Department went so far as to consider revoking Doris's passport for the duration of the war.

To make matters worse, Eleanor Roosevelt was in Italy around the same time that Doris Duke arrived. Harry Hopkins, Special Assistant to the President, was also present and spoke derisively about the "richest girl in the world" being on the Italian front. However, Doris was granted a security clearance in March, put on the payroll at $2,000 a year, then assigned to the Air Force Hospital. There her duties were much like those on her previous job.

Doris Duke busied herself giving piano lessons and helping the hospitalized Americans make recordings about themselves and the war that were part of the propaganda effort. Each recording was sent home to the soldier's local radio station where it would be broadcast for friends, neighbors, and family.

Bored by the "non-work" for the OSS and worried about being sent back to Washington for training to appease those who were against her having a job, Doris decided to create a crisis.[1] Captain Henderson, whom no one knew but Doris and no one had ever met, suddenly died. He was killed in action, a valiant end for a valiant figment of her imagination.

Doris staged a complete breakdown, something she considered her finest hour of acting. She needed to deal with the crisis through hard work, work that would be far more involving than what she was doing for the Air Force Hospital. The trouble was that the OSS had nowhere else to send her since she had received no other training.

A friend of Doris's contacted publisher William Randolph Hearst's son, a personal friend, to see if Doris could become a war correspondent. She would be teamed with Mike Chinigo, bureau chief for Hearst's International News Service (INS) in Rome. Tex McCrary, head of photo reconnaissance for the OSS in Italy and the man who helped get her the job, agreed to provide Mike and Doris with tips when possible.

The choice of Doris Duke was not completely out of line. She had gained experience interviewing soldiers and sailors for both the USS volunteer work and for the OSS. She was not a good writer, but she was accustomed to asking questions, had an eye for detail, and was willing to work. She was also pleased to receive $25 a week from the Hearst organization.

As it turned out, Chinigo was one of the early breed of spies who used his reporter's credentials as a cover. The vast majority of journalists would come to hate such a ruse. Postwar reporters felt that their objectivity was critical. To be in any way connected with a government agency was to compromise their ability to gather and report news. Those journalists who went on the payroll of the OSS (or CIA, as it came to be known), the FBI, or any other government agency were held in disdain. But at the moment the world was at war, and Chinigo's double duty was still considered honorable.

The INS made clear that Doris's role would be publicized. She would be listed as a secretary but would also be expected to turn in articles to be heavily rewritten by an INS editor. She agreed, and soon articles appeared under her by-line.

Doris was able to locate the widow of Benito Mussolini, who was living in exile, and interviewed her for a story. She also was sent to look at what was happening to the average family devastated by the war. She went to the former motion picture capital of Italy, a place called Cinecittà, where children were being housed, as well as to soup kitchens and shelters for those made homeless by the war.

Doris was fascinated by writing and the life of a working woman. She took a small apartment on the Via Lima, a working class area of the city. She used a bicycle, had no staff, and wore old slacks. But when she needed any assistance, she could rely on the advice of Clare Booth Luce.

When she went to work as a war correspondent in Europe, Doris Duke was a rarity among American women. Most women in journalism were stateside, and most of those who came from backgrounds like Doris's were employed by newspapers such as the *Washington Times* and were located in major cities. Many prominent men had daughters who also worked as journalists (Joe Kennedy's daughter Kathleen was a writer for the *Washington Times*), and the established journalists mocked them. When Hearst made a practice of finding jobs for the daughters of the famous, usually stateside, they were derisively called "debutramps." They were considered adventure seekers.

Although Doris did not stick with writing for long, initially she was intensely committed. She fought to gain War Department credentials and dutifully covered even the most boring of stories in order to prove her seriousness. She may have used every method possible to gain her job, but she was determined to keep it based on hard work.

During this period Doris also did manage to return briefly to London where she was reunited with Cunningham-Reid. But he offered Doris Duke no future. He was committed to his British wife, to raising their child, to maintaining the dignity required of a member of Parliament.

Doris allegedly was willing to do anything necessary to regain the affection of her former lover. She offered to be his mistress. She offered him money, depositing whatever sums of money he requested in the secret bank accounts she knew he retained. She knew he was a cad, but unlike Jimmy Cromwell, he was a sexy one who could delight her in bed. To his credit, Cunningham-Reid turned her down.

Doris returned to her work as a writer with intensity. She offered to take any assignment, an unusual situation at the end of the war. Victory in Europe would soon be achieved, but this did not make the world a safer place. Occupying forces who had defeated the Germans were still facing violent pockets of resistance. Reporters were not welcome.

Doris did not care. The only respect she earned herself was as a journalist, and though she may not have been a good writer, she could get the facts and the quotes. She sought the chance to interview four-star general George Patton, who was on the Russian front.

Patton was no stranger to Doris. He was an odd character, a wealthy, aristocratic soldier who could wage war or play polo with equal ease. He was happily married and delighted to commit adultery at every opportunity. He and Doris had traveled in the same social circles when he was stationed in Hawaii, and he was aware of her "work" with the OSS.

Patton was big news because of risks he had taken, which were either deemed foolhardy enough to warrant his being court-martialed or lauded as heroic. He had marched across France, freeing Bastogne from Nazi occupation and capturing 750,000 soldiers. Finally he had linked his troops with the Soviet forces under the command of Field Marshal Feodor Tolbukhin.

Doris and Patton met by chance in Linz, Austria, four days after V-E (Victory in Europe) Day. He was more relaxed and happy than he had been in many months. When he learned that Doris was no longer on the OSS payroll (at least not directly), he told her she should do a story about him. Then the two of them went to his headquarters where they partied and made love. Several days later she returned to Rome. Doris Duke, physically sated, decided to get on with her life. That meant finding a second husband, and her choice was one of the most unusual men of the twentieth century.

# 10

~❦~

# *Notorious Stud Seeks Wealthy Wife*

*P*ORFIRIO RUBIROSA knew little about the physical sensations a man experiences when making love to a woman. His penis, though six inches in circumference and perpetually in a state of moderate erection, was insensitive to touch. He wielded it with the frequency and enthusiasm of a nymphomaniac locked in solitary confinement with a dildo. But it was the woman of the moment who left sated, enormously satisfied, and certain she had experienced the world's greatest lover. Rubirosa's satisfaction came secondhand, from the breathless enthusiasm of his grinning partner caught in the sweating afterglow of the moment as well as from her open checkbook. This was because, whenever possible, Porfirio Rubirosa sold his swordsmanship to the highest bidder.

Rubirosa was more than a superb lover. He was also one of the deadliest men in the world, the possible model for the James Bond character author Ian Fleming created. Although Fleming had Bond as a part of the British Secret Service (007—Licensed to Kill), Rubirosa's exploits were probably the inspiration for the character.

Rubirosa was a short man, several inches shorter than Doris. Extremely intelligent, he was the son of a Dominican general. He was raised in Paris and studied law for a while. When General Rafael Trujillo was elected president of the Dominican Republic, Rubirosa joined the army.

Trujillo may have been legally elected to his position, but he would hold onto it through fear. There were to be no living enemies within the Dominican Republic, and Rubirosa, who was named Trujillo's aide-de-camp, was to help ensure the dictator's continued power.

Rubirosa, who became a captain in the Dominican Republic Army, knew what he wanted in life. He was a tough sophisticate, a man who understood the quality of a custom-tailored suit made from the finest cloth available as well as the value of marrying well. He saw that sex and marriage could lead to money and a position where you could be protected from people who might otherwise become your enemy. This was especially clear with Trujillo, who had a sixteen-year-old daughter named Flor del Oro. The girl was nine years younger than Rubirosa, then twenty-five. The age difference was not that unusual, but the marriage was a deliberate coup on Rubirosa's part. It was 1932, and in a single, simple ceremony, he found himself a member of his country's wealthiest, most powerful family.

Trujillo decided to seal his son-in-law's loyalty to the current regime. An insider could be dangerous if he had no reason to feel that his interests were best served by protecting the interests of his in-laws. Rubirosa was about to become both a political assassin and an arranger of violence.

Exactly whom he killed has never been determined with certainty, although there are a number of clues. Rubirosa traveled to New York in 1935 in order to hire his cousin, Chi Chi de La Fuentes Rubirosa, to kill Dr. Angel Morales. Morales and Sergio Bencosme shared a home in Manhattan, and Chi Chi killed Bencosme by mistake.

The murder had international implications. The Du Pont family was involved with Dominican politics at the time. They had made loans to the Dominican government so substantial that when Trujillo came to power and refused to repay them, the Du Ponts were allegedly involved in an overthrow attempt. They were rumored to be shipping arms and ammunition to men working against the dictator, and after the murder they sought to increase their efforts.

Following his indictment for the murder and attempted murder, Chi Chi fled to the Dominican Republic, where extradition was not permitted. In appreciation of his efforts, he was given a position as an army lieutenant in order to ensure a steady income. However, Chi Chi, unlike his cousin Porfirio, did not understand the need to have total loyalty. He decided that the lieutenant's pay was not enough. He wanted to be captain, and if he wasn't promoted, he would tell what he knew about the assassination. Supposedly Porfirio permanently silenced Chi Chi.

As the Nazi government became increasingly powerful and Trujillo sought favor with Hitler, he sent Porfirio Rubirosa to Berlin as third secretary of the Dominican legation. From there he went to Paris, womanizing so blatantly that Flor became outraged. She divorced Rubirosa in 1936, which cost him much of his power although he was allowed to keep his diplomatic passport, a valuable asset in those prewar days.

Trujillo did not like what Rubirosa had done to his daughter, but she was only a girl and Porfirio had proven his total loyalty. When he realized that the young man was not going to talk, was instead dividing his time between bedding wealthy women for a fee and committing crimes, the president chose to ignore the past. However, his former son-in-law needed more income.

With the turmoil in Europe, wealthy men in exile would pay to regain possessions left behind in the land they fled. Rubirosa involved himself in such an action at least once, then murdered his partner and stole a portion of the merchandise he had been sent to retrieve. But his greatest wealth came from the results of a job Trujillo gave him during the war. The dictator named him Dominican Chargé d'Affaires at Vichy, France, from which position he began selling visas to wealthy Jews who otherwise would have been sent to a concentration camp. Rubirosa also used his diplomatic pouch to smuggle jewels, money, and other valuables for the Jews so they could have a fresh start away from the horrors of the Nazis. However, he frequently stole the valuables, claiming they were "lost." It is believed that Rubirosa killed a number of wealthy Jews following these transactions. Apparently they were never sent to the camps, nor were they seen after Rubirosa sold them visas and secreted their valuables.

Rubirosa's attitude toward the Nazis became obvious, in part, due to his next marriage, to Danielle Darrieux, a Nazi sympathizer who was the highest-paid actress in the French film industry. They married in 1942, a fact that placed him in jeopardy, because the French Resistance movement had marked Danielle for death and made at least one attempt on her life because of her Nazi connections. When a gunman shot at Danielle, Rubirosa threw his body over hers and was struck three times near his kidneys. He had long been an amateur boxer to build up his body, and he survived due to his excellent physical condition.

Shortly after the liberation of Paris in 1945, Rubirosa and Danielle had to move to Rome. He was banned from Paris because of his relationship with the Vichy government during the occupation, and she went with him. It was there that Doris interviewed him in her capacity as a reporter for the INS.

Doris Duke was fascinated by Rubirosa. He was sexy, dangerous, and handsome. He also was delighted by Doris's interest in his body, for she had more money than Danielle. More important for the moment, Doris had none of the enemies who seemed to be constantly lying in wait to shoot Danielle.

It was with Rubirosa that Doris started a pattern that would affect her relationships for the rest of her life. Possibly Doris Duke never loved anyone other than her father. She could respect an individual for his or her skills, either sexual or professional. She could love the fantasy that someone was interested in her, not her money. But, after Jimmy Cromwell shattered her few illusions on their wedding night, apparently it was impossible for Doris to truly give her heart. His question about his allowance reinforced every warning Buck Duke had ever given her.

Instead of love, Doris turned her relationships into business ventures. She chose to buy someone, give that person a lifestyle so opulent that he would stay with her, meeting her demands, yielding to her desires, until she tired of him.

Rubirosa understood that he could benefit himself by pleasing Doris in ways that went beyond sex. He gave her a gold ruby-studded compact and diamond earrings, the most expensive gifts she had ever received from a man. The cost of the present was minor when compared with the potential benefits. And because men did not routinely buy Doris Duke gifts of a type they knew she could better afford herself, Doris allowed herself the fantasy that Rubirosa wanted her regardless of her money.

Doris may have enjoyed her fantasies, but she was not a fool. She knew that no matter how much Rubirosa might love a woman, he loved money more. He would walk away from the greatest love any man had ever experienced if he could profit financially by doing so. Pragmatic Doris decided to buy him.

The down payment on Porfirio Rubirosa was $1.5 million. The first million dollars went to Danielle, who was ordered to divorce him on the grounds that he was, had been, and would again be an adulterer. Danielle was smart enough to know that Rubirosa would soon tire of being married to her and leave her. She also knew that her career in French films was essentially over. Her wartime, pro-Nazi activity cost her any future she might have had. With $1 million in American money, she could live quite well anywhere in postwar Europe. Danielle took the money and went off to buy her own kind of love.

The remainder of the money was a bonus for Rubirosa for going along with the negotiations. It was also meant to assure him that he would be well cared for even though Doris demanded a prenuptial agreement to protect her assets.

The United States State Department was outraged and considered canceling Doris's passport. The war might be over, but there were many issues surrounding Rubirosa and his position that could cause the U.S. government embarrassment. Doris was ordered to return briefly to the United States for what would later be called an "attitude adjustment."

No one in the federal government understood how sophisticated Doris Duke was when it came to her understanding the business and politics of her "boy toy" purchase. They did not understand that she had no illusions about Rubirosa.

Doris Duke understood that Rubirosa was not a man who could be bought in the normal way. When he went after someone's money, he would do whatever was necessary to get it. There was little doubt in anyone's mind—from the State Department to Doris Duke and her attorneys—that if he became her equal through marriage without a prenuptial contract, he would kill her and take it all. A government hit man would then own a power company that supplied much of the South, including military bases. He could take over her Texaco Oil Company stock, and she was a major shareholder. He could control her aluminum manufacturing business at a time when the metal, previously underused, was suddenly wanted for the aircraft industry. Important businesses and sections of the nation would be beholden to Rubirosa and, indirectly, to the corrupt, violent political leadership of the Dominican Republic.

Rubirosa wanted nothing to do with a prenuptial agreement when Doris discussed it with him after returning to Europe. She had visited her mother. She had visited Hawaii. She had even continued to bed Duke Kahanamoku, but it was more for friendship's sake. She wanted to buy Rubirosa, who was so unlike any other man she knew, and she was willing to pay the price.

First, Doris needed a job that would justify traveling into areas the State Department might not approve of. Although working with the INS at the time, she used her wealth to create a "front" for herself. She provided almost $40,000 in loans to help three correspondent friends start a newspaper called *The Rome Daily American*. In exchange, she was given the title "society editor" in order to force the State Department to see she was doing substantive work. Later she would sell her stock in protest against management decisions on hiring, then go to work for *Harper's Bazaar*, which was delighted to have a famous name working for them. For *Harper's* she would do research in the fashion industry as well as contribute an occasional article. The magazine had an excuse to exploit Doris's famous name, and she had an excuse to stay in Europe with Rubirosa, regardless of the State Department's concerns.

In the midst of all this, Doris was still dealing with the financial problems posed by her ex-husband. Jimmy Cromwell had never stopped fighting the divorce agreement. The Nevada divorce was recognized in forty-seven states. It was not recognized in New Jersey. He wanted money from Doris, and if he couldn't get it, he felt that ultimately the New Jersey courts would prevent her from marrying anyone else.

Jimmy had been fighting for Doris to establish a $7 million trust fund for him that would shield the money from taxes. Naturally he would be the person in charge of the fund, earning $50,000 a year for his work. His brother and other unnamed staff people would also be hired. The fund would be formed with Doris receiving debentures at 1 percent interest for thirty-five years. There would be 10,000 shares of stock, Cromwell and his designees having 9,970 of the shares.

The money requested was never paid. However, a settlement

was reached and Jimmy Cromwell received money until his death at age ninety-two. Exactly how much is not known for certain, although it was probably far less than Doris spent fighting any other settlement. It left her bitter, and she made clear to friends in the OSS that they were to make certain Rubirosa signed the prenuptial agreement on September 1, 1947, the day the wedding ceremony was to be held at the Dominican Republic legation in France.

No one on either side of the marriage trusted the other. The Trujillo regime feared that the OSS would kill Rubirosa to prevent his gaining any control over Doris Duke's holdings. Likewise, the OSS and Doris feared that Rubirosa might murder her. The answer was to force a binding prenuptial agreement that would protect Doris.

The OSS drugged the whiskey highballs Rubirosa was consuming before the ceremony. Then two men, allegedly lawyers who undoubtedly worked for the OSS, handed Rubirosa a prenuptial agreement. They explained that he could sign it or they would kill him. With such an incentive and with his mind clouded by the drug, he signed.

The timing was perfect. The ceremony began, both Rubirosa and Doris taking the vows. Then he slipped a ruby wedding band on Doris's finger and she slipped a custom-designed gold band on his. He glanced down and saw that it was a hint of his future—the ring was shaped like a miniature handcuff, a reminder that she had just purchased him. As the couple was declared man and wife, he realized that he belonged to Doris for as long as she desired him. Then the drug took full effect and he passed out. He never had a chance to walk back down the aisle, and he never consummated their wedding night. He just slept for hours, then was outraged on the honeymoon until Doris agreed to buy him a Paris mansion at 46 rue de Bellechasse. The price was $100,000, far more than the sum might seem because the French franc was in shambles and Doris paid in American dollars, which were worth far more. She spent $500,000 for an interior designer's work on the place. And because Rubirosa was a pilot, Doris also gave him an airplane.

The price was reasonable by her standards. She also knew that she had won the sick game they both were playing.

The OSS kept a nervous distance from the couple, anxious to

protect Doris without pushing too hard into her private life. Rubirosa owed many people large sums of money. The debts had been written off as uncollectable, as Rubirosa customarily spent everything he earned. With the marriage, there was a chance some people would try to collect.

Rubirosa ("Rube" as he was known to Doris, "Rubi" in the press) believed that he could do anything to please a woman. He was well known for agreeing to any sex act a woman desired. He was also totally devoted to each woman he bedded, at least during the time he needed to seduce her. Before their marriage, Doris often kept him waiting for her, showing him as much disrespect as possible to remind him of his place. Once together, they spent the first six weeks with Doris delighting in her new husband's body. Sated, having explored every sexual idea she wanted to try, they soon became bored with each other.

The marriage was difficult after the physical passion ebbed, and Doris became extremely jealous of Rubirosa's time. She did not want him dancing with anyone else. She did not want him talking with other women. She wanted to be the focus of his attention. At the same time, she expected to be able to do anything she wanted, including leaving their Paris home alone and going to jazz clubs and bars.

Doris never went to the clubs with an entourage. She never told anyone who she was, wore flashy clothing or expensive jewelry, never showed large sums of money. So far as anyone could tell, the tall American blonde was just another expatriate jazz lover, probably lonely, who shared an appreciation for music.

Doris's favorite locations were the cheap clubs where there was a piano in one corner but paid talent only once or twice a week at the most. A patron could sit at the piano and play without the management being upset, provided the person was a competent musician.

Doris began going to such clubs, sitting at the piano, and playing jazz. She was good, certainly good enough to be hired to play for the cocktail and early-evening dinner crowd in upscale American restaurants, and so the club owners were pleased. Frequently an empty glass would be placed on the piano top and patrons would drop in tips. At the end of the first evening of earning money, she realized that she had become a professional musician. She knew it was her life's calling, as much as anything could be said to be a vocation in her world.

For some people, the Paris experience would have been a turning point. They would have done whatever was necessary to continue their career. Certainly Doris had seen that there were plenty of places in the world where the name Doris Duke did not gain her entrée, but instead it was her skill on the keyboard that caused people to be interested in her. Those around her might still want something from her, but it was the sound of her playing, not the money in her checkbook. She had become an entertainer, and while the fact would rarely be mentioned, she would one day play on Grammy-winning records. For the moment, though, Doris found relief from a marriage that offered no joy and a personal life that focused on her inheritance, not her soul.

For his part, Rubirosa was frustrated by Doris's nighttime meanderings. She frequently brought jazz musicians back to the house so they could have after-hours jam sessions, which he hated. He contacted Trujillo to see if the president had any jobs for him, and while waiting for his former father-in-law to decide how to use him, he also went to nightclubs. However, he was prowling for women to entertain in a very different way and often serviced them for days as a way of getting back at Doris.

Rubirosa was named Dominican Republic ambassador to Argentina, which required that he and Doris move to Buenos Aires. The State Department did not want to give her permission to travel there, though, because she would be in a country that might not protect her from attack. She could be convinced to change her prenuptial agreement in a way that would be legal under United States law, then she might be murdered so that Rubirosa and, indirectly, Trujillo could have her assets.

Doris was required to return to the United States. She bought a war-surplus B-25 bomber, had it refurbished and converted into a luxury transport for Rubirosa so he could visit her, and had it dispatched to Buenos Aires. Shortly after that, Doris was given permission to join him.

Rubirosa felt that if he treated the Argentines properly, they would support his country. Since many of the most powerful fig-

ures were women, including Eva ("Evita") Peron, he let his penis
handle the diplomacy. Unfortunately, he acted with no sense of discretion, which upset Doris. She informed him that he could either
be quieter about his "diplomacy" or start paying his own way in
life. As a result, Rubirosa agreed to return to Paris to work for a
while, and Doris, determined to exact revenge before joining him,
flew to Hawaii for servicing by Duke Kahanamoku. Then they
tried for a reconciliation of sorts until both she and Trujillo discovered that Rubirosa had renewed his sex life with Flor de Oro, his
ex-wife.

Despite the prenuptial agreement, at first Rubirosa was unwilling to let Doris get a divorce. He felt that it was best to kill her, then
see if he could expect better terms when the estate was being settled.

The first fight occurred in their Paris home. She had begun taking three German shepherd dogs with her, pets she had enjoyed in
the United States. These animals were welcome everywhere because the Parisians, then as now, considered dogs to be appropriate companions in restaurants and other public gathering places. It
was not unusual to go into a café and see someone sitting, eating
with a friend, their dogs perched on adjoining chairs. But the Duke
pets were also trained attack dogs, and to Doris they may have
been potential weapons.

Doris was also physically quite strong, and though Rubirosa
was a boxer, an enraged Doris could be a match for him in any
fight. Thus word came out that they had had a fight that left bloodstains spattered about the Paris mansion; while no one was certain
of the exact details, what was clear was that, either to end the marriage or in the height of violent passion, Rubirosa had physically
hurt his wife.

The second incident was different. Doris was supposed to be
traveling to New Jersey aboard the B-25. She decided to not fly at
the last moment, alerting no one to her change of plans. The plane
took off without her and crashed in a manner that implied tamper-
ing. There was no proof other than the maintenance and refurbishing records, which indicated that the plane should have been
able to fly without incident.

Finally Doris became ill. The distraught Rubirosa rushed his unconscious wife to a hospital known for long-term rest cures. The OSS learned of it and removed her, never knowing if she was sick and had recovered, or was drugged and would have been held a prisoner.

Doris returned to Reno for another divorce, providing Rubirosa with $25,000 per year for life or until he remarried. It was a more than generous settlement since he only married wealthy women. And though Doris Rubirosa was a target for murder, Doris Duke was not, so she and Rubirosa could remain friends, neither having to be wary of the other any longer.

The marriage officially lasted from September of 1947 through October of 1948, at which time the Reno action declared that Rubirosa was being sued for divorce on the grounds of "mental cruelty" so severe that it had affected Doris's health.

The law was more conservative toward divorce in those days. Even when both parties desired the action, as Doris and Rubirosa did, someone had to be declared the wronged party. A gentleman to the end, at least when he found he couldn't succeed in stealing her money through murder, Rubirosa let Doris be the innocent victim. They each showed the other how much they appreciated the ultimately civil divorce by Rubirosa's making periodic visits to Somerville and elsewhere in order to "service" his former wife. She also kept pictures of Rubirosa in all her homes. The marriage was unsuccessful, but the sex was unforgettable.

# 11

⚜

# *Doris Duke in Transition*

*A*s Doris Duke approached forty, her life was moving in several different directions. She had traveled the world. She had indulged in every form of sexual activity that intrigued her, frequently using the skills of men who took pride in their willingness to please the women they were with. She had begun experimenting with drugs. And she had become seriously devoted to music.

Her physical needs were ministered to by two men, Joey Castro and Louis Bromfield. Joey was the younger lover, approximately fifteen years her junior, and one of the outstanding young jazz pianists of his day. Bromfield was the older man, sixteen years her senior, a Pulitzer Prize–winning author and internationally known conservationist.

The relationship with Joey Castro began first. He had been born in the small town of Miami, Arizona, was raised in Pittsburg, California, and attended San Jose State College before joining the army in 1946. With the war over, and having played jazz piano professionally since he was fifteen, he was placed in the army band and combo. He completed his education after his discharge, then began performing up and down the West Coast and in Hawaii. Among the places he played was the Los Angeles Mocambo Club where Doris was a regular.

Doris had first heard Joey in Hawaii, but it was in Los Angeles that she truly began to appreciate his music. He was one of the most brilliant players of his day, a student of the music of both the classical Maurice Ravel and the jazz innovator Charlie Parker. Experts in the field felt that his reputation never matched his actual skill, and the reason, according to some musicians, was his relationship with Doris Duke. This was not because she hurt him in any way. However, once they were together, his travels became more limited, and though by 1952 he was playing the London Palladium, much of his work was limited to the areas where Doris was living and traveling.

Doris Duke's jazz training was in a style of music that was becoming dated by 1950. Innovations during and immediately after World War II were bringing new names into the field, and with them came styles Joey knew and Doris wanted to learn. He agreed to tutor her when she was living in Hawaii.

Soon Shangri-La became the place for musicians playing in Honolulu to drop by after hours for jam sessions. Sometimes they gathered for fun. Sometimes Doris paid them for their time. But Joey was her favorite, her friend. He also understood a problem Doris had that most others overlooked.

Doris Duke was terrified of crowds. Put her on a piano stool in a dark club, filled with smoke and noisy drinkers who would listen intently to her playing, use the music as background, or tune her out completely, and she was fine. She relaxed and played with all the skill of a seasoned professional. Likewise, her singing, never a strong point, could be blended with others to make her a solid backup and chorus performer.

Otherwise, she suffered from a kind of performance anxiety. The pressure of playing for a large, attentive group of listeners was overwhelming to her. She could not comfortably sit alone on a stage without fear affecting her playing style. It was a problem shared by many top professionals, some of whom overcame it with therapy or intense willpower, while others stopped performing. Instead they taught, composed, or worked backup. But when playing with Joey and other professionals, the performance anxiety vanished and Doris came alive, just one musician interacting with her fellow performers.

Doris added a music room and full recording studio to her Somerville estate, gradually having jam sessions there as well. Her proximity to New York, Philadelphia, and other major cities resulted in Duke Farms being a popular stopover for such greats as Duke Ellington and Pearl Bailey, among many others. She would also treat the musicians as friends, putting on records when they were finished and serving champagne.

The full story of Joey Castro has never been told. He refused to be interviewed for this book, claiming that he has always been misquoted by writers and saw no reason to risk it happening again. He lives and works in Las Vegas, a highly respected performer who never became the household name of jazz that his playing warrants. Joey's musicianship is well documented. His relationship with Doris Duke is vaguer.

The first area of confusion concerning the Doris Duke/Joey Castro relationship is the marriage. There is a serious question as to whether Doris Duke had a legitimate marriage ceremony with Joey Castro, civil or religious. However, there did come a point in their relationship when she declared herself to be his wife. Certain cookbooks in her kitchens were found to have her surname and the last name of Castro in each one. And by state and federal laws related to common-law marriage, they definitely qualified for husband-and-wife status.[1]

However, an actual marriage license for Doris and Joey has never been found. This does not mean that a ceremonial marriage did not take place. And whether ceremonial or common law, a traditional divorce is necessary to dissolve the relationship.

Whatever the relationship, Doris decided she needed a regular place to stay in Los Angeles when she was there with Joey. She first rented a two-bedroom suite, complete with piano, at the Bel-Air Hotel. A small stove was added so her maid could cook for the couple. Joey also maintained a small apartment nearby, but the two usually spent their nights together.

At first Doris kept a distance from Joey, at least in public. When he was in New York, Doris introduced him to her mother and others as her piano teacher. Doris was not ready to bring Joey completely into her life during the early weeks of the affair. As a result, she would go to glamorous Hollywood parties, her money assuring her acceptance as a celebrity, then leave, change from expensive clothes to more casual wear, and go club-hopping with Joey.

For two years, Joey Castro seemed to be a secret part of Doris Duke's life. Then, in June 1952, she threw a party where she entertained such celebrities as Charlie Chaplin and Gilbert Roland. Joey and his band played, but the couple's behavior together made it obvious that he was her escort. She was so in love with his playing that she wanted others to share the experience.

By New Year's Eve, when she and Joey went to the Mocambo as guests, there was no question that Doris was in love again. Ironically, among the guests was Peggy Lee, who would later hire butler Bernard Lafferty, the man who came to control access to all aspects of Doris's life during her last days.

⌇

IN 1953 DORIS AND JOEY grew tired of sneaking around the Bel-Air Hotel. They decided to buy a house, and the one they chose was as eccentric as Doris.

George Read originally built the house Doris purchased at 1436 Bella Drive in Beverly Hills. He was a real estate developer, and after constructing the mansion, he sold it to actor Rudolph Valentino. Secluded on a hilltop in Benedict Canyon, the home was called Falcon's Lair. It changed hands several times. Bob Balzar, a writer and expert on wine, owned it when Doris began looking. Previously restaurateur Gypsy Buys had owned the place, and prior to that, actress Ann Harding. It was the third owner who was the most interesting, though. Virginia Hill, "bag lady" for organized crime and the woman who helped established the mob's drug shipping routes into Mexico, had lived there. Eventually she gained massive notoriety as the girlfriend of Bugsy Siegel, the man who fronted for Meyer Lansky and other mobsters in building the Flamingo Hotel. Allegedly to please Virginia, Siegel had stolen $650,000 from the Flamingo and used it for his own purposes. When he refused to pay it back, a hit was ordered. Virginia arranged for Siegel to stay at the Beverly Hills home, then went to Paris so her role in helping set up the death would not be known. An expert marksman using an M-1 army carbine shot Siegel through the window.

Hill brought the house infamy. Valentino brought it fame. He was considered the greatest screen lover of his time, and when he died in 1926, thousands of fans attended his funeral. His ghost was supposed to haunt Falcon's Lair, though none of this mattered to Doris. She liked the mansion, and she liked the adjoining guest house, which she remodeled specifically for Joey Castro's use.

The house purchase implied a commitment to Castro, one she made only after it became obvious that her other lover, author Louis Bromfield, was not going to marry her.

Bromfield was as close to Doris emotionally as any man she had ever known. He was a farm boy, raised in the small town of Mansfield, Ohio, and educated at Columbia University's Cornell School of Agriculture.

Mansfield was an unusual city in pre–World War I America. The steel industry was just beginning to be important in ways that would make some men multimillionaires and create a steel, tire, and car manufacturing region out of Detroit, Youngstown, Cleveland, Akron, and Pittsburgh. The owners bought mansions on the outskirts, the equivalent of today's suburbs; Mansfield was one. This was a time of social snobbery, and Bromfield was attracted to the daughters of many of the newly rich industrialists.

World War I saw Bromfield going to war in France. Lonely and excited about seeing action, he joined the European battle before the United States was officially involved. However, instead of becoming a fighter, he drove an ambulance and began working at becoming a writer.

*The Green Bay Tree* was Bromfield's first novel, published in 1924. It was semiautobiographical and drew enough interest that his second book, *Early Autumn,* won the Pulitzer Prize in 1926. Then, two years later, his short story *The Apothecary* won the O. Henry Short Story Award, and Bromfield was looked on as a man who could do no wrong. He began writing books and movies, including such well-known works as *Mrs. Parkington* and *The Rains Came.* His personal fortunes rose, and his Hollywood contracts usually were better than those of the actors, earning him large sums of money in residuals from the showing of his films. He married New York debutante Mary Appleton Wood, moved his wife to Paris, and bought the type of home he had envied in Mansfield.

Bromfield had great success, a devoted wife, and four daughters. He was highly respected, wealthy, but had a poor sense of timing. He settled into Parisian life just as Hitler began his march across Europe. The Bromfields returned to the United States in 1939, the Nazis having confiscated his Paris home.

Bromfield's success was ensured by the continued demand for his work, so he bought approximately a thousand acres of Ohio farmland on which to grow crops and raise animals. He had been trained in agricultural methods, and then he immersed himself in the latest literature concerning both farming and land conservation. He also remodeled the farmhouse that sat on the land into a mansion.

The remodeling was eccentric. He used oak and pine obtained from the trees on his land, keeping much of the house in tune with the surroundings. At the same time, he wanted to be certain that his agent and business manager, a man who felt uncomfortable anywhere other than Manhattan, could spend time at the farm helping him with his writing. To give him reason to tolerate the smell of flowers and the sound of birds instead of the aroma of car exhaust and the cacophony of honking car horns, Bromfield added a secret passage connected to his library. Upon entering it, a staircase led up to a guest apartment. The apartment, a duplicate of the agent's Manhattan living quarters and reserved solely for his use, and the secret passage assured he would have both privacy and a touch of the familiar.

When he moved his family into the house in 1941, Bromfield was a conservationist seriously interested in running a working farm. However, because he did not need money from the crops, his primary focus was esthetic. The land was cultivated in a manner that was both practical and beautiful. It was as if the grazing area for the cattle and horses, the cultivated fields, the trees, the water, and the other aspects of the land were sculpted so that, from above, they would look like a still-life painting. In fact, Bromfield delighted in giving tours of the beautiful area to friends who came to visit, and because he was well known in Hollywood, those friends included major movie stars such as Humphrey Bogart and Lauren Bacall. In fact, Bogart and Bacall were married in the entrance hall of Bromfield's home, and they spent their first night together as husband and wife in his guest room.

Bromfield soon found himself writing about his home. *Pleasant Valley* and *Malabar Farm* came out in 1945 and 1946, respectively, and were read by Doris Duke. At the time she was concerned with Dutch elm disease devastating many of the trees on her Somerville

estate, and Bromfield's works convinced her that he had the expertise to help her. She decided to consult with him, and if she liked
what he had to say, to add him to the string of men she had purchased over the years.

Doris had a staff member contact Bromfield to let him know
that a private plane would be dispatched to the nearest landing
field to take him to Somerville. Naturally there would be a check.
Surprisingly, Bromfield ignored the woman.

There was more correspondence, and finally Bromfield sent
Doris a note telling her to cut down the trees and burn them. At
least that would slow the Dutch elm disease. Ultimately all the trees
might die, but if any were saved, it would be because of the drastic
action. He was not interested in coming to see her estate.

Still unwilling to settle for a note, Doris invited herself to the
farm. She flew to Cleveland where she chartered a limousine to
drive her the three hours into the country to where Malabar Farm
was located.

Doris was instantly taken with both Bromfield and the beauty of
the land. He was the first man she had met who reminded her of
Buck Duke—self-made, satisfied with his wealth and status in life,
and in love with agriculture. Buck had built Duke Farms. Louis
had Malabar Farm.

Doris was serious about saving her trees and improving her
holdings, something that gradually changed Bromfield's attitude
toward her. He spent hours explaining his work and theories about
agriculture. She made notes like a dutiful student. And always they
were followed by Prince and Baby, his two boxers who constantly
fought with each other. Years later, when Bromfield was dead and
his home became a tourist attraction, visitors to his writing area
saw his typewriter and the darkened bloodstains left many years
earlier during one of the dogs' fights.

The writing area also reveals Bromfield's eccentricity. Bromfield
ordered a large, expensive desk custom built, yet his typewriter sits
on a rickety card table. After having the desk delivered, he discovered that it was the wrong height for working. Rather than having
it redone or ordering a new desk, both of which he could well afford to do, he set up a card table.

The dogs were used in a Scotch whiskey advertisement that ran in the *Saturday Evening Post* during a time when writers held celebrity status and a writer's endorsement could increase product sales. Bromfield was withdrawn, an observer of people rather than particularly social himself, and he was mildly alcoholic. Scotch was his favorite drink, one he used to numb his emotions at the end of the day, giving him an excuse to lie down on the couch in his library rather than joining his wife in bed. He had a comfortable relationship with her, each tolerating the other, neither feeling much passion. And though he delighted in sex, he much preferred having affairs with the wealthy wives and daughters of the type of men whose homes he had once found so forbidding.

Bromfield's wife died in 1952, and since Doris had been having an affair with him, she fantasized about their possible marriage. He had no interest in her money, as he had more of his own than he needed, and she loved the man who was so much like her father. Both talked about the possibility of a committed life together, but neither was truly serious. The relationship was intense, and Doris for many years after his death kept a picture of him, but it was ultimately Joey Castro and the lifestyle of a performer with which she felt more comfortable. As for Bromfield, he died in 1956, heavily in debt. Doris and he had always remained friends.

With Joey came Doris's first professional musical experiences since playing in small Parisian clubs. In April of 1954, Joey created a special combo that was scheduled to play in Geneva, Switzerland, at a club called the Paladium. Doris, Joey, and some trusted sidemen would perform, with Doris playing under a pseudonym and her blond hair covered with a black wig. When the group needed a publicity photo, Paul Castro, Joey's brother, had his girlfriend Darlene put on the black wig. That way no one from the press could see the picture and recognize Doris.

It was during the two-week engagement in Switzerland, a difficult time for Doris, who was both excited and frightened by performing, that she heard the news that Barbara Hutton had married Porfirio Rubirosa. He needed money and either she needed sex or wanted to upset her rival, Doris Duke; or perhaps both. By then Hutton was degenerating into alcoholism, her life was falling apart, and apparently she found it worthwhile to pay Rubirosa $1 million to entertain her. Barbara also gave him $250,000 to buy himself an airplane, which he did—for $200,000. He pocketed the $50,000 change, an amount that, at the time, represented well over ten years' salary for the average working man with a family of four.

The problem for Hutton was that she had purchased Rubirosa from actress Zsa Zsa Gabor. He had been almost monogamous with Zsa Zsa, with only two men naming him as corespondent in their divorces from unfaithful wives. Gabor saw Hutton as no different from the two minor affairs and didn't understand why she and Rubirosa could not continue their relationship, despite his marriage. Rubirosa agreed but Barbara did not. Their marriage lasted a total of seventy-three days, during which time Trujillo also made him minister to Paris.

The reality of that marriage and Rubirosa's attitude toward it are best illustrated by the brief description in his *New York Times* obituary when he was killed in a car crash on July 5, 1965, at the age of fifty-six.

> On Dec. 30, 1953, he took his fourth wife, Barbara Hutton, who was then celebrating her fifth marriage, at 1100 Park Avenue in a civil ceremony conducted by the Dominican consul general.
>
> Mr. Rubirosa was reinstated in the Dominican foreign service on the day of his marriage to the millionaire heiress. The couple chartered an 86-passenger Super Constellation for a flight to Palm Beach, for themselves, two servants, and a crew of six, at a cost of $4,500.
>
> They settled into the sublet splendor of the 14-room villa of the Maharaja of Baroda, filled with great vases, bronze pieces and incense burners. A company of flamenco dancers whirled at their first dinner party and Mr. Rubirosa's favorite troubadour, an itinerant Cuban guitarist named Chago Rodrigo, strummed love songs.
>
> In December of 1954, Mr. Rubirosa sold the story of his 73-day marriage to Miss Hutton to the *New York Journal-American*. He said that he had liked an athletic, socially active schedule and that she had preferred a secluded life. . . .

Interestingly, although Rubirosa was enough of a cad to sell the story of a marriage he never took seriously, he never wrote about his marriage to Doris Duke. They remained friends throughout his life, with Rubirosa always respecting Doris's privacy. He considered only Barbara Hutton a target for his ridicule.

Doris was furious and deeply hurt at the news of the wedding. While she did not expect him to remain celibate between his special times with her, she did expect him never to remarry.

It has been alleged that both Castro and Doris began experimenting with drugs, including LSD, during this period. As mentioned, Castro has refused to comment on anything to do with Duke, but it is known that Doris Duke included mind-altering drugs among her coveted sensual experiences. She tried hallucinogenics, uppers, downers, and milder stimulants such as marijuana. Later she would become addicted to the use of enemas, allegedly for her health. The drug use would leave her anorexic, vitamin deficient, and at high risk for heart attacks and other problems.

At the same time that Doris was involved with drugs, sex, and professional jazz, she was also exploring the spiritual side of life. Raised a Methodist, fascinated by the teachings of Gandhi, perhaps seeking some connection with her dead child Arden, and educated in the idea of reincarnation by her father, Doris began studying Eastern religions, mysticism, and other spiritual philosophies.

Although she would later be closely connected with a Baptist church in Nutley, New Jersey, during the Castro years she became most interested in the Self-Realization Fellowship in Los Angeles. The organization dates back to September 1920, when Paramahansa Yogananda came to the United States as India's delegate to the International Congress of Religious Liberals being held in Boston. He was only twenty-seven at the time, a graduate of Calcutta University and a monk in India's Swami Order. He decided to stay in the United States, traveling and lecturing before setting up what became the international headquarters in Los Angeles. In 1946 he wrote the book *Autobiography of a Yogi,* which was read by Doris and many others. The book is still in print today. Twenty days after his death, on March 7, 1952, he was reported to have a body that showed no physical deterioration.

Faye Wright, a close friend of Doris's and one of the few friends allowed to see her the day before she died, became a disciple of

Paramahansa Yogananda's in 1931. She eventually took the name
Sri Daya Mata (Mother of Compassion) and was made president of
the Self-Realization Fellowship in 1955. That same year she met
Doris, and from that time forward, Doris utilized her for both religious teaching and friendship. They talked by telephone every
week or two, and the women visited in each other's homes when
Doris was in Los Angeles. They also had dinner together every
time Doris was in the city. Faye's sister, Virginia Wright, was also a
friend to Doris, though not quite so close.

The Self-Realization Fellowship teachings fell nicely into place
with Doris's ideas because the followers believe strongly in reincarnation, seeing it as "the justice of God," according to Daya Mata.

Their teachings are summarized in Fellowship literature. According to their writings, the teachings of Paramahansa Yogananda
follow *raja yoga,* the "royal" or highest yoga path, which combines
the essence of all the other paths (*hatha yoga,* consisting of bodily
disciplines for physical and mental well-being; *karma yoga,* right
action or selfless service; *bhakti yoga,* devotion to God; and *jnana
yoga,* attainment of wisdom through discriminative reason).

"Central to Yogananda's teachings are scientific methods of
concentration and meditation, including an advanced technique
called *Kriya Yoga.* These methods automatically quiet both body
and mind, and make it possible to withdraw one's energy and attention from the usual turbulence of thoughts, emotions, and sen-
sory perceptions. In the clarity of that inner stillness, one comes to
experience a deepening interior peace and attunement with oneself
and with God. (The term *Self-realization,* as used by Yogananda,
signifies realization of one's true Self, or soul—the individualized
expression of the one universal Spirit that animates and informs all
life.)"

Doris did not necessarily practice all the teachings of the Self-
Realization Fellowship as explained by Lauren Landress, a spokesperson for the organization. She did take counsel with her friend
Faye Wright, and she respected the work enough to donate substantial sums of money to the organization over the years. But
Doris ultimately did not seem to fit into any one religion; rather,
she pulled aspects of many together in her philosophy of life,
death, God, and creation.

Her attitude toward philanthropy underwent changes during this time, changes that might be considered the result of her spiritual search.

The value of the Duke fortune in the 1950s is unknown, but it may already have approached the $1 billion Doris was credited with having at the time of her death. (Doris Duke's wealth has long been underestimated. Doris believed herself to be worth $7½ billion in 1990. The idea that she was worth close to $1 billion forty years earlier makes sense given that she could account for every penny she had.) Her ownership of Duke Power Company was worth between $400 million and $500 million alone. This had nothing to do with holdings ranging from treasury bills to real estate, a variety of businesses, precious gems, museum-quality art objects, and the like.

In the 1950s, her private contributions amounted to only a few hundred thousand dollars. At the same time, her gifts through the Doris Duke Foundation (originally called Independent Aid, Inc.) totaled less than $3 million. As for Duke University, it received less money than other pet projects, such as the Center for Self-Supporting Women and Students of New York. She also contributed to groups so diverse as New York University's Institute of Fine Arts and Planned Parenthood, the latter a seeming natural given her propensity for taking lovers.

A Manhattan office was established at this time to serve as the screening point for Doris's donations, and she regularly used two independent investigators to check the legitimacy of an organization or individual seeking help. The ones that were doing excellent work, such as the Narcotics Rehabilitation Program in East Harlem, had no problems passing the tests. Others failed to pass.

Doris was personally interested in five causes: artists and musicians in need of help; Southern black churches, many of which were poverty-stricken; Appalachian communities where the citizens were in crisis; the rundown residential section of historic Newport, Rhode Island; and agricultural experimentation. Only with the latter cause did she fail to find an effective use for her money and ideas.

As mentioned, Doris believed the officials of Duke University held her in some disdain, trying to honor her enough to get her money without truly caring about her. If Duke University would not take her seriously, she worried, what other institution would? As a result, Doris lacked the courage to take her money and plans anywhere else.[2]

When Doris walked away from Duke University, she continued to honor her father's wishes about the school. However, instead of staying personally involved, she asked her cousin, Mary Duke Biddle Trent Semens, to take over. Mary was living in Durham, the mother of a large family, and a quiet housewife who had inherited approximately $300 million. She eventually became chairman of the board of trustees of the Duke Endowment, worth approximately $1.4 billion at this writing. Thus Doris could rest easily about her obligation to her father without having to be overly concerned about Duke University.

One failed experiment of Doris's was a result of her relationship with Louis Bromfield. Doris was a self-taught expert on orchids, which she developed in Somerville. *She* was the expert, and whatever work she did not do was done under her close scrutiny. Yet while students of botany are familiar with her contributions to the science, others are not. To her regret, this included the people at Duke with whom she tried to share her research program.

Doris wanted to use land at Malabar Farm, Duke Farms, and in Hawaii, and large parcels to be purchased in regions with different climate and soil conditions—the combination to be made into a Duke University agricultural school. In this way she could develop hybrids and new breeds of critical food crops—wheat, oats, corn—as well as improving livestock, all of which would benefit people throughout the world.

Doris's ideas were sound and probably would have resulted in fine programs. She wanted to name the school the Louis Bromfield School of Ecology and Agriculture. (A portion of Malabar Farm was named "Doris Duke Woods" and the land, now the Malabar Farm State Park, has a section called the Doris Duke Nature Trail.)

Doris had other problems with Duke University. She felt that her family had donated enough money to the school that it could indulge her curiosity about matters related to health. She was fascinated by research into science, counterculture medicine, and metaphysics. Often people who claimed to have cures for one illness or another approached her for money; most of them were frauds.

But Doris felt that it was better at least to listen to the less obvious frauds, then have their schemes scientifically analyzed. One idea might have something of value. And if the ideas didn't, then she wanted to be able to show the person who proposed it that real experts had told her the concept was fraudulent.

Once again she trusted Duke University to back her efforts. She assumed that the school would handle the rejections, giving her sound reasons to turn away the people who approached her, rather than seeming either coldhearted or overlooking something legitimately promising. Unfortunately, Duke University continued to ignore what they perceived to be her foolishness. Again the officials estranged themselves without meaning to do so.[3]

By the early 1960s, the relationship between Doris and Joey Castro was becoming strained. After Louis Bromfield died, Joey had wanted to marry Doris. Though Joey was convinced that he had in fact done so, Doris's cousin Pony Duke later said that the marriage his cousin arranged for herself was a sham. She never wanted to be legally committed to anyone again. Still, she was working hard to promote Castro's career, buying him clothing and cars, financing a record company promotion, and generally trying to help him. Oddly, the help was both good and bad since he often found himself limited to gigs in those cities and venues that fit her whims, not what was best for his career.

In hindsight, Doris and Joey probably had the best relationship that either had experienced up to that time, as well as the most destructive. They both were becoming violent. Fights, sometimes physical, occurred with some frequency. Each allegedly hurt the other at one time or another, and it would only be a matter of time before a divorce (or palimony action, depending on whose story can be believed based on press and court accounts) would take place.

Needing an outlet for her emotions as she was moving out of the relationship with Castro, Doris began to involve herself in another interest that would enhance her wealth considerably.

At this time, corruption in Southeast Asia was extensive. The French had been defeated by the North Vietnamese in 1958, and the Americans were beginning to become involved in what would be known as the Vietnam War. In the meantime, corrupt government officials in Thailand, Cambodia, and South Vietnam were willing to sell the treasures of their past to the highest bidder. There were few collectors, and even the most sophisticated of American museums did not fully recognize or seek out these treasures. Most focused on Chinese and Japanese works, a fact that made Doris Duke's efforts richly rewarded. She was able to acquire inexpensively the greatest works of a culture in which others soon would develop an intense interest. As a result, she not only dramatically increased her art holdings, most of which were kept in Shangri-La, she provided herself with a basis for even greater wealth. The value of almost all that she bought would skyrocket in the last years of her life.

In the midst of all this, Doris's life was filled with lawsuits, charges, and countercharges related to her ending her relationship with Joey Castro. By 1964 they were in court with some frequency.

First Joey said he was married and wanted a divorce. Then, on May 11, 1964, Joey told a Honolulu judge that he never said he was Doris's husband. Yet the following month he and Doris again traveled together, using the names "Mr. and Mrs. Castro." Doris had also formed the music publishing company Jo-Do and the record company Clover Records with Joey. The first release had been *Lush Life*, a solo album of Castro's that combined previously recorded works and new songs. Unfortunately, because Joey was not well known except among serious jazz aficionados, most radio stations failed to play cuts from the album. Most record stores did not bother stocking it, and it didn't sell well in those that did. Since there was no advertising budget, the album failed.

There were other albums, though not with Joey. He became increasingly estranged from Doris, the two of them seemingly happy in public but increasingly at odds in private. Perhaps she would have stayed with him longer had other problems not entered her life.

First there was Edward Tirella, a man of many talents. Tirella was best known as an interior designer and landscape architect in Hollywood. He would later make a reputation in films such as *The Sandpiper*, starring Elizabeth Taylor and Richard Burton. He de-

Doris Duke and Barbara Hutton were the leading heiresses of their day. Although neither friends nor rivals as the press would make them out to be, they did share occasional lusts, including the "buying" of Porfirio Rubirosa, the man who was the model for James Bond. Hutton's life was self-destructive and ended tragically. (*Archive Photos*)

Doris Duke's home
at 1 East 78th Street
in New York City.
*(AP/Wide World
Photos)*

*Right:* An aerial view
of Doris Duke's
estate in Newport,
Rhode Island. *Below:*
The home of Doris
Duke in Hawaii.
*(Both photos from
AP/Wide World
Photos)*

The unhappy honeymooner, Doris Duke, tolerates yet another press photo with her new husband, James Cromwell. She wanted privacy and intense intimacy. He destroyed the romance by asking about his allowance the first night of their marriage. And the privacy was marred by his arranging with the Hearst newspaper people to be photographed at every port of call, an unpleasant surprise for his bride. The Hawaii arrival changed everything, though, for she would soon build an estate where Cromwell was barely tolerated, and she would delight in the first of many lovers. (*AP/Wide World Photos*)

Duke and Cromwell with a dragoman on a sightseeing tour in Cairo.
(*AP/Wide World Photos*)

Porfirio Rubirosa was Doris Duke's one marital indulgence. She "bought" Rubirosa, as had Barbara Hutton and others, in order to enjoy his sexual prowess. Although probably lacking in the ability to have an orgasm, his unusually long sexual organ and his affliction with a condition that left him partially erect at all times enabled him to spend hours sexually satisfying women. He was also a political assassin who, it was feared, planned to kill Doris to gain access both to her money and her power-company holdings, the latter potentially affecting national security.

(*Top photo: Archive Photos. Bottom photo: AP/Wide World Photos*)

A merchant seaman, injured while delivering needed supplies to the war fronts, dictates a letter to Doris Duke, who was training to go overseas as a worker for the USS. (*AP/Wide World Photos*)

Doris Duke arrives at LaGuardia airport after visiting her in-laws in the Dominican Republic. (*Archive Photos*)

The most controversial incident in Doris Duke's life came with the death of Edward Tirella. She apparently deliberately tried to startle or hurt him with her station wagon as he opened the gate to her New Jersey estate. (*AP/Wide World Photos*)

Later Duke (shown here leaving Superior Court with her attorney, Aram Arabian) fought a $1.2 million lawsuit brought by Tirella's siblings. She was found negligent and ordered to pay a judgment of less than $100,000. (*The Everett Collection*)

Doris Duke and Elizabeth Taylor first met in 1948 when the
young Taylor was the star of the film *National Velvet*. Years later,
when Duke was dying, Bernard Lafferty provided the actress
with a million-dollar gift from Doris for AIDS research work.
Lafferty hoped the gift would lead to his being accepted
in the actress's private world. (*AP/Wide World Photos*)

The most meaningful time of Doris Duke's life came when she
gained acceptance as a professional musician. Long a competent
jazz pianist, she found friendship, acceptance, and spiritual guidance
when she joined the Reverend Lawrence Roberts's Angelic Choir.
She never had the skills of a soloist, but she knew how to effectively
blend her voice, and her musical knowledge was such that he could
rely on her to help instruct others. (*AP/Wide World Photos*)

The late Bernard Lafferty *(right)*, a man considered either Doris Duke's best friend or the betrayer who was responsible for her isolation late in life, which led to her changing her will in his favor. Although said to have worn Duke's clothes and jewelry and to have slept in her bed, he never got a chance to truly enjoy her money. Alcoholism, drug abuse, and obesity took their toll not long after the Surrogate Court agreed that he could receive at least $500,000 for life. *(AP/Wide World Photos)*

signed the oceanfront home in which Taylor lived in the film. Because he was also tall and handsome, he was given a brief scene of his own. Tirella was also a set designer for *Don't Make Waves* (Tony Curtis and Claudia Cardinale) and *Eye of the Devil* (Deborah Kerr, David Niven, and Sharon Tate), all three MGM films.

Joey Castro met Tirella before Tirella met Doris. The designer was also a nightclub singer and worked some clubs where Joey played. Tirella didn't meet Doris until he was introduced in 1959, because of the greenhouses she owned on Duke Farms.

The greenhouse work would be Tirella's first test. Doris maintained twenty adjoining greenhouses, which she had stopped using for anything serious. They were so large that she wanted them converted to what would become a tourist attraction.

The modification was unlike anything that could be seen elsewhere in the world. Each greenhouse was converted to a garden based on a different part of the world, including different climate and soil conditions. But beyond re-creating natural foliage in a beautiful design, Doris applied the ideas she had been using for her orchids. Using her own and her gardeners' expertise in developing new hybrids, she improved upon nature.

What made the Somerville estate different was the number of different gardens, each perfect. One was Indian, another English. There were French, Chinese, and Italian gardens. The designs and the plants were all authentic, and they could be viewed by outsiders during weekdays by appointment. By 1965, the gardens were so impressive that *House & Garden* magazine did a feature praising the work, although it omitted Tirella's name. It is not known whether Doris ever gave him credit, although to be fair, she did most of the physical work and research. He was the designer who accompanied her on buying and sketching trips throughout the world.

Despite Doris's desire for privacy, she opened the gardens to the public, because doing so made the work nonprofit and tax exempt. Some critics feel that this was why Doris involved herself with restoring Newport, since she was earning at least $1 million *per week* from her investments, and the ownership of the Newport houses provided a tax shelter.

Tirella's background was quite different from Doris's. He was raised in New Jersey, attending Dover High School, approximately twenty-five miles from Duke Farms. He became a dancer and amateur artist before graduating and joining the infantry during World War II.

The first job Tirella found after his discharge was as a hat designer working at Saks Fifth Avenue, where his customers included Mae West. He was always involved with the rich and famous. When he became a gardener, Alan Ladd and Peggy Lee were among his clients.

Tirella was one of the most successful failures in Hollywood at the time he became involved with Doris. The high point of his career came in 1952, when he earned approximately $500 a week as a stage set designer. He had a three-year job with one play, making excellent money for the time.

From the stage he began working for a real estate developer, designing home layouts and color coordinating interiors. But when he went to Hollywood, he either did not qualify for union membership or did not apply, which limited the work he could do. He seemed to be as impressed with the stars he met as they were with him, charging little for his talents and rarely making more than $4,000 per year. He was constantly in debt, constantly borrowing money he could not afford to repay.

Despite this, Tirella managed to own a small car and two apartments, one in Big Sur, the other in Los Angeles. He spent all the money he made, although probably some of his clients and friends helped underwrite his lifestyle. Certainly he was taken to dinner with great frequency. However, had he truly made a business of his work, he could have become quite well off.

Tirella was with Doris on July 5, 1965, when she got word that Porfirio Rubirosa had died in a car crash. The one-car accident was a suspected suicide, in part because Rubirosa was a trained and experienced race car driver, among his other skills.

Rubirosa was forty-seven when he again abandoned Zsa Zsa Gabor, this time for a French teenager, the actress Odile Rodin. She was neither rich nor famous, but her bust was impressive. Apparently he was faithful to her, though not because he had changed. Rubirosa was feeling a decline in his sex drive, probably the result of destructive high living. He may have lost his constant "half-mast" erection. He may have been ridiculed by one of his lovers. He may have been the victim of his own paranoid fantasies about his declining sex life. Whatever the cause, he was depressed about the change in what had once made him world famous.

At 8:00 A.M., Rubirosa took his Ferrari sports car on the Avenue de la Reine-Marguerite, accelerated to 100 miles per hour, sideswiped a car, and smashed into a tree in the Bois de Boulogne. He managed to keep from being thrown from the car, but his chest was impaled on the steering wheel. He died on the way to the hospital.

Joey Castro was essentially out of Doris's life by this time, so Doris turned to her friend Tirella for comfort. This was one relationship that was never physical, a fact that seemed to increase their closeness.

Tirella was a homosexual who avoided committed relationships, preferring casual sex as the desire arose. He also was not doing enough work in Hollywood to make him want to stay there. As a result, he was willing to tackle any project Doris conceived for him to do anywhere in the world. These ranged from redecorating the kitchen at Falcon's Lair to refurbishing a hotel that became the headquarters for the Self-Realization Fellowship. They went to fashion shows together, then Tirella would take her to shops in Manhattan that sold knockoffs of the clothing by the same designers. He saved her thousands of dollars for items of equal quality.

Doris gave Tirella a room in each of her homes and apartments so he would have privacy wherever they were together. However, he was uncomfortable with her smothering attitude, with her dominating his time. He asserted his independence like an adolescent seeking separation from a parent. He changed his first name to "Eduardo" in order to give himself a more distinct personality.

Doris had concerns other than Eduardo's attempts at independence. In March of 1966, she discovered that one of her buyers had bilked her out of a large sum of money by buying flea market items, then lying about their cost, as well as stealing the priceless treasures she had obtained from Southeast Asia. In May she closed Clover Records, making clear to Joey that their relationship was ending.

To try to bring some positive change to her life, Doris took Tirella to Rough Point that summer. She wanted to restore the estate, including obtaining the original furniture and artworks. Much of the restoration work would be done in Somerville, then shipped back to Newport. The grounds of Duke Farms were so extensive that she could set up any sort of workshop that was needed, no matter how elaborate.

This same summer Doris became interested in restoring the rundown homes of Newport. Other than the occupied mansions, many of the early homes were in disrepair. She wanted to buy them, restore them, and then arrange for people to live there so that the community could be reinvigorated. Newport was in danger of becoming the nation's wealthiest semighost town, a beautiful area filled with abandoned houses.

By the end of the summer, Tirella decided that the glamour of his life with Doris Duke was not worth it. He wanted to return to Hollywood, and it was then that he took the job on *Don't Make Waves.* He saw it as his comeback chance, something he could parlay into a revitalized career. The fact that the other films had brought him neither recognition nor the union membership critical for regular work in a guild-dominated industry made his fantasy unrealistic.

Tirella was afraid to admit to Doris the real reason he was returning to Hollywood. He claimed that he needed dental work and he wanted to use his own dentist. Doris felt that he should use hers in New Jersey and became angry with him.

Finally she used her ultimate weapon. She said she would give Tirella money. Cash had motivated her lovers; perhaps it would work with the broke designer.

The ploy was successful. Tirella was behind in his taxes, which was more serious than the situation with his other creditors. Doris would save him and he would work with her until he was debt-free. Then he would change his lifestyle for good, returning to Los Angeles permanently.

What happened next has never been adequately explained. Although much has been made of Doris Duke's healthy regimen and careful diet, the truth was that she frequently drank to excess, choosing fine wines and champagne over adequate meals that might have reduced the alcohol's effect on her. She also delighted in trying the latest drugs as well as such standbys as marijuana and Quaaludes.

Doris was also experiencing intense mood swings that seemed related to the daughter she lost. She contemplated the meaning of motherhood and worried about where her life was going. Feeling the need to immortalize the baby in some way, eventually she wrote a song about the girl. The reality was that Doris's mental state was not very good.

Adding to the pressures, Doris stopped sleeping normal hours at Somerville. One day she might start working in the greenhouses at midnight. Another day it would be after breakfast. There were no set hours, no pattern to her waking and sleeping.

Although the establishment of the Newport Restoration Foundation began to include the rich and famous who had lived in the area, among them Jacqueline Kennedy, neither this nor any other project managed to sustain Tirella's interest.

Joey Castro was also cause for pain. As had been the case with Rubirosa, Doris did not want to live with him, but she did not want anyone else to have him. She became depressed and angry when she learned that he was engaged to be married to a singer named Loretta Haddad.

On October 7, 1966, Doris was faced at forty-four with many harsh changes in the world around her. Castro's impending marriage meant an end to that phase of her life. She had been undergoing periodic cosmetic surgery to retain what she felt was a youthful appearance, yet she was keenly aware that she had passed into middle age. Eduardo Tirella was unhappy enough that even the lure of her money would not hold him. And she was probably drinking and taking drugs. Whatever the case, if her actions that day were extremely suspicious, the results were deadly.

Doris Duke rented a Dodge station wagon with a push-button automatic transmission. This innovation replaced the column shift or floor stick with a series of buttons that controlled the different gears. The vehicle was a well-maintained rental with nothing wrong with either the transmission or the brakes. A station wagon was practical for the work Doris and Eduardo were doing together. It was roomy enough to transport what they needed, and it was sealed, unlike an open-back truck.

A little before 5 P.M., Doris and Eduardo got into the station wagon. Doris was driving. When they reached the gates of the

Somerville estate, Tirella stepped out to open them so they could drive onto the street. When he was between the stopped car and the gates, the car started moving. With Doris behind the wheel, the car accelerated. One later explanation was that Doris accidentally hit the gas instead of the brake. Theoretically this could have happened—except for the way witnesses described the scene.

The car struck Eduardo, pinning him between the car and the gates. However, the motor continued to race. Doris's foot was firmly on the gas pedal, never moving off it or attempting to brake.

Then the gates began to shake from the stress. Each gate weighed approximately 2,000 pounds. They were almost twenty feet high and had no special counterbalance or electric opening device. They were properly hung and would not fall without intense pressure.

The gates shook harder, then fell. Doris's car kept traveling, rolling over Tirella, crushing him almost beyond recognition, then rolling over the gates with Tirella still caught in the wrought iron and steel. Finally the car came to rest against a tree across the street.

Doris left the car. Witnesses said she seemed incoherent, in shock. She said nothing, returning to the house where she entered, then began screaming Eduardo's name. An ambulance was called to take her to the hospital, where her lawyers arranged for her to be placed in seclusion. The police also arrived, clearing the scene of the car and the pieces of Tirella's body as quickly as possible.

The Duke staff began to eliminate all evidence of what occurred. First they cleaned the street and grounds, eradicating all marks in the street made by the car and the dragging of the corpse and gate. They carefully located all trace evidence—bits of glass, metal, clothing, and the like—and took it away.

Everything was done in a way that assured that if someone was foolish enough to bring charges against Doris Duke, there would be no evidence for conviction. Doris was kept from talking right after the accident. The police investigation was limited. She was not tested for drugs or alcohol. The only information Doris Duke was known to have given anyone at the time was that she had stepped on the gas and not on the brake. This explanation was hard to believe, given the fact that just taking her foot from the gas pedal would have slowed the car's momentum enough so that the gates would have stopped it. The fact that witnesses were convinced that whoever was inside never took her foot from the gas pedal indicates something other than an accidental slip of the foot from the brake to the gas.

The Duke staff claimed that they had never heard Tirella and Doris argue or fight, that they seldom drank. However, there is a good chance that Doris was far from sober when the accident occurred.

So what happened that late afternoon? The best guess is that Doris Duke deliberately struck Tirella. She was angry, probably intoxicated, and probably did not mean to kill him. But she did mean to scare him, possibly to hurt him physically, and she either panicked or was not sober enough to stop once she hit the gas. She was guilty of what, in most parts of the country, would have been involuntary manslaughter. Quite likely she could have been charged with second-degree murder (first degree is premeditated).[4]

Doris Duke's lawyers understood all this. They also insisted that she fight any payment to Tirella's family, something that apparently she disagreed with. She knew she was responsible for his death and wanted to compensate them in a manner that was greater than the final settlement. However, she was not allowed to make an offer, for the lawyers stated "her" position that nothing was owed for the death. This forced the heirs to take her to court, where she was sued for $1.2 million. The jury forced Tirella's family to settle for less than 10 percent of that figure—$96,000. This represented $75,000 in payment and $21,000 in interest for the time between the death and the July 1, 1971, jury verdict. When the Tirella family appealed the initial settlement to the Rhode Island Supreme Court two years later, the court sided with the lower court's verdict and settlement.

The original fight against the settlement made sense. Any willingness to settle would possibly have been enough to prove her guilt in the eyes of the law. This would have enabled criminal charges to be brought, and though it was doubtful that Doris Duke would be convicted, a lesser person would have to serve jail time at least.

The advice was good, though hardly necessary. In New Jersey, Doris Duke could do no wrong. Her money meant jobs and influence.

The first official statements concerning the case were made when Doris was forced to take the witness stand. Prior to her speaking, her defense lawyer tried to make Tirella appear negligent for failing to set the hand brake when he left the car. The extra precaution would have either prevented the car from moving or slowed it considerably, they stressed. The fact that he was *not* driving, and that the driver, Doris, was the one who should have set the brake was not mentioned.

While Doris was under oath, she claimed that her foot was on the brake and she had no idea how the car shot forward. She suggested that perhaps the car went forward on its own, no one touching the gas pedal. While this is not a mechanical impossibility if the car was damaged in some way, a thorough investigation of the engine, transmission, brakes, and other critical parts revealed that the car was in perfect operating condition.

The case took six years to resolve, but in the end, Doris Duke found herself benefiting from the same influence purchased by wealth that shielded Nanaline when she deliberately let Buck Duke freeze to death.

---

THE DEATH OF Eduardo Tirella changed Doris in other ways. It was in 1967, the following year, that she became seriously involved with the Reverend Lawrence Roberts and the First Baptist Church of Nutley, New Jersey. Although some have seen her involvement as a way of gaining attention for herself, it is far more likely that Tirella's death caused her to rethink her life. Certainly she underwent a spiritual change that cannot be explained any other way.

The Reverend Roberts was an unusual man in the music world. He was the first black producer for a major record label—Savoy Records—in the United States. He worked for Savoy for twenty-seven years and was well known among the major jazz musicians in this country, including Duke Ellington and Ray Charles. He also was pastor of the church in Nutley, ran the group known as Reverend Lawrence Roberts and the Angelic Choir, and composed for the choir. Roberts's choir sang regularly with gospel great James Cleveland, and their group won two Grammy Awards, the record industry's highest honor.

Well-known jazz musicians sent Doris to the Reverend Roberts for possible inclusion in his choir. He was not told who she was, only that she was a skilled musician interested in gospel music.

The reverend quickly learned three things about Doris Duke. The first was that she was a skilled professional musician. The second was that she was a weak singer who, with effort, could properly blend her voice with others to be a competent choir and backup singer. And the third was that because of her skills outside of the vocal area, she could master the words and music of whatever they were working on as a group, then teach the others when the Reverend Roberts was away.

Doris was made a member of the choir, her participation limited to blending her voice with others. "She had a great desire," said the reverend. "But, of course, in my estimation she was . . . how can I put this genteelly . . . she was a fair singer that worked out in a choir but would never make it as a soloist. I put her in a trio, and I have recordings that we did nationally, and she was a great voice to hold a part, and it blended in with the other voices. But I would never put her out on her own to do anything."

The Reverend Roberts said, "She just didn't have a crisp sound. She sang, but she just wasn't a great singer by any stroke of the imagination. She had a great desire, but not the voice. She was equivalent to any Baptist church, what we would call a good senior choir member."

"I took two very strong voices . . . but her voice was blended in with theirs and they overshadowed her.

"Doris was not by any stroke of the imagination not one who was not aware of her limitations, but she had a gusto to want to try, that everyone who knew her had to appreciate.

"She took pride in being bright and early, I think, because she said prior to meeting me, she never sang before any group of people. And I asked her what she was singing for. I said, 'If you have it and want to do it, you have to do it before people, to be accepted by them. Just to be in your house, singing in your theater, singing in the bathtub . . . I mean, everyone does that.'"

Once the Reverend Roberts and the choir members knew who Doris was, she invited them to her studio in the Somerville estate. They could rehearse there, make a recording if they so desired, and generally take advantage of a full professional facility where they could prepare for their performances. She was frequently asked to teach her fellow altos because she understood the music and how the reverend wanted it performed. "She carried the tune of the song well enough, and knew the melodic line we were singing well enough to teach those right quick. And then they got the basic idea and didn't overshadow her."

"She was a fantastic pianist," Roberts explained. "She had a very good ear and she was a great dancer. . . . She stayed with me from 'sixty-seven until she got involved with Lafferty. As a matter of fact, I was in touch with her until eleven months before she went to California, where she died. And wherever she was, she would always call me. I knew where she was and was one of the very few folks who could reach her."

Doris was good enough that the Reverend Roberts was delighted to include her in a major Madison Square Garden concert in honor of Duke Ellington's birthday. The Angelic Choir, including Doris Duke, performed along with Sammy Davis, Jr., Ray Charles, Duke Ellington, and others.

The Angelic Choir also worked with the Alvin Ailey Dance Company, which allowed Doris to experience her two passions. They traveled throughout the country, Doris incognito, singing as just another member of the choir. She was on the group's Grammy-winning recordings, her voice always blended with those of others.

The Reverend Roberts also found her to be ". . . a very spiritual woman, but her spirituality was involving several phases of religious beliefs. You couldn't pinpoint her to the one thing. She found some goodness in everything as well as giving you a reason why something couldn't work with her or for her, alone. She loved the Methodist church. She loved the Baptist church. She had an ideal feeling for certain phases of Catholicism, and we would discuss much about religion.

"A very, very dear friend of hers was involved with Transcendental Meditation—she was involved in that. And so Doris was a multianchoring person. She would get involved in so many things, it was unbelievable.

"And then there was a phase of her life with me when she—I wasn't a part of it, naturally—she would go to séances, or have them I should say, and try to call her father back from the grave." In addition, Doris explained that if you traced back her various incarnations, she was certain that she had originally been a fish, the reason that she would one day be buried at sea.

The Reverend Roberts did not share such theology, but each felt comfortable enough with the other to discuss his or her own beliefs. Doris also raised the issue of cremation, wondering if there was anything wrong with it. Roberts explained that the body ultimately deteriorates to dust and cremation essentially speeds a natural process. There was nothing wrong with it spiritually, a fact that pleased her. Although Doris expressed an intense fear of the pain of being burned to death, she was quite comfortable with the idea of being cremated, her ashes thrown in the ocean where she could return to the water from which she felt she evolved.

———— ✦ ————

THE REVEREND ROBERTS REPRESENTED the "legitimate" side of her spiritual life. Doris also became involved with religious charlatans during this period, the most notorious of whom was Norbu Chen.

Chen played nicely into some of Doris Duke's special interests. Her principal pleasures were from singing, dancing, and playing the piano. She performed professionally—anonymously, often wearing a wig and other disguises when with the Reverend Roberts—and had as close to a career as she would have with anything she did.

The other interests that brought her to Chen were spiritual understanding and a desire for endless youth. He may have helped a bit with the former. As to the latter, his treatments may have begun a lifelong addiction pattern that caused her health to seriously deteriorate.

Norbu Chen led two lives. He was a crook who had been jailed for rape, arrested for grand larceny, and spent time in a psychiatric hospital. He was also a serious student of the form of Buddhism practiced in Tibet and Mongolia called Lamaism, eventually traveling with Doris and his wife to Bhutan, India, and Sikkim, where he was able to locate his old teacher.

Lamaism is practiced with elaborate rituals and has an elaborate hierarchy. Chen, while only a student, was able to gain additional respect by declaring himself the reincarnation of a previous high lama. The Tibetan leader in exile, the Dalai Lama, reinforced this idea when he met with Doris and Chen and proclaimed the latter to be "Nalijorpa," or a reincarnated high lama.

If Chen was genuine in his religious practices, the rest of his actions were questionable at best, outright destructive at worst. They seemed to follow the same thinking that made him a modestly successful con man before he changed his name.

Norbu Chen was originally known by such names as Richard Michal Johnson, Michael Lee Alexander, and Carle Clayton Johnson. He was a brilliant man who became well known among those interested in parapsychology and nontraditional healing. Grape juice was his nutritional treatment for any sort of medical problem. The juice, which was the only nourishment allowed during the treatment periods, was said to end bodily pain, grow hair, and otherwise correct whatever was wrong. Chen added the spiritual touch by personally chanting and meditating by the patient's side. This therapy was always combined with enemas for cleansing the body, and it was the enemas combined with laxatives that created the problem for Doris Duke. She enjoyed having them so much that for the next two decades she would be addicted to them, using them as often as several times a day to control her weight. (She was severely anorexic for the last few years of her life.)

Chen created the Chakpori-Ling Foundation in Houston as his headquarters. Doris provided an estimated $30,000 per month for its operation and journeyed there for her treatments. She was also named to his board of directors.

Chen's followers included such well-known people as Edgar Mitchell, the *Apollo 14* astronaut who was traveling the world to learn about alternative healing methods, and the late actor Yul Brynner. The latter, a chain smoker who developed cancer, was "cured" in December 1974, according a story covered by that premier news journal, *The National Enquirer.* Despite Norbu Chen's brilliance, Brynner died October 10, 1985, from the same condition from which he had suffered eleven years earlier. However, he fared better than Chen, who met his end on June 9, 1977, just as an autobiography was to be published, written with former tabloid editor Tom Valentine, assisted by Doris.

Mitchell was the person who gave Chen legitimacy. In the early 1970s, astronauts were the greatest of American heroes. They risked their lives to experience the unknown. Mitchell parlayed a successful speaking tour into the creation of the Institute for Noetic (related to the mind) Studies. How knowledgeable he might have been in his evaluation of healers is not known. However, in his speeches, the people he discussed were given more credit than they might have deserved.

It is not known if Mitchell knew Chen's past, nor is it necessarily important. Chen was well trained in Lamaism, and his teachings, though a little odd, were still often within the framework of Buddhism. That was one reason why Chen's Chakpori-Ling Foundation attracted men such as the late adventurer/writer Lowell Thomas. Because he seemed credible, Doris sought him out on the recommendation of a friend.

Chen claims to have cured Doris from "Oram's syndrome," apparently a reference to Holt-Oram's syndrome (congenital heart or upper extremity defect), which no doctor ever diagnosed Doris as having. She was enough of a believer to take follow-up treatments on a monthly basis.

Norbu Chen may have studied Lamaism, but he also understood American show business. He went to his "patients" while wearing Tibetan clothing and carrying a jeweled dagger, a human thigh bone, and other ritual items probably never used by a genuine high lama. He would erect a portable shrine, then meditate on a tapestry he carried with him, chanting the words, "Om Mani Padmi Hum."

Doris would lie on her back on a bench or flat table, her feet bare. After meditating and chanting, Chen would grab her feet, one in each hand, inhale deeply, then rapidly exhale in order to fill her with tantric energy. He would repeat the action as often as necessary, though in an extreme case he would also hold her head and breathe in the same manner. Those who witnessed the Chen approach with people who genuinely were sick claimed that they had seen obvious improvement.

By this time, Doris's focus on her health was becoming obsessive. She bought salves and creams, worthless electrical gadgets, and had regular cosmetic surgery to keep her body looking attractive. She was able to maintain a tight rear end and firm bust through dancing and surgical changes, but her skin had lost its natural color, developing brown and white sections, as well as white splotches. Her hair was thinning noticeably. Every time she looked in a mirror, she was reminded of her age.

———— ❧ ————

DORIS'S ACTIVE SEX LIFE also may have related to her search for youth. In the early 1970s, disco dancing was popular. Exclusive nightclubs such as Studio 54 sprang up in New York and were patronized by well-known stage actors, movie stars, and other wealthy celebrities, including Doris. Cocaine was as available as breath mints. Sex acts were rumored to take place in darkened corners and private rooms. You could not enter these clubs unless you were either "somebody" or dressed in appropriately outlandish attire with the right attitude evident to the doorman and bouncer. This was theater in which the participants were also the show, and the visitor mix was carefully choreographed.

Doris became well known in Studio 54. At the time she was engaging in a series of meaningless sexual conquests, and picking up a willing partner at one of the clubs was simple. However, she did not want them to know who she was so she used a penthouse in the Ritz Tower on Park Avenue. It was a suite decorated for sex.

Doris seemed always to dedicate her living quarters to the arts. In New Jersey, Rhode Island, and Hawaii, her homes were museums of artwork in different styles and from different nations. They reflected her investments, her love of beauty, and her taste for the exotic. At the Park Avenue address, the interior was dedicated to the art of fornication.

The floors were of black enamel. Silver wall coverings gave the room the look of a nightclub. The sofas were covered with fake fur, columns were filled with multicolored glass, and the bedroom was decorated with chiffon. Black and maroon were the colors of choice, and there were mirrors everywhere. Doris could obsess over her looks, spend time altering her appearance with makeup, or watch herself in the midst of casual passion.

The men who came to the apartment were, for the most part, uninterested in the surroundings. The rooms were not really meant for seduction. The heat of dancing and the stimulation of one or more drugs served as foreplay. The men she brought back from the clubs rarely stayed more than half an hour. There were few, if any, repeats. She was just a wild older woman who could give as well as get when it came to playing in bed.

———— ﷽ ————

IN THE MIDST of this troubled life, one that was simultaneously invigorating and destructive, spiritual and hedonistic, she met a young woman named Chandi Heffner. The new relationship would be the start of the downward spiral leading to her untimely death.

# 12

## *The Trouble with Chandi*

ALKING WITH PEOPLE about Chandi Heffner is like experiencing a mystery play told from the viewpoint of three different suspects, each of whom is believable, two of whom are lying. The difference is that with a mystery play, there must be a resolution. The liars must be unmasked.

In the case of Chandi Heffner, all that is certain is that Doris Duke loved her. She wanted Chandi to replace Arden, to be the daughter she had denied herself through the self-induced abortion so many years earlier.

Perhaps more than ending the pain of her childlessness, Doris also wanted Chandi to be her closest friend. She wanted Chandi to be a companion who would provide a bridge through three existences—the present, death, and reincarnation.

Because Chandi was almost two generations younger than Doris, there would be plenty of time for Doris to die of old age, be reincarnated, and then grow old enough to walk, talk, and recontact Chandi at the Hawaiian estate Doris bought for her. At that point Doris, using whatever body she had been assigned, would whisper a code phrase—a Sanskrit message the two women memorized during their happiest times together. Once spoken, a delighted by then elderly Chandi would welcome Doris to her new life, the two of them enjoying the fortune Doris left to Chandi before crossing over to the other side. (Presumably this arrangement could work for each of them over several lifetimes, although it is not clear if either woman thought that far ahead.) Or such was the plan that Doris revealed to others. What was not revealed at the time was the full history of Chandi Heffner. But even before

Chandi can be understood, it is necessary to look at the changes in Doris Duke's life that made her vulnerable to the unusual relationship.

The Chandi Heffner story actually begins thousands of miles from where the two women met. Doris Duke had matured in many ways by 1971, the year that Chandi, then known as Charlene, graduated from Notre Dame Academy, a private Catholic girls' school in Maryland.

Doris had experienced sex and marriage. She had traveled the world. She had acquired great art. She had dined with the wealthy, the powerful, and the infamous. And while she still craved the love that had eluded her throughout life, she realized that there were more important areas of concern for her.

The first was music and dance. Doris was involved with Reverend Lawrence Roberts in both artistic and religious endeavors. She was studying many forms of dance, including ballet, modern dance, as well as traditional African and Middle Eastern styles. The latter had long been an interest, she later confided to Ibrahim Farrah, one of her teachers. As a little girl she had taken some of her mother's silk scarves and tried moving to Middle Eastern music. Then, while in Lebanon in 1945, shortly after the end of the war, she was able to see Tahia Carioca, a practitioner of what is most properly called "danse Orientale" and more commonly known as belly dancing. By 1968 she was becoming seriously involved in the dance form and was involved with mastering the art.

The other serious interest was Newport. Doris took a course in restoration so she could properly maintain her collection of Islamic Persian art. She also began looking at the eighteenth-century Newport homes as objects of art.

The first house was a 250-year-old, two-bedroom, three-story dwelling first rented to Charles O'Loughlin, dean of Continuing Education for Salve Regina College-by-the-Sea, and his wife. They moved into the home in August of 1970, paying $275 a month rent. The colonial cost so much to restore that it would have been impossible for them to afford the house without the unique program Doris created.

Approximately fifty houses were purchased in the program's first phase, then they were restored a half-dozen at a time. The newest home dated to 1812, and many had been abandoned. Doris personally mastered all phases of the restoration and frequently worked with the laborers.

She personally joined the crew that made certain the house could be saved. If the land could not be purchased with it, then the house was moved. No expense was spared in the re-creation. The bathrooms and kitchens were obviously not original, but Doris ordered that materials and designs that would complement the original houses be utilized. The kitchens were done in natural wood, usually pine planks as wide as 28 inches, just as in the originals. The only difference was that a nylon-formulated wood sealant was added for a waterproof finish.

Paints were limited to twenty interior and fourteen exterior shades, to match the original colors. And the bathroom washstands had marble tops. One man who worked for the foundation had the job of traveling everywhere original marble, chandeliers, old wood, old flooring, and similar items could be found. The homes looked like museums when they were finished, with the rebuilding matching the colonial methods, such as visible nails in the clapboard siding.

To assure the integrity of the property, no tenant was allowed to make any changes, such as adding air-conditioning units, washing machines, clothes dryers, and outside television antennas. The restrictions were compensated for by the rents—$125 to $150 for a small one-bedroom house all the way up to $450 for a home featuring six bedrooms and five baths.

The foundation employed approximately forty people, including architects, landscape gardeners, five carpentry crews, a painting crew, and a mill crew that made window sashes, door jambs, and any other parts that were no longer available. Renters were selected based on the instincts of the foundation personnel who interviewed them. In order to ensure control over the care of the properties, they could not be sold. However, it was presumed that the rental arrangements could be for life, assuring a caring involvement on the parts of the renters.

In addition to the fifty properties owned in 1970, the foundation had the money to buy the remaining 145 eighteenth-century homes in the area. The houses were watched until they came up for sale, at which time those in good enough condition to be saved would be purchased.

In keeping with Doris Duke's interests, the homes were all in an area that had become disreputable at the time. Known as The Point, the area was a slum combining colonial houses and asbestos-shingled shacks. She chose to restore the original homes and leave the shacks, a concept that helped people understand the way the area could be transformed without displacing the low-income families living there. As a result, a blend of people of different incomes and educational backgrounds not only lived in harmony but became the focus for tourists. The result was an influx of visitors who greatly increased the tourism industry in the area.

Doris had also become a serious businessperson. She was keeping track of her investments, running a highly profitable orchid business, and enhancing her wealth. But in spite of all this, she was lonely. That loneliness would soon end with a chance meeting with Charlene "Chandi" Heffner.

———— ❧ ————

CHARLENE HEFFNER'S FAMILY was financially extremely comfortable although not greatly wealthy. William J. and Barbara Heffner raised Charlene and her sisters in Spring Lake, Maryland. He was a bank vice president as well as an attorney. She was a surgical nurse.

As with so many young people growing up without money worries in the 1960s, Charlene was drawn to the suburban version of the counterculture of the day. She favored torn jeans before they became fashionable. She liked loose Indian-style blouses. And she had an attitude that made her come across like a hybrid mix of "biker chic" and "hippie." She had a tattoo on her arm, was a loner in school, and fled the state for California and Hawaii after graduation.

Heffner and a friend reached Hawaii in 1972, taking a job on a horse farm where they worked grooming and exercising horses, while living in the owner's tack room. The two young women were followers of the Hare Krishna movement, an Indian-based religion requiring chanting and meditation throughout the day. It was an interest that would later endear Charlene to Doris because they both studied and respected Eastern religious teachings. Unlike Doris, Charlene chose to stop eating meat and become a vegetarian. She also periodically wore the saffron robes traditionally used by members of the religion.

While in Hawaii in the early 1970s, Charlene met Gary Winslow McElroy, a leader in the Hare Krishna movement. He was eight years older, a priest, and, like Charlene, seemed to have little interest in material possessions. They lived on five rented acres of land next to Kolopa State Park on the Big Island, their shack of a home shared with other Krishna members. They hand-built a temple and lived quietly, paying $180 a month for rent.

It was in 1977 that Charlene Heffner received the name Chandi. She and Gary traveled to India to see A.C. Bhaktivedanta Swami Prabhupada, the leader of the International Society for Krishna Consciousness. He declared her to be "Chandi," a Sanskrit name meaning "female energy personified." Gary and Chandi may also have been married, though both this and Gary's marital status at the time are uncertain; it is known that he was married when he first moved to Hawaii in 1968.

The Krishna enclave proved reasonably successful, with the group being able to buy the acreage for $60,000 in 1979. It was a private arrangement with the owner, to whom they made mortgage payments. Within the next three or four years they also added horses, which Chandi loved.

Eventually Chandi seemed to grow tired of the simple life. Her younger sister, Claudia, married Nelson Peltz, president of New York–based Triangle Industries who, with the help of junk bond king Michael Milken, later jailed for his dishonest activities, bought out National Can. The purchase was a remarkable feat since Peltz had previously been a small-time copper wire and vending machine company CEO. National Can was a much larger corporation, and the purchase made Nelson and Claudia extremely rich. They traveled by chauffeur-driven limousine, which impressed Chandi. They also gave her father a position on the board of directors of the Peltz businesses.

Chandi seemed to tire of the communal life and began traveling to Oahu to watch the polo games. Her interest is usually described as if it had a sinister twist, as if the former stable girl was suddenly trying to meet wealthy Hawaiians. The fact that Chandi had always loved animals, including the horses she spent many months caring for, is overlooked in all this. Polo is a game that uses beautiful, well-trained animals working in precision with their riders. Many men and women who enjoy horses also enjoy watching the games. Since there is no indication that Chandi tried to meet the owners of the horses or any of the wealthy patrons, the criticism seems unfounded.

Chandi also became interested in belly dancing, again a situation that seems within character but would later be given a sinister twist. She was fascinated by the exotic, from Eastern spiritualism to Near Eastern music and dance. She had been trying to lose weight during this period, and the danse Orientale seemed to fit perfectly into her plans.

It was during a visit to her sister, Claudia, that Chandi contacted the Eastern-style dance company run by Bobby Farrah and founded with the help of Doris Duke. Farrah had a studio on 47th Street and Eighth Avenue in Manhattan, and Chandi apparently had both the drive and the ability of a competent professional. She dressed poorly, though, a sharp contrast to her sister, who was wealthy through marriage and had done modeling. Claudia tried to buy her better clothing, but this was not one of Chandi's interests.

Chandi allegedly claimed to be an heiress uninterested in money when she talked with people at the polo games. By 1984 she was allegedly telling at least some people in the dance field that she had been cut off from a trust fund by parents who disapproved of her lifestyle.

The facts are that Chandi had a history of interests similar to those of Doris Duke long before she tried to meet the heiress. Chandi was a Hare Krishna, a member of an Indian religion. Doris was a student of the teachings of India's Paramahansa Yogananda. Chandi loved animals and kept a baby pig she nursed with a bottle. Doris loved animals, owning everything from dogs to camels over the years. Chandi was devoted to Eastern dance forms. Doris was devoted to professional dancing in all phases, having been involved with Eastern dance forms for sixteen years prior to meeting Chandi. And both Doris and Chandi loved Hawaii.

Had Chandi and Doris been a woman and a man, friends and associates would have thought they were meant for each other. They would have talked about how their shared interests overcame their age difference. They would have seen in Chandi's lifestyle, in the years before Doris, a woman who was comfortable without money. And they would have laughed at her enjoyment of the wealth Doris shared with her because they too would have been seduced by so comfortable a lifestyle. They might have felt she was a bit of an opportunist given Doris's age, yet they would have believed her motives to have been reasonably pure when the two first became close.

There is every indication that had events in the lives of Chandi and Doris taken a different turn, the "sinister" nature of their first meeting would have seemed innocent.

At the end of 1984, Chandi arranged to bring Bobby Farrah and Phyllis "Phaedra" Saretta to Hawaii to put on a seminar in Honolulu. Saretta was part of Farrah's company and one of Doris's teachers. Farrah was also editor of the dance magazine *Arabesque,* which gave his presence a double appeal for those interested in the art form. Together they were considered a major draw anywhere they performed or taught.

Doris returned to Shangri-La in January, so it was natural that she and Sarretta and Farrah would expect to get together.

Chandi had a horseback riding accident during this time, seriously injuring her leg. It was placed in a cast, and although the injury was extremely painful, she never planned to change the date for the seminar.

When Doris returned to Shangri-La, her interest was in dance and especially Farrah's company. He spent extensive time in her home, though he promised Chandi he would have dinner with her alone the night before he left to return to New York. Since he would be visiting Doris the same day, he asked Chandi to meet him just outside the gates of the mansion.

Chandi did not bother staying in the car, as Farrah had told her to do. She was curious about the house, had a walking cast so she could maneuver on crutches, and decided to use her meeting with Farrah as an excuse to go inside. She walked through the gates and was met at the door by house man Johnny Gomez. When Doris realized what was happening, she was gracious enough to invite Chandi to have a glass of sherry.

The conversation was casual and focused on Chandi's injury. Doris told her that she knew a Japanese doctor who probably could heal the leg without the surgery Chandi had been warned might be necessary. The two women exchanged telephone numbers, then Chandi left with Farrah as planned.

Chandi made the first telephone call, thanking Doris for her hospitality. The women met again, this time for lunch, and Doris was soon delighted with the younger woman with whom she had so much in common.

Friendship turned to obsession. When Doris could not make contact with Chandi for a few days, she called New York hoping that Serrata or Farrah would be able to get the message to her that she was missed. Finally Chandi decided to leave the commune and, at Doris's request, move in to Shangri-La.

Doris Duke's money subverted anyone who was allowed to experience the luxury it could buy. Beyond the lavish living quarters, the vast wealth made literally anything possible. If you wanted to adorn your dinner table with a rare flower grown solely in a mountain region thousands of miles away, you could order a private jet to deliver it. You could have a taste for a sandwich you enjoyed in a Santa Monica delicatessen and have it prepared to order, then sent to your apartment in Manhattan. There was no material possession that she could not buy. The party never stopped and to be invited to participate was to call all your past values into question.

Chandi's enemies say that she began exploiting Doris's weakness the moment she arrived. Doris was frightened that her new friend would leave, and resigned to the fact that everyone had to be bought to stay with her. Chandi allegedly understood this and did whatever was necessary to gain some of the wealth, according to her detractors.

Chandi's supporters point out that Doris Duke always was neurotic about those whose love and loyalty she desired. Jimmy Cromwell had taught her that she had to spend money to hold someone close to her. Porfirio Rubirosa reinforced this thinking. It had become routine for her to be excessively generous to a select few in order to ensure that they would not leave her. Chandi may not have been manipulative, just willing to accept her friend's largesse, knowing Doris could well afford anything she wanted to do for her.

Whatever the circumstances, certain facts justify both versions. First, in February 1986, Chandi called the holder of her mortgage in Hawaii and arranged to pay off the remaining portion. She wanted control of the property and gave McElroy more than $30,000 for his share, assuring herself clear title. Then, a few weeks later, Chandi made a successful $1.5 million bid for a Kohala Mountains ranch. The 290 acres were purchased for cash, and the owner was certain that Doris Duke had provided the backing. Since Chandi had no such personal wealth, there seems little question about who financed the transaction.

Was such a purchase characteristic of Doris? Only when it involved husbands and long-term lovers. It certainly fit the pattern of Jimmy Cromwell and Porfirio Rubirosa. However, it happened only if there was a deep attachment that Doris wanted to protect.

Friends of Doris's became suspicious because they felt that Chandi was constantly trying to imply she was someone she wasn't. Chandi, they said, alleged that she was from a wealthy background. Chandi, they said, alleged that she was related to the *Playboy* magazine publisher with a similar last name (Hefner, with one "f").

But Chandi was also seen as compliant, a devoted companion, someone who was giving Doris pleasure at the same time that she was enjoying the new world to which she was exposed. In other words, at least for the first several months, Chandi offered Doris true devotion, something the older woman desperately wanted and reveled in experiencing.

There probably also was a sensual side to the relationship, one about which no witnesses are certain. Talks with security personnel reveal stories of the two women being in the same bed together, of their holding hands, of Chandi caressing Doris's feet. One of the security guards tells of a time when Doris and Chandi were allegedly undressed and dancing at a window where they knew the men would be looking. They were not touching each other. The guard felt that it was more in line of a college sorority/fraternity prank, but the fact that Doris was in her seventies and was the richest woman in the world troubled him. She simply did not care about propriety.

It is hard to know when Chandi was seduced by Doris's wealth. Her detractors feel that she knew about the money, wanted the money, was determined to get the money even before she met Doris. But there is nothing in Doris's history that indicated she would be an easy touch. Certainly there was no reason for Chandi to believe she would become "family" and an heir to the estate.

Yet the truth is probably the simplest explanation. Chandi Heffner, like probably every other person in Hawaii who had ever heard of Shangri-La, wanted to see the Duke estate. She was drawn to wealth, drawn to the unusual lifestyle it could buy, and she took advantage of an opportunity to meet Doris. When the women found they genuinely liked each other, it was probably a friendship based on mutual interests. Chandi was almost certainly not a sophisticated con artist who had mastered the interests of Doris Duke before meeting her in order to win her over.

Rather, like so many others in Doris's life, Chandi changed. She was seduced by the wealth and all that it could bring. She allegedly began telling different stories about her life in order to seem to fit in. Then, if the allegations are true, she seems to have been unable to stop herself.

If there was a specific turning point, Pony Duke feels that it was when Doris and Chandi journeyed to the ranch on which Chandi had been living with McElroy and the others. According to Pony, they smoked some "unusual pot" and used at least one other hallucinogenic. Then Chandi allegedly channeled the spirit of the long-dead Arden, a spirit who declared Chandi to be the reincarnated daughter of Doris Duke.

The story, if accurate, indicates a probable con game. The problem is that, like so many accusations made against Chandi, there is reason to question whether it occurred. If Doris was convinced that Chandi was her daughter reincarnated in some manner, she never said this to any of the staff. None of the men and women interviewed by either author of this book could recall hearing Doris claim that Chandi was Arden.

By contrast, staff members witnessed incidents that implied an aggressive intimacy on Doris Duke's part. Whether this was a same-sex relationship or a sensually charged friendship with unconsummated sexual overtones, only Doris and Chandi could say with certainty. Doris is now dead and Chandi has vehemently denied there ever was a sexual relationship.

Doris Duke's apologists like to say that Chandi set her up. The young woman deliberately created the impression of a lesbian relationship whenever she knew that a staff member would come upon them. However, there are other indications that these moments of intimacy were unplanned.

For example, Tom Rybak recalls one August in 1986 when he had been working approximately three weeks as Doris Duke's private chef. It was Chandi's birthday and Doris asked Tom to prepare a triple-layer Belgian and bittersweet chocolate layer cake with "Happy Birthday Chandi" in white icing. This he did, and when he was finished, he brought it to Doris. He was not expected, and when he entered the room where the women were resting, he saw Doris leaning back, her bare feet on Chandi's chest, the younger woman sucking Doris's toes. It was an intimate act, sensually charged, and probably instigated by Doris, not Chandi.

Oddly, Rybak remembered the incident because it was the first time he had a good look at Doris Duke's feet. Her toes were splayed, perhaps from a birth defect, perhaps from arthritis. And their unusual configuration startled him.

The next morning the maid mentioned bringing a breakfast tray to Chandi and finding both women in bed together. This was unusual for them, which is why she mentioned it. Presumably they spent the night that way.

Rybak and others would later comment that they never heard Doris Duke compare Chandi with Arden in any way. They felt that the relationship was one of two intimately close adult women. If Doris came to look upon Chandi as a daughter, it was because of the age difference rather than because of a reincarnation theory.

What must not be overlooked, though, is that Doris Duke was not a vulnerable, addled old lady. She was not the type to fall for a séance, even if she was under the influence of drugs. Even if she had been stoned out of her mind, she was also sober for long periods before ever acting to benefit Chandi. Doris Duke might have been misled at that stage in her life, but only if she chose to be. Chandi may have been intensely manipulative as she became Doris's favored companion. She may have decided to take Doris for all she could. But at this time, Doris was aware of everything taking place and did not stop it. All she asked of Chandi was total loyalty, the same request she had silently made of her first great love, Jimmy Cromwell. He had betrayed her and, ultimately, Chandi would as well.

Chandi was allowed to take an increasingly active role in running the Duke estates, and it was in this position that criticism of her increased dramatically. She became the employer from Hell, firing a long-term employee without warning, yelling at staff members who failed to perform to her satisfaction, and working to end pension plans to save money. She spoke for Doris, something of which Doris was well aware and saw no reason to correct.

Chandi also began shopping sprees with Doris, the younger woman delighting in Chanel designs, both women delighting in lingerie, luggage, shoes, and other indulgences. They also purchased a Boeing 737 and hired a private pilot in 1987 in order to travel more readily between Hawaii and New Jersey.

———— ❧ ————

CHANDI HEFFNER SEEMED to have found the good life. She had power on the Duke estates, a close relationship with a woman willing and able to indulge any whim, the choicest food, the most opulent surroundings, and the chance to "shop till she dropped" on a Platinum American Express Card whose credit limit could not be achieved in one lifetime. It was a life that every girl who has ever obsessed over a Barbie doll could imagine as the epitome of good times. Instead of Malibu Barbie, there was Shangri-La Chandi. Every day was dress-up day. Every day was a new adventure in her very own Ford Bronco. (Barbie's Corvette was impractical for her lifestyle or she would have had one too.)

The trouble is that being someone else's Barbie doll gets very old very fast. Chandi Heffner was bored. Doris Duke was possessive, insisting that the two be involved with the same things constantly. They shared similar interests. They enjoyed similar activities.

And Doris could not stand the idea of Chandi becoming enamored of anyone else during their time apart, an experience she had endured with great sorrow during the early days of her marriage to Jimmy Cromwell.

In the 1950s, writer Rod Serling created a television series called *The Twilight Zone.* In one episode, a smalltime hood who had made his living as a thief is shot and killed in an alleyway while running from the police. He dies and is ushered into opulent surroundings. Waiting for him are beautiful women who hang on his every word, are delighted to give him every indulgence. The unspoken implication is that he merely has to tell them how he wants sex and they will oblige enthusiastically.

In addition, there are the casinos. In life, he had loved to gamble. In death, he just has to alert the casinos that he is coming and he will win everything he plays. He is the master of blackjack, roulette, or any other game in which he wishes to indulge. His skill is legendary within the casinos, his successes applauded by everyone in the room. And always the adoring women are willing to take him aside and reward him as he chooses.

So long as he tells them. So long as he makes a specific request.

Finally the man admits his frustration. Gambling was exciting when the adrenaline would flow over a game of change. It was the excitement of never knowing if you would win or lose, never knowing when you approached a woman if you would be scorned or if you would "score."

The casino host, the man's tour guide into death, is understanding. He tells the former thief that he can lose any time he desires. Each time he enters the casino or makes a reservation, he should just say when he wants to lose and how much, and it will happen. He can win or he can lose based on his desires. He is in charge.

The man becomes outraged. He doesn't want to be in control of his fortunes. He wants to be surprised. The women have become meaningless to him because they are no more than toys with no minds of their own. Gambling is not gambling if you know the outcome of every wager, every toss of the dice, every spin of the wheel. He thought he wanted to spend eternity indulging in his two loves in life—women and games of chance—but he was wrong. He is bored, intensely bored, mind-numbingly bored, bored enough to commit suicide just to see what that would be like, though obviously it is too late.

Finally, unable to stand another minute, he apologizes to his host for his disrespect but says that he can't stand where he is. As much as he's thrilled to be in Heaven, it's so boring, he wants to go to the other place. The idea of boredom for eternity is the worst punishment he can imagine so the other side, no matter what that means, has to be better.

The host begins laughing hysterically. He looks at the man and asks him what makes him think he is in Heaven.

Living with Doris Duke, for Chandi or anyone else with whom Doris wanted an intensely close relationship, was very much like the Rod Serling version of Hell. Life held no surprises, no challenges. The surroundings were exciting. No whim went unmet. But there was no time to be alone. No time for personal thought. No chance for spontaneity. No chance to develop an interest or activity not shared with Doris. Chandi was in a gilded cage, and though the bars were built with love, they were still bars.

Chandi became authoritarian. She was determined to stay the course, knowing Doris loved her, knowing Doris was increasingly willing to share everything. She was young. If she could endure a few years with Doris—and ultimately she was with her almost until the final decline leading to Doris's death—she would benefit beyond her greatest dreams.

Fortunately, Chandi had patience. She would endure anything. Her gentleness of spirit and the quiet she had honed through meditation and study made her a passive partner in the relationship. The boredom, though, brought out the very human frustration that led her to explode against the staff, to demand what amounted to perfection, to tinker with life on the estates because she had nothing else to do.

There would be two diversions for Chandi during this period, one that would cost Doris Duke millions of dollars, the other of which, occurring a few years later, would be viewed as a total betrayal.

Doris had broken with her usual pattern before returning to Hawaii. Over the years she had become a close friend of Philippines' President Ferdinand Marcos. He was quite similar to Buck

Duke in temperament, and ironically Marcos originally came from the province of Ilocos Norte, the tobacco-growing capital of the Philippines.

On a pragmatic level, a friendship with Ferdinand Marcos was also essential for any multinational tobacco company such as Doris's wishing to do business in the Philippines. However, Doris's relationship transcended the needs of her inheritance.

Doris also knew Marcos's wife, Imelda, but their relationship was not close. Imelda was more obsessed with material possessions than anyone Doris had ever encountered. Her fetish for shoes alone led her to own, at any one time, more than 1,700 pairs. Her concern about assassination led her to also buy custom protective clothing, including a bulletproof brassiere.

Together, the Marcoses acquired property throughout the world. Yet technically the Marcos family was poor. Their official income for many years was the equivalent of $100 per week. However, their holdings were believed to be worth $1.6 billion, most of which was controlled by Imelda. Obviously they were robbing their country, stealing money meant for other purposes. Little was said about all this in the United States or the Philippines. Marcos's country was situated in an area of strategic importance to the United States, and dissent within the Philippines could result in death.

The only common bond between Imelda and Doris was music. Imelda Romualdez had been a beauty queen at eighteen ("The Rose of Tacloban"), parlaying the win into a short-lived singing career. The latter resulted in her being named the "Muse of Manila" at the age of twenty-four when she was asked to perform at the 1953 Philippines International Fair and Exhibition. The following year she went to work for a bank where she met Marcos, then a young congressman. Eleven days later they were married, Marcos giving her an eleven-carat diamond engagement ring and an eleven-carat diamond wedding ring.

Marcos went to the Senate in 1959, became president in 1965, and consolidated his power seven years later in 1972 by declaring martial law. Then Imelda was given positions of power such as minister of Human Settlements and governor of Metro Manila.

Imelda did not prosper solely at the expense of the people. She used some of the money for good works and was rightfully hailed for improving the nutrition of the populace and for being an ardent supporter of the arts. However, she also was known to travel to New York City with 300 pieces of luggage and 40 assistants, making her one of the most aggressive shoppers the world has known.

Imelda continued to sing, but her skills seemed to wane a bit as she became more interested in money, and Doris used to mock her efforts. She had no respect for Imelda. Instead, Doris's friendship was with Ferdinand, and there were rumors that they had enjoyed casual sex together. If true, it would have been in character for both of them.

Imelda Marcos was in trouble as early as 1983. Opposition leader Benigno Aquino was the one man in the Philippines who could successfully challenge President Ferdinand Marcos's iron control of the country. He had been imprisoned, then allowed to travel to the United States for essential heart surgery. Feeling healthy and recovering without complications, he decided to return even though Imelda Marcos warned against such a move. Many people hated him for challenging their beloved leader. The Marcoses could not be certain they could keep him safe. Certainly he was welcome, but it would be best if he did not return at least until new elections assured Marcos's continuing in power.

Aquino, determined to stop the ongoing corruption, flew back to his homeland. A 1,200-man military security force had sealed off the landing area at Manila airport that is adjacent to the Villamor Air Force Base. When the plane landed, Aquino emerged, and despite the security, he was murdered.

Officially the killer was Rolando Galman, known to be a small-time criminal allegedly hired by the Communists. Unofficially the killer was someone in the military acting under orders from the Marcos family. Galman was set up, allegedly by air force colonel Arturo Custodio, who had removed Galman from his home four days before the murder. The two men had allegedly been seen dining at the air force base as well.

With the exception of seven witnesses, including Galman's nine-year-old son, no one would come forward and speak on the record. Their reluctance was not because the official story of the murder was accurate. Instead it was because immediately afterward, armed men, presumably from the military that arranged the death, kidnapped the three people Galman held most dear: his common-law wife, his girlfriend, and his sister.

The murder seemed unnecessary. The Marcos family could easily control the elections as they desired. The nation was a dictatorship disguised as a democracy, and the viciousness of the repression resulted in an investigation and great anger against Imelda and Ferdinand by 1984.

Doris Duke cared about none of this. She was Ferdinand's friend, and even if he ordered the murder, she knew that her own father was as ruthless in business as Ferdinand was in politics. Buck Duke would never kill anyone directly, but he understood the necessity of eliminating a rival.

By November of 1985, Ferdinand and Imelda Marcos were accused of stealing money and hiding it in real estate purchases throughout the United States. The *San Jose Mercury News* had begun a series of articles earlier in June of 1985 showing that the couple allegedly owned buildings ranging in value from $500,000 to $2 million in California, all the way up to the Lindenmere estate on Long Island, which cost $5 million. Imelda Marcos allegedly worked through a holding company in the Netherlands Antilles and a series of agents acting on her behalf but without using her name. For example, the purchasing agent for four Manhattan apartments bought in 1977 for just under $1 million was Vilma H. Bautista, Imelda's personal secretary in New York. The most expensive property, also in Manhattan, was a $51 million building.

The administration of President Ronald Reagan got into the dispute, trying to find a way to settle the problem. The United States had two military bases in the Philippines that were of strategic importance. Rather than lose them, efforts were made to alter the financial aid routinely given the Philippines as well as to negotiate a way to gain a new, honest election.

In 1986, with Philippines elections having become a sore point for the Marcos family—Ferdinand was opposed by Corazón

Aquino, widow of the slain Benigno—New York congressional representative Stephen Solarz claimed the couple had $350 million in New York real estate alone. It was all money that should have belonged to the Philippine people, and Solarz was eager to help the opposition seek criminal indictments.

Imelda Marcos, a one-time beauty queen who owned hundreds of dresses and fabulously expensive precious gems, dismissed the anger in her country by saying "Cory Aquino doesn't use makeup; she doesn't do her nails. Filipinos ask only one thing from life—beauty. Beauty is the supreme value, above money and power. And Filipinos who love beauty will vote for Marcos."

Still, there was a chance that the joyride would come to an end. She commented to American reporters that "One of these days, you will see me hanging from a tree. So what else is new? I don't want to be an old, ugly corpse. The beauty about me is that I'm not attached to anything, not even to life."

Corazón Aquino did win the election, and the Marcos family was immediately flown into exile to a 4,500-square-foot, $2 million mansion in Hawaii. By Imelda's standards, the home was a hovel.

For the first time the holdings of the Marcos family were revealed. While the accuracy of the exact figures is in doubt, one thing is certain: the huge amount the Marcoses had stolen. Gold hidden in the Philippines was expected to be worth $14 billion. Various holdings recovered by the Philippine government during the early days of the forced exile totaled $2.6 billion, and the government had identified another $2.7 billion in holdings. Another $1.5 billion was believed to have been located in the Swiss banking system; the Swiss government even took the unprecedented step of sealing the accounts until lawful ownership could be verified. Although the couple publicly denied having such wealth despite their lavish spending, reportedly Ferdinand Marcos offered to give the opposition access to $5 billion in exchange for letting the couple return to the Philippines.

The U.S. government brought charges against Imelda and Ferdinand, charging them with a fraction of the crimes their accusers believed them to have committed. These included their plundering of $103 million in Philippine government funds and taking U.S. banks for another $165 million in fraudulent financing arrangements resulting in the purchase of four Manhattan buildings. Even during their Hawaiian exile they were supposedly working on illegal financing schemes utilizing Saudi Arabian arms dealer and billionaire Adnan Khashoggi as well as several fronts. They were both ordered to appear in court in Manhattan for an arraignment, but Ferdinand was too ill to leave Hawaii. Imelda went alone, flying in Doris Duke's private plane to New York, then staying in an $1,800-a-day suite at the Waldorf Astoria Hotel.

Ironically, the plane was one that Imelda had helped find for Doris. Doris had mentioned her interest in purchasing a plane while visiting Ferdinand, and Imelda thought she knew where to obtain one. She went to her friend Khashoggi, who sold Doris one that was owned by a Kuwaiti friend. It had been completely refurbished to hold eighteen passengers in great comfort and supposedly was an excellent buy at $25 million. Besides, as a bonus, Chandi negotiated the addition of two Mongolian humpbacked camels, which both she and Doris adored. These were named Princess and Baby in honor of the late Louis Bromfield's boxers.

The plane was apparently overpriced by $15 million, and Doris was led to believe that Chandi and Imelda split a $2.5 million commission from the sale. While Imelda undoubtedly benefited, it is unlikely that Chandi took advantage of Doris. Although Duke family members and friends read sinister motives into Chandi's activities, she had access to whatever she wanted. She had already been given a Hawaiian estate. Taking an unapproved commission, an action that Doris might have discovered, was an unlikely risk. She could lose everything for a tiny fraction of what might otherwise be hers.

### LAST WILL AND TESTAMENT OF DORIS DUKE
Dated: July 28, 1987

Page 5: "I give Five Million Dollars ($5,000,000) to CHARLENE HEFFNER ('Chandi'), of Somerville, New Jersey."

Page 18: "I name CHANDI and a New York City bank or trust as Executors of, and Trustees under, this Will. Any bank or trust company selected by Chandi must be a Trustee of personal trusts having aggregate assets exceeding Three and One-Half Billion Dollars ($3,500,000,000). If no corporate Executor or Trustee selected by Chandi within the period specified is acting, I name CHEMICAL BANK, of New York, New York, to fill the vacancy."

There are also mixed stories concerning Doris's motivation for helping Imelda when she was in New York being arraigned. Bail was set at $5.3 million, a sum Doris tried to pay quietly. Given the notoriety of the case and the fact that the Marcoses' known assets were frozen, it was impossible to avoid publicity. At least Imelda fared better than her alleged co-conspirator, Adnan Khashoggi, who had to post $10 million bail and wear an electronic ankle bracelet that allowed law enforcement officers to keep track of his movements.

Without question, Doris meant her effort to help Ferdinand. Both he and his wife were in trouble, facing the same penalties. Doris could not help one without the other, and her statement, released through her attorney, Donald A. Robinson, linked the two together. The statement said: "I shall do all I can to help my friends, the Marcos family, in this terrible time of need. I am disgusted, embarrassed and ashamed of my country's mistreatment of Imelda and her ailing husband, Ferdinand. Why should America spend millions and millions of dollars prosecuting two people who for a generation have been our closest allies, including our Pacific outpost against Communism?"

Imelda was quoted by *People* magazine writers James S. Kunen, Scot Haller, Maria Wilhelm, and Victoria Balfour as saying "Doris Duke has saved my faith in America." She made clear that she felt abandoned by the Reagans with whom she had been friends for many years before he was elected president. "Doris Duke is the realization of that beautiful lady, the Statue of Liberty, who says at the threshold of this great country, 'I embrace the oppressed, the deprived of mankind.'" In a rather humorous aside, Marcos was quoted as saying that although Americans may not know it, she was fighting for all of our rights.

Despite the self-aggrandizement, the Marcoses and Khashoggi

were acquitted. Although at least some assets remained, Imelda made no effort to repay what Doris Duke considered a loan, not a gift.

---

On November 10, 1988, Doris Duke again made headlines, this time because of her relationship with Chandi Heffner. She made the younger woman her daughter.

By that year, the idea of adult adoption seemed outrageous. Often it was viewed as a way of avoiding taxes or a scam on the part of the adoptee. But, in fact, adult adoption had once been routine in much of the United States, and child adoption was the unusual situation.

Until the late 1940s and early 1950s, many Americans felt that children bore the sins of their parents. If a mother was a drug addict, an alcoholic, or otherwise unfit, the child taken from her care was somehow tainted. The child might be seen as the demon seed, a crisis waiting to happen. Even an orphan could not escape prejudice and ridicule. There was something wrong with a child who allowed his or her parents to die young.

As ridiculous as such thinking seems today, it was a reality for more than a century. Homes for orphaned and abandoned children were located primarily in rural areas, where the children could work the surrounding farms. In that way they earned their keep, learned a trade, and could grow up to be self-supporting.

The families who took in the children to help with the chores often worked with them for several years. They got to watch the children grow and mature into responsible teenagers who, by the standards of the day, were adults. Many a family came to love the children who worked for them on arrangement with the orphanage or children's home. When the children were old enough that it was obvious they were "different" from their birth parents, somehow having escaped the taint, the families often adopted them. Although the boys and girls might be only teenagers, they were old enough to marry and have children of their own. They had earned the rights and expectations of adults, and the adoption that took place was considered adult adoption.

Only recently have families adopted children while very young.

After the pioneering studies of how children grow, which were begun during and immediately after World War II, adults came to realize the importance of a nurturing environment on the development of character. Thus, while Doris Duke's adoption of Chandi Heffner was shocking by the standards of the day, it had a history that was far more common than people realized. In one sense, Doris Duke was rewarding Chandi's behavior in the same way that farm families rewarded the years of service the children had provided them.

Doris and Chandi expressed other reasons at the time as well. Chandi stated that Doris had treated her like a mother, and she made clear that she saw the older woman in such a light. She explained that when Doris was hospitalized, at times only blood relatives were allowed to visit, even though Doris wanted Chandi by her side. Adult adoption would assure that Chandi, who changed her name to Chandi Duke Heffner, could always be close when needed.

The adoption assured something else. Among the trusts established by Buck Duke was one that would pass from Doris to her immediate descendant. That would have been Arden, had Arden lived. With the adoption, Chandi was assured of benefiting from the trust that would reach approximately $180 million by the time Doris died. While this was a small portion of the Duke estate, it represented greater wealth than most people experience in their lifetime.

Not that Chandi was poor. The land Doris had bought her was free and clear—and also worth well over $3 million. No matter what happened between the women, Chandi would never be poor again.

Others have questioned whether the adult adoption took the place of a marriage. The issue of lesbianism and bisexuality constantly arises in regard to the two women, and Chandi refuses to discuss the matter beyond making a firm denial.

Whatever the relationship between Doris and Chandi, there is no question that Doris wanted to solidify it in a legal manner. Many believe that Doris wanted to marry Chandi, although same-sex marriages were not recognized anywhere in the United States. The closest they could come would be with a formalized commitment ceremony being offered by some religious leaders for gay and les-

bian couples, primarily in San Francisco and Hawaii. Such cere-
monies gave the couples the sense of sanctification without any of
the legal rights of a marriage. Since inheritance rights were a prime
consideration of Doris's, the answer was adult adoption.

Judge Wilfred Diana was on duty in Somerville's family court
when Doris and Chandi arrived at 4 P.M. on November 10. The paperwork was complex enough that preparations had to be made
over a few days. However, the time and date of the actual court
appearance were not scheduled so as to ensure there would be no
leaks to reporters.

Some witnesses claim that Doris seemed confused, as if mentally not quite right. She had a little trouble walking as well. Later
there would be talk that she may have been under the influence of
drugs. However, the idea that Doris was against Chandi's becoming part of her family is probably the result of anger by those who
opposed the adoption, not objective reasoning. Certainly the
power Doris gave Chandi the year earlier in her will indicated an
intense closeness and a respect for the younger woman's ability to
handle the administration of the estate. Also, the only assured benefit of the adoption was the right to income from a single Duke
trust. Doris wanted Chandi to have far more and had felt this way
from the time she drew up the earlier will. Undoubtedly the adoption was a reasoned decision, regardless of how she may have felt
later.

Doris Duke's physical state can be called into question. However, her difficulty walking and the slight confusion noted at the
time of the adoption was consistent with Doris's behavior at the
time and for well over a year. Tom Rybak noticed the problem
when he became the chef for Doris and Chandi more than a year
earlier. He felt that it was related to a combination of alcohol abuse
and problems caused by what was supposed to be a health regimen.

Before Rybak was hired as Doris's chef, she and Chandi had
been on a tour of the Slavic countries and had stopped at a health
spa in Romania. The location was an odd one and their faith in
their program might have been humorous had it not held so many
health risks. At the time Romania was in turmoil, led by a violent
dictator. Many children were malnourished and abused in orphan-

ages where they had been sent after their parents were tortured and/or killed. Yet the spa allegedly held the secret for longevity, and the two women returned with large bottles of yellow pills. The pills were stored in the butler's pantry refrigerator in Newport and in kitchen refrigerators in Somerville and Hawaii. In addition, there were small bottles of liquid suitable for injection. Each bottle had a thin rubber seal that could be penetrated by a needle, the liquid then drawn into a syringe.

Tom was told that the pills were lamb placenta. He was never told what the vials of liquid were, though they looked identical to the liquid vitamin B-12 that his mother had been given by her doctor. The vitamin, which had to be injected, came in the same size vial. He assumed that it must be the same.

In addition to this, Doris Duke insisted on having a glass of liquefied wheat grass every evening. The wheat grass was grown on the Somerville farm on a ridged platform Tom estimated was three feet by five feet. The platform held soil and six to eight inches of rich green wheat grass.

The wheat grass was placed in a special machine that appeared to be a hand-crank version of an electric juicer. It was old and apparently had been used for many years, although Rybak never knew how long the wheat grass regimen had gone on.

Rybak was told to fill a glass with what he estimated was six ounces of the liquid. Doris would consume it after breakfast as part of what she called a cleansing ritual. In fact, the juice caused violent diarrhea. It was yet another of her laxatives.

The diarrhea caused electrolyte and vitamin loss that her diet could never make up. Doris was eating next to nothing. She had soup and salad for dinner, but she usually left most of her lunch. If she wanted chicken breasts, for example, the chef was expected to prepare an entire chicken, then carve what was desired. It was delivered to Doris, then returned largely uneaten.

Every day it was the same. A meal large enough for two was prepared for Doris, but she ate only a small quantity. Chandi, a vegetarian, always ate everything prepared for her. But Doris was seriously underweight because of a combination of her laxative abuse and her refusal to eat an adequate portion.

Heavy drinking that probably amounted to alcoholism com-

pounded the problem. Each night between seven thirty and a quarter to eight Doris would have a bottle of La Ina Sherry (eight to
nine glasses) sent to her room on a silver tray, along with a dish of
fresh pecans, lightly salted and toasted. Doris drank the entire bottle herself, then had dinner delivered, occasionally with a few
glasses of champagne. Her attention span and motor skills often
were directly related to how much alcohol she consumed beyond
the nightly bottle of La Ina.

THE NEW JERSEY ADOPTION shocked the trustees of the Duke Endowment and many people connected with Duke University. Under New Jersey law, accepted throughout the United States,
Chandi Duke Heffner would probably forever be considered the
legal, lineal descendant of Doris Duke. She would have the same
rights as a birth child, and this meant that money that would otherwise revert to the university and its trust fund for want of a Duke
heir would now go to Chandi.

Compounding the questions about the adoption is an incident
writer Bob Colacello related in an article for the March 1994 issue
of *Vanity Fair.* He wrote: "After a two-week rejuvenation cure in
Romania with the controversial Dr. Anna Aslan, they stopped in
London. One night at dinner, Heffner told me, 'Doris said to me,
"You're my daughter reincarnated. You're Arden." ' "

Colacello also said that when Chandi Heffner planned to return
to Hawaii toward the end of that same summer, Heffner claims
that Duke made the oral promise. . . . "We were sitting on the
rocks, and she [Doris Duke] said, 'I will take care of you and all of
your animals for the rest of your life. We'll travel together. We'll
have a great life together. You don't have to go back. You can live
in the manner that I live and have this lifestyle. It will be wonderful.' "[1]

IT HAS BEEN SAID that Chandi Heffner changed after the adoption,
although it is more likely she felt approval for the actions she had
been taking ever since the two women became close. Her life was
limited to people such as Imelda Marcos, who became a regular at

Shangri-La, even using the estate for an occasional party. Ferdinand was dying and Doris was making frequent visits to his bedside, often giving him a massage she felt could help heal him. Her efforts were not successful, though. Ferdinand Marcos died on September 28, 1989; thereafter Imelda never received the same warm reception at Duke's estate.

The story of Doris Duke and Chandi Heffner made headlines as it continued to unfold. But there was another story that had begun three years earlier without publicity or notice, one that was of much greater importance. It concerned Bernard Lafferty, and although no one realized it at the time, a new employee would ultimately become embroiled in allegations involving money, power, and death.

# 13

✦

# *The Chef, the Butler, and the Golden Girl*

*D*ORIS DUKE'S LIFESTYLE might be compared with that of the head of a major corporation. In order to maintain her properties, oversee her orchids, and tend to her personal needs, she required a full- and part-time staff of approximately 500 people. Duke Farms alone employed 400.

And like any corporation, there were hierarchies of employees. For example, the butler was ideally a middle manager. He would answer the telephones, answer the door, serve meals, and oversee parties. He would also act as a liaison to the staff. If Doris wanted to have some maintenance work done on Shangri-La while she was living in Newport, she might ask her Newport butler to coordinate the work or to contact the Hawaii butler to do it. If she wanted the maids alerted to the fact that unexpected house guests would be arriving, the butler would relay the message and oversee the preparations.

Other members of the staff, such as Doris's personal secretary and her chef, acted somewhat independently. Yet a butler with good administrative skills would be likely to coordinate all employment, arranging for an employment agency to locate the applicants, then handling some of the prescreening before presenting the most promising candidates.

Long-term domestics are well paid for their skills. An experienced professional couple—the wife a combination cook and maid, the husband serving as butler and chauffeur or butler and handyman—command $6,000 a month plus room and board. Individual maids, depending on skills and job requirements, earn between $300 and $450 per week. Personal chefs and the best butlers are paid between $500 and $1,000 per week.

Due to the money, the benefits, and the chance to work closely with the rich, the famous, and the powerful, many such skilled employees are happy to make a career out of domestic service. In fact, for many years it was difficult to gain such jobs because, unless someone died or retired, there were few openings. Men and women did not see the work as a stepping-stone to another career nor as an interim job while training for a different field. Domestic work required professionalism and was well paid.

The situation changed in the 1980s. A takeover mania struck the business world. The junk bond market was invented, and creative financiers found ways to purchase a business with many different divisions, then sell off assets whose values individually totaled an amount exceeding the debt for the whole. The buyer then kept the core business he desired, profiting handsomely. Instant millionaires abounded, several of whom eventually would be jailed for actions that were clever but illegal.

With money pouring into Wall Street and couples wanting to enjoy the trappings their new wealth allowed, domestic help was suddenly in greater demand than ever before. People interested in domestic service had their choice of job offers. Rarely did someone with any degree of competence not have three or four offers to choose from. Some of the wealthiest families fought over someone with great skill, who often was approached with job offers by the friends of the people for whom he or she worked.

In such a market, it was natural for there to be an employment agency specializing solely in domestic service. The premier such agency in New York, the one that had the highest-paying clientele, was the Pavillion Agency on 40th Street in Manhattan. It was a clearinghouse for the best, advertising in the *New York Times.* Employers could trust the agency's screening, and the workers were loyal because the agency fee, twelve weeks' pay per person placed, was charged to the employer, not the employee.

In 1986, Tom Rybak came to the Pavillion Agency from Quail Hollow Restaurant, forty-five miles outside of Manhattan in Washingtonville, New York. He was a master chef, commanding top money, but the restaurant where he was working could not afford to increase his salary. He knew that the opportunities as a private chef were greater, and he loved the idea of working for someone wealthy enough to afford such a luxury. He had come from Erie, Pennsylvania, and though he was college trained, he saw himself as an unsophisticated, small-town boy who wanted the chance to see more of the world.

The agency was interested in Rybak. His experience was excellent, and he had even written a food column on a part-time basis while still living and working in Pennsylvania. He seemed capable of handling everything desired by one of their best clients, Doris Duke.

Tom had never heard of Doris Duke. He was in his early thirties, and Doris had left the celebrity spotlight by the time Tom was old enough to read the papers. He had no idea that she was the richest woman in the world. He also had no idea that he would fall in love with her—to care about her as he would about a beloved aunt.

Chandi Heffner did the preliminary interview by telephone with Tom, arranging for him to be driven to the Newport estate by truck. The driver, part of the security force, was a cynic. He warned that the dogs he would encounter were vicious and that the house was run by "two lesbians." He added that if Tom could "stomach it, you can watch them dance nude at the windows."

Tom ignored the "warning," concentrating on the drive. When they approached the estate, at first he thought he was entering an office compound. Then came some of the dogs he had been warned about—four massive St. Bernards, each weighing 200 pounds or more. Two of them decided Tom was the nicest, most wonderful human they had ever encountered. The other two seemed to be contemplating having his head for lunch. It was like being in a police interrogation room with men playing good cop/bad cop.

The staff members Tom met made clear that he was to respect the dogs and any other animals he encountered. This was not because they were trained to kill, but because they were beloved pets. He was informed that a security guard for the estate had become fed up with the animals, and when he felt they were bothering him, he kicked at them to make them go away. The man was fired on the spot.

"The dogs *live* here," Tom was told. "If you're hired, remember that you only work here." It was a distinction Rybak never forgot.

The staff area was large and extremely pleasant, but the kitchen was a surprise. The crocks for sugar, coffee, and tea each bore Nazi symbols. He learned that they did not reflect any anti-Semitic feelings on Doris Duke's part. Rather they reflected the eclectic mix of characters she had met over the years. The crocks had been a gift from General Hermann Goering with whom she had lunch while staying at the Ritz Hotel in Paris during the German occupation.

Tom was asked to cook a sample meal for Doris Duke and Chandi, the latter of whom met him after he arrived. She was thirty-four years old, just Tom's age, and had wavy black hair accenting the most beautiful blue-green eyes he had ever seen. She was wearing a white tennis outfit, her usual form of dress when at home.

Tom was wearing his hair long enough to have it in a little ponytail. Chandi did not care about such an eccentricity, though she was pleased that he was single, could travel, and loved going to different cities. There would be travel with the chef's job, some planned well in advance and some on his employer's whim. Chandi wanted to be certain that whoever was hired would be comfortable with the demands of the position.

The interview and the sample meals were enough to convince Chandi that Tom was right for the job. He was also comfortable with the idea of handling extra work, such as helping to train some of the staff who served meals. The only drawback, a minor one, was Tom's need to give notice at the restaurant. They hoped he could start that Saturday, preparing a dinner for Chandi, Doris, and Chandi's sister and brother-in-law. Chandi explained that they were currently shorthanded and would need to hire a butler, so having someone experienced at the party would be a blessing for them.

When Tom met Doris Duke, he was surprised by her height—approximately four inches taller than his five foot ten. He was also surprised by her unkempt appearance. She was wearing a long, white terry-cloth bathrobe, her skin was splotchy, and her hair was matted. She was delighted with what Tom considered a simple lunch—stuffed chicken, whipped potatoes, and fresh-picked corn.

Dessert would be peaches also freshly picked from her estate and poached in champagne. Chandi, a strict vegetarian, was to have vegetables and a salad.

Later Doris sent him back home on a seaplane that landed at the 52nd Street Pier. He was paid $200 and expenses for his day's work. He was also told that he would receive $275 to $350 per day when he worked for private parties. Tom had found a new home.

----

FOR TOM RYBAK, Rough Point was almost beyond comprehension. Having grown up in Erie, Pennsylvania, a kid interested only in being a chef, he was always an outcast, always a little different from others. He was respected in his field, a trusted professional, but he never thought he would have a chance to do more than work in fine restaurants.

Doris Duke and Chandi Heffner were giving Tom a chance to see the world. He would travel with them among their estates, and he might be requested to go elsewhere with them as the need arose. He would be paid well, given his own quarters and the chance to serve some of the wealthiest, most powerful people in the world. Previously he had wondered if he would be able to save enough money to travel the few hundred miles to Washington, D.C., to take a private tour of the White House. Suddenly he had found employment at a place where he would find Jacqueline Kennedy Onassis walking into his kitchen to thank him for the delicious meal she enjoyed as Doris's guest.

For Tom, Doris Duke seemed like the eccentric rich aunt in one of the screwball comedies so popular with Hollywood in the prewar years before he was born. She would show him the world, and as long as he always remembered who was the employer and who was the employee, he would be able to enjoy life as few people ever experience it.

The exterior of Rough Point was already familiar to Tom as it was to millions of Americans, although they did not realize that fact. He had seen it on the Gothic television series *Dark Shadows*. The science fiction soap opera, still playing in reruns and available on videotape, involved a vampire and his troubled life. Doris's home seemed to fit the type of estate a wealthy, blood-sucking immortal might enjoy when he wasn't spending the daylight hours in his coffin.

Inside, Tom discovered that the third-floor staff rooms, fifteen in all, comprised a space larger than that to which most homeowners could aspire. His own room was, he guessed, twelve by eight feet, with its own private bath. Smaller than the first room he was offered, it had a view of the ocean that he preferred.

The third-floor wing also held a section for Doris that included the music room and piano on which she practiced every day. Other private rooms contained her collections, such as exquisite pieces of valuable porcelain. Tom also discovered that she studied maintenance and restoration of her holdings so she could take care of them properly. Unlike some wealthy collectors, Doris did not acquire possessions without developing personal expertise in their history, maintenance, and value.

The entryway of Rough Point was massive, an estimated fifteen by twenty feet. A staff room was large enough to have a good-sized dining table, sofas, a television set, and plenty of room to hang out and relax.

The kitchen was nicer than most commercial kitchens, and at twenty-four feet by thirty, it was large enough to use to run a restaurant. The Vulcan stove and other appliances were all of a type you would expect to find in high-quality dining facilities. There were cabinets everywhere, along with a butler's pantry that held dishes, glasses, and linen.

The silverware and silver serving pieces were stored in an eight-by-eight-foot room kept under lock and key. Many were the finest examples of French, British, and Near Eastern craftsmen, among others. They were specially wrapped and regularly polished. The staff member employed to maintain the holdings worked eight hours a day, five days a week. Yet so massive was the collection of silver serving pieces that the maid could polish the entire room of valuables only once every six months.

Doris and Chandi preferred plain English flatware, each having her own set. But even the simplest pieces were of great value and beauty.

The dining room was positioned to face the ocean. There was a grand stairway and a ten-foot-tall painting of a very young Doris

Duke by the late portrait artist John Singer Sargent. Other paintings included two of thirteen known efforts by an obscure Renaissance artist whose work was greatly desired by museums and knowledgeable, very wealthy collectors.

The library held a small sofa, a coffee table, and many books, most of them personal choices rather than Duke family holdings. Doris was well read in many fields, and the library reflected her tastes.

Larger parties and formal balls were held in the biggest room Tom had ever seen in a private home, easily fifty by one hundred feet and at least two stories high. Large, very rare rugs, flags, and other decorations made it look like a cross between the banquet room of a five-star luxury hotel and a museum display area.

Next to that was a smaller solarium—twenty by twenty-four—in which Doris and Chandi frequently had lunch. And near that was an even larger area of seventy-five by one hundred twenty-five feet with eight or nine complete groupings of furniture, most of which traced their origins to Versailles. There were porcelain vases from China and so many other valuable pieces that museums seeking to acquire the items regularly courted Doris.

It was obvious that Doris Duke knew beauty, value, and investments. Her holdings brought great pleasure to the eye but could easily have been worth far more than her official net worth based solely on cash assets, financial investments, and property. For example, one Van Gogh was the companion to a painting that had just been sold at auction to a Japanese buyer for $43 million, and the Duke example was considered superior.

There were seventy-nine rooms in all, Tom was told, including ten master bedroom suites on the second floor and another eight bedrooms in one wing. The house was designed so that each had a special view. Chandi's bedroom, for example, overlooked a beautifully planned and tended flower garden on one end and the sea on the other.

In all, the Newport house was as large as a city block, yet Tom was to discover that it was only a third the size of the New Jersey residence. That home, he would discover, had indoor tennis courts and a swimming pool, among other amenities. Tom later tried to compare the New Jersey place to the high school he had attended in a building so large that it accommodated 3,000 students without overcrowding. The Somerville mansion was larger, and there were sixty to eighty more houses on the grounds just for the workers who tended the 64,000-acre estate.

But Somerville and the Hawaiian house, Doris's favorite, would become familiar later. For the moment, Rybak would have to learn about Doris Duke's life and the machinations of those around her from the Newport estate.

Doris respected her chefs and expected her guests to do the same. When she entertained a famous guest who was late for the meal, the meal was not delayed. She explained that her philosophy was that her guests will wait for her chef, but her chef will not wait for her guests.

The relationship between Duke and Rybak quickly became a strong one. She treated him no differently from many other members of her closest staff, but for him, it was an exciting time. There was the travel among the estates, of course, but there were personal touches. Doris was sensitive to the fact that he and Chandi were close in age and background, while all other adults with whom they came into contact on the estates were much older. While Doris always referred to Chandi as "Miss Heffner" when addressing the staff (to this day Tom Rybak and other former staff members think of Doris solely as "Miss Duke"), Tom and Chandi were on a first-name basis.

When appropriate, and so long as Tom did not forget his place, he was included in various outings involving Doris and Chandi. For example, they went to a ZZ Top concert together and shared pot, which both women enjoyed. They sometimes went shopping together, such as to select videos. Tom got in the habit of calling Miss Duke when he was going into town to see if she wanted him to pick anything up for her.

Doris was an expert swimmer who frequently attached herself to heavy-duty ropes and swam in the water by the Rough Point estate. This area was considered too dangerous for anyone except the most expert of swimmers, and even then there was a high risk. Tom did not swim here, but he did know how to scuba dive and he taught Doris.

Frequently Doris would drive the three of them to wherever

they were going, always using a worn pickup truck when they were in Somerville. Periodically there would be tour buses outside the estate and they could see the people on board ignoring them while craning their necks to see if they could spot the wealthy Doris Duke. She would laugh at them, Tom remembered, commenting "There goes Doris Duke in her fucking limousine."

During the months following Rybak's hiring, there was a crisis in the Duke household staffing. The butler who had been on duty was dismissed because of some problem with his background. Although the chef could serve when necessary, important in New Jersey where the maids, the next in line after the butler for such a job, did not know the proper method, a butler was critical for managing the household staff.

Bernard Lafferty registered with the Pavillion Agency in September of 1986. He was not a U.S. citizen, though he was a legal immigrant from Ireland who had lived in the country since the 1960s. He had been born in 1945, and among his jobs in America was employment in Philadelphia's Bellevue-Stratford Hotel from 1972 to 1983 and at the Sands Hotel and Casino in Atlantic City from 1983 to 1985. His employment also included time with singer Peggy Lee, who had met him when singing in the Versailles Room at the Bellevue-Stratford. He managed the room and the two became friends. She hired him in a variety of capacities, from general assistant to major-domo to butler.

Bernard Lafferty, about six feet tall with reddish-blond hair and an Irish accent, was considered an excellent employee by everyone who used him, including Chandi's sister and brother-in-law, Nelson and Claudia Peltz of Philadelphia, where he worked as a butler. The problem, and it was a major one, was that he was a periodic alcoholic. Sober, he was hardworking, well liked, and although only semiliterate, considered extremely intelligent. Drunk, he was a major problem. He had gotten drunk while working for the Peltzes, something of which Chandi had apparently been unaware at the time.

The Pavillion Agency also was not originally aware of the drinking problem, although the director heard about it after it affected his employment with the Peltzes. When Chandi turned again to the Pavillion Agency, the president of the company, Glenn Scott Greenhouse, was said to have mentioned the drinking. He did not want to hurt Lafferty; he just did not want to be less than honest with so important a client. (Again, stories conflict. If Chandi and Doris did know about Bernard's periodic binges, they were respectful enough of the man to give him a chance to prove he had the drinking under control. They never mentioned this detail to Tom, who was surprised by Bernard's drinking.)

Doris Duke hired Lafferty in May 1987, for a salary of approximately $500 per week plus room and board. He immediately proved himself to be an excellent butler.

Lafferty had other skills as well, embroidery being the most important for the estate's needs. Doris used him to repair fabric and old costumes of hers. Then, as would happen later again and again, Lafferty started drinking.

The incident was an unexpected surprise. Lafferty had fallen into the routine of the Duke estate almost immediately. When he and Tom had a day off together, Tom suggested that they get in the Triumph Spitfire he owned and drive to New Hope, Pennsylvania, where Tom was familiar with the bar scene.

Lafferty agreed, though he stated that he did not drink. He proved this by ordering only Coca-Cola in the bar where they spent the evening playing pool and talking. By the time they drove back, Tom was convinced that whatever problems Lafferty may have had with alcohol were behind him. He had gained the self-control needed to no longer drink.

Shortly before the first incident of binge drinking, Tom, Doris, and Chandi flew to Shangri-La for what was supposed to be a week's stay. Lafferty was to remain in Somerville.

The butler was extremely disappointed, according to Tom. He wanted to see the estate and enjoy Hawaii. However, he was not needed there, and Tom tried to show him that Doris's trips were paid vacation time for those who stayed behind. Work was minimal, if there was anything to do, and everyone was paid as if he worked all day.

The one-week Hawaiian trip stretched to three weeks. Then, although Tom returned to Somerville, Doris and Chandi spent two days in Falcon's Lair, the home Doris used in Los Angeles. She hated the jet lag caused by a six-hour time difference between the islands and the East Coast. She liked to reduce the stress by staying in Los Angeles, three hours' difference from both the islands and the East, for a couple of days before moving on.

Tom had called Duke Farms around 10 P.M. the evening before the three of them left Hawaii. Even with the stopover, Tom wanted to alert the staff, through Lafferty, that it was time to prepare for Miss Duke's return.

Lafferty sounded tired to Tom, though he thought little of that fact. Two maids had quit in order to take a better-paying job with hotel owner Leona Helmsley, and a new maid, a Polish immigrant, had been hired. The transition easily could have accounted for the exhaustion.

The day that Chandi and Doris were due to arrive, the Polish maid stopped Tom late in the morning and said that Bernard had been nasty to her. Not knowing what was taking place, Tom did nothing, figuring he would observe first.

The two women arrived in the early afternoon, and Doris could tell Lafferty had been drinking. It did not seem serious, but it was certainly inappropriate. He was not allowed to drink on the job, and it was disrespectful to be doing so at all when his employer returned from what had stretched to almost a month away. Doris had Tom talk with Lafferty, the confrontation harsh though in line for the staff regulations the butler had broken. Then, Tom drove to the store to buy food for the evening meal as well as for some of the household pets.

That same evening, Tom prepared a tray for Doris Duke that Lafferty, as usual, was to take up to her. This was the most boring part of the butler's job. Because of Doris's heavy drinking before her meal, and because she liked to eat leisurely courses, the butler was expected to sit outside her room, waiting to remove each tray as she finished. Under the best of circumstances, the wait would be an hour and a half. At other times it could be three hours.

That evening Lafferty was nervous taking up the tray and dropped one he had brought back down. Tom felt he was drinking and asked the new maid to remove the last of the dinner trays from Doris's room when she finished.

The next morning Tom expected Lafferty to be working by 8 A.M. A menu for the day's meals accompanied breakfast. Doris would approve Tom's choices, modify them, or put down her own desires. Then he would gather the vegetables he needed from the farm produce, when possible, and from the town markets when necessary.

That morning Lafferty did not report to work on time. He showed up around 11 A.M., when Doris was around. She was quite concerned that Lafferty seemed to have been drinking. By evening he was unable to hold the tray, dropping Doris's evening meal and forcing Tom to prepare a second tray.

According to Tom, Lafferty did not appear until late morning the next day. He said he was not well and he looked terrible. He returned to his room, where Tom and the head of security found him around four that afternoon. He had passed out and was surrounded by what Tom remembers as twenty-eight empty bottles of sherry, as well as some Grand Marnier that Buck Duke had placed in the cellar. Lafferty may have matched the alcoholic Doris's evening regimen of a bottle a day while she was away in Hawaii. Whatever the case, he had obviously been drinking heavily and needed hospitalization. Tom remembered a four-week absence during which Lafferty went through detox and a treatment program. However, according to journalist Bob Colacello, Somerville hospital records indicated that he was a patient from July 1 to July 14, 1987.[1]

Doris felt that she should be compassionate, but she also knew that Lafferty was a new hire. He could be dismissed immediately without such an action being challenged. She was not certain what was the best thing to do, and since he had to work closely with Tom, she asked him.

Today, Tom Rybak regrets his decision. At the time he felt only compassion for a person he felt was highly troubled. From what he had learned about Lafferty, the man had no family except for one relative in Philadelphia. His work was excellent, and at the time of the hiring, only two candidates had met the initial criteria for the job Doris had established. The other man was a graduate of the highly respected Ivy Spencer Butler School, but he was inexperienced. This would have been his first job after training.

The two applicants were tested. The evening of the day they were interviewed, they were both shown how to deliver dinner trays. The Ivy Spencer graduate was selected to do the serving, although he had problems because he was fatigued from jet lag. All he wanted was a bed where he could rest.

The next morning Lafferty and Tom went to town to run errands. The Ivy Spencer man seemed nice, although he did not like Lafferty. This was not a concern because Tom planned to hire them both, one to stay in Newport, the other to work in New Jersey. They would then be tested before anything was finalized. In that way, both men might get jobs.

The butler from the Ivy Spencer school decided he did not like Lafferty and did not feel that he could work with him. He returned to the Pavillion Agency to see what other jobs might be available. Lafferty was hired, and even though he subsequently proved himself to be a problem, Tom felt he deserved another chance. Perhaps some unknown pressures had added to the problem. One more chance would not hurt any of them. Or so he thought.

There was another reason for the altruism, Tom later admitted. He needed help. While he had to prepare for fewer meals than when he worked in a busy restaurant, the demands were quite different. He had one vegetarian menu to maintain for Chandi and a second menu for Doris. No menu item could be repeated for two weeks, quite a different situation from a restaurant, where the manager decides upon the food choices, then establishes a menu where the prices will be altered more frequently than the food items.

In addition to the meals for Chandi and Doris, Tom was involved with the preparation of food for the staff (a full meal for lunch, cold cuts for the lighter dinner fare). He also was expected to prepare stew for the dogs, a concoction that the vet felt was best for their health. It involved a combination of regular dogfood mixed with elbow macaroni, boneless, skinless chicken chunks, corn, and spinach. He had to make forty gallons at a time, which added to his work.

Shopping in Newport was a nightmare. Out of season, the community could be traversed in two minutes. In season, the traffic was so intense that it took an hour and a half to go from the estate to the store and back. The butler's job included relieving some of the pressure from the chef, and Rybak wanted the help. It would take more time to locate and train someone than to take a chance on a known butler who was under treatment.

When Lafferty was hospitalized, there had been no relief for Tom. He was working every day, and though Doris and Chandi recognized the pressure he was under, paying him extra for his efforts, he wanted time off. Instead, he could do little more than drive around, talk with the estate guards, and sit in his room, relaxing with a beer and television. For a man who liked people, liked to get out, it was a frustratingly boring period.

When Lafferty returned, Tom began spending less time with him, since the friends he had in Newport did not care for Lafferty. Tom could now enjoy the town's nightlife on his own.

Lafferty began spending more time with Chandi. There was nothing special about the relationship, though he seemed to be healing the distrust that existed after the binge drinking incident.

What happened next is uncertain. There is enormous animosity between many people involved with Doris Duke and Bernard Lafferty during this period. In fact, it would be Tom who, when Doris Duke died a few years later, would be among the first to go to the media with questions about whether Doris was murdered. He would become obsessed with the idea that Lafferty may have killed Doris by neglect or was deliberately involved with her untimely death. However, because he stopped being objective, his hindsight analysis of events must be considered in that regard.

While many Duke employees from this time and later were placed in Doris Duke's will, Tom was never considered for an inheritance. He was paid when he worked there. He was given proper severance pay when he left. There was no expectations of anything more, and certainly no complaints on his part. He had simply come to love and revere the woman for all that she had enabled him to experience and did not want to see her death go unavenged.

Whatever the full truth, given the events that would follow, Rybak was not present. He could not be certain he understood the mind of Doris Duke in her later months. He had no way of knowing when staff people were carrying out her wishes.

Certainly after Rybak left, after Doris Duke was dead, Lafferty wrote notes to himself, revealing some of his feelings of aggression toward Chandi as well as the head of Doris Duke's security force, her accountant, and one of her doctors who was also a longtime friend. He wrote, in part:

> "Dr. Demoplis [sic] has to be destroyed. Heffner. Bloom. Levey. . . ."[2]
>
> "I have been abused by Miss Heffner for 5 year [sic]. It was a nightmare."[3]
>
> "Papers for Heffne [sic] to file a undueinfluce [sic] against me. It will be me against her. So will take to my hands. What to do with her. It is time for some bad press for her."[4]

———— ❧ ————

ACCORDING TO TOM, it was during the summer of 1987 when food started being returned by Chandi and/or Doris. He would prepare a hot meal, as he had been doing for many months. Then he would send it up as usual, secure in the knowledge that the two women would enjoy it. Nothing had changed in his preparations and actions. Nothing should have changed for them. Instead, though, he was getting complaints two and three times a day. He was told that food that should have been served cold was arriving warmed. Food that should have been served hot was arriving lukewarm at best, cold at worst.

Chandi was outraged. She complained to Lafferty who commiserated with his employer.

Tom, suspicious of the butler though not understanding why the man would sabotage the meals, periodically arranged for the house man, Vincent Cohelo, to serve the food. Each time Cohelo made the delivery, the meal was perfect. When Lafferty brought it, there were usually problems.

Tom believed that the only explanation was that Lafferty was deliberately sabotaging the meals. There was plenty of time and plenty of places where Lafferty could alter it. Just delaying for several minutes going in with the hot food would drastically reduce its temperature, changing the taste.

Given the problems the women had experienced with Lafferty's drinking, Chandi became suspicious that Tom had become a closet alcoholic or drug addict. She contacted Steve Levy, the head of security, and asked him to arrange for a blood test to be administered to Rybak.

Tom was both hurt by the unfounded accusations and touched by the fact that Doris, no longer trusting him, wanted to help him with his "problem." When the test came back clean, she had him return to Newport from the Somerville estate where he was living, awaiting the results.

The return to the Newport estate was a nightmare. The food had been fine for almost two years, yet suddenly nothing was right. Tom would fix it to what he knew was perfection. Then Lafferty supposedly would take it directly to Doris. Time would pass, Tom would be relieved, and suddenly it was returned. The mashed potatoes were wrong.

Tom replaced the mashed potatoes only to have them returned. He replaced this second batch, and again it was returned.

Lafferty suggested that another chef be hired. Tom was obviously no longer competent. After all, Bernard took whatever he was given directly to Miss Duke, and it seemed almost always to be wrong.

Chandi began to talk about hiring another chef. Perhaps Tom was overworked. Perhaps Tom had lost his touch. Perhaps there was something else causing such bizarre behavior in the kitchen.

Finally the pressure was overwhelming. The food was returned once again and Tom's heart began racing. His breathing was labored, his chest felt constricted.

Tom looked at the plate. It had been perfect when he prepared it, perfect when he gave it to Bernard Lafferty.

Yet Chandi and Miss Duke wouldn't lie. Neither woman was the type to play games with the staff. The food was good or it wasn't, and until Bernard Lafferty returned from alcohol detox, it had always been excellent. He was a master chef, after all, a man with an education, great skill, and experience in all phases of fine dining. He could follow any recipe or improvise and create great tastes from ingredients mixed with his own unique flare.

Tom closed one eye, still staring at the plate. The pain in his chest made breathing difficult. He began to shake uncontrollably, his body seeming to go into shock or convulsions. No one was certain what was happening, but Steve Levy, the head of security, knew it was serious. An ambulance was called and Tom was rushed to the hospital in the throes of what everyone feared was a heart attack.

The hospital staff gave Tom an electrocardiogram. There had been no damage to his heart. His body was fine. He had experienced a stress attack so severe that he had what are known as bronchospasms, a condition that is as painful as a heart attack although lasting much longer and without any subsequent physical damage.

Tom knew he had been lucky. He also knew that no job was worth his life. The next time he was overwhelmed his heart could be in danger. He was not going to die for the richest woman in the world. He also realized that he was no longer in a position where Doris or Chandi would believe what he felt was the truth. Rybak was concerned that Bernard Lafferty was making certain that the food would be unacceptable to Doris to ensure that he would be fired.

There seemed nothing to be gained at the time. Bernard Lafferty was a butler. He had come from a family with nothing, and the money he was making was more than he had ever experienced in his life, perhaps more than he would ever know again. He was semiliterate, a known alcoholic with an uncertain future. The idea that he could be involved with any sort of intrigue seemed ridiculous. Telling what he believed to be the truth would only make Tom look foolish at best.

What no one understood was that being semiliterate did not mean that Bernard Lafferty was not intelligent. With the departure of Tom Rybak, someone whose presence had been enjoyed by both Chandi and Doris, Lafferty was perceived by his enemies as starting to isolate Doris from the people closest to her. It was believed by those hostile to him that his next target would be Chandi Heffner. After that, it was impossible to say. All that seems certain in hindsight is that Bernard Lafferty had found a home. He apparently wanted to become indispensable to Doris Duke, and to gain the prestige and importance that had eluded him in the past. With the departure of those closest to the elderly billionaire, such an end could be achieved.

# 14

## *Butler Rises*

*T*HE RELATIONSHIP BETWEEN Chandi Heffner and Doris Duke began to deteriorate after Rybak left their employ and Ferdinand Marcos died. Imelda Marcos had not realized how much Doris disliked her until after Ferdinand's September 28, 1989, death, when the relationship between the two women grew cold. Imelda also seems not to have considered repaying the loan she was given for her bail, keeping the money when it was returned to her following her acquittal. This so upset Doris that she made certain that her Last Will and Testament included a mention of the $5 million loan and the request that it be collected if still outstanding at the time of her death.

Doris was also once again making news because of her eccentric friends. Among these was comic actor Paul Reubens, who became famous for creating the character Pee-Wee Herman. Reubens, as Pee-Wee, had an extremely successful children's show on which he played a man with a child's sensibilities who had all manner of adventures with people, animals, and a variety of contraptions that made his home seem like a Rube Goldberg cartoon. In his private life he was openly homosexual, living with a male lover in a Hawaiian home rented from actor Jim Nabors.

While Doris was on the mainland, Reubens and his lover wanted to have a commitment ceremony, since marriage between men was not legal. Chandi allowed the men to use Shangri-La for the event, at which Nabors sang love songs usually reserved for weddings.

Chandi's enemies like to use the well-publicized incident to imply that she was abusing her power, at a time when Doris was thousands of miles away. However, Doris certainly would have approved, since she too was close to Reubens. In fact, many months later, when Reubens was arrested by plainclothes vice officers for masturbating in an adult movie theater, Doris gave him refuge in Somerville. She genuinely cared about the man and felt the arrest was out of line given its location and the fact that Reubens was bothering no one. She was especially sympathetic due to the fact that the publicity cost him his very successful children's shows and a budding motion picture career.

At this time Chandi was becoming even more unpopular with the staff. She was demanding, imperious, and generally disliked. She had taken control of many of the day-to-day operations of the estates, and though she did so with the knowledge and approval of Doris Duke, the staff focused their anger on her, not their employer.

Chandi also began using professionals and service career personnel with whom she or someone close to her was familiar. Although later seen as sinister, especially since she used her sister and brother-in-law's accountant, Irwin Bloom, and their former butler, Lafferty, the actions were practical ones. Her friends knew the reputable suppliers, such as Pavillion, and they were wealthy enough so that their accountants, lawyers, and advisors were likely to be trustworthy. If later there were problems Doris and Chandi would be in good company since others among the rich and powerful would also be victims.

Doris had a history of hiring people based on friends' recommendations. For example, for a while her health care was overseen by Ferdinand Marcos's physician, Dr. Rolando L. Atiga, on Marcos's recommendation. Such actions were no different, nor any more sinister, than when a family moves to a new community and uses friends they make on the job, in church or synagogue, and elsewhere to find a dentist, pediatrician, and the like.

The real problem for Chandi and Doris came when Chandi hired a bodyguard named James Burns. He was handsome, a martial arts expert, and experienced in security. He also became Chandi's lover for a brief period, or so Doris believed. The relationship with Burns led Doris Duke to break with Chandi. Duke also perceived it as a betrayal on several counts.

As mentioned, the degree of intimacy between the two women has always been questioned. Staff members who spoke about what they saw felt there was a lesbian relationship. Others, including Chandi when interviewed by Bob Colacello for *Vanity Fair,* claimed otherwise. If Doris considered Chandi her lover, then she had to have felt betrayed if Chandi became involved with someone else.

Tom Rybak felt that the hatred Doris Duke came to feel toward Chandi was definitely related to an intimate relationship. It was matched only by her hatred for Jimmy Cromwell, her ex-husband, whom she felt was very similar to Burns. Both were handsome, powerful men interested in martial arts, and in her mind, both were causes of betrayal. Rybak also feels it is possible that Chandi didn't realize that Doris would be upset, either because she was not engaged in a physical romance or specifically because Burns was male. In some same-sex relationships, one partner does not feel threatened if the object of his or her affection takes a lover of the opposite sex. If the sexual allegations were true, Chandi may have believed that Doris would not object.

It's also possible that Doris was acting as a mother concerned about her daughter's involvement with the wrong man. Even though they were quite different, Burns and Cromwell were similar in Doris's eyes. Doris could easily have been outraged that Chandi would make such a mistake after all she had heard about her mother's (Doris's) problems with Cromwell.

Whatever the circumstances, the two women became estranged. In addition, the bored Chandi was becoming a harridan, yelling at the staff, many of whom were leaving, after which Bernard Lafferty would handle their replacement.

Finally Doris became convinced that Chandi was trying to poison her. Her health was declining and she worried that Chandi was giving her medicines that were actually causing her degeneration. But staff members have shown that the way in which Doris received the food and drink that might have been tainted made it impossible for Chandi to add anything. Equally important, what Doris did not realize was that her addiction to laxatives, her heavy drinking, and her recreational drug use were the probable cause of her rapidly deteriorating health. Colin Shanley, the chef who followed Tom Rybak, was worried about her anorexic condition, but though he made every effort to improve her diet, Doris still ate less than she needed to remain healthy. So long as she could swim regularly in currents that tested the strength of even the best athletes, she felt certain she was doing nothing wrong.

### Last Will and Testament of Doris Duke
#### Dated: November 4, 1991

I declare that, despite my 1988 adoption of Chandi Heffner (who was 35 years old at that time), it is my intention that she not be deemed to be my child for the purposes of disposing of the trust property described in Subdivision A of this Article SEVEN, or for any other purpose of this Will, or otherwise, and that this will and all trusts and other entities in which I have an interest shall be administered accordingly. I am confident that my father, who created certain trusts for my lifetime benefit, would not want Chandi Heffner to have any interest in any such trust, even if I wanted her to have such an interest (which I do not).—p. 20

If BERNARD LAFFERTY shall survive me and shall at my death be in my employ or the employ of a foundation of which I am a member, director, trustee or officer at my death, I give and bequeath to my Trustees a sum which my Executors, in their absolute discretion, determine shall be necessary, assuming that such sum will generate interest at a rate of seven percent (7%) per annum, to produce income on an annual basis which shall equal the sum of (i) two (2) times the annual salary that BERNARD LAFFERTY received from me or such foundation, as the case may be, for the twelve (12) month period immediately preceding my death plus (ii) Eighteen Thousand Dollars ($18,000). Such sum shall be held by my Trustees in a separate charitable remainder annuity trust, with income and principal thereof to be disposed of in accordance with the provisions of Paragraph 5 of this Subdivision C.—p. 11

Eventually Dr. Atiga seemed to concur with Doris's concern that she was being poisoned. In a letter dated December 11, 1991, Dr. Atiga said that during 1989 and 1990, when Doris complained of weakness, he was shown cartridges of what appeared to be heparin, a substance meant to slow the clotting of blood.[1] He did not have them lab tested, did not check to see where Doris got them, and apparently did not know about Doris's general drug and alcohol abuse. He also stated that Chandi was apparently giving Doris digoxin (Lanoxin), which would slow Doris's heart rate.

The problem with all of these stories is that no single physician was involved with primary care. It is not known where Doris went for treatment, where she acquired medication, and what she insisted upon taking herself. The closest she had was her longtime friend Dr. Harry Demopoulos, but even he often was not aware of the variety of treatments she was seeking and the medication she was using. Add to this her dependence on laxatives and a nightly fifth of sherry, and blaming anyone other than Doris for her decline seems unrealistic.

Perhaps the most provable counter to Doris's allegation against Chandi was the allegation that she poisoned the nightly bottle of sherry. Yet the strict, unvarying routine Doris Duke demanded of staff members, including Tom Rybak, his successor Colin Shanley, and others makes such an action a physical impossibility.

Doris would call down to the kitchen at approximately 8:20 P.M. to request that La Ina Sherry be sent up to her sitting room, where she regularly ate dinner. The chef or the butler took the bottle from the locked liquor cabinet; only they had keys. The bottle was placed on a table and the person who removed it from the cabinet would remove the black plastic wrap from around the bottle top. The plastic-topped cork that sealed in the sherry was not removed.

Next, the bottle was set on an ornate silver serving tray along with one crystal glass and a silver bowl filled with freshly buttered, salted, and roasted pecans. Then the butler or a maid would take it upstairs to Doris Duke, placing it on a small table between Chandi and Doris. Whoever delivered the tray would ask to pour for Miss Duke, and then the cork would be pried from the bottle. If Doris chose to do it herself, the staff person would be dismissed. At no time would anyone else be alone with the bottle, and only Doris Duke would drink the sherry. When she was finished with the entire bottle, or as much as she wanted to consume before dinner, she would ring for the meals to be brought up. This always was from one hour to an hour and fifteen minutes later.

This routine was followed seven days a week, 365 days a year, in every one of her houses. The only variation came when she was traveling, not a concern since the allegations of possible poisoning by Chandi related only to when the women were living in one of the homes.

The poison issue may have been nonsense, but the tension over Chandi's management style was causing staff members to quit. Among those who fled Chandi was chef Colin Shanley, who worked from August of 1988 through November of 1993, returning as house man from January 1994 through July 1994. "In October 1989, I told Miss Duke that I could not work for her any longer because of difficulties I was having with Charlene Gail Heffner, who was disrupting my work." He stayed away until early in 1991, when Doris, by then extremely sick and paranoid about Chandi, was so convinced that the younger woman was trying to kill her, she severed her relationship with her. However, she could not change the adoption or alter the fact that Chandi Duke Heffner had become her lineal descendant and the proper claimant to one of the trust funds.

"After Heffner was gone, Miss Duke never even mentioned her name. Nor could anyone else mention her name. I was instructed by Miss Duke not to prepare any foods that were in any way reminiscent of Heffner, such as Krishna dishes or pizza."

Shanley explained the role Lafferty held in the house at the time. He said: "Before Miss Duke terminated her relationship with Heffner, Lafferty had a very limited role as the butler. Lafferty was responsible for polishing the silver (a task which he often passed off on other, elderly employees), answering the door at the households (there were, however, very few visitors), and serving Miss Duke's food to her on a tray (each day, while she was eating, Lafferty would be required to wait—sometimes for hours—in the hall outside her room until she rang her bell, at which time he was allowed to come into the room to remove her tray).

"Miss Duke never had a meal with Lafferty. When she rang her bell, that was his signal to come into her room. She would not permit him to enter the room until she rang the bell. Like the rest of the employees, he always called her 'Miss Duke' or 'Madame.' He never would have been allowed to call her 'Doris,' as she was called by her friends and guests.

"When Miss Duke was well enough to be aware of her surroundings, Lafferty was required to wear a formal butler's uniform that included a white jacket, white shirt, bow tie, and black pants, all of which were adorned with many buttons. (When we were in Hawaii, Miss Duke made Lafferty wear Filipino butler's shirts.) Miss Duke devoted no attention to Lafferty's clothing because he was required to wear a uniform. On the rare occasion when Lafferty would wear other clothing, Miss Duke never got involved in the selection of Lafferty's clothing.

"I recall the one and only occasion when Lafferty went with Miss Duke to a social event. He assisted Irwin Bloom in attending to her at an event that was held at the New York club, Tatou. I went with Lafferty to Macy's to help him select the sweater he wore that evening.

"Miss Duke knew that Lafferty was a very simple, illiterate man. When she had possession of her faculties, she never asked Lafferty for any advice. Indeed, she was almost intolerant of his illiteracy—his inability to verbalize or understand things. . . ."[2]

Shanley continued, "Miss Duke never included Lafferty in her social plans. If she allowed him to attend an event with her, he did so in his capacity as her butler, to provide assistance to her. He did not attend as her 'guest.'"[3]

Shanley told of the change that occurred in the house when Chandi left. He said that "Lafferty spent more time with Miss Duke. He began to enhance his role in the household outside her presence and without her knowledge. Miss Duke still treated him as the butler (for example, she never had meals with him as she would with a guest or with Heffner). Nonetheless, he was taking advantage of Miss Duke's depression, which resulted from her concern that she had been deceived by Heffner. He would tell Miss Duke very bad things that Heffner had done to him and her in order to ingratiate himself to Miss Duke. He would claim that

Heffner had been cruel to him, in order to gain Miss Duke's sympathy. He positioned himself to be the only [one] who would be passionate enough to 'do battle' with Heffner in the future. He began to fill Miss Duke's head with all sorts of 'conspiracy' theories about Heffner and others. He tried to convince Miss Duke that she needed to implement elaborate security systems, such as bullet-proof glass in the Newport mansion, in order to protect herself from Heffner.

"By the fall of 1991 and early 1992, Lafferty began to 'call the shots' as to who would speak with Miss Duke. If a telephone call came in, he would make false statements about Miss Duke's frame of mind, whereabouts, or activities, to either mislead the caller or to make the caller believe that they should check with Lafferty before speaking to Miss Duke. He often refused to put calls through to her. As time went on, he effectively cut her off from the outside world."[4]

Shanley was upset by Lafferty's lack of ability to understand their employer's passions. He later explained, "Miss Duke loved African-American culture and music. Lafferty couldn't stand music by James Brown or Aretha Franklin, or other African-American artists. When Miss Duke played music by black artists, he would say, 'she has those wailing niggers on again.'

"Lafferty also could not understand Miss Duke's interest in Islamic art. Miss Duke had a vast collection of Islamic art, including tapestries and plates. Lafferty would point to one cracked Islamic plate (which was in a case in the dining room in Honolulu), and say 'can you believe this piece of shit is worth millions of dollars?' Lafferty would say the Islamic art was made by 'sand niggers.'"[5]

The changes that followed Heffner's departure and the gradual isolation seemed to come to a head in 1992, when Shanley stated: ". . . it became obvious that Miss Duke no longer was involved in her day-to-day affairs. From 1988 to early 1991, Miss Duke was intimately involved in the day-to-day management of her properties. She would receive daily reports from each of her estate managers and from the Duke Business Office. She would get involved in relatively minor details, such as the purchase of a piece of lawn equipment or the color paint that would be used on a minor item. She was completely in control of all such matters.

"By late 1992, and certainly by the time she was hospitalized in February 1993, Miss Duke was incapable of handling those details. She no longer understood, and no longer was interested in, the management of her properties. This was a remarkable change for a woman who had devoted much of her life to preserving and maintaining her estates and who knew every detail regarding the management of those properties."[6]

Doris Duke's deterioration was noticed by others not connected with her daily life. The Reverend Lawrence Roberts feels that she was rapidly declining as early as 1991, for example. He was surprised that she was as healthy as she was because of the way she had abused her body over the years. What was changing was the way the estate was being handled. Colin Shanley stated:

"Lafferty then took control of the management of Miss Duke's estates. He directed the activities of Miss Duke's employees by claiming to act under authority granted by her. In fact, Miss Duke never granted, and never would have granted, such authority to anyone. On many occasions, when Lafferty received an inquiry from one of the estate managers, he would act as though he had presented the matter to Miss Duke and had obtained her approval. In fact, he would not even discuss such issues with her and never obtained such approval. He would put a caller on hold, saying 'let me talk to Miss Duke about this.' He would then wait a few minutes. He would then get back on the phone and pretend that he obtained approval from Miss Duke.

"By early 1993, Lafferty regularly told me that he had complete control over Miss Duke and her affairs. He said that he could get her to do whatever he wanted her to do."[7]

## APRIL 16, 1992, CODICIL TO THE WILL OF DORIS DUKE
### Dated November 4, 1991[8]

[P. 1] *TEN:* A. Subject to the provisions of paragraph B of this Article TEN, I nominate, constitute and appoint WALKER P. INMAN, JR., BERNARD RAFFERTY [*sic*] and THE BANK OF NEW YORK, or such of them as shall qualify and be serving hereunder as Executors of this my Last Will and Testament.

B. The appointments of WALKER P. INMAN, JR. and BERNARD RAFFERTY [*sic*] are conditioned upon their accepting, respectively, a maximum commission equal to Two Hundred Fifty Thousand ($250,000.00) Dollars for the performance of their respective duties as an executor hereunder.

The appointment of THE BANK OF NEW YORK is conditioned upon its accepting the maximum commission equal to Seven Million ($7,000,000.00) Dollars for the performance of its duties as an Executor hereunder.

C. If THE BANK OF NEW YORK fails to qualify or ceases to serve as Executor hereunder, I authorize and direct WALKER P. INMAN, JR., or if he fails to do so, then I authorize and direct BERNARD RAFFERTY [sic] to name a substitute or successor bank or trust company to serve hereunder, provided that such bank or trust company is among the ten largest institutions (measured by its aggregate assets) authorized to do business in the State of New York, and that it agrees to the maximum limit on commissions set forth in paragraph B of this Article TEN. The nomination shall be in writing and filed in the Court in which this Will is probated. . . .

E. The appointment of WALKER P. INMAN, JR., is conditioned upon his accepting a maximum commission equal to Two Hundred Fifty Thousand ($250,000.00) Dollars in the aggregate for the performance of his duties as a Trustee of all the trusts hereunder.

The appointment of BERNARD RAFFERTY [sic] is conditioned upon his accepting a maximum commission equal to Two Hundred Fifty Thousand ($250,000.00) Dollars in the aggregate for the performance of his duties as a Trustee of all the trusts hereunder.

With the appointment of Bernard Lafferty (or "Rafferty," as she spelled it at the time), Doris Duke acknowledged that her health was failing. Her Last Will and Testament from December 1, 1980, clearly defines the type of person she insisted upon as an executor or director of her trust. The description shows that when she was fully rational, there is no way that a man with Lafferty's education would ever be considered. She stated on page 10 of the will that:

i) The replacement must be not less than 50 years of age, nor more than 70 years of age.

ii) The replacement must be a graduate of an accredited university or college.

iii) The replacement must have either banking, accounting, legal, financial or business experience, and

iv) The replacement must be a person of good moral character and standing in the community.

The story of the last months of Doris Duke are about something more than money. There are those who claim that the problem with the people involved with her last days was that they stood to financially benefit from her death. Yet even for some of those who might benefit financially, the money was often not all that meaningful. They were already financially well off by the average person's terms. The real benefit Doris Duke's death could bring was national respect and prestige in a way few people ever achieve.

———— ⚜ ————

BERNARD LAFFERTY WAS SIMILAR to the Irish immigrants who came to the United States following the nineteenth-century potato famine. They were an agricultural people, self-sufficient, with a culture quite different from the Americans they encountered after their arrival. They were also unwilling immigrants, people who enjoyed a life that the destruction of their crops made impossible to continue. They moved to America to survive, not because it had been their long-held dream for the future, as was the case with many Eastern Europeans of the same era.

The hatred that greeted the Irish immigrants upon their arrival was accompanied by violence. An early witch trial in the New England colonies began when an Irish woman was caught praying in her native Gaelic before a statue of the Virgin Mary. She was accused of using a witch's tongue to condemn the good Protestants of the area.

Toward the end of the nineteenth century, Boston newspapers frequently ran ads such as: "*Wanted.* A Cook or a Chambermaid. They must be American, Scotch, Swiss, or Africans—no Irish." "*Wanted.* A woman well qualified to take charge of the cooking and washing of a family—any one but a Catholic who can come well recommended may call." While the second advertisement did not obviously exclude the Irish, all of the Irish immigrants were Catholic.

The Irish were different in another way—they lacked access to art and education. They might be highly intelligent, but they were not exposed to "culture." They entertained themselves by playing hard after working hard—drinking, dancing, and brawling. While the modern equivalent of the nineteenth-century immigrant was often far better educated, a man like Lafferty was quite similar to those early Irish. He was barely literate, a heavy drinker, and bawdy in his enjoyment of entertainment.

At the end of the nineteenth century and start of the twentieth, the Irish were relegated to the most menial jobs available, frequently working for city government. They collected the trash, cleaned the streets (remember, that this was in the days when horses were the major form of transportation, and horses relieved themselves wherever they might be), fought the fires, and policed the city. The "good people" of a community did not want to dirty themselves with such jobs. They lived in large homes, frequently commuting into the city, and they wanted the Irish to ensure that everything would run smoothly for them.

The leaders among the Irish quickly learned that their power came from the work they dominated. While they would never be socially acceptable to the elite, they could extort money and gain a higher standard of living for their families. All they had to do was go on strike. By not doing the jobs no one else wanted, the Irish won concessions that enabled many of them to obtain a far better standard of living for their children and grandchildren.

Later, among Irish union members, the extortion took a different form. For example, in some cities the Irish glass workers' leaders would ride down a business district, breaking windows with bricks, to ensure work for their members. If the business owners paid a fee to the union leaders—a fee that rarely, if ever, ended up anywhere but in the leaders' pockets—the windows were not broken.

There were payoffs on both sides. Irish political bosses assured those who would work with them that the voters would turn out on election day. Men frequently went from precinct to precinct, voting twenty and thirty times each before the polls closed. So civic-minded were the Irish that even the dead voted, or at least the names of men long laid to rest appeared on the records as having cast their ballots at least once.

Votes also could be bought. When John "Honeyfitz" Fitzgerald became the first Irish Catholic mayor of Boston, he campaigned in part by handing out cigars to every man who turned out to vote. Each cigar was wrapped in a dollar bill, and the men who had the good sense to vote frequently for Honeyfitz were well paid for their efforts.

In the end, status among these early Irish immigrants and their children came from their standing with the social elite. An industrialist did not respect a city mayor. But the industrialist needed the city services the mayor and/or his political party bosses controlled, so the industrialist would wine and dine him. Ironically, being a servant enabled you to walk through the front door of many a mansion. And if you were good at your job, you would be "courted" to accept a new position from men who otherwise would want nothing to do with you.

Bernard Lafferty was a man who seemed to want to achieve self-esteem through his relationship with the social elite. Barely able to read or write, to some people, he was from that worst of all worlds—a hard-drinking, Irish immigrant servant. The fact that he was highly intelligent despite lacking an education and was delightfully affable when sober meant nothing. His sense of self-worth seemed to come from the people for whom he worked, and in Doris Duke he had achieved a status almost impossible with any other employer.

Just by answering the telephone each day, Bernard Lafferty was able to talk briefly to heads of state, major industrialists, movie stars, society leaders, and numerous other rich, powerful, and intellectual giants. True, he was only a conduit between them and Doris, the person to whom they wished to speak. True, he was treated as a servant by all, not an equal. But he was in the midst of a world to which almost no one has access, and the more he could solidify his importance, the greater his status.

There was nothing devious about such an attitude or action. It is possible that, at the time, all Bernard Lafferty wished to accomplish in life was to be Doris Duke's second in command. While the rich life was desirable by anyone's standards, money alone would never buy him the status of working for Doris Duke. As her butler he would have the status of a big-city mayor whose favor is constantly being sought. With the departure of Chandi Heffner as a "rival" at the same time that Doris was in declining health, the future looked very bright to him. But only as long as she lived. If she died, he would be penniless and unemployed. The rich, the powerful, and the wealthy would no longer speak to him.

There were other societal factors in play at this time as well. When Doris Duke died, the trustee of her estate would be in a position to appoint directors of the various foundations.

There is money involved in being a foundation director, the income usually depending on the size of the holdings. In Doris Duke's estate, a foundation director could receive a fee ranging somewhere between $10,000 and $20,000 *per week*. Yet ultimately the men who would become the focus of allegations of improper actions in handling her last days were not ones to whom income of this size was unfamiliar. One of them, Dr. Harry Glassman, a Beverly Hills plastic surgeon with an international reputation and income to match, was married to actress/entrepreneur Victoria Principal. Between them, they were accustomed to a lifestyle that far exceeded what a half-million to a million dollars a year could buy.

The reason for coveting a position on one of the trusts was quite simple—the social elite needed money from the trusts just as the old Boston socialite industrialists relied on sanitation workers to ensure their businesses ran smoothly.

Few people understand the ways in which charities, museums, and universities need money. The cost of acquisitions, staff, and maintenance for a museum often exceeds both its endowment income and the total of any admission charges. Universities have such high expenses that were they to attempt to break even based on student tuition, the cost per year would be prohibitive for all but the wealthiest in society. Worse, courses requiring extremely expensive equipment might be impossible to offer.

Foundations act as a bridge between the money earned through admission, tuition, endowment interest, and similar sources, and the true cost of operation. Gifts may range from a few thousand dollars to many millions of dollars each year. All are necessary, though obviously the more that is received, the more that can be accomplished.

Most foundations have directors who are extremely humble people, modestly paid, hardworking, and equipped with a background that allows them to make effective judgments within the parameters of whatever money they are administering. Most are also extremely ethical. For example, in researching for this book, the Kellogg Foundation was repeatedly cited by professional fund-raisers as an example of a organization with very strict guidelines for the staff. The foundation pays all travel, food, and other expenses. No gratuities of any kind can be accepted. Staff members must be scrupulously honest, or they will not be allowed to continue in their jobs.

By contrast, members of old-line families such as the Whitneys, Vanderbilts, and Astors sometimes talk about occasional trustees who are quite different from the Kellogg personnel. They are not individuals who want bribes—this is not a world where there are kickbacks for giving money. Rather, they want social access.

Followers of the society pages of major city newspapers frequently see mention of lavish parties held on oceangoing yachts, in the ballrooms of major hotels, or in museums or concert halls. One of the guests of honor will be a man or woman who is a trustee of a major foundation. That person may be photographed with the social elite of the community, the leading politicians, and business executives. In such cases, the trustee will be feted by people who otherwise might never talk with him or her.

For an insecure status seeker, the power that comes from position is more important than money, more important than the perquisites of the office. It is a chance to "be somebody" when before you might have perceived yourself as merely rich or renowned in the "wrong" social circles.

Every community has its status symbols. Sometimes this has to do with the church or synagogue to which one belongs. There can even be subsections of status, such as which pew a family occupies within a religious institution. One church group, for example, assigns pew locations based on a number of status factors, including donations. The family name is attached to the pew, and the closer to the altar the pew is located, the higher the status. Then, when the service is over, the church is emptied by rows, with the front-row families leaving first so that they will be seen and presumably honored by all.

In Beverly Hills, California, status is accomplished in many ways. The size and location of one's home are important, as is the car that is driven. But when someone is a service professional, money is second to the source of clientele. For example, a doctor who lives and works in Beverly Hills and treats the studio executive, the A-list stars, and the like is a very high-status person. By contrast, a doctor who lives and works in Beverly Hills but has a patient list of wealthy individuals from throughout the world may make far more money than the high-status doctor but will not be treated with the same reverence and respect if he or she does *not* treat the A-list residents.

With many lawyers, it is again the client list, not just the income, that is everything. But when someone is concerned with status, the driving force may not be money, may not be the things that money can buy. Rather it may be the chance to be treated as an equal or better by people held to be the elite in the society in which the person is traveling.

Bernard Lafferty wanted a servant's idea of prestige. He would soon encounter wealthy, well-educated, seemingly successful individuals who apparently wanted the type of prestige that comes from socializing with the East Coast society "establishment." They wanted to be welcomed at the front doors of the families whose children and grandchildren attended the same gatherings as Doris Duke, men and women who previously neither knew of nor cared about their existence.

In hindsight, there were those who came to see Doris Duke's gradual decline as playing into the worst insecurities and blind ambitions of men whose job it was to protect her. These critics believed that decisions may have been made for reasons other than Duke's best interests. A problem is that this *was* hindsight. It did not take into account the day-to-day pressures of handling an elderly, severely ill woman with an estate worth more than many major corporations. And so a mystery was created in ways that might otherwise not have happened.

# 15

# "Disoriented to Time and Place"

$\mathcal{D}$ORIS DUKE WAS determined to die better looking than she had lived. Not that she knew she was dying on April 16, 1992, when Dr. Harry Glassman gave her a face-lift, then altered her eyelids (bilateral lower blepharoplasty) and cheeks (bilateral malar augmentation) using Proplast implants. She was seventy-nine years old, and according to medical records, when she was admitted to the hospital with a fractured right hip two days later, she was anemic enough to need a blood transfusion prior to surgery. She also was severely malnourished and had heart disease. When she was discharged on May 17, her mind was confused enough that she needed both written and oral instructions in how to handle the medication prescribed for her.[1]

As Colin Shanley remembered the incidents, "Dr. Glassman performed a face-lift on Miss Duke in his office on April 16, 1992. I drove her to Dr. Glassman's office for that procedure. We left the house at approximately 11:30 in the morning. There were no visitors at the house that morning. Miss Duke and Lafferty said the surgery would last about an hour and one-half. In fact, Miss Duke did not leave Dr. Glassman's office until late that evening. I carried her to the car with Madelyn, her nurse, and Lafferty. Her head was wrapped completely in bandages. I drove her home, where she was cared for by Madelyn.

"Shortly thereafter, as Miss Duke was recuperating at home, she had what one of the nurses, Madelyn, described as a drug-induced 'psychotic episode,' or 'hallucination.' This occurred in the evening. Madelyn went to Miss Duke's room, where she gave Miss Duke her medication. A short while later, when Madelyn was in the kitchen, we heard a crash. Miss Duke apparently had climbed out of bed. She was found on the floor. She had broken her hip."[2]

Had Doris Duke been of average means and of no interest to the press, her life might have been prolonged for years. Everyone who was close to her knew that she abused alcohol enough probably to qualify as an alcoholic and enjoyed recreational drugs with some frequency. She was also rich enough that extensive medication was routinely prescribed for her so that she would have no discomfort. Rich meant being pain-free, even if the freedom from the mildest pain might lead to an isolated existence and premature death.

Under the best of circumstances, the ability to prescribe multiple medications is part art form, part science. Medicines theoretically relieve a symptom (aspirin used for headache, inflammation of the joints, and the like), correct a biochemical imbalance (lithium salts for manic-depressive illness), or help treat an ongoing, perhaps life-threatening problem (beta blockers for certain types of chronic heart conditions). On a one-to-one basis—one problem, one drug—the science of pharmacology is fairly exact. However, when more than one drug is being used routinely, problems can arise. The patient's body chemistry combined with the chemical interaction of two or more drugs in the bloodstream can result in a seemingly unrelated, perhaps life-threatening problem in a part of the body unrelated to the area being treated. The medication becomes a potentially greater danger than any of the original conditions being treated.

In the last few years, pharmacy experts have been studying these crossover effects and helping doctors find safer alternatives when possible. Certainly this knowledge was available to the physicians treating Doris Duke. However, it was still so new that many established doctors were not aware of the concerns or the expensive, regularly updated reports to which pharmacists can subscribe. Instead, most relied on the *Physicians' Desk Reference* (*PDR*), which is far less thorough, if they consulted anything.

There was no indication in Doris Duke's medical records that the interactive effects of the many medications with which she was being treated were being analyzed at the time. In the years immediately prior to Duke's death, pharmaceutical experts learned that two or more seemingly harmless drugs could combine to create complications masked because of their location. For example, someone taking a prescription headache medication and a beta blocker for his or her heart condition might complain of an extremely painful foot condition. In the past, with a hypothetical case like this, doctors would also treat the foot, probably with still more drugs. But by the time Doris Duke was dying, it was known that the interaction of two or more drugs with the human body could lead to seemingly unrelated complications. There is no indication that any of the physicians treating her were knowledgeable enough in this area of human biochemistry to know to seek an expert's opinion of what the combinations of medications were doing to her. Apparently no medically and pharmaceutically skilled, objective third party was ever consulted on this issue prior to having Doris Duke sign papers drastically altering her previous wills.

On any given day, Doris Duke received a combination of essential medications, vitamins to counteract her malnutrition, and other drugs, such as tranquilizers, which were given for comfort, not for health. In many instances knowledge of the number of drugs is limited at best because Dr. Charles Kivowitz, the Beverly Hills physician whose internal medicine practice has a subspecialty of cardiovascular disease and who was her primary care provider in 1992 and 1993, refused to keep complete notes about Doris's full history. The hospital records show staff administered medication as they should. But Kivowitz avoided documenting her history of alcohol use and recreational drugs, enemas, laxatives, and the like that were a part of her lifestyle prior to admission. He said, "The only notes I made would be notes in the admission history and physical. I recall also other information regarding a rather extensive history of medication taking, including the extensive use of diazepam-type tranquilizers [like Valium], including the use of assorted stimulants, including the extensive—extensive use of alcohol. But, to the extent that I had any other notes or . . .

"I don't think I had any other notes . . ."[3]

The reason why Dr. Kivowitz did not keep extensive notes seems valid. Cedars-Sinai Medical Center is the Beverly Hills hospital of choice for the rich and the famous. It is not unusual to see television crews with satellite uplink vans parked in the hospital lot or on the grounds outside. News helicopters often can be heard slowly circling overhead. And reporters constantly dog the steps of the public relations staff whenever a celebrity is staying there. Every effort is made to protect the patients, including special security arrangements. But lower-level staff members frequently are offered large sums of money as bribes, and though leaks are not common, the possibility constantly exists.

Dr. Kivowitz was apparently thinking of this, for he explained, "Miss Duke is a celebrated person, was a celebrated person, and medical records at Cedars-Sinai Hospital have been known to show up in places like *The National Enquirer*. So any information that I had that might in any way be detrimental to her image as a person, I would not include in the medical record." And among such omissions was her heavy use of alcohol, even though many prescriptions come with warnings that they must not be used with any alcoholic beverage. The hospital records lacked complete prior history information concerning her alcohol and drug use.[4]

Whether or not the decision not to include everything in the medical records was a mistake is uncertain. What is clear is that it was one of a number of acts taken for the perceived good of Doris Duke that may have contributed to her increasing decline.

The April treatment was a lucrative one for Dr. Kivowitz. Although she was only one of several patients he saw that month, and though he kept no notes concerning the time he spent on her case, he decided to charge her $50,000 for his services alone.

Why such a high fee? "It was essentially arbitrary. I had put in a great deal of time and effort. I had a very successful outcome, and I felt that this was a deserving fee, if in fact a high fee, for the services performed."[5] He estimated the time as "probably in excess of 100 hours," or about two-and-a-half weeks of normal work. At such a billing rate for all his patients, his income would have been $80,000 for the *month*.

Doris Duke had not been swimming or otherwise exercising prior to her face-lift, and by the time she left the hospital the second time, she was walking with a cane. She had constant knee pain and was told that she might need knee replacement surgery.

But the biggest problem of all following her recovery from the fall that occurred two days after the cosmetic surgery seemed to be the fact that she was constantly malnourished. She had to be admitted to Cedars-Sinai hospital on July 7, 1992, because her body, now shrunken to approximately five foot eleven inches, weighed less than 100 pounds, more than 55 pounds less than what was considered optimum for her height.

There would be other hospitalizations, including August 4 and September 9, by which time she was down to 96 pounds. She was still anemic, and among other statements, it was noted that she had "hypertrophic cardiomyopathy with atrial fibrillation and mitral valve insufficiency." Despite all this, she underwent replacement of both knees on January 21, 1993, then was admitted to Cedars-Sinai Medical Center on February 25 "in a state of extreme dehydration and malnutrition," according to Dr. Charles Kivowitz.

Doris was given even more medication, thus increasing the potential for interaction as well as negative side effects. She received eighteen different pharmaceuticals and vitamins on February 25[6] and twenty-two the following day.[7] Another half dozen were on the list by February 28.[8]

Obviously the medical staff deemed the volume and variety of medications necessary, but the risks of the different drugs varied. Sometimes there was a risk of an adverse reaction, such as with the tranquilizer Valium; some people become *more* anxious and agitated on it than they were before treatment. The cumulative effect of the different medications could be problematic as well. Each person is different, but a hospitalized patient on a great deal of medication often does not have the good judgment that he or she will show prior to entering the hospital.

From Doris Duke's medical records:

> 2/26/93—"drowsy . . . apathetic . . . unsteady." "patient forgetful at times."
> 2/27/93—"remains drowsy . . . ate 50% of lunch." "frequent reminding necessary," "forgets short memory information and recent information"[9]

William "Bill" Doyle, Jr., was a partner in the law firm of Katten Muchin & Zavis (KMZ), based in the firm's Chicago office. Doyle was the former co-chairperson of the law firm's Tax and Estate Planning Department. He was also an instructor of advanced estate planning courses for practicing attorneys seeking to better educate themselves in that field. In an affidavit for the probate proceeding he stated:

"On the evening of Tuesday, March 2, 1993, I received a telephone call at home from Alan Croll, a partner in KMZ's Los Angeles office, advising me that we might be asked to represent an elderly woman of immense wealth with respect to her estate plan. Mr. Croll did not give me her name at that time, saying only that she was hospitalized and wanted to meet with a trusts and estates lawyer to discuss her affairs. He said that one of her physicians [Dr. Harry Glassman, a tennis partner of Croll's] had recommended him, but because Mr. Croll's specialty is not estate planning, he called me to ask if I would assist him. Mr. Croll said that he did not know if the woman would take her physician up on his recommendation, but stated that he would get back to me if he heard anything further."[10]

> Nurse's Notes 3/1/93—"drowsy" "Maximum assist" "communication ability impaired." "noncommunicative" "depressed"
> Doctor's Notes 3/2/93—"neurology . . . seen for fluctuating confusion, general weakness and dysphagia" [difficulty swallowing, not to be confused with "dysphasia, which would imply more severe communication problems] . . . oriented X3."
> "metabolic/toxic encephalopathy [brain disease] *aggravated by Haldol/Reglan* [emphasis added], recommend MRI brain . . ."
> Nurse's Notes—"drowsy" "apathetic" "depressed" "needs teaching" "oriented to place, person, time" "able to answer questions . . . simple one-two word answers."[11]

Doyle continued: "The next evening, Wednesday, March 3, 1993, Mr. Croll called again. He identified the woman he previously told me about as Doris Duke. Mr. Croll said that he had spoken again with the physician, Dr. Harry Glassman, who had spoken with Miss Duke and that she said she would like to meet with us the following day. Mr. Croll warned me that he had been told by Dr. Glassman that Miss Duke had an imperious style and that the trip to Los Angeles might be for nothing if she did not like the way we looked, the way we answered her questions, etc. He also told me that Miss Duke was 80 years old, not married, did not have any natural children, and was estranged from a daughter, Chandi Heffner, whom she had adopted as an adult five years before.

"Mr. Croll said that it was Dr. Glassman's understanding that Miss Duke wanted to disinherit Ms. Heffner. Mr. Croll also advised me that Dr. Glassman was familiar with her medical situation and that although she was ill and hospitalized, she was competent and very much in control of her affairs . . ."

Doctor's Notes 3/3/93—"Neurology . . . MRI moderate to severe atrophy and small vessel ischemic white matter disease . . ."
"Impression . . . Underlying Organic Brain Syndrome (OBS), vascular"
Nurse's Notes 3/3/93—"Ate well without difficulty, in good spirits."[12]

According to William Doyle, Jr., he traveled to Los Angeles on Thursday, March 4, 1993, meeting with both Croll and Dr. Glassman. Then the three men went to Cedars-Sinai Medical Center. "When we reached Miss Duke's room at the hospital, Dr. Glassman left us in the hallway and went in to speak with Miss Duke. After a few moments, the nurses left Miss Duke's room, and Mr. Croll and I were invited in to meet Miss Duke. Miss Duke was sitting up in bed and smiled as she greeted us. Mr. Lafferty was also in the room."

Dr. Glassman handled the introductions, and according to Doyle, the conversation moved to her estate, her limited family, and Doris Duke's concerns about Chandi Heffner. "During that first meeting on Thursday, March 4, which lasted approximately two hours, Miss Duke repeatedly stated her strong desire to have Irwin Bloom, her accountant, removed from his responsibilities. She stated that while she believed he was a good accountant, she felt that he thought he was running her various estates and her financial affairs. Miss Duke said that Mr. Bloom was mistaken in that regard because *she* [emphasis in the original affidavit] was in charge of things and Mr. Bloom simply worked for her." Note: According to the nurse's notes for the day, Doris was "Drowsy," "needs teaching," and was "extremely sleepy."[13]

Doyle continued, "Miss Duke also told me that Dr. Demopoulos told her that she had not been properly advised when she adopted Ms. Heffner, and accordingly, that she should hire new lawyers to handle her affairs. She said that Dr. Demopoulos suggested she use the Los Angeles law firm of Howarth & Smith to oversee her legal affairs, including seeing to it that Ms. Heffner was disinherited."

Doyle alleged that he had been told by Doris Duke that a few months after working with Howarth & Smith, her former accountant felt she should make yet another change. The new firm was that of William Zabel, a New York trusts and estates attorney. When she terminated her relationship with Bloom, she allegedly wanted also to end her relationship with the firm he recommended.

Attorney Doyle explained that Doris Duke went into rather extensive detail concerning her properties, her philanthropic interests, and her previous wills. "After meeting for an hour and a half to two hours, we decided to take a break. As I recall, the nurses or a therapist wanted to spend some time with Miss Duke. At that point, Miss Duke handed me two documents which she had on her lap or on the hospital tray table throughout the discussion. She said it was her will and a codicil and that she wanted me to review them during the break and then come back and resume our meeting with her in a half hour or 45 minutes.

"Mr. Lafferty stayed with Miss Duke. Dr. Glassman had to leave. . . ."

From Nurse's Notes 3/4/93—"New orders given and noted, *patient's chart removed from cart and placed behind desk, hidden*" [Emphasis added.] There was also a notation that twenty-three medications were given that day, although neither Haldol nor Reglan were on the list.[14]

Was the removal of the medical chart on the fourth of March significant? Philip Zakowski, M.D., a consultant on the infectious disease case of Doris Duke (listed as Norma Jane in the records to hide them from prying reporters), wrote a report of his examination on March 4. He stated, in part: "At this point in time, the patient is relatively emaciated and wasted with an indolent history of Leukocytosis," *"She reportedly has had some declining mental status for the last week."* [Emphasis added.][15] That fact alone might cause someone concerned with Doris Duke's best wishes to question the meeting with the lawyers.

The disappearing/reappearing chart is an enigma. The doctor's consult notes on Doris Duke's decline were not removed, and they raise enough questions about the appropriateness of Duke being encouraged at this time to sign a new will to have concerned investigators looking into her eventual death. Yet there really seems no reason for anyone to think the chart's handling was critical. As questionable as the timing for signing the will may have been, the chart's presence or disappearance seems a minor concern.

———————— ❦ ————————

ATTORNEY DOYLE RETURNED to Doris's room and explained that he would have to review all documents, including her father's trusts, in order to see what could be done about Chandi Heffner's inheritance. He and Croll were alone with her, Lafferty and the medical staff staying out of the room. She said that she wanted to make all changes before she had a gastrostomy tube inserted in her stomach the following week.

Doyle continued: "The next day, Friday, March 5, 1993 I further reviewed the documents Miss Duke had given to me. . . . Based on my lengthy discussions with Miss Duke the day before, I was sure that she was mentally competent to execute a codicil to her will."

Doyle also had a meeting that afternoon with Doris Duke, the first time her chart is at all positive. It states that she is alert, oriented, and active. The twenty-three medications remain in effect.

Doyle continued with his explanation in the affidavit, saying "I also questioned the appropriateness of the $250,000 limit on Mr. Inman and Mr. Lafferty's executors' commissions given the substantial work I envisioned for the executors of her immense estate, particularly in light of the potential that a will contest might be brought by Ms. Heffner. Miss Duke agreed that $250,000 limitation was too low."

On March 6 and 7 there were other meetings. "In general, Miss Duke said she still wanted the bulk of her estate to go to charity as set out in her existing November 4, 1991 will, and that the only changes she wished to make related to certain individual bequests, the executors, and she wanted to strengthen the provision in her will relating to Ms. Heffner to make certain she could not take anything from her estate. . . . With respect to Bernard Lafferty, Miss Duke told me she wanted him to be well taken care of. Miss Duke and I discussed the bequest of $350,000 to Mr. Inman, and she said that she wanted Mr. Lafferty to receive more than Mr. Inman. After some thought she directed me to provide Mr. Lafferty with $500,000 annually for life from a fund that would revert to her charitable foundation upon his death.

"With respect to the executors who would be responsible for administering her estate, Miss Duke said she wanted Mr. Lafferty in control, along with a bank. . . .

"As to the bank which was to serve with Mr. Lafferty as co-executor, Miss Duke said she did not want to name Chemical Bank because of its ties to Mr. Bloom. After discussing various alternatives, she said that she would leave that decision to Mr. Lafferty, although at my suggestion she agreed to name U.S. Trust Company of New York as the corporate co-executor in default of a contrary selection by Mr. Lafferty.

"Miss Duke decided the compensation of her executors by reviewing the following compensation provisions which appeared in her November 4, 1991 will. She said that the $7.5 million limit on fees for the bank should continue to apply, although she felt that since Mr. Lafferty would be less involved in the tax and financial aspects of the administration of the estate than Mr. Bloom would have been, she felt that Mr. Lafferty should only receive $5 million, rather than the $7.5 million she had provided for Mr. Bloom in the November 4, 1991 will." She also decided to give Lafferty an additional $500,000 for life, according to Doyle.[16]

Nurse's Notes for 3/7/93—"Dr. Glassman visiting—patient alert and oriented, complains of fatigue and dozed off."[17]

Chef Colin Shanley disagreed with the attorney's evaluation of Doris Duke by the time Doyle was preparing the codicil to her will. As he recalls, "From late 1992 until her death, Miss Duke's physical and mental condition declined rapidly. . . ."

Shanley continued, "During the February 1993 trip to Hawaii, I observed that Miss Duke's mental deterioration had progressed. She did not know where she was or what day it was. On a rare moment, she would seem to be in control of her faculties, but then minutes later, she would return to her incoherent state.

"Miss Duke returned to California in late February 1993, when she was hospitalized at Cedars-Sinai. She was in terrible condition when she arrived at the hospital. She was very weak and completely disoriented as to time and place.

"Miss Duke was hospitalized for the last few days of February, the entire month of March, and several weeks in April 1993. During that hospitalization, Miss Duke was quite disoriented. She did not recognize many of her employees and others around her. She insisted that she could do things that had become physically impossible. For example, she said she could walk and use the toilet, when in fact, she could not get out of bed. She had to be told on many occasions that she was in the hospital. She had to be reminded that she had been operated on a few months earlier, that she had a feeding tube and the like.

"Lafferty told me, in early March, that Miss Duke had suffered a stroke.

"On many occasions in March and April, Miss Duke did not know she was in a luxury suite at a hospital. She thought she was in an apartment in New York. She would announce that she was in Brooklyn. (Indeed, when Miss Duke was having a particularly bad day, the shorthand phrase used by the nurses, doctors, and Lafferty was 'She's gone to Brooklyn again.') Miss Duke made repeated statements about what she apparently believed to be her Brooklyn 'apartment.' She complained that the neighbors were too noisy. She said the plumbing in the building was not good.

"At times, Miss Duke could give the impression of being alert when in fact she was confused and disoriented. Lafferty often devoted entire days to coaching and preparing Miss Duke for a short meeting, so that she would give the impression of being alert and competent. He would drill her on the facts that were relevant to an upcoming visit and would rehearse with her.

"Often, when Miss Duke had visitors, she would not say anything, but would simply look around the room as if she understood what was happening around her. Moments later, she would make some statement that would indicate that she did not know what was happening."

Although much of what Shanley says is readily corroborated in the medical notes and the statements of others, it must be noted that he, like several of the staff members, was named in an earlier will. The changes being brought by William Doyle and KMZ would benefit Lafferty as well as Shanley and the others. The fact that, through his attorney, Shanley challenged the later will at the time he made the statement adds to his credibility, since the outcome would reduce what he received. In addition, the medical records appear to corroborate too much regarding her daily fluctuations of orientation to dismiss his statements. However, all facts must be weighed when trying to understand what was happening among the men and women who would be closely associated with Doris Duke's financial planning and care from the first will change through to her untimely death.

———— ⋅❧⋅ ————

THE NEW CODICIL for the will was signed on March 8, 1993, a day on which the nursing notes give no information about Doris Duke's mental capabilities. The records do say that her "appetite remains poor," though her "spirits are up" and she "needs teaching."[18] However, in his law firm internal memorandum for that date Doyle states that he proceeded with the signing only after conferring with Dr. Kivowitz about his patient's mental and medical condition.

When the codicil was prepared, Bernard Lafferty was named executor for a maximum fee of $5 million. He was given the right to appoint a bank or trust company, although the one named was United States Trust Company of New York.

A statement meant to deny Chandi Heffner all money was added to the codicil: "As indicated in Article *SEVEN*, it is my intention that Chandi Heffner not be deemed to be my child for purposes of disposing of property under this my Will (or any Codicil thereto). Furthermore, it is not my intention, nor do I believe that it was ever my father's intention, that Chandi Heffner be deemed to be a child or lineal descendant of mine for purposes of disposing of the trust estate of the May 2, 1917 trust which my father established for my benefit or the Doris Duke Trust, dated December 11, 1924, which my father established for the benefit of me, certain other members of the Duke family and ultimately for charity." Yet the adoption was no longer contestable. New Jersey, unlike some other states that allow adult adoption, takes it as seriously as child adoption. Chandi could be disinherited from Doris's personal largesse, but she might forever be legally the lineal descendant under the law. Certainly Doyle knew, and according to his staements he advised Doris of the fact, that Chandi probably would contest the will. He wanted Doris to understand that there was a good chance Chandi would legally inherit a portion of the estate no matter what roadblocks Doris tried to create in her will.

The greatest question at the time the will was being changed was Doris Duke's mental condition on March 8, 1993. Even if her body was responding to treatment, her mind probably was affected by the twenty-five different medications she received that day, according to the medical chart.[19]

Far more controversial was a second codicil signing on March 14, just six days later. This mostly had to do with the establishment and operation of a number of her charitable foundations, as well as creating foundation structures that would be most effective for tax purposes. However, of greatest importance for what came next in the will were such changes as:

> I nominate and appoint Bernard Lafferty as Trustee of each trust created hereunder other than any wholly charitable trust held pursuant to the provisions of Article *EIGHT-A* of this Will. If Bernard Lafferty shall fail to qualify or cease to act as Trustee of any such trust hereunder and if he shall not have theretofore effectively appointed a successor Trustee, then I hereby nominate and appoint UNITED STATES TRUST COMPANY OF NEW YORK, New York, to serve as the sole Trustee of each such trust created hereunder.[20]

The nursing notes for March 14 have limited information concerning Doris Duke's mental state. She was described as "drowsy" and "agitated and angry during respiratory therapy."[21] Again, twenty-five medications are listed as being given on that day.

According to Doyle's affidavit, "On the afternoon of March 14, I met with Miss Duke at the hospital. Before meeting with her, however, Dr. Kivowitz explained to me, Mr. McCarthy and Mr. Croll that Miss Duke was experiencing some difficulties with her gastrostomy tube that day. I asked Dr. Kivowitz if there was any problem with having Miss Duke sign legal documents with witnesses and a notary. Dr. Kivowitz said that she was perfectly capable of attending to her business affairs and that we could go ahead after the medical personnel finished their work. Accordingly, at my request, Ann Bostich and Colin Shanley were called and asked to come to the hospital to attest to the new codicil. Pearl Rosenstein, the afternoon nurse, agreed to be the third attesting witness.

"While we were waiting for the witnesses, I was told that Miss Duke asked to see me and I went into her room. She and I met alone and I explained the technical reasons for the changes in the March 14, 1993 codicil, and asked if she wanted to sign it at that time. She said that she did."[22]

"In March 1993, I was asked to serve as a witness to a codicil that was being signed by Miss Duke," Ann Bostich, a minor beneficiary in an earlier will, would later state in an affidavit given on January 13, 1995, as part of the Probate Proceeding for the Will of Doris Duke.[23] "Lafferty told me that Miss Duke's doctors had told her to 'get her affairs in order.' Lafferty told me that she had suffered a stroke; he said that she was dying.

"When I arrived at Miss Duke's room, Makasiale [Nuku Makasiale, Doris's maid] and Alan Croll, Esq. [an attorney with KMZ & W], were waiting in the hallway. I entered the room where Lafferty and William Doyle, Esq. [another KMZ & W attorney], were waiting. Miss Duke's bed was raised so that she was in an upright position; she was not talking, moving, or even looking at anyone. Doyle asked Miss Duke some 'yes' or 'no' type questions, but Miss Duke's voice quavered and strained and was difficult to understand due to the strokes. I believe there were three witnesses, including me and Shanley. We were in the room for no more than 10 minutes. During that entire time period, Miss Duke did not look at anyone or speak to anyone with the exception of answering Doyle's three or four 'yes' or 'no' questions in a very shaky manner. He did not discuss the terms of the codicil with her or the nature and extent of her assets.

"Doyle gave Miss Duke the document which he wanted her to sign. Miss Duke appeared to start to sign the document, but Doyle stopped her. Doyle said 'let me put my briefcase on your lap.' Doyle then did so. He slid his own hand under her wrist. He propped her hand up with his hand. Doyle then pushed her hand along the page, guiding the hand [which held the pen]."

(Doyle later countered, "I am aware of Ann Bostich's . . . Affidavit, and the statements in paragrphs 33–35 of that affidavit to the effect that I guided Miss Duke's hand as she signed the codicil. That is not true. . . .")[24]

Bostich continued, "I don't believe Miss Duke was capable of understanding the process of re-doing and signing the codicil. Throughout her hospitalization, according to what I was told by Lafferty and Nuku, she was quite often disoriented and confused. She did not know who she was, where she was, or why she was there. Prior to her February stroke, Miss Duke at one point woke up and thought she was in Brooklyn. From that point on, when the household staff referred to her confusion or disorientation, we would say 'She's in Brooklyn.'

"After the codicil had been signed, I told Lafferty that *I would never agree that Miss Duke was of sound mind when she signed it.*" [Emphasis added.]

From the Second Codicil to Last Will and Testament of Doris Duke, March 14, 1993—Page 12:

Each of the undersigned, individually and severally being duly sworn, deposes and says:

The within Second Codicil was subscribed in our presence and sight at the end thereof by Doris Duke, the within-named Testatrix, on the 14 day of March, 1993, at Cedars-Sinai

Hospital, in the City and County of Los Angeles, State of California. . . .

. . . Said Testatrix was, at the time of so executing said Second Codicil, over the age of 18 years and, in the respective opinions of the undersigned, of sound mind, memory and understanding and not under any restraint or in any respect incompetent to make a codicil to her will.

The statement was signed by Colin Shanley, Pearl Rosenstein, and *Ann Bostich*. This does not mean that Bostich was being honest when she signed the codicil or that she understood the import of the statement. It does mean that one of her statements was false, either the one made at the time of the signing or later, when she gave her statement to the attorneys.

The conferences with Doris Duke continued. The two codicils were a stopgap measure, correcting alleged problems and supposedly assuring that her wishes would be carried out if she died before a new will could be prepared.

Then the final will was made ready, and as Doyle would later attest, "Shortly after noon, I met alone with Miss Duke to discuss the alternative funding factors. Miss Duke approved use of the 5% factor. Miss Duke and I discussed non-business matters while we waited for the witnesses to arrive. I told Miss Duke that I was planning a trip to Italy, and she made some recommendations on places to stay and things to see. Mr. McCarthy joined us at the tail end of our conversation, and I confirmed for him Miss Duke's decision on the 5% funding factors for the charitable remainder trusts. The will ceremony then proceeded. . . ."[25]

Consultant report for April 5, 1993, by Allan Metzger, M.D.— "The patient has a history of being admitted for progressive weakness on admission, decreased appetite, and fatigue. Intermittently she has reported to have been confused by the many people who work for her. . . .

". . . The patient has had an MRI of the brain which has revealed moderate cerebral atrophy which may be contributing to her *poor mentation* [emphasis added] and her toxic metabolic encephalopathy."

The actual medical chart allegedly had critical portions of the assessment left blank. Twenty-four different medications were listed as being given to Doris on that day.

On April 14, at 8 p.m., nurse's notes indicate the "patient forgetful and disoriented to time and place."[26] The next day Doris was discharged from the hospital, already making plans to begin her travels again. She was in need of skilled medical care, but her homes could be adapted to her needs, and care would be provided by professional in-home health care services. What she did not realize was that she would all too soon be cared for only in Falcon's Lair, the Beverly Hills mansion that she looked upon as the least desirable of her homes. What had once been a brief stopover point when traveling between her beloved Shangri-La and the equally beloved Duke Farms would become the only environment she would know until she died.

On December 21, 1994, Steven E. Hyman, M.D., director of Psychiatry Research at Massachusetts General Hospital, associate professor of psychiatry and neuroscience at Harvard Medical School, and researcher on the effects of pharmaceuticals and the mind for the National Institutes of Health, was asked to review Doris Duke's medical records during her stays at Cedars-Sinai Medical Center. Dr. Hyman had originally been retained by the attorneys for Irving Bloom, a fact that does not alter his expertise but must be noted since he did not enter the proceedings before the surrogate as a neutral party. His summation of the period during which Doris Duke was alleged by her attorney to have adequate mental capacity to prepare and sign a new will stated:
   "Overall, the notes give compelling evidence of the classic picture of delirium with waxing and waning levels of consciousness (from drowsiness to agitation), waxing and waning orientation to person, place, and time, and episodes of forgetfulness and confusion. This is not surprising given what we know of the patients [*sic*] health status. Based on the MRI, showing atrophy and other abnormalities, on the patient's age, and on her severe state of malnutrition and debilitation, she was in the very highest risk group for toxic-metabolic encephalopathy (delirium). When her irrational and

excessive regimen of psychoactive drugs is taken into account—
even limited to the prescribed drugs that we know about—a toxic-
metabolic encephalopathy (delirium) would be almost inevitable.
In this regard, the fact that she was permitted to drink champagne
in the hospital, as documented in one note in the record, suggests
cavalier treatment at best.

"The patient was also described in multiple places in the record
as severely depressed. I find it extraordinary that there is not a single adequate mental status examination in the hospital record. Was
this depressed, delirious patient seen by a psychiatrist during the
hospitalization? Was she seen by house staff? Was her mental status ever appropriately investigated or was it ignored? Within the
records only Dr. Braunstein's consultative notes seriously raised
questions about the roles of prescribed medications and abused
drugs in the etiology of Ms. Duke's abnormal mental status. Dr.
Wolfe, the pulmonary consultant, also expressed concern about
the sedatives and recommended tapering them. This was appropriate
given the well documented risk that oversedation creates for aspiration pneumonia. Unfortunately, a long-acting benzodiazepine drug,
diazepam, was actually added subsequent to these consultations.

"In summary the hospital record testifies with a great weight of
data that Ms. Duke suffered a serious toxic-metabolic encephalopathy (delirium) throughout her hospital stay, including the period during which she conferred with her attorneys and signed the
codicil and her new will. There are not adequate mental status ex-
aminations in the record to document her competence; remarkably
I do not find a single adequate test of attention, concentration, or
short-term memory in the record. The records we do have, however, leave it essentially impossible to imagine that Ms. Duke could
process the information needed to understand her affairs. It is important to note that the natural course of delirium is for symptoms
to wax and wane during the course of the day, but superficial improvements in alertness or orientation while patients pass from
drowsiness to agitation and back again are not accompanied by
normalization of cognitive function. The time course of substantial
cognitive improvement in severely ill 80 year old would be very
slow, and would have required, at a minimum, her detoxification

from sedatives and narcotics. Unfortunately for Ms. Duke, she remained on an irrational combination of psychoactive drugs throughout her hospitalization that prevented mental clearing and may well have initiated the delirium to begin with. Sedation must also be considered a prime suspect in her life-threatening aspiration pneumonia. The care provided by Dr. Kivowitz is well below any standard of practice, likely contributed to the patient's downhill medical course, and at best, reveals ignorance about the appropriate treatment of an elderly patient with diminished mental status. . . ."

⌘

WITH THE SIGNING of the April will, butler Bernard Lafferty stood to gain not only financially but in terms of prestige. He had enjoyed the power that a butler can experience when Doris Duke was still healthy enough to travel and lead an active social life. She had given him the authority to recruit, hire, and train some of the staff, so he was able to ensure their loyalty to himself almost as much as to the woman who paid their salaries. He was able routinely to converse, albeit superficially, with the rich, the famous, and the powerful. Occasionally he was photographed by the press when they covered the events Doris Duke attended. And he had the chance to live in homes greater than some of those experienced by royalty. So long as he gave the impression that he was constantly alert to her interests, he could continue as a trusted servant for what would hopefully be years to come.

With the change in the will, a situation existed that could lead outsiders to fantasize about the potential for Duke insiders to turn against Doris Duke. Some of the people with the greatest influence and power over Duke's life and health no longer had a financial incentive to be her advocate or to keep her alive. This was regardless of their professional and/or personal responsibilities to Duke. However, such thinking also overlooks the moral and ethical values and attitudes of those people, something few critics considered in the period immediately after her death.

Bernard Lafferty now would benefit financially far more by Doris Duke's death than he would by her continuing existence. Alive, he was classed as a servant. Dead, he would become the conduit for money from the charitable trusts. The man who once served the wine and the dinner would become the person who had to be wined, dined, and courted by those seeking foundation money. He would become an instant equal with the biggest names in philanthropy, if not in reality, at least in the way he was treated by people who previously saw him as a servant.

As an outsider, it would seem that William Doyle, Jr., and his law firm might have been remiss as Doris Duke's advocate since she had long made clear her standards for an executor for her funds. Certainly the advice made public did not match the well-reasoned ideas for an executor's background that she had long held in the past:

   i) The replacement [Executor] must be not less than 50 years of age, nor more than 70 years of age.
   ii) The replacement [Executor] must be a graduate of an accredited university or college.
   iii) The replacement [Executor] must have either banking, accounting, legal, financial or business experience, and
   iv) The replacement [Executor] must be a person of good moral character and standing in the community.

But did Doris Duke change her mind? Did she find that Lafferty and people like him had a native intelligence that made them valuable despite a lack of formal education? And did she prove this to her law firm's satisfaction even if she never set such an idea in written form? While some questioned Duke's decisions, William Doyle and his law firm were adamant that they were carrying out her recent wishes.

The law firm would receive set fees for its work while Doris was alive, a proper remuneration yet all the money it would receive from the heiress. However, when Doris Duke died, the fact that the firm represented the co-executors Bernard Lafferty and U.S. Trust meant that it would be generating large sums of money for a long time. One or two attorneys might work for a living Doris Duke. Several more would be able to participate in the handling of the estate, advising the executors, and otherwise benefiting when she died.

Only Doctors Kivowitz and Glassman would seemingly be losers. They made their money treating the living, not the dead.

Certainly this was the case with Charles Kivowitz. The fees he charged for Doris Duke's care seemed outrageous at the time compared to physicians doing the same type of work and still seem outrageous in hindsight. However, her death would cut off any future income.

Dr. Harry Glassman was possibly in a different category, even though the dead have no need for plastic surgery, especially if they were cremated. Dr. Glassman was richly rewarded by a gift from Doris Duke for his friendship, according to his statement. Rumors among former staff members indicated that he would be named a Doris Duke Foundation Trustee, a fact that, if true, would garner him the type of respect even his lucrative Beverly Hills practice and marriage to actress Victoria Principal had not brought.

Age, infirmity, and declining mental competence had caused Doris Duke to let down her guard. She signed a will that was unusual for her. She changed her mind about the appropriateness of an executor's background. She ensured that, with her death, some people who had lacked money and/or national prestige would suddenly achieve it in a manner that would otherwise have been impossible for them. The question that arose later was whether or not the people most responsible for her care in her declining days acted for or against her expressed wishes.

# 16

⚜

## *Oh What a Tangled Web We Weave . . .*

FROM NURSE'S NOTES 3/4/93—"New orders given and noted, *patient's chart removed from cart and placed behind desk, hidden."* [Emphasis added.][1]

From the Deposition of Charles Kivowitz, M.D., April 19, 1995:[2]

Question: Dr. Glassman was removing records from the hospital?

Answer: [Kivowitz] I don't believe that Dr. Glassman ever removed any record from the hospital.

Q. He called you and told you he did, didn't he?

A. No.

Q. Didn't you testify that Dr. Glassman called you and told you he took some records out and put them back?

A. He said he took them out of the chart and put them back.

Q. Do you have any explanation for why Ms. Duke's records were hidden?

A. None records [*sic*] of Ms. Duke were hidden.

Q. Did you ever see a notation of that in the records?

A. No.

MR. BARNOSKY: Objection.

In notation that the records were hidden?

MR. HOWARTH: Yes.

THE WITNESS: No, I've never seen any such notation.

From the Affidavit of Colin Shanley, January 13, 1995:[3]

"When Miss Duke was at Cedars-Sinai Hospital, I ran back and forth from the house to the hospital many times each day. On oc-

casion, I would take a break in lounges near her room. On one occasion in 1993, when Miss Duke was in the Respiratory Intensive
Care Unit, Lafferty and I had just returned from one of his shopping sprees. I went to the lounge and lay down on a couch.

"Shortly after I arrived, I heard Lafferty and Dr. Glassman talking in the lounge. (Even though they were at another seating
arrangement perhaps ten feet away, they apparently did not see me
as I was lying on the couch, concealed from their view.)

"Lafferty and Dr. Glassman began to have a heated conversation about some papers Dr. Glassman was holding. Dr. Glassman
said 'you told me to destroy them!' Lafferty began to hem and haw,
saying things like, 'well, I really don't know.'

"Dr. Glassman said 'I'm doing what you told me to do. Here are
the records you asked me to get for you.' Dr. Glassman said something to the effect that he had already destroyed some of them and
he now had the rest of them. Lafferty apparently did not want the
rest of them. Dr. Glassman said to Lafferty, 'why are you double
crossing me?' Dr. Glassman stated that he could not return the
records. It sounded like once the documents had been removed,
they could not be reinserted in the records.

"At about that point in the conversation, I got up from the
couch. Dr. Glassman started to shout at Lafferty, at which point
Lafferty pointed his finger at me and said 'you better not repeat
anything you've heard here. You are a dead man if you repeat anything.' I responded by saying 'I don't know what you're talking
about' and began to leave the room.

"Lafferty then said, 'don't leave, I want you to stand here and
witness this.' Dr. Glassman then abruptly left the room with papers
in his hand. Lafferty said, 'All right. I'm going to call Bill Doyle. I
want you to witness this phone call.'

"Lafferty then went to the pay phone and called Doyle, who apparently was at his home. (His decision to use a pay phone was unusual, because we both had cellular phones.) When Lafferty
reached Doyle, he began to discuss the removal of the records
without even discussing the background. From my observation of
Lafferty's part of the conversation, it appeared that Lafferty and
Doyle must have discussed the issue previously. Lafferty said to
Doyle: 'Everything is fine. Harry put the records back.' I knew that

what Lafferty had told Doyle was false, because Dr. Glassman had said that he had already destroyed some records and could not put the remaining records back.

"Lafferty then explained to me what had happened. He said that Dr. Glassman 'wanted to get rid of the records' from the dates that Miss Duke signed documents in the hospital, because they wouldn't look good in the future if people 'were going to start contesting her will.'

"Lafferty told me that Doyle 'didn't want any part of this.' Lafferty also told me that Doyle discussed Dr. Glassman and Alan Croll, Esq., with him. Mr. Doyle had told Lafferty 'to watch out' for Glassman and Croll, because 'they are just trying to trick you into their being indispensable to you.' He said 'don't be in a situation where you owe them anything or they have any goods on you.'

"Lafferty later told me that he believed that the records that had been removed included records that residents would have put in Miss Duke's files on the dates that she signed important documents. Lafferty told me that residents and others were 'writing stupid things' in Miss Duke's charts. Lafferty did not know about those charts until Dr. Glassman read them and told Lafferty about the comments. Lafferty said there were notations in the charts that she was disoriented, was not aware of her surroundings, and that sort of thing. He said these statements were in records for dates on which she executed critical documents, such as her April 5, 1993 will.

"In or about January 1994, Lafferty told me that he had directed that a $500,000 check be issued to Dr. Glassman. I was concerned about that payment because I suspected that it related to the conversation I had overheard in the lounge the previous summer."

From the statement of Harry Glassman (unsigned), May 4, 1995.[4]

"Doris urged me on many occasions to submit a bill to her for my services which I refused to do. I told her that I was a friend and that whatever I was doing for her was out of friendship. She and I exchanged gifts on birthdays and holidays. Several times she expressed her interest in giving me a special gift. I told her that it wasn't necessary.

"Several weeks before she died, during one of my visits to her home on Bella Drive, she asked me to sit at her bedside. She handed me a small pink stationery envelope. Inside was a check made payable to me in the amount of $500,000. When I opened it and saw the amount of her gift, I first protested that I could not accept it. She told me to please consider it a gesture of her appreciation and a gift from one friend to another. I accepted on that basis. I did not solicit her gift, and I was not expecting it. Although she was ill and exhausted at the time, she was alert and very much aware of what was going on."

The problem for everyone involved with Doris Duke's presumed last requests is that her new lawyer was seemingly too eager to get her to sign the revised will. Had William Doyle waited until she was on drastically reduced medication following her discharge from the hospital, probably no one would have questioned her ability to act. Instead, at any moment of each day during Doris Duke's hospitalization she might have been lucid and aware, or she might have been incapable of sound judgment. The chart and anecdotal evidence from witnesses indicate both conditions existed. The attorney certainly may have acted at a time when she was lucid and clearly in control of her actions. But there were enough times when the combined trauma of surgery, illness, and medication caused her to be out of control that it would have been more prudent for the attorneys to have waited until she was discharged from the hospital. Then, acting while she was recovering at home, they would have avoided any suspicion that they were taking advantage of a helpless old woman.

Did this mean that the last will did not represent her desires? Although those who have contested the validity of her will say that it is the product of greedy people seizing a window of opportunity when Doris was defenseless, there is no absolute proof of this contention. However, her failings were as much the result of the many years of medication, medical treatments, and the forced inactivity as they were the result of her stroke or other permanent disability. It is possible that she had changed her mind concerning her standards for an administrator of her estate, that the person's education in money management, business, and philanthropy no longer were critical to her. It is possible that she saw Bernard Lafferty, the semi-literate butler with a history of alcohol abuse, to be an ideal executor. It is possible that she wanted to make him wealthy and powerful beyond his greatest dreams. Certainly there is adequate anecdotal and photographic evidence that indicates they seemed to have a fondness for each other during her healthier days. It is also possible that she wanted the KMZ law firm and U.S. Trust to have major influence on her estate. But because men like Bill Doyle and Dr. Charles Kivowitz allowed the finalization of the will to be made when some objective, dispassionate professionals would consider Duke potentially mentally incapacitated has resulted in serious questions being raised. And when, in the weeks that followed that first discharge, decisions were made to gradually stop procedures ensuring the longest possible life, the men and women who may genuinely have been following Doris Duke's wishes created an environment later giving rise to suspicion and distrust. They allowed actions to transpire that created a cloud of suspicion that required serious, potentially career-threatening investigation. They should have had the patience to wait, since that might have led to the same will being accepted fully. Once Doris Duke was out of the hospital, her obviously better heatlh would have implied to the potential challengers that the new will truly was her intent. In the hospital, the changes and the signing seemed to some, in retrospect, to have been tainted by possible fraud.

For Dr. Harry Glassman, who declined through a spokesperson to be interviewed for this book, suspicion was raised following the acceptance of a $500,000 check. That check, which would be dated 10-4-93 and drawn on a new account from the United States Trust Company of New York,[5] was completely out of character for Duke. An examination of her income tax records for the years just prior to 1993 indicates that she did not give this type of personal gift. In fact, other than her secret philanthropy and occasional loans to friends, ranging from Dr. Rolando Atiga to Imelda Marcos, bequests of even a few thousand dollars were placed in the will so that they would be given following her death. Glassman was the exception to this arrangement, and since men and women far more important to Duke than the doctor would only be gifted in the will, that exception was out of character for Doris Duke during this period of her life.

By contrast, if Doris did not authorize the check, or if she was misled about the nature of it, there can be an implied logic to the gift's timing. By arranging for the issuance of the check, it could be alleged that Bernard Lafferty would gain the support of Dr. Glassman.

At this writing, nothing is 100 percent provable connecting any "hidden" or missing records to Dr. Glassman. There are no known witnesses, and the bulk of the evidence comes from allegedly overheard conversations and a nurse's notation about the "hiding" of the chart for reasons unknown. The $500,000 then has the appearance of a payoff, prior to the ultimate payoff of being named a Duke Foundation director. It certainly was not a payment for what would otherwise likely be the most expensive elective, nonessential cosmetic surgery on record. Yet Doris Duke could have changed, could have genuinely wanted to give such a gift in person and during her final days.

Dr. Glassman has thus been tainted in some people's minds because Doris Duke's attorneys did not wait for her to be weaned from her medication and returned to a more active life.

Doris Duke did both seek and achieve a more active life following her discharge, though the periods of illness were becoming more frequent. She needed surgery for removal of a blood clot (arterial embolectomy) on April 20, five days after leaving the hospital, but she was hospitalized only until April 22. Then, a week later, she resumed her travels, flying to Morristown, New Jersey, by private jet. A helicopter took her home to Somerville, where her fight for life was evident. The records indicated that at 3 A.M. the nurses had to deal with her wetting herself (incontinent of urine). Yet just three hours later, at 6:05 A.M., a nursing note indicates that she was "reading newspapers and conducting business with Bernard."

Doris Duke's mental abilities were no longer so impaired. She was in obvious command of her surroundings, and though she had trouble moving from her bed to the commode and frequently was incontinent, she was taking charge of her life again.

After staying in Somerville for a day, she had questions she wanted answered about her condition, according to the nurses' notes.[6] Reportedly, she was aware that her health had deteriorated, and she decided to return to California where she could talk with the doctors who had been treating her.

As Doris grew stronger, she felt comfortable returning to her old habits, many of which were self-destructive. By May, stronger than she had been in months, she began using Falcon's Lair as she had done in the past, just as a stopover point where she could adjust to jet lag before moving on.

This time her destination was Shangri-La, where she traveled on May 5, once again going swimming in her pool. The nursing notes indicate that she required assistance in the water, but the fact that she made the effort showed how she was fighting for a better quality of life and was determined to continue the rituals of years past. The only problems she was exhibiting were those of alcohol and Valium abuse, which had been part of her lifestyle when she was physically healthier.

Lafferty also seems to have returned to heavy drinking. On the weekend of May 8, he allegedly was too drunk to handle his chores effectively,[7] a situation apparently known to Dr. Kivowitz.

Over time, Lafferty's role in the drama that was being played out concerning changing the disposition of Doris Duke's estate would be questioned. Some of the hospital staff viewed him as intensely loyal to Doris, staying in or near her room throughout her hospitalizations. But Colin Shanley challenged that idea. He stated, "Lafferty claims that he cared so much for Miss Duke that he slept at the foot of Miss Duke's bed when she was ill. That is a sham. In fact, every night, Lafferty would leave Miss Duke's hospital room, or her bedroom at home, to go to commercial sex establishments, such as bars, bathhouses and porn shops. I know, because he insisted that I drive him to such establishments. These trips occurred wherever Lafferty was: in New York, New Jersey, Newport, Honolulu, or Los Angeles. In Los Angeles alone, Lafferty made hundreds of trips to places such as the 'Bunkhouse,' the 'Spa,' and the 'Melrose.' He would spend large amounts of money at each of these establishments and maintained memberships there. He would frequent such establishments from 9:00 at night until 1:00 in the morning or later. When Miss Duke was hospitalized, he would then return to the hospital, where he would sleep for four or five hours. When she was at her homes, he would return there in the early morning hours.

"Lafferty always tried to be back near Miss Duke's room in the early morning. He slept in Miss Duke's hospital room because he wanted the doctors to believe that he was entirely devoted to her care and wanted to keep control over the medical situation."

Although the statement from Shanley's deposition is negative, there is no indication that Lafferty created problems for Doris Duke. He was present when needed, and although he may have misled others to ingratiate himself further, there was nothing essentially sinister about such actions. He was not endangering her recovery, which was progressing better than might have been expected, given her years of drug, alcohol, and laxative abuse.

Doris flew to New Jersey on June 2, and though she needed assistance because her legs were no longer strong enough to hold her upright, she had regained the ability to control her bladder and bowels. The diarrhea that had plagued her was over, and she may have helped herself further by stopping the use of laxatives.

Whether the change was a fluke or whether it was a plateau before a natural deterioration is unknown. All that is certain is that when she returned to California on June 9, she began to decline. A medical note by Nurse Pearl Rosenstein on June 14 read "forgetful—conversing with Bernard—has forgotten all activities taken place today—i.e. attorneys & Business matters." The decline continued through the first part of July. She was confused about events happening around her and frequently forgetful. Yet despite this she had surgery on her left knee on July 9. The surgery, approved by Doris, who was no longer able to think clearly, Bernard Lafferty, and Dr. Kivowitz, put her at higher than normal risk for a stroke. Between her past medical history and the fact that she was not taking anticoagulants while she was in the hospital, the decision, at least in hindsight, was a poor one. However, having the knee surgery would help her walk again, giving her both a physical and psychological boost.

Doris returned home in what has been described as an "agitated state" on July 13, then had a stroke two days later. She immediately lost sight in her left eye. The following day she vomited and inhaled some vomit into her lungs, which forced an emergency room visit to Cedars-Sinai. She was treated, then placed on a respirator in the intensive care unit. She would not leave the hospital again for more than two months, due to difficulty breathing without special support, infections, and other problems. When she recovered sufficiently to return home, it was to a bedroom set up for intensive medical care.

Controversy and varied interpretations have surrounded exactly what happened between the return home and Doris Duke's death the following month. Much of the information, which will be discussed in later chapters, was learned after the fact and could not always be fully documented. What matters is that if Doris Duke was of sound mind, the nurses' notes indicate that she suspected she was becoming the victim of foul play. If she was delusional, then the lawyers' claims that she understood their discussions and paperwork may have been unduly optimistic. Or she may have been drifting between lucidity and a delusional state, raising a question about her condition during all her conversations.

For example, on September 20, Doris Duke is reportedly "glad to be home," "in no distress," breathing normally ("respirations . . . even . . . unlabored"), and tolerating food that had previously been a problem for her. Assuming she is as healthy as this seems to indicate, there is a troubling note on the chart. It reads that Doris Duke "states she's afraid of being murdered."

The chart shows only continued improvement with her lungs clear and healthy sounding, and Doris being "awake, alert, conversive & pleasant" on September 22. She was in no pain, was taking food easily and working well with the physical therapist. Then, on September 24, the notes again raise a concern about those around her. They state that her "breath sounds clear," that she "denies pain," that "respiratory therapy completed, tolerated well," and that she "wanted to make telephone calls." But also in the notes is the statement for the same day: "patient agitated, and angry, accusing Bernard of her being ill."

The admittedly arguable fact of the medical charts is that each day Doris Duke seemed to be rallying, both mentally and physically. She was almost certainly terminally ill, but the timing for her impending death might possibly have been extended. Doctors agree that though they can tell when the body is failing, there is generally no way to say accurately when a patient will die. This is why there are frequent anecdotes of patients being given the last rites, then dancing at their children's weddings months later. They die from the condition they had when first diagnosed, but not when the doctor expected them to die.

As for Doris, all that can be determined is that, for September 27 when the lawyers stopped by to question her ("patient pleasant & slightly confused at times, but cooperative"), everything pointed to Doris's health being restored. The notes stress "patient stronger," "more alert," "denies any pain," "patient awake, talkative," "responds to questions appropriately," "denies pain," "patient very cooperative," "respiration non-labored," "breath sounds clear," "states she is pain free and comfortable," "alert, in pleasant mood," "more alert," "patient up in cardiac chair."

Day after day the notes reached similar conclusions. Duke was stronger, healthier, more animated, and experiencing no pain. She also wanted to leave Falcon's Lair.

Doris Duke spent her life traveling the world. If she had to be limited to one home, her preference would have been either Shangri-La or Duke Farms. Yet there she was in Falcon's Lair, and for Doris, now more alert, healthier, and able to move about with whatever assistance was required, it was time to leave.

On October 6, 1993, a pain-free Doris was noted as "asking Bernard to take her out in the car." This was quite realistic, even if she needed a private ambulance. She was the richest woman in the world, and if she chose to spend a million dollars each week for the next several years allowing herself to have the support necessary to provide a bit of freedom, it would be less than the interest she would earn from a portion of her holdings.

But Bernard Lafferty refused to take Doris Duke for the drive she requested. The note reads "angry mostly toward Bernard, but cooperative with me [one of the nurses, unidentified] in nursing procedures."

And on October 7, Doris, though "responsive and cooperative" with the nursing staff, was "talking, asking to leave the house." Finally, at 3 P.M., she was fed up. "Patient awake, angry, wants to go to either Cedars Sinai Med., or Duke University Hospital."

For the first time a decision is made concerning her medical care that, in hindsight, has raised questions much like the gift to Dr. Glassman. Doris is suddenly restrained through chemistry. At 3:55 P.M., "Valium given intravenously." At 4:30, outraged by her treatment, "patient remains awake, angry, and agitated 'wants to go.'" Instead, Dr. Kivowitz arrived and Doris was given 25 milligrams of Demerol. The next note reads "medications effective as patient becoming drowsy, Demerol intramuscular also." She awakens at 8:30 that evening and is given another 50 milligrams. Then the drugs were increased so she received 2 milligrams of Haldol every six hours around the clock, 2.5 milligrams of Valium every three hours around the clock, and 50 milligrams of Demerol around the clock.

Based on later testimony, Dr. Kivowitz justified his actions on his conclusion that Doris had begun to fail. He wanted her comfortable, and this meant, to him, relieving her agitation and keeping her more heavily tranquilized and sedated.

Later, some former staff members were angry. They wondered why, since Doris was dying anyway, they didn't just rent her a limousine, ambulance, or other vehicle in which they could lay her by windows and let her go out. She could afford anything she wanted. Why not let her have the pleasure of seeing more of the world, even if she died during the outing? Yet they never talked with Doris about such a possibility. Indeed, they knew little about anything taking place until well after her death. They also did not consider the doctor's position that the shock of attempting to move her could have killed her far sooner than when she did pass on.

On October 8, Dr. Kivowitz increased the Haldol by 50 percent to 3 milligrams every six hours. The Valium was doubled to 5 milligrams, the Demerol was left as it had been, and Meprobamate (if needed) was added to the chemistry.

The question that will probably forever be debated is the reason why such pharmaceuticals were prescribed. At this writing, questions from the author have gone unanswered; however, Dr. Kivowitz has said in deposition that he viewed Doris Duke's care as essentially a hospice situation for a terminally ill patient. Dr. Kivowitz later stated in a court affidavit that he explained to the nurses, household staff, and Doris's attorneys the hospice principles. Death was imminent and she needed to be kept free from pain and quiet.

The long-term acquaintances feel that Doris would have wanted to remain as active as possible within her physical limitations, nearing the end of her life. However, an active patient could endure great emotional trauma when faced with severe, existing limitations that are likely to increase during the final days of the illness. A sedated, tranquilized patient is not suffering.

By October 9, the once affable Doris Duke could barely stay awake. The notes have her sleeping soundly all night, something that had not been a problem. But instead of the notes showing her awake, alert, and happy during the day, they have statements such as "08:30 A.M. 'Demerol given as ordered. Patient responds to touch by opening eyes and mumbling.'" At noon she would awaken to touch, but she was staying awake only "intermittently." She constantly denied pain or discomfort but was obviously frustrated by the continued sleeping and failure to leave the house. At 4 P.M. that afternoon, the notes indicate "patient drowsy," "asking Bernard to 'get her out of here.'"

Still, no one responded the way she seemed to desire and soon she was rarely awake. Nursing notes have her "Sleeping soundly" at 10 A.M. and "patient asleep" at 3 in the afternoon. From that day forward, the notes are no longer filled with Doris Duke's increasingly lively responsiveness and desires to travel. Instead, there are charted painkillers and depressants despite the fact that Dr. Kivowitz or the nurses never mention the need for them. In addition, there are constant references throughout the day and night that Doris Duke is either sleeping or drowsy. This situation increased when she was given Vistaril.

Finally, on October 18, the first sign of emotional depression creeps into the chart. At 1 P.M. it is noted "Patient semisleeping denies pain." "I want to die. Pt. states how she feels."

Later, questions will be raised about this statement and Doris's October 7, 4:30 P.M., comment that she "wants to go." The defenders of the medical care and the actions Dr. Kivowitz would soon take want to imply that she meant that she wanted to die. In their minds, her one mention of death while in a depression possibly caused both by the medication and the fact that this once-active woman, being forced by pharmaceuticals to endure an almost immobile existence, reflects an unchanging desire for death. However, it may reflect the type of depression physicians frequently see with such patients, and it is the rare exception who in these instances has such feelings for very long. Hospice workers and others dealing with the terminally ill regularly tell of even the sickest of their patients embracing life for as long as they can, even though they experience periodic depression. Dr. Kivowitz later said in a court affidavit that he decided to begin hospice-type care on October 7 in accordance with Doris's previous oral statements made to him in the course of her care. According to the doctor, she said she didn't want her life artificially prolonged if she could not return to a lifestyle she enjoyed prior to her rapid decline.

For the most part, the chemical control of Doris Duke was effective. She was not in pain and she spent much of her time sleeping. On October 20, for example, a note made at 10:30 P.M. states that her "Eyes open blinking but mostly a blank stare, no verbalization, no physical mobilization." Only on two days is there a note concerning an attempt to talk. It is also the last such note in the record.

To a layman, it would seem that it was on October 26 that Dr. Charles Kivowitz made a decision that would allow Doris Duke to die. He was already convinced that she had only hours to live when he deliberately removed her from the feeding that was a part of her life support system. As Dr. Nicholas T. Macris later explained, "Dr. Kivowitz canceled the pulmonary therapist's visits and he stopped the pulse oximetry which was used to monitor her blood oxygen. This meant that the nursing staff would no longer have this objective guide as to the amount of oxygen the patient may need. He also discontinued her TPN, total parenteral nutrition therapy. *This action will lead to starvation and hasten Ms. Duke's death.*" [Emphasis added.][8]

Demerol, theoretically meant for pain control, was increased despite the fact that she was in no pain according to the notes. Dr. Kivowitz later explained that he did not want his patient to be in pain, the administered pain killer apparently meant to avoid a problem in the last few hours.

When Doris Duke did not die, morphine was added at 4:00 P.M.

on October 27, then increased when she continued to live. The first two doses were 5 milligrams; the amount rose to 15 milligrams at 3:30 A.M. on October 28, 25 milligrams at 4:30 A.M., and 25 milligrams more at 5:30 A.M. One hundred milligrams of Demerol were added to the last morphine drip. Doris Duke was dead eighteen minutes later.[9]

According to Dr. Macris: "Ms. Duke stopped breathing at 5:48 A.M. on October 28, 1993 as a result of the large doses of Morphine administered to her and was pronounced dead at 6:20 A.M. by Dr. Trabulus. The death certificate signed by Dr. Trabulus gave as the immediate cause of death; 'Septicemia—Hypertension, Atrial Fibrillation.' There are no physicians notes during her home care from September 20, 1993 to October 28, 1993 to document the diagnosis of Septicemia and Urosepsis. The nurses notes do not support this diagnosis. . . ."[10]

Dr. Kivowitz later responded in a deposition on January 4, 1995, "One has to understand what cause of death means. Everybody dies essentially the same way. Their heart stops and they stop breathing. As an immediate cause of death, that is somewhat obvious.

"You can go back a few steps, and one step would be acute pulmonary edema which is a mechanism of death. Another mechanism of death present in this situation was Septacemia Urosepsis. Septacemia Urosepsis preceded pulmonary edema in Doris Duke. Both would be legitimate, immediate causes of death as far as the State of California is concerned."

~·◈·~

Tammy Payette was an employee of the Saratoga Nursing Registry, a service that placed her for short- and long-term assignments in hospitals and homes where private medical care was needed. She had a Bachelor of Science in Nursing degree with a concentration in Psychology from Husson College in Bangor, Maine, and served in the U.S. Navy for two years prior to graduation. She was one of the nurses assigned to care for Doris Duke during the last weeks of her life. There were six nurses per day in all, teams of two nurses each working an eight-hour shift. In addition, respiratory and physical therapists came to the house to assist with what Payette felt would be Doris Duke's eventual rehabilitation.

Payette, who would later be convicted of stealing from some employers, stated that "based on my observations and past experiences with patients and general nursing knowledge, Miss Duke's life expectancy was at least five years, if she had been kept on the rehabilitation plan."[11] This conflicts with what Dr. Kivowitz later stated when he caused Doris Duke's death: "I increased the morphine so that she would not linger, that she would not suffer, and ultimately that she would die perhaps shortly or sooner than she would have otherwise died from her medical conditions, which I judged within a 48-hour period were of a terminal nature."[12]

Payette's discussion of Doris Duke's last days would eventually come to the attention of law enforcement officers who otherwise were not aware that Duke had died by something other than natural causes.[13]

"During the entire period from September 20 to October 28, 1993, Miss Duke's vital signs were stable, her pulse was strong and she had little, if any, respiratory discomfort or trouble. She was not anxious or combative, except as would be expected from a person who was impatient to get better and get out of bed.

Payette explained that Duke used Bernard as a trouble shooter when she thought things weren't going right with her care.

"Bernard often asked me to increase Miss Duke's sedation and to keep her quiet. Dr. Kivowitz instructed me and Pearl Rosenstein to give Miss Duke sedatives on the instruction of Bernard, to give her whatever Bernard wanted. Bernard also took Miss Duke's Valium for himself."

Payette said that toward the end of September and first part of October 1993, Duke was talking and interested in her appearance. Despite this, she was only allowed to see Lafferty-approved visitors and receive Lafferty-approved telephone calls. She remembered lawyers from Doyle's office and Dr. Glassman stopping by. She also remembered that when Duke had been home from the hospital a couple of weeks, "she became very agitated and said she wanted to return to Cedars Sinai or go to Duke Medical Center. Bernard heard these statements and called Dr. Kivowitz. . . ."[14]

"At this time, Dr. Kivowitz ordered that Miss Duke be given injections of Demerol, *although Miss Duke was not in pain.* [Emphasis added.]

"The injections of Demerol were increased, until eventually Miss Duke was put on a Demerol drip intravenously. Miss Duke began to have body spasms, and Dr. Kivowitz said those were due to the high doses of Demerol."

Payette said that the vital signs remained good ones during this time, her breathing and pulse strong. She was recovering consciousness despite the effects of the Demerol. Payette then said, "On October 27, 1993, Dr. Kivowitz had a long meeting with Mr. Doyle, Bernard Lafferty, and Dr. Glassman. I was not present in the room, but they were all at the house. They all came into Miss Duke's bedroom, and *Dr. Kivowitz told me and Pearl Rosenstein that it was time for Miss Duke to go. At this time, Miss Duke's vital signs were still stable, she was not in distress or pain.* [Emphasis added.]

"Dr. Kivowitz then directed me to prepare an intravenous bag under the instruction of Dr. Kivowitz, Morphine was placed in the solution. He directed that Miss Duke should receive 15 milligrams per hour. *Mr. Doyle and Bernard asked Dr. Kivowitz how long it would take for Miss Duke to die. After he injected her, Dr. Kivowitz answered, 'less than an hour.'* [Emphasis added.]

"Dr. Kivowitz then left the house saying he would be out of town, and Dr. Trabulus should be called when Miss Duke expired. . . ."

Payette explained that despite large doses of Demerol and morphine, only Duke's breathing slowed. Otherwise she was quite stable. Payette added that the fact that Duke was lingering caused Lafferty to become "excited and impatient." According to Payette, he telephoned Dr. Kivowitz to explain what was happening.

"Dr. Kivowitz returned and injected a needle into the IV tube and began to 'push' the morphine. This increased the rate of the flow and further slowed down Miss Duke's respiration. Miss Duke's respiration slowed down progressively as the morphine doses were increased. Eventually, as a result of the morphine IV Miss Duke's kidneys began to fail, her lungs filled up with fluid and her circulation began to deteriorate. Miss Duke did not have pulmonary edema, and no doctor had diagnosed pulmonary edema.

"Despite the massive doses of morphine, Miss Duke still did not expire until several hours later at about 5:30 A.M.

"Mr. Doyle and Bernard remained at the house all night.

"Miss Duke did not die of natural causes and was not in danger of dying until the large doses of morphine were given to her. She was asleep, medicated with a large amount of Demerol and certainly was not in pain when the morphine was administered.

"Morphine is a very potent respiratory depressant and rapid injection increases its effect.

"Miss Duke expired as an immediate result of the morphine which was given to her on October 27 and 28."

From the *New York Times,* May 25, 1995: "The nurse who alleged that billionaire heiress Doris Duke was murdered with overdoses of morphine was charged Wednesday with stealing jewelry and art works from six wealthy patients—including Duke and cosmetics magnate Max Factor. . . .

"Detectives who led Payette away in handcuffs from the West Los Angeles Courthouse said they have tied the nurse so far to nearly $450,000 in missing jewelry, artwork and other items, and that the actual value of the stolen property could be much higher when their investigation is complete."

The article, by Paul Lieberman and John J. Goldman, indicates that the alleged thefts came to light after private detectives began following Payette because of her claim that Doris Duke had been deliberately killed. It states that she admitted to the reporters that she had "stolen some ivory statues and other items as a 'nervous reaction.' "

Later Pearl Rosenstein would be quoted in the press as denying Payette's reports. She felt that the care was excellent, although the nursing notes and medication listing would later be the basis for questions raised by some. The increases in morphine and Demerol were difficult to justify in some reviewer's eyes based on the evidence in the charts of little or no pain for Doris.

Pain control is always a judgment call on the part of the physician. The trauma of pain is exhausting. It can weaken the immune system and/or slow recovery. Some physicians, knowing a patient is experiencing periodic, severe pain, may start the pain medication to either delay or reduce the severity of that periodic pain when it returns. It is possible this was the physician's judgment call in Doris Duke's case.

The last curious note was the taking of the medical records. Colin Shanley noted, "On the morning of Miss Duke's death, Doyle was in the house (I believe he had been there all night). He had a meeting with Lafferty. He then confronted the nurse, Tammy Payette, who was packing the medical equipment. Doyle said, 'I need your logs, your records.' Ms. Payette said 'no, I can't give them to you.' Doyle persisted, saying 'can I make a copy?' She eventually said, 'All right, but I need them back right away.' Doyle then disappeared for several hours; he later returned only a copy, and not the original, of the nurse's records."[15]

Tammy Payette noted that "At the time of Miss Duke's death, Mr. William Doyle took the originals of the nurses notes which were kept in Miss Duke's room. I asked him not to remove these records. Mr. Doyle told me he would take thee records, make a photo copy and give me the original back. In fact, I was given a copy of notes.

"On October 28, Mr. Doyle gave me a copy of at least some of the records he removed from Miss Duke's room.

"I have reviewed these records. I recognize my handwriting and notes. These appear to be a true and correct copy of my handwritten nursing notes and those of other nurses regarding Doris Duke's condition and medical care."[16]

Doyle later explained that the original notes were in the KMZ files. He said that no one had asked for them.

And so Doris Duke was allowed to die before her time. But was Doris Duke's premature death by her physician a crime? As it turned out, the story would become stranger as the days passed following her death and cremation and as more details emerged.

# 17

## *Dead to Rights*

T HE NEW YORK TIMES Obituaries of Friday, October 29, 1993, B11: "Doris Duke, 80, Heiress Whose Great Wealth Couldn't Buy Happiness, Is Dead." Eric Pace wrote:

> Doris Duke, the tobacco heiress and philanthropist whose bittersweet life was woven of luxury, disputes and interludes of deep unhappiness, died yesterday at her house in Beverly Hills, Calif. She was 80 and had her main residence in Somerset County, N.J. She also had homes on Park Avenue in midtown Manhattan, in Newport, R.I., and Hawaii.
>
> The cause was progressive pulmonary edema resulting in cardiac arrest, said Howard J. Rubenstein, a spokesman for Bernard Lafferty, a friend and adviser to Miss Duke who was with her at her death.
>
> Her manifold interests as a philanthropist ranged from animal rights to AIDS, historical preservation to orchids. . . .
>
> Late one evening in Rome in 1945, Miss Duke, who was then 33 years old, told a friend that her vast fortune was in some ways a barrier to happiness.
>
> "All that money is a problem sometimes," Miss Duke told her companion, a young American journalist, over a glass of wine at the Hassler Hotel. "It happens every time. After I've gone out with a man a few times, he starts to tell me how much he loves me. But how can I know if he really means it? How can I ever be sure?"

There were whispers and rumors almost from the moment of Doris Duke's death in Falcon's Lair. The body was rushed to be cremated, allowing neither an autopsy nor a chance for Chandi, Duke blood relations, or anyone else to be notified so that the cremation could be challenged. If she had been murdered, the evidence might have been destroyed in the fiery furnace. And because of the rush to burn the body of a woman who lived in terror of fire, it was "obvious" she had been murdered.

Not that anyone knew for sure. Yes, Doris Duke had talked about being fed to the sharks. Chandi said that Doris lived in terror of cremation, a feeling that, if true, apparently changed after Chandi and Doris separated.

It was some time after the years with Chandi that Doris discussed with the Reverend Lawrence Roberts the religious and moral significance of cremation versus any other form of disposing of her body. He knew that she had accepted the idea as a practical one. He also understood that her fear was of burning in life. She did not care what was done to her physical remains in death.

The fact that the butler would be the primary inheritor was also subject to speculation, ridicule, amazement, and jealousy, depending on who was discussing the situation. Since the butler is also the stereotypical villain in many older murder mysteries, Bernard Lafferty received close scrutiny by the press and regularly came up wanting.

Ironically, it was not something so major as Doris Duke's unnatural death that exposed men of wealth, power, fame, and influence to embarrassingly close scrutiny. Rather it was the simple action of a young man only five years out of Fordham Law School and still closely connected to friends he made while trying to pay for his education as a waiter.

Raymond Dowd is a deceptively quiet man when discussing a case in his office. Place him behind a desk and he seems able to melt into the anonymous near invisibility of a clerk who can work forty years for the same firm, then retire without anyone knowing his name.

Yet the quiet, seeming passivity encountered by a friendly visitor to Dowd's law office can be replaced by the cocked-chin toughness of a man who has seen too many troubled lives, too many street fights, too many putdowns based on race, religion, or ethnic heritage. Yet his is not the pugnacity of the barroom brawler. Instead, his is the courage of a man who knows where he is going and will not tolerate challenges from anyone whom he believes is wrong to question his actions. He has traveled the notorious New York subway system in the early hours of the morning, oblivious to the dangers that cause other Manhattan residents to huddle under lights near exits. He is streetwise enough to know that the hours he must keep and the suits he must wear make him a target for muggers and robbers. Yet he lives his life without fear, confident that he will deal with whatever is thrown his way. He will not cede his freedom to predators who might be lurking in the shadows of the streets at night or in the boardrooms by day.

Ray Dowd is first and foremost a moralist, a man who truly believes in truth and justice even when the proper pursuit of a case ensures an outcome that may be detrimental to his client's desires. Some lawyers take pride in winning a case even though the win is a corruption of justice. Dowd seeks fairness, and if a client wants more than what is rightfully due, the client needs a different lawyer. As a result, Dowd is tenacious in the way that only a man of ethics and integrity can be. He does not think too hard about the consequences of his actions, only whether the actions themselves are appropriate for the championing of a righteous cause.

The result is that Ray Dowd is often on the receiving end of verbal put-downs that are meant to wither the heart and shatter the nerves of attorneys deemed inherently inferior by more experienced lawyers. For example, Tom Barr of Cravath, Swaine & Moore, a high-powered firm with the right skills and connections to be hired by United States Trust Company, wrote to Dowd, saying, in part: "Young lawyers are sometimes in a hurry to make fools of themselves. You have greatly exceeded the norm."

Outside the office, Dowd's charisma is evident to friends who join him at one of the Irish bars near his office. Women come on to him, and he is as comfortable with the boisterous rowdiness of men who consider hard drinking a proper end to a day's rough labor as he is with the staid formality of the courtroom.

Colin Shanley did not realize all this when he came to see Dowd. His visit was as much as a friend as a client. The two men had worked in restaurants together and, in the manner of employees working shifts that end when most of the world is asleep, so-cialized together. Their lives were leading them in radically differ-ent directions, yet the restaurant work had been a common ground neither had forgotten.

The discussion Shanley held with Dowd led to allegations that Doris Duke had been murdered, a crime outside the attorney's le-gal expertise. What was within his scope of training, interest, and skill were breaches of employment agreements consummated in the State of New York. Shanley, along with fellow Duke estate em-ployees housekeeper Ann Bostich and maintenance worker Mari-ano De Velasco, asked Dowd to represent them. Their legal action would be taken against William Doyle, fellow attorney Lee Ann Watson, their law firm, Katten Muchin & Zavis, and "Bernard (a.k.a. John Mason a.k.a. Peter Malone) Lafferty."

The suit revolved around the claims that each of the plaintiffs' jobs had clearly defined descriptions and specific work weeks of forty hours each. According to the action filed by Dowd, Bernard Lafferty and William Doyle insisted the employees perform duties well beyond those spelled out on their job descriptions. The com-plaint stated that: "These services included being on-call round-the-clock assisting Lafferty in dressing, driving, shopping, eating, moving furniture, assisting in arranging for his personal entertain-ment and shopping expeditions and making improvements for his personal benefit on the Mansion located at 1436 Bella Drive, Bev-erly Hills . . ." (Falcon's Lair). In exchange for this work, which went beyond the nature of the job description, "Lafferty and Doyle promised compensation in the form of lifetime employment and pension and a variety of promises made to each Plaintiff person-ally."[1]

Each person had specific claims, the importance of them some-times exceeding the issue of direct compensation. For example, Shanley, a chef, was paid $41,600 per year, with medical and dental care provided as part of a benefit package worth approximately $3,600 annually.

Shanley's compensation was in line with what he might earn at a higher-priced restaurant, but the guarantee of lifetime employ-ment that Doyle and Lafferty allegedly offered could not be matched elsewhere. In addition, he was receiving housing worth approximately $20,000 per year, one perk not likely to be found anywhere except as a private chef for the very wealthy. He was allegedly promised enough money to enable him to purchase a house on the water in Amagansett, Long Island, where homes cost at least $1,500,000.

But the most important promise which Shanley claimed had been made had to do with his mother, a paraplegic in need of therapy. He was allegedly told that part of his employment benefit for working beyond his job description would be "five months of top medical care and rehabilitative treatment at Burke Physical Rehabilitation Center. . . ." The value of the treatment was placed at $150,000.[2]

Helping his mother had been a driving factor in Shanley's life long before Doris Duke's death. In a statement by Harry B. Demopoulos, M.D.:

"Sometime during the Summer of 1991, I had lunch with Doris Duke at her Somerville, N.J. residence. My wife and son accompanied me. During lunch, Miss Duke discussed with me the situation of her Chef Colin Shanley's mother. Miss Duke informed me that she had Guillain-Barre Syndrome and discussed with me an article on GBS that had recently appeared in the *Wall Street Journal*. She told me that Colin's mother, due to financial reasons, was having difficulty receiving quality treatment and that she wanted to remedy the situation and would do anything she could to help. I told her that I knew the director of the Rusk Institute for Rehabilitative Medicine and felt certain that with her backing, I could get Mrs. Shanley into the Institute quickly.

"We discussed the costs which I told her would run at least $1,000 a day for two to three months, and she said that was fine."

Dr. Demopoulos said that he spoke to the director of the Rusk Institute concerning the situation. The director agreed to begin treatment when he received a letter from Duke accepting financial responsibility.

According to the doctor, Doris Duke was comfortable with the arrangement and said that Irwin Bloom would be authorized to release the money. Dr. Demopoulos also contacted Laura Shanley,

Colin's sister, so she would know what was happening. However, the promises were not kept and the troubled physician called the accountant to learn why. "Bloom told be [sic] that Miss Duke no longer wanted to finance the physical therapy," said the doctor.

"I was shocked, because of Miss Duke's obvious enthusiasm and willingness to help. I did not inquire further into the situation, since I did not feel that it was my place, but it did strike me as very odd, especially since during the years that I knew her, she was especially proud of Shanley."[3]

Demopoulos went on to recount other incidents where Doris Duke had allegedly offered to help both employees and inner city youths in Newark, New Jersey, the offers countermanded by Irwin Bloom. This failure to get money to help his mother greatly upset Shanley. It had also been a major motivating factor in getting him to continue with his employment. It would also be an issue in the breach of employment contract charges being brought by Dowd.

The circumstances surrounding housekeeper Ann Bostich's complaint were equally emotional but concerned dental work. Around June 1993, she was in the process of getting a dental implant. A temporary prosthesis had been installed but, Bostich claimed, Lafferty refused to pay for the remainder of the necessary dental surgery. The cost would be approximately $4,000.

The complaint further alleged that "on or around August, 1993, to induce Bostich and De Velasco to continue providing extra services to Lafferty, Lafferty promised to provide Bostich and De Velasco with sufficient funds to purchase a home with sufficient space to have a woodworking shop as soon as the will of Miss Duke was probated.

"Lafferty pointed out some homes that he thought might be suitable in West Hollywood.

"Such a home would have a value of at least $300,000."[4] There were also claims of lifetime employment and pension rewards for the couple.

There were other charges brought out, including that the witnessing of the Doris Duke will had been an act made under threat of physical harm. Shanley left the employ, having become emotionally upset and an alcoholic.[5] He went through an alcohol and drug treatment program from November 1993 through January 1994, then began attending Alcoholics Anonymous meetings. At that time Lafferty tried to rehire him, and Shanley agreed.[6]

During this same period, Bernard Lafferty was using his position to get access to more money than he had ever experienced. Although only the "nominated individual Executor" of Doris Duke's April 5 will, he made clear in a letter dated October 31, 1993, that he would be appointing U.S. Trust Company of New York as corporate executor in the original probate of the will. He noted that he also would be establishing compensation for the work. The letter, sent to Anthony P. Marshall, senior vice president of U.S. Trust, gave the company a commission "calculated at 1/2 of 1% of the date of death value of the gross estate as finally determined for federal estate tax purposes." Some other fees were mentioned, all seemingly small, but because of the size of the estate, they represented millions of dollars in income.

On November 22, 1993, Karen Unger of U.S. Trust, responding to a call she received from Marshall at 2:30 P.M., sent a memo to the company's Gerri McNamara and John Hover. She was extremely concerned with the ethical situations she felt were being raised and was acting, in effect, as the moral conscience of the company. Her concerns would be dismissed by others.

Unger explained that Marshall asked "if we would provide Bernard Lafferty with a loan of approximately $300,000 plus interest to accrue until repayment. Tony needs an answer by 8:30 A.M. when he has a conference call with Lafferty's Chicago lawyers. Lafferty may also be amenable to pay interest monthly, but in that case, would ask for a higher loan, to cover the interest payments. The interest rate itself was not discussed."

Unger said that the purpose of the loan would be to enable him to receive $30,000 per month for ten months "for living expenses." She noted that he would be inheriting $500,000 per year for the remainder of his life *once the estate is settled*. She also pointed out the fact that though he was co-executor of the estate, with U.S. Trust, he also *"has the right to fire us."* [Emphasis added.]

After explaining the payment of the loan, which could not be certain since the will had not been probated yet, she noted: *"Lafferty has no assets in his own right. Tony [Marshall] said that the es-*

*tate can not lend him the money. He did not give me the reason."* [Emphasis added.]

To her credit, Karen Unger raised the question of a conflict of interest, a question that would haunt U.S. Trust. "Tony disagreed, saying that we would be lending on the basis of expected income, and we could structure the loan so that Lafferty would pay interest monthly if we lent him the interest amount.

"Tony indicated that the loan was Jeff Maurer's idea and that Dick Covey had OKed it, as no conflict of interest existed."[7]

The memo was followed up by another one the next day, further outlining the risks. One of the concerns was the repayment of the loan should Lafferty die. Another was whether there would be a problem if Lafferty was not paid his executor commission by the end of 1994, though that was apparently a risk only if he committed a crime.

On November 26, 1993, Lafferty was offered "a $300,000 unsecured non-revolving line of credit." The rate was to be prime + 1 percent, "charged monthly to your checking account to be opened at U.S. Trust." They agreed that he would have $30,000 applied to his account each month for 10 months. Another $200,000 was authorized in April of 1994 ($25,000 per month for 8 months). There was $200,000 more authorized September 16, 1994, $30,000 more on October 31, 1994, and $95,000 more on January 4, 1995. The total had reached $825,000—despite the fact that the will had not been settled in any way. It was noted that "our informal understanding is that the outstanding balance on the line will be repaid in full the earlier of March 31, 1995 or from the disbursement of your executor commissions."

All but the earliest sums would be provided to Lafferty in the future. While Bernard was convincing U.S. Trust to lend him money despite having no real way to pay it back if the challenges to the will were successful, other events were putting pressure on him. In February 1994 *Vanity Fair* magazine made the death of Doris Duke and the bizarre circumstances surrounding her estate the subject of popular gossip. Writer Bob Colacello interviewed everyone involved with Doris in her last years who would talk with him. Tom Rybak told of his regrets concerning letting Lafferty return to work following his hospitalization for alcoholism.

Chandi stressed that she and Doris ". . . discussed cremation, and she said, 'Never, never, ever let anyone cremate me.' She had this terrible fear of fire."

Nelson Seabra was quoted as saying "A very close friend of Doris's said that she committed suicide. She was taking so many pills at the end and, knowingly or not, killed herself.'"

While Dowd maintained that he was bringing a breach of work contract action, he knew that his action, coupled with challenges to the last will, could force law enforcement to look more closely at Doris Duke's death. He also was challenging the fitness of Lafferty and U.S. Trust to be executors of the estate. And always he returned to the seemingly simple premise that all he wanted was for his clients to have their jobs back, along with back pay, since Doris Duke's will indicated that they should have remained as employees.

At this writing Ray Dowd is still fighting for his clients despite a loss in court.

The claims Shanley brought were dismissed. Shanley had gone into a rehabilitation program for his alcoholism, a recovery effort sponsored by his employer. However, when he returned to work, he was told he was out of a job and could not return for his personal belongings. The only way he could have his possessions would be if he signed a paper giving up all rights to claims he had as an employee.

Shanley felt that his condition was precarious at the time. He was sober yet knew that he could easily slip and start drinking. As with many recovering alcoholics and drug addicts, he became obsessed with his possessions, determined to get them back at all costs. They seemed more important at that moment than anything else. It was not a well-reasoned decision nor would it have been one he would make when fully recovering. But instead of waiting or consulting a lawyer, he was so convinced he had to get his belongings that he signed the agreement.

As Ray Dowd sees it, the issue is, in part, whether or not Shanley's emotional health was such that the request improperly placed him under what is called economic duress. If he was, then the agreement Shanley signed would be invalid.

Unlike Shanley who signed an agreement that is in contention. Bostich and her husband allege that though they signed no papers,

Lafferty's behavior was so improper that they left their jobs under duress. The initial trial court ruling also disagreed with their allegations and dismissed their case. Dowd is now pursuing his clients' claims in other venues. Thus the fight continues.

⋯⋰⋯

Bernard Lafferty was not handling the stress of all that was taking place well. He traveled to the Breakers Hotel in Palm Beach, Florida, taking a suite and rapidly working his way through the stock of liquor provided for all adult guests. According to the admissions report for the Good Samaritan Medical Center in West Palm Beach for February 11, 1994:

"This 48 year old gentleman was brought to the emergency room from the Breakers Hotel, where he is on vacation. Apparently, he was unresponsive. The EMTs [emergency medical technicians] felt that the patient was having difficulty breathing and instead of taking him to an alcoholic rehabilitation center in Wellington, he was brought to the emergency room at Good Samaritan Medical Center. The patient apparently initially was difficult to rouse but subsequently was aroused, became combative and required restraints in the emergency room. He apparently came close to if not actually biting a nurse. He is currently unemployed but appears to be a man of means. He admits to owning five homes. He is currently residing in New Jersey."

The report, by Dr. Israel Wacks, lists Lafferty under the name "Brian O'Conner" whose address is listed as 515 W. Monroe, Chicago, Illinois. The KMZ law firm's offices in Chicago are at 525 W. Monroe, and Dr. Wacks notes: "I have spoken to the patient's attorney, Mr. Doyle, and he says that the patient does have a history of previous alcohol abuse and says that the patient does require detoxification and alcohol rehabilitation in spite of the patient's protestations to the contrary. These will be arranged at the light of day."[8]

Doyle had flown to Florida with Colin Shanley, who was asked to help care for Lafferty when the butler/heir was still in the hotel and becoming out of control. It was Doyle who was forced to call the EMT unit and eventually arrange for Lafferty's transportation back to Duke Farms. From there he flew to Los Angeles via

Chicago with Dr. Harry Glassman on board to supply medical care as needed.[9] In Los Angeles, he was placed in Cedars-Sinai hospital.

There would be other problems that year for Lafferty. His public behavior was creating difficulties for those around him. For example, on June 2, 1994, Lafferty, who had no driver's license and was not skilled in driving a car, crashed the Duke Farms–registered Cadillac while in the West Hollywood, Beverly Hills area.[10] When giving his statement to the investigating officer, he admitted he had always had a chauffeur.

By August, Lafferty was being heavily medicated in his fight to end his periodic alcohol abuse. His physician, Michael Horwitz, M.D., was prescribing for Lafferty almost as many medications as Doris Duke had received. These started with 100 milligrams of Toprol XL on July 22, 1994, and escalated on August 26 to 2 milligrams of Klonopin, 100 milligrams of Toprol XL, 5 milligrams of Ambien, 75 milligrams of Effexor, 300 milligrams of lithium carbonate, 150 milligrams of trazodone, 5 milligrams of diazepam, and 10 milligrams of Baclofen. In September he also was given 125 milligrams of Depakote on the eighth, 250 milligrams of Depakote E.C. on the sixteenth, and a Midrin capsule on the twentieth.[11]

Richard Kuh's report provides seemingly contradictory information. As to the alcoholism, he states: "The above episodes [the Florida incident as well as alleged alcohol abuse problems in July, October, and December 1994] notwithstanding, it was reported to me that both during Duke's lifetime, and since her death, Lafferty is generally able to function effectively within the parameters of his skills." However, he also included a letter from Dr. Ralph N. Wharton, a psychopharmacologist and psychiatrist at Columbia University's College of Physicians and Surgeons. Dr. Wharton was asked ". . . to try to objectively evaluate the mental status and function of Bernard Lafferty from September 1992 through [*sic*] January 1995. During this interval, Mr. Lafferty has required the use of substantial dose of a number of major anti-depressants and anti-psychotic medications for mood disorders, sleep disorders, and transient thinking (delusional) disorder:

"(3)  sleep medications included: Halcion, Restoril, Ambien

"(7)  anti-depressants included: Prozac, Effexor, Paxil, Imipramine, Pamelor, Desyrel, Lithium

"(3) anti-psychotics included: Tegretol, Risperdal, Haldol

"(6) anti-anxiety medicines included: Klonopin, Xanax, Valium, Depakote, Phenobarbital, Ativan.

"Ordinarily, an anti-depressant is used one at a time; the combined use may be interpreted as a more malignant depression.

"In addition, he also used a number of minor muscle relaxants.

"As far as I can tell, he was treated by three primary physicians, Drs. Horwitz, Kivowitz and Pallay. There is no thorough mental exam reflected in any of these records and as far as I know none of these physicians is a qualified psychiatrist."

Dr. Wharton concluded: "It is likely that further episodes of alcohol abuse will recur given the recent history. The patient requires a current complete psychiatric and neurological examination. A full psychiatric exam requires a richly detailed assessment of appearance, mood variability, thinking, orientation, memory capacity (recent and remote), arithmetic function, judgment, insight, etc. It would be likely that (given his ongoing need for anti-depressant and tranquilizer [*sic*] treatment for at least the next 18 months) he would have difficulty managing any complex financial matters. However, to be thorough and fair, complete examination would reveal the impact of these binge episodes and the seriousness of his mood disorder."[12]

By contrast, Dr. Horwitz, who has a subspecialty in addiction medicine, took exception to the Wharton report. He did not believe that Dr. Wharton was able to give a fully informed opinion regarding Bernard Lafferty's abilities without close observation of the former butler. Dr. Horwitz made clear that his counter opinion came from such observation.

Despite the growing concerns, U.S. Trust was committed to advancing Bernard Lafferty hundreds of thousands of dollars for his use. The money to be advanced was based on what he would eventually receive if the final will was approved. The request for the loan came from U.S. Trust's Senior Vice President Anthony P. Marshall, and although it originated in 1993, additional sums would be granted while Lafferty's alcoholism and prescription drug use escalated, raising questions about what the trust company knew and how responsible it was being with estate funds. This time the questions were both about conflict of interest, the issue that Karen

Unger had raised, and also whether or not Lafferty's drug and alcohol problems might ultimately result in his being denied a portion from which he could repay the loans.

On January 12, 1995, Ray Dowd, acting on behalf of clients Colin Shanley, Ann Bostich, and Mariano De Velasco, filed a motion in New York's Surrogate Court to obtain a temporary stay in all proceedings related to the probate of the April 5, 1993, Last Will and Testament of Doris Duke. At this time the press first became aware that there was a strong suspicion of foul play in Doris Duke's death, a suspicion that might be justified.

Dowd wrote: "On December 5, 1994, when I reached the personal conviction that Doris Duke had been murdered for profit, and upon consultation with my clients who were willing to cooperate, I contacted the U.S. Attorney's office in the form of a letter to Mary Jo White, U.S. Attorney for the Southern District of New York to which I received no response.

"On December 13, 1995, Colin Shanley called me and informed me that an eyewitness to Doris Duke's death had told him that Doris Duke had been murdered. Ann Bostich confirmed that she had spoken to the same eyewitness."[13]

Dowd, stating that he feared for the eyewitness's life, refused to provide the name, although he did offer to present it privately to Surrogate Court Judge Eve Preminger. He also explained that he had contacted Ann Ryan, chief of the Major Crimes Section of the U.S. Attorney's Office for the Southern District of New York, scheduling an appointment with both her and Ron Gardella, a Federal Criminal Investigator. That led to a December 13 meeting lasting five hours. Three days later Colin Shanley spoke with them, and on December 19, Ann Bostich was flown to New York to speak with both them and a "Mr. Schecter," who was allegedly in charge of the investigation. Dowd said, "Schecter told me that the U.S. Attorney's office did not wish to proceed, since a witness (not a party to the present action) that I had supplied to them could be a possible homicide defendant." However, Ann Ryan said that a report would be sent to the authorities in Los Angeles.

Gradually the various court actions challenging the wills led to

Surrogate Court Judge Preminger's assigning attorney Richard H. Kuh as limited temporary administrator. He was asked to investigate the death, the wills, and the other allegations surrounding the settlement of the estate. His investigation, begun on January 20, 1995, allowed him unrestricted access to all documents, books, and records relating to the estate. It would uncover everything from the copy of the canceled $500,000 check payable to Harry Glassman to medical records whose review led some medical experts to question the treatment Doris Duke received at the end of her life.

Then, on January 21, the *Los Angeles Times* carried an article by John Goldman and Robert Lopez under the headline: NURSE ALLEGES HEIRESS WAS GIVEN FATAL MORPHINE DOSE. It reported that Tammy Payette had come forward the day before to allege that the death was the result of an unwanted lethal dose of morphine. Four months later, Payette was arrested for allegedly stealing jewelry and artworks from six patients, including Duke and cosmetics magnate Max Factor. Although the allegations of theft would color the allegations of murder, the combination of Ray Dowd's challenge on behalf of his clients, the challenge by former major heirs written out of the final will, and Tammy Payette's statement resulted in the opening of cases on several fronts. For the first time, the men and women involved would be required to tell their story under oath. Apparently the true story of the last days of Doris Duke would be resolved.

But what really happened?

# 18

❧

## *Death and Suspicion*

*I*F DORIS DUKE's death had been fiction, it would have had all the elements needed for any number of clichéd endings. There was the luxury-loving butler—semiliterate, alcoholic, heavily using pharmaceuticals at times, and spending Doris Duke's money while she lay dying. Yet with Doris dead, it was all too easy to ignore the possibility that such spending was authorized and well within his duties on her estates. Instead, some observers of his actions created the image of a man so eager to grasp her wealth that he could not wait until the probate of her estate to reward friends and acquire personal luxuries.

The butler went from salaried servant to executor controlling billions, consulting with the new lawyers who handled the will changes and signing. He also arranged for the seclusion of his mistress while she was confused and sometimes comatose from an array of drugs, including painkillers and sleeping medications some doctors would later say were unnecessary and/or improper. At the same time, by keeping Doris Duke at Falcon's Lair, she was saved the stress of a terminal hospital stay while never being far from any special medical help she might need. While others saw her as isolated when they were denied a chance to telephone or visit her, such separation from the stress of even the most casual conversation may have kept her from becoming dangerously tired when her body was in a severely weakened condition.

At her death he mourned her loss, yet there were allegations that the mourning included the wearing of her clothing and jewelry, as well as the sleeping in her luxurious bed. He was alleged to have talked as though death was a blessing for Doris since she would no longer be suffering.

Hindsight was easy, of course. Bernard Lafferty was the wrong man in the wrong place at the wrong time, according to his critics. But with the eccentricities of his employer in the two years before her death, it is also possible to see him as a lucky man, gaining a reward that his employer wanted to give him. The fact that this was a radical change from her past actions and desires did not mean that she was coerced. It just means that the Doris Duke of her late seventies was a radically different woman from the Doris Duke of her fifties and sixties.

Regardless of Lafferty's actions or desires, longtime friends agreed she had, indeed, changed. And Lafferty would later maintain he spent his time carrying out her wishes, however that might make him appear when she could no longer speak for herself.

There was the Beverly Hills glamour doctor, a man who cuts and sews, nips and tucks, suctions and injects so that men and women with more money than values can stand in the face of the Grim Reaper and lie about their age. They are people determined that when the breath of life leaves their bodies, their corpses will have the tautest skin, firmest buttocks, tightest thighs, and best endowed chests in the funeral home. Married to an actress who was graciously shifting from starring in ingenue and glamorous "women of that certain age" types of roles to becoming a major star on infomercials, he accepted a $500,000 check drawn in Doris Duke's name.

There was the less glamorous physician, providing Doris Duke's primary care, making decisions about her physical therapy, her feeding, her oxygen intake. He was a man who never made notes about patients receiving his home visits, creating for some a trail of suspicion of incompetence, and suspicion of deceit. Had he left a properly complete paper trail, the facts would have been known and the death would have been fully understood.

And there were the weak links: nursing staff, cleaning staff, all manner of staff personnel. Some were witnesses to the death. Some claimed to be witnesses to the alleged machinations of one or more of the prime suspects. Some were simply backroom whisperers who put two and two together, then cried murder most foul without checking their addition.

Other potential villains abounded. There were the lawyers, a profession believed to supply a rich, full life for practitioners willing to sue widows, orphans, and even their own mothers, if they have the requisite "deep pockets" for collection. And there were the bankers, similar in perceived character to the lawyers, except that they have favorable press every Christmas when television reruns Jimmy Stewart as the blessed banker in *It's a Wonderful Life.*

But whispers of murder, allegations of cover-up, celebrity doctors, a high-living former butler, and all the other characters in a story whose alleged villains are too trite for pulp fiction writers do not necessarily make a chargeable crime. This was certainly the concern for investigators who would spend approximately twenty months seeking evidence and weighing facts as they tried to determine what happened and whether or not the events leading to her death were criminal in nature.

That Doris Duke's death was premature has never been disputed. As Dr. Charles Kivowitz stated in his deposition, "I increased the morphine so that she would not linger, that she would not suffer, and ultimately that she would die perhaps shortly or sooner than she would have otherwise died from her medical conditions, which I judged within a 48-hour period were of a terminal nature."[1]

The question that mattered was who knew what and when they knew it. Dr. Kivowitz claimed that he discussed the idea of not continuing to provide the most extensive possible care for Doris Duke "once it was determined that further medical care would be of no use."[2] He also claimed that he had discussed this idea with her several times during late September and early October when she was at home.[3] Yet there were no records to this effect, no notes, and the nurses' notes seem to indicate that informed consent by Duke might have been impossible. What they do not reflect were private discussions between Dr. Kivowitz and his patient prior to her reaching her final weeks of life.

Dr. Kivowitz would later explain, "I have never maintained a record of notes on a patient in the home."[4]

Despite the lack of notes, Dr. Kivowitz was very specific about the painful condition he said he believed Doris Duke to be experiencing. "The tracheal tube was infiltrated with granulation tissue. It was very painful to her. She was trying to tear it out of her throat. She had to be restrained and sedated in order to simply maintain the airway. When she did reach the tracheal tube and pulled at it, it bled.

"She had arthritis in virtually every joint in her body with multiple joints swollen.

"She had, as a result of several strokes, near quadriplegia and flexion contractures in most of her—in all of her extremities. Any movement of any extremity, whether it was a distal extremity, meaning the fingers or the hands, or proximal extremity like the arm or the shoulder or her legs, to either position her in bed or clean her or—generated pain, substantial amounts of pain.

"And for those reasons, medications were prescribed to help her remain alive with the pain that she was suffering."

The problems seem horrendous and make the doctor's actions compassionate. The questioning of the doctor's actions that occurred in the months following her death stemmed from the fact that the nursing notes did not reflect the difficulties he described under oath.[5] And as always, Dr. Kivowitz said, "I don't have a record of it."

"There were no household physician notes kept. It's not my practice to do so in the household, and I don't believe that any of the other physicians have it as their general rule to keep notes in the household."[6]

Based on his professional assessment of his patient's condition and prognosis, Dr. Kivowitz took steps that would lead to a death sooner than if he sustained basic life support. First, he stopped having the pulmonary therapist provide treatments that the nursing notes seem to indicate she was tolerating quite well. "I felt, as I had thought for approximately three weeks by this time that Miss Duke was dying and that the problems that she had were progressing, that she had additional new problems that I didn't intend to treat in any vigorous way, and I felt that she was dying, and everything was, in short order, going to just fall apart. I didn't think it was appropriate to give her additional pulmonary therapy as I thought she had an infection from her urine and was probably at the time becoming septic. She was comfortable, and she was asleep as per her request."[7]

Kivowitz continued to stop monitoring and treatment that might have prolonged the quantity of her days. "To this time, Miss Duke had a device on her finger [pulse oximetry] which measured her oxygen saturation in her blood. It measured only part of her respiratory status. Her respiratory frequency was measured or monitored by the nurses in their record of vital signs, but her carbon dioxide content was unmeasured.

"I felt that at this time Miss Duke was dying, this was an expected phenomenon, and it was a consequence of her medical problems."[8]

Then Dr. Kivowitz commented that Doris Duke's death was the result of a combination of her various illnesses, her deteriorated condition, and the trauma of necessary invasive procedures such as a feeding tube. Thus her death resulted, in part, as ". . . a consequence of her treatment for her medical problems . . ."[9]

The doctor then admitted that he had not consulted with any medical professional concerning his decision to end Doris Duke's food and water while providing lethal doses of morphine and Demerol.[10] He explained that, "It is understood by anyone in the State of California who is involved in a hospice situation that the medications may be involved—may be, in part, responsible for some brief shortenings—shortening of a patient's life."[11]

Numerous questions remain.

At the very least, the lack of note-keeping by a physician is an unwise move that can lead to a successful medical malpractice claim. For many years one of the coauthors of this book was a contributing editor for *Physician's Management,* a financial journal for doctors. He frequently wrote about the issue of medical malpractice, and consistently throughout the nation—including in California—attorneys specializing in the field warned about the necessity of complete records. For Dr. Kivowitz to make neither complete records to be added to the nursing notes kept within Falcon's Lair nor complete records to be retained in his office provided an open invitation to a lawsuit. It is not that the doctor was necessarily doing anything wrong. There are many instances where a competent physician treating a patient in an acceptable manner, achieving expected results has still lost a medical malpractice suit. This is not because the physician did anything wrong. It is because he or she was not careful to document what took place.

When Dr. Kivowitz began making a practice of not keeping full personal records of in-home patient care, he created the potential for serious problems. As it is, the investigations by Kuh and others have led a number of skilled professionals to challenge Kivowitz's judgment. Yet no one could say with 100 percent certainty how right or wrong he was because only the nurses' notes exist and they may not reflect all his decisions.

The second problem is the issue of medical ethics in the case of a terminally ill patient. Los Angeles County has an ethics committee to both help physicians with their decisions and review alleged violations. Physicians on the committee work in conjunction with legal ethicists connected with the county bar association. They were contacted for their opinions about this type of case, though the specifics could not be identified because they may be called upon to judge Dr. Kivowitz's actions at some later time.[12]

According to the ethicists, Dr. Kivowitz may have pushed the ethical boundaries to the limits without violating them. They explained that if the person who is next of kin or otherwise closest to a clearly dying patient is deeply grieving, the physician may look after that person's concerns when deciding on a treatment plan. In this instance, instead of the next of kin, who would be Chandi Heffner, or a blood relative such as Pony Duke, Walker Inman, or someone else, the closest person to Doris seemed to be Bernard Lafferty. He was apparently grieving deeply. He was also seemingly the closest person to her based on the will with which Dr. Kivowitz was familiar.

The ethics experts said that if Dr. Kivowitz felt that Doris was terminal, and if Lafferty talked about how she would have hated her condition, hated her inactivity, would have preferred death to permanent helplessness, Dr. Kivowitz would not have been unusual in hastening the death. Other Los Angeles area doctors had made such compassionate decisions, establishing a precedent which Kivowitz did not violate.

The idea of a physician prematurely taking the life of the person he or she is hired to help is still upsetting to most Americans. Dr.

Jack Kevorkian's assisted suicides in the state of Michigan have gained international attention. Having assisted approximately twenty-five suicides by the time Doris Duke was dying, he would go on trial three different times, being acquitted in every instance.

By contrast, hospice workers and others caring for the terminally ill all report that most people cling to life, though they may go in and out of depression. And the role of a doctor rather than a family member who orders a respirator or other life support equipment turned off is extremely controversial. The Hippocratic oath taken by every new physician in the United States has as its core the idea that a physician should first do no harm. Yet both the precedents of physicians who have quietly taken lives and the reaction of the jurors who supported Kevorkian despite his violation of the oath indicate that the public is uncomfortable with eliminating the option of doctor-induced premature death for the terminally ill who wish to die.

At the same time, when a terminally ill patient is in intense pain and either living fitfully or drugged into unconsciousness, there are doctors who may skirt the ethical issue by simply supplying more medication than a patient needs. Someone who needs one sleeping pill a day may be given one hundred, for example. The patient thus has either a one hundred days' supply or the means to personally choose death when the doctor is not around.

The doctor can rest peacefully. He or she has provided the means for the death, knowing that the patient has reached a point where suicide is a viable option within that patient's belief system and experience. Some patients use the medication. Other patients endure, comforted by the fact that if there comes a time when living is intolerable, there is a way out. And among the latter, it is believed that most die before they feel they have reached an intolerable situation. The availability of death enables them to better endure the seeming injustices of their last days of life.

California has no law allowing assisted suicide. More important, there is nothing in writing that indicates that Doris Duke ever wanted to have her life ended. The final decision by Dr. Kivowitz was apparently unilateral as to day and time. He decided when and how she should die, claiming his action was justified based on the pain and suffering, which were *not evident in the nurses' notes* and which he failed to record anywhere else.

Did this mean that Dr. Kivowitz's actions may have been criminal? If Doris Duke was truly terminal, and if Dr. Kivowitz genuinely believed that a slight change in care would hasten her death by only a few hours or days at the most, then what he did had precedent. If he could state that the comments of the grief-stricken Lafferty, coupled with the fact that Doris Duke would never again leave her bed, convinced him that the increased painkiller was justified, he would probably not be found in ethical violation. This is the pragmatic side of medicine as it involves the terminally ill and their families or closest friends.

Would Doris Duke have wanted such treatment? It is hard to know with certainty. Dr. Kivowitz has been quoted as saying that Doris Duke would have wanted such treatment based on her discussions with him.

Prior to her growing debility, there is no question that she ardently embraced life, would never have considered premature death. Certainly there is no written record to show that she approved what eventually took place. Likewise, while she did not want heroic methods used, it is hard to consider the removal of oxygen-monitoring equipment, the ending of feeding, and the increase in a painkiller without written indication of pain as heroic methods.

Once again, as with the change in the will, it can not be determined with certainty that what took place accurately reflects Doris Duke's desires.

The allegations of murder by Tammy Payette and others seemed at the time to bolster a case against Dr. Kivowitz, and to possibly implicate others who benefited, such as Bernard Lafferty. Thus with the combination of Payette's charges and the questions raised about the appropriateness of Dr. Kivowitz's care, the Los Angeles authorities felt compelled to begin their investigation. Yet former staff members, who felt compelled to champion Doris Duke's cause, demanding to anyone who would listen that a full investigation be made before a final will is determined, have one question. Why did it take approximately fifteen months for the staff members to act?

Tom Rybak, for example, constantly has questioned why Colin Shanley, Tammy Payette, and every other "good guy" close to the case at the time of her death failed to seek outside help. He wonders why they didn't contact other family members and friends. He wonders why they didn't call the police. He has made himself seem like an obsessed extremist by harping on the issue, yet the fact is that it was many months before anyone came forward. Even when they did, had it not been for the courage of Ray Dowd, the allegations might never have reached the authorities.

There is no fully appropriate answer.

To the credit of some of the people aware of the premature death, they were being told that the situation was appropriate by men with medical degrees. In American society, most people look upon doctors with respect. Physicians have often had as much as twelve years' education after high school, and while they specialized in narrow areas of science, they are still viewed as sophisticated intellects. Doctors also hold a special place in our emotions because they represent life and death. They have the power to stay the hand of God, to ease the burdens of Job, to cheat death or assist it. Most people view doctors with a sense of awe. And when they are wealthy from their successful practices, we feel that we are somehow lesser beings for our more pedestrian lifestyles.

Doctors told the Falcon's Lair staff that what was taking place was right and proper. Doctors told the Falcon's Lair staff that they were acting in Miss Duke's interests. And equally important, the doctors spoke to people who came from servant work which, no matter how skilled, still carries an implication that the servant is a lesser person. Thus there was the added, subliminal message that the servants could not fathom the wisdom of their "betters."

Another problem was the money involved. There were alleged promises of lifetime job security, help for Colin Shanley's mother, and other significant offerings. Were these purported offers meant to be bribes to cover up improper activity or a continuation of Doris Duke's largesse? Certainly she wanted benefits for the staff members involved. The alleged promises could have been the equivalent of someone comforting a survivor by explaining that there would be a continuation of what had always been expected.

Or they could have been ways to control people who may have witnessed an improper action.

The money, if allegations were true, also could have been seen as hush money for potential witnesses. Bernard Lafferty, according to the Shanley allegations, made threats of violence against people he disliked, especially when he had been drinking. Some of those allegedly threatened might have feared that someone would be hired to hurt them or kill them. The fact that the alleged words had never been accompanied by any physical action was not comforting to people who also were aware that Lafferty had gone from being a co-worker to a man with access to hundreds of thousands of dollars. Yet to an outside observer, the fact that a man of his wealth could have hired a thug to commit a violent act with little likelihood of getting caught tends to make the seriousness of his alleged threats quite questionable.

It was because of Ray Dowd's courage that allegations were examined for any possible factual basis instead of being improperly shouted or equally improperly ignored. As Dowd explained:

"Basically, when Ann and Colin came to me, they didn't even know each other's accounts of the events leading up to Doris Duke's death," explained Dowd. "They had not ever had the opportunity to sit down together to say, 'What did you know about this? What did you know about that?'

"I personally watched them getting together on the phone in the fall of 1994 to compare notes on a household that was totally segregated and separated, and in which everyone was terrorized. People had suspicions about something, but with so many doctors and nurses around, how could anything go wrong?

"Doris Duke's staff members were in a position where loyalty, discretion, and basic subservience to doctors and lawyers is not only expected but prized. So for the chef to be questioning Dr. Kivowitz about giving a prescription is even more preposterous in that kind of environment."

Dowd continued, "Colin, Ann, and Mariano had intimations of things being wrong, or suspicions, or half-heard conversations that made someone go, 'Hmmm, I don't know about this.' But it would have been irresponsible to start shouting about foul play before learning more. Even when my clients came to me last. . . . almost two years ago, they said to me, 'You know, we've got some suspicions here.' And my first response was, as a lawyer, I can't deal with suspicions."

Dowd said that when he got them to tell him what they knew regarding evidence of alleged foul play, he felt that available evidence didn't "add up to a hill of beans." Dowd said they commented, "Well, we think Lafferty this. We think that. . . ."

None of the comments meant anything because there were no documented specifics. "With all due respect as a lawyer sitting in New York, I've got to advise you not only will you get your butt sued off, but to even say anything critical of the doctors would be irresponsible on your part. Proceeding without investigation could really destroy innocent people's careers. So I said, my advice is you may have suspicions, but they needed evidence before going public. They were saying things like, 'Oh, we *know* something is wrong.'

"[I said] Tell me what you know, what you witnessed, and when we got down to it in a legal sense, they didn't know anything. 'Well, you know, they were acting funny.' Well, acting funny . . . People act funny when people die, when coming into a million dollars. . . . It really didn't add up to a hill of beans."

Dowd explained that he told them that he was an attorney who handled civil work. "I don't know anything about this criminal stuff and I'm not going to pretend to be something I'm not." He said, "If I come upon one piece of evidence that convinces me in any way that something was wrong, that went on with Doris Duke improperly, I will bring it immediately to the proper authorities. That I can tell you. Honestly, to my thoughts, at the time it sounded like a far out hypothetical. And lawyers, we deal in some hypotheticals, but to proceed we must focus on what is concretely before us."

Dowd said that "during the course of a discovery we might turn up something, and okay, that's a whole different scenario. But why are we worrying about that scenario today?"

This was why Dowd brought the original suit based on work-related issues of unfulfilled employer promises. He explained, "First of all, Ann and Colin and Mariano had been totally used, abused, and ripped off in their work situations." Dowd felt that they were working more than forty hours a week without proper pay for the additional hours. Dowd also mentioned the promises allegedly made to Shanley concerning his quadriplegic mother's needed medical care. Shanley felt that working for Doris and, later, for Bernard, would help assure that Doris's alleged promises of medical care would be fulfilled. Yet over time, when nothing came through, Shanley felt he had to come forward.

Shanley also explained the frustrations he felt in knowing that his employer was ill, knowing that nothing was quite right, yet working in isolation in the kitchen. "I just sensed things were wrong, but it wasn't as if I could put myself forward on these positions. I'm basically slapping together meals for people I've never met before, who have never been in this woman's home before, and you have the most prominent physicians in Beverly Hills driving Bentleys and Jaguars all coming in to do their business. It was not my place to question or inquire."

Shanley said that he had been told by Lafferty that Doris Duke had leukemia. "Starting in June . . . I guess it was June, 1993," he was told many times by the butler, "that she was going to succumb from leukemia."

He explained, "See, there were times I asked the nursing staff about her [Doris Duke's] leukemia. They looked at me puzzled. I remember saying to Pearl [Rosenstein, one of the nurses], 'God, leukemia, how does this affect you?' I really didn't know what it was. I'm not well versed in medical things at all.

". . . And I remember her looking at me, puzzled, and saying, 'Leukemia? What are you talking about?'"

Colin assumed from the nurse's reaction that the issue was a very personal one, that it was wrong for him to be asking about something like that. "I didn't pursue it and she didn't pursue why I was asking that question. It kind of was awkward."

Shanley continued, "I could have gone to one of the doctors and asked him, but there are very definite lines defining what protocol becomes. I mean, I felt quite badly because, quite frankly, I liked her."

Shanley explained that the doctors came through the front door rather than passing through the kitchen dining area. There was a little contact with Dr. Kivowitz, but nothing that made him feel comfortable prying into Duke's health. "The few times I spoke with him was about when she was eating, what she was eating. But other than that, I would call them 'doctor' and they would call me 'Colin.' 'Hi. How you doing?' That sort of thing."

The doctors and nurses never bothered with the staff. Instead, Lafferty assumed the role of liaison, telling the staff what was happening. This was true even when the nurses or other medical professionals requested that the Duke staff obtain supplies such as rubbing alcohol. "Everyone had to go through Bernard."

The staff talked among themselves. Shanley was concerned as much as anyone. Yet the manner in which the household was run, the way the doctors and nurses were separated from the staff, and the role Lafferty played all prevented any serious questioning. Even when she died, the staff members were either in such shock, grief, or concern about their own future that contradictions between published reports and what they had been told were overlooked. The failure to come forward was more understandable than originally believed by former employees and other outsiders who cared about Doris Duke.

———— ❧ ————

NO MATTER WHAT the situation with Dr. Kivowitz might have been, and following Doris Duke's death he became the primary focus for questions about her final days, the greatest beneficiary was Bernard Lafferty, whose lifestyle changed even while his employer was alive. During the months when Doris Duke was frequently unable to think clearly, he began making personal purchases and distributing sizable sums of Duke's money, something for which there was no precedent. Attorney Richard Kuh investigated Duke's tax returns for several years prior to her death and found that she did not publicly give money in the way Lafferty did in her name that last year.

In September of 1993, a loan of $900,000 was made in the name of Doris Duke to Dr. Rolando Atiga. This was not the first money she had loaned him. He was already in debt to her for more than $400,000, a fact that normally would have been likely to cause her to cut off further funding.

On October 4, 1993, Dr. Harry Glassman was gifted with $500,000, the check signed by George Reed, who worked for the

Duke Business Office.[13] Attorney Richard Kuh would later report that "On March 2, 1995, Lafferty said that when he had spoken to George Reed ("Reed") at the DBO, and instructed him to send $500,000 check payable to Dr. Glassman, Duke was listening on a speakerphone. When again interviewed by me a month later, on April 13, 1995, Lafferty was told that the previous day (April 12, 1995) Reed, who had kept contemporaneous notes, had said he had not been told that Duke was on a speakerphone, and knew nothing of such first-hand Duke knowledge—*all his dealings having been with Lafferty and Doyle* [emphasis added]—Lafferty said maybe nothing had been said to Reed about it."

From Reed's notes concerning the $500,000 gift to Dr. Harry Glassman:

> Bernard sending me authority to draw a check for Dr. Harry Glassman for $500,000 and send to him overnight so he has on Tuesday—it's a gift.
> Also he's sending a list of contributions to go out from *Miss Duke personally by overnight mail on Tuesday*—
> $2,000,000 to Duke University for AIDS cure
> $1,000,000 to Eliz Taylor for " " "
> $1,000,000 to Michael Jackson for [no note as to what it was for]
> $1,000,000 to PETA [People for the Ethical Treatment of Animals]
> Large donations to local fire cos. etc."
> *Bernard said:*
> Besides the check for Dr. Glassman, the contributions to
> PETA
> Michael Jackson
> Eliz Taylor
> Duke University
> are to be from Miss Duke Personal.
> The other contributions should be made by DDF [Doris Duke Foundation][14]

There was more to Lafferty's lifestyle than ingratiating himself with the rich and famous. While he arranged to give money to Elizabeth Taylor and singer Michael Jackson, the latter an action not completed after Jackson received extensive publicity concerning possible child molestation, he also was personally spending money.

Ann Bostich commented that beginning with the summer of 1993, Lafferty would spend a portion of each day shopping. "He began to wear extravagant clothing and jewelry. Almost every day he would spend substantial sums of money. He would go on shopping sprees, buying paintings, artwork, furniture, jewelry, clothing, shoes, socks, and knick-knacks.

"Lafferty wanted everyone to believe that Miss Duke made enormous household expenditures so that he could continue them after she died. He made extravagant expenditures, such as a $40,000 lighting system and $3,000 silk curtains for a small French door. All of these expenditures did not make much sense to me, because I understood that Falcon's Lair was to be sold after Miss Duke's death."[15]

Bostich mentioned that, "At one point in early 1994, Doyle and Lafferty had a disagreement over a $9,000 bill for living room curtains. I was in the room when Lafferty responded to Doyle's call. In a conversation that lasted about one hour, Doyle told Lafferty that he could not spend money making improvements on the house. Lafferty responded with what can only be compared to a child's temper tantrum. He screamed at Doyle. That conversation took place just as Lafferty was leaving to go to a Patti Labelle concert. He was wearing a black Armani outfit. Makasiale had applied makeup, including mascara, eyeliner, pancake makeup, and lipstick to Lafferty. By the time Lafferty was done screaming at Doyle—and crying—the makeup had run down his face, streaking it. He was screaming that Miss Duke left him her houses and her money to do with as he pleased.

"Whenever Doyle or someone from the bank tried to rein in Lafferty's spending, he would tell them, 'Well, I can always find another law firm. I can always find another bank.'"[16]

Attorney Richard Kuh did an examination of Bernard Lafferty's spending on his American Express card alone. In December of 1993, for example, more than $5,000 was spent in each of three luxury-item stores—Cartier, Giorgio Armani, and Louis Vuitton. In the following year, the total for Cartier was just under $50,000 and for Georgio Armani was more than $66,000. The total spending on the American Express card for major department stores was $20,153.47 for December 1993 alone. It reached a high of $41,527.41 for the month of October 1994, and a low of just $406.37 for April 1994, one of only two months in the course of the year when his spending dropped below $1,000. The total for the year, unrelated to expenditures for food, transportation, or housing were charges of $155,272.67.[17] That same year, the total of all American Express card personal charges totaled $266,652 with another $90,915 charged for estate items.[18] And as late as February 25, 1994, Lafferty charges on the American Express account of Doris Duke, totaled $5,303 for the month. And all of this by a man whose position with the estate remained uncertain before the probating of the will, and whose income was well below what was appropriate for the charges made.

Karen Unger had been concerned about the ethics and propriety of having her bank, U.S. Trust, loan Lafferty money prior to the settling of issues revolving around the will. Certainly it was obvious that Lafferty was delighting in using whatever money he could get his hands on. And always he acted without anyone challenging or stopping him.

The story of Lafferty gradually became fodder for gossip columnists throughout the country. His outrageous antics led both photographers and reporters to seek him out. For example, on July 13, 1995, columnists George Rush and Joanna Molloy wrote in their *New York Daily News* column:

> First, he wears her jewelry. Now, Doris Duke's butler/trustee, Bernard Lafferty, reportedly has been wearing her clothes.
> Mind you, we're told the 45-year-old pony tailed Lafferty has been raiding Duke's closet strictly to find vestments that will allow him to channel with the billionaires from beyond the grave . . .

Cindy Adams's *New York Post* column for May 9, 1995, first described Lafferty's drug use, then mentioned:

The Butler couldn't drive. Court papers claim he "recklessly drove and totaled a Duke Cadillac." Later, with Duke funds, he bought an identical car. Sole purpose? "To escort Victoria Principal."

Victoria, whose husband got Dr. Harry Glassman half a mil from The Butler, managed to place her skin care cosmetics at Duke's bedside. Nurses rated this "tacky."

Elizabeth Taylor's name also was introduced into the aftermath. She had received a $1 million gift for the fight against AIDS from Lafferty in Doris's name. Taylor also attested that Doris had been mentally competent when the changes in the will were made, explaining that they had known each other since Elizabeth was eighteen. Ironically, the supermarket tabloid press ran a photograph of Bernard Lafferty and Taylor, the outrageously false implication being that they might have a romantic involvement.

And as always, the lawyers were the greatest beneficiaries. By February of 1995, Richard Kuh had determined that the fees were approximately $13,000,000.[19] Bernard Lafferty was a client of Katten Muchin & Zavis, and there were often two or more attorneys present with him when he had to be involved with depositions or litigation. When KMZ (then Katten Muchin Zavis & Weitzman) began working with Doris Duke, the estate planning fees were noted to cost $325 per hour for Alan Croll's time and $275 per hour for Bill Doyle. The prices were subject to change at any time and did not include the charges for others involved.[20] It would have been cheaper to hire experts in each field of concern and put them on annual salary than to work through the law firm.

So what really happened to Doris Duke?

ONCE THE INVESTIGATORS began looking into Doris Duke's last days, there were several questions they had to explore. An obvious one came from the admission by Dr. Kivowitz that he deliberately shortened Doris Duke's life. This was certainly within precedent established among members of the medical association, provided he acted alone or with professionals following his orders. But investigators would have to consider whether there could have been others working with him to plan her premature death. Could there have been a conspiracy to benefit from her will, to perhaps commit murder as some had alleged?

Dr. Kivowitz deliberately ordered the stopping of food and water at the same time that he increased her morphine and Demerol to fatal levels. Although controversial and seemingly an outrage to many who knew her, if he believed his actions were meant to ease Doris Duke's pain, suffering, and terminal helplessness, he would not be reprimanded within his profession, nor would he be criminally charged.

The nurses carrying out the orders were acting in the belief that the physician overseeing Doris Duke's care had her best interests in mind. He was the one who presumably had conversations with Doris Duke concerning her desires if she ever reached a state of unstoppable decline. He was the one who presumably had read any living will she may have made concerning her treatment after entering what the doctor judged to be a terminal state. They acted according to their medical training as it pertains to the hierarchy of caregiving in medicine, even if they did not agree with what was happening.

But what of Dr. Harry Glassman, a specialist in plastic surgery, not the primary-care physician? Was he in a position to understand Doris Duke's condition or to see any discrepancy between the nurses' notes and the actions Dr. Kivowitz was taking?

What of the attorneys whose law firm would profit handsomely from the estate work?

In addition, investigators would have to consider the less likely possibility that Doris Duke's life was deliberately taken, not for humanitarian reasons but to shut her up before she could protest the changed will. The medical records that were kept in Doris's home indicate that sedation increased when she began complaining about Bernard and being trapped in the house.

FOR MONTHS the Los Angeles Police Department, working with the district attorney's office, investigated the death of Doris Duke. The report of Richard Kuh and the allegations of Tammy Payette required an intense look into all aspects of the death.

On July 22, 1996, a letter was sent over the signature of Richard L. Jenkins, Head Deputy District Attorney for the Los Angeles County District Attorney's Office, Bureau of Special Operations, Major Crimes Division. It read:

> As you are aware, an investigation was conducted by the Los Angeles Police Department with the assistance of this office regarding the circumstances surrounding the death of Ms. Doris Duke.
>
> The results of the completed investigation disclosed no credible evidence of criminal homicide. The facts developed during this investigation and the results thereof will remain confidential.

# Epilogue

RAYMOND DOWD REMAINS a thorn in the proceedings. Attorneys are considered to be officers of the court. This means that truth must be paramount, that justice must prevail. This does not always happen in a criminal courtroom where the adversary method of deciding cases before a jury can lead to emotional manipulation, not necessarily truth. But in a civil proceeding, a lawyer such as Dowd believes his first allegiance is to what is right.

Ray Dowd's clients fare best with the last will in place. The changes in the wills handled by KMZ each tend to reward certain employees a little better than with the previous wills. This means that when he challenged the last will, he felt Doris Duke could not have understood what she was signing the day she signed it. He felt that the will should be declared invalid. This was done despite the fact that the previous will naming his clients would award them fewer benefits if he were to win their civil action. Yet as Dowd saw it, justice would prevail for all involved, including Doris Duke, assuming she was not competent when she signed her will in the hospital. And since he takes seriously his role as an officer of the court, acting for truth rather than a client's self-interest, he could be the noblest warrior in the battle. (Note: Dowd's clients would benefit from the breach of employment contract action, a separate issue for the estate.)

Certainly he was the most unlikely challenger to the rich, powerful interests engaged in legal combat. And though a man of greater integrity, Dowd's tenacity was so much like Buck Duke's that Doris Duke probably would have approved of his challenge even if he was wrong. (If her belief in reincarnation is a valid one, there may be time within her next lifetime and his current one for her to congratulate him for his efforts.)

Ultimately, the last will to be written was approved as valid by the court with modifications. Tragically, the money already spent in probating the will would have outraged Doris Duke. As Surrogate Court Judge Eve Preminger has stressed from time to time, the money that was left was meant for causes that reflect the public interest. The trusts and foundations were designed to improve the lives of many, and nonessential costs charged to the estate would have incurred her wrath.

At this writing, some civil battles continue to be waged. It has been reported that under the terms of the modified will that the surrogate approved, Bernard Lafferty accepted a multimillion dollar settlement.

Dr. Demopoulos has become one of the trustees of the Doris Duke Charitable Foundation. U.S. Trust is sole executor of the estate.

And as is too often the case, tragically in this instance where Doris Duke always wanted her money to be used for the public good, an ever-growing sum is being taken by the attorneys. Ultimately they are proving to be the true victors, their fees having reached millions of dollars.

Doris Duke spent decades buying anything and anyone she desired. She developed a corporate executive's expertise in business, a museum curator's expertise in art, a botanist's expertise in orchids, and a slut's expertise in sex. She lived life to the fullest, trusting no one, using everyone, being vulnerable to love only a half-dozen times—with Jimmy Cromwell, Porfirio Rubirosa, her music, her dancing, her dogs, and Chandi Heffner. It was only with the ravages of age compounded by alcohol, pills, laxatives, and surgery that she dropped her guard. The high-living butler, the massive legal fees, and the delays in disbursing the first of the grants expected to come from the trusts and foundations clearly would have saddened and angered Doris Duke.

In the end, the death of Doris Duke was a massive tragedy for all concerned. That she died before her time is a certainty. That she could have recovered enough to travel, at least to one of the homes she loved, is unknown. She might have remained, in an almost certainly terminal condition, bedridden and miserable, frustrated by an active mind and a rapidly declining body.

Equally tragic are the questions that will forever haunt the others involved. Dr. Kivowitz is not being charged with any criminal wrongdoing or any ethical violations. But he has had his medical judgment questioned by some physicians who never knew his patient, nor were present during her final days. He has explained that he acted with compassion, his decisions in the best interest of a terminally ill patient.

Why was $500,000 given to Dr. Harry Glassman prior to Doris Duke's death when all similar bequests were left in her will? Was it simply a gift of friendship as Dr. Glassman contends? Doris may have deviated from the manner in which she benefited other friends because she knew she had little time and enjoyed seeing his reaction.

Allegations were made in court proceedings by former Duke staff members that Bernard Lafferty was not always a faithful servant, but a schemer for position and power. Or was he a gentle, compassionate man, troubled, a periodic alcohol abuser, yet a true friend to the woman who gave him repeated chances to abandon his self-destructive actions?

Was Chandi Heffner a scheming opportunist or a person wronged by all, including the woman she loved in the manner of a committed friend or, perhaps, a surrogate parent? Certainly the more than $60 million she eventually gained from the trust Doris's father established seems in line with the rules of that trust. But was the money her ultimate goal? And even if it was, was Chandi another plaything Doris wanted to buy, just as she had purchased lovers over the years? Was Chandi someone whose price Doris determined from the start and would have been comfortable paying had she remained healthy?

Bill Doyle was well-to-do by most people's standards, a relative lightweight in terms of hourly billing for KMZ when he landed the Doris Duke account. In addition to potentially increasing his own income, he would become a far more respected member of the law firm. Yet the rush to change the will while Doris Duke was still in the hospital, her mental state inconsistent on any given day, gave rise to questions about the appropriateness of the will signing.

U.S. Trust, as Karen Unger pointed out, had to confront ethical questions of possible conflict of interest when it justified loaning Bernard Lafferty more than $800,000 from an estate that had yet to be settled in the courts. He had no assets, and his future remained in question because of the ongoing litigation. Yet U.S. Trust also wanted to keep its client happy given the vast size of the portion of the Duke estate brought under its management. Millions were waiting to be made or lost, and those millions had to be a concern for the bank. It is a profit-making organization, not a public-service or government agency. The instant influx of a billion dollars or more in readily liquefied assets is enough to alter many a career for the better. Yet the publicity about the action also tainted this major corporation.

———— ⚜ ————

ON MONDAY, NOVEMBER 4, 1996, Bernard Lafferty suffered a massive heart attack, ending his life. A few weeks before his death, Patricia S. Lawford, sister of John F. Kennedy and widow of the actor Peter Lawford, was at the same hairdresser used by Lafferty. He was preparing to travel to New York for yet another court appearance relative to the Duke estate and his role in handling it. He was also so high on drugs and severely impaired by alcohol that he had trouble walking and talking, his speech slurred to the point of being almost incomprehensible. He was obese, sloppily dressed, yet adorned with so much jewelry that he was a grotesque parody of a bon vivant, a man about town. To Patricia, an acknowledged former addict and alcoholic who had straightened out her life after her husband, Peter, died of alcoholism and drug abuse, he seemed in dangerously bad health. She was amazed his heart had not failed him then and wondered how long he could live without intervention. The surprise to those who knew him was not that he died on November 4, but that he survived so long.

With Lafferty's death, a retrospective look at his actions seemed warranted, although all the facts will undoubtedly never be known.

By the time of Doris Duke's death, some of the employees closest to Bernard Lafferty felt he wanted to *be* Doris Duke, not just hold power among the staff. He had achieved a position and a lifestyle well beyond anything a semiliterate, orphaned immigrant could have imagined for himself. Yet when Duke became ill, her health declining in what seemed an irreversible downward spiral, Lafferty began creating a future that was an odd blend of servant and master.

Lafferty was always viewed as being intelligent despite his lack of education. He had spent his adult years having to anticipate the whims of the people around him. He was a man whose career was to please others while remaining as invisible to them as possible. He was frequently in the midst of the rich and famous, witnessing their behavior in private gatherings. He listened to them talk, discussing their true feelings, revealing the best and worst of their character traits. Each of these moneyed, powerful celebrity guests had reason to protect the others present because they all had weaknesses members of the media, as well as their rivals, were anxious to exploit.

Staff members on Doris Duke's estates may have watched and listened to everyone, but they kept to the background, fading to seeming invisibility in ballrooms where those of low status were perceived as no more a threat than the furniture. Some of the staff signed confidentiality agreements when they obtained their jobs. Others did not. But to their credit, most staff members maintained a loyalty and respect that justified their employer's trust.

Lafferty was not looking to betray Doris Duke and her guests to the tabloids. Instead, he seemed to be learning information he could use later to better his position or curry favor with someone he admired—to gain without blackmail or betrayal. That was why, like any good servant, he studied the actions, attitudes, and language of the famous guests. And because the events were private, the guests revealed aspects of their characters in ways they would not have done under other circumstances.

Lafferty allegedly used this knowledge to begin isolating Doris Duke as she became ill. He knew which of her friends and acquaintances she expected to contact her and whose absence from her life would be troubling. He knew which individuals could be denied access without his mistress's suspicions being aroused. And he knew how to talk with them all in a manner that would be most effective in keeping them from looking too closely at her health, her care, and her declining quality of life.

Increasing responsibility was given to the butler. But though he may have been intelligent, the handling of great art treasures, large quantities of gold, vast businesses, and heavily endowed philanthropic organizations cannot be done by someone who is untrained in such fields. Likewise, there are no self-help books to teach someone what to do with a billion dollars.

Doris Duke was also without extensive formal education, though she had far more schooling than Lafferty, including from her father. When the estate was relatively small, Buck Duke helped educate his nephew, his business heir apparent, over many months. The youth had college training, but he held the equivalent of a Ph.D. in Duke enterprises when he drowned. Buck then switched the schooling to his daughter, a less desirable alternative only because she was so young. Fortunately, she was eager to learn, bright, and became a woman who would pursue self-education throughout her life.

More important, although Buck Duke was an extremely wealthy man, the holdings were simpler, the business less complicated than it would become through Doris's guidance over the next sixty-plus years. There were also advisors specifically appointed to keep the estate flourishing while Doris was educated to run things on her own.

Perhaps as critical, Buck and Nanaline instilled in Doris a love of reading, of research, of questioning those with extensive knowledge in fields of interest so she could master any subject about which she was curious. That was why her early wills and powers of attorney selected individuals learned in one or more of the areas with which they would be involved. That was also why Doris Duke, in her earlier years, would not have given personal or extensive estate management power to Bernard Lafferty, a man who could barely read and showed no interest in bettering himself intellectually.

The butler undoubtedly understood all this, as did the other servants who regularly interacted with Doris Duke. They all knew that either she had changed her thinking in her last months of life or she had become so weakened by illness, bodily deterioration and/or drug reactions that she entertained ideas she would have rejected earlier.

Doris Duke seemingly had the constitution of an athlete when Bernard Lafferty first began working for her. He was also in the throes of alcoholism, early on having the binge that caused Duke to pay for residential treatment. Any fantasies of gaining power and influence relative to her estate undoubtedly lay dormant in the butler's mind, never forgotten yet never entertained as a serious possibility.

That all changed when it became obvious that Doris Duke was not well. She had indulged her whims in drugs and alcohol in a less destructive, more controlled way than Lafferty, yet it was still in a destructive manner. Her diet was less than her body needed for proper nutrition, regardless of the best efforts of her chefs to make appropriate food, flawlessly prepared, available to her. And only her physically active life kept her body functioning in ways that belied the underlying deterioration.

Doris Duke's pursuit of physical beauty through the skillful sculpting of the plastic surgeon's knife led her to subject her body to trauma unhealthy for a woman of her years. She accelerated problems that were developing from her lifestyle, and she compounded her troubles with medication often used improperly. By the time she had entered the hospital and was considering a new will, Bernard Lafferty had managed to obtain power a younger Doris Duke would never have given him.

At the same time, Lafferty had learned how to utilize men of great learning involved with his employer's care. He recognized that while they might be friends with Duke, her wealth and status caused them to extend a certain deference to her. They were seemingly uncomfortable acting against her desires, even if her expressed wishes seemed radically different from those she had expressed in the past. Certainly this was true with the powers of attorney, including for medical care, an area where previously she wanted only MDs involved.

Lafferty was a man who spoke with authority, and that authority seemingly came directly from Doris Duke. As a result, others treated him as more than a servant. The doctors and lawyers, along with some staff members and friends, perceived Lafferty as a key gatekeeper. Orders were passed through him, and his word was taken. He was at times a source of information about Doris's condition. For example: Lafferty might assure the lawyers that Doris was in good shape, as he did on June 14, yet as was mentioned in Chapter 16, Nurse Pearl Rosenstein's note indicated that Doris was "forgetful—conversing with Bernard—has forgotten all activities taken place today—i.e. attorneys & Business matters."

Again as previously shown, the medical chart for September 20 reads, in part, that Doris Duke "states she's afraid of being murdered." Two days later the notes read "patient agitated, and angry, accusing Bernard of her being ill."

The tension between Lafferty and Duke appeared to grow at times when Doris seemed most like her former self. Yet this was seemingly recognized only in hindsight. While treatment was taking place and business was being conducted, Lafferty was seen as solicitous, respectful, and selflessly concerned with Duke's interests.

Later, when decisions had to be made about Doris Duke's care in what everyone realized would be the final days of her life, Lafferty was seen as a man who loved her. He gave the impression to outsiders of being ever present by her side. He seemed to harbor a special relationship that had already led him to be trusted to spend estate money, to carry out arrangements for her medical care, and for gifts to made in her name. Thus, if he talked of Doris Duke's pain, of how she would rather be dead than trapped in bed, declining by the minute, others would listen. He had become the equivalent of the next of kin in the minds of those hired to care for her. He spoke, they listened. And when Lafferty allegedly was irate that Duke was not responding to the increased morphine the way he expected, no one thought it odd that he was so comfortable with the imminence of her death.

Once freed of the burden of Doris Duke, Lafferty took advantage of his access to the Duke estates as well as Doris Duke's clothing. He became imperious with the staff, making demands that were well out of their job descriptions. And after barking out orders in a caricature of what Doris had only rarely done in life, Lafferty adjourned to her bedroom, adorning himself with her night clothes, her jewelry.

"Having it all" did not improve Bernard Lafferty's life. Besieged by lawyers seeking Duke Estate business, lawyers challenging the changed will, even lawyers investigating him, Lafferty returned to the heavy drinking and drug use that had plagued him in recent years. When he died, he was alone in bed "in the affluent Bel-Air section of western Los Angeles," the *New York Times* obituary reported.

Among the few supporters of Lafferty at the end was author Stephanie Mansfield. She was quoted in the *Times* as saying, "He was not in it for the money. Bernard didn't have a life beyond Doris, and she showed a side of herself to him that she showed to few others, that was warm, funny and loving."

The truth of the Lafferty/Duke relationship in this life ended as it began, with more questions than answers. Yet if he did betray her, and if her religious beliefs are accurate, Bernard Lafferty is likely to be facing the uncompromising wrath of his former employer. In that event, unless there is a mellowing of humanity in whatever the afterlife proves to be, Lafferty's judgment by God will be far more compassionate than anything meted out by the woman who, in the end, would have finally understood why her father always warned her to trust no one.

# Notes

CHAPTER 1: TOBACCO BARONS

1. Quote from William J. Cooper and Thomas E. Terrill, *The American South: A History* (New York: Alfred A. Knopf, 1990), p. 493.

CHAPTER 2: BLOODLINES

1. Farms have changed over the years. When Duke bought his property, the acreage was not unusual for a larger farm. Many that were in the eastern and midwestern farming country were larger. But in recent years, such property would be massive. In Michigan, for example, there were many farms larger than Buck Duke's property at the time he purchased it. But by the time Doris Duke died, farms larger than 1,000 acres—less than half her Somerville estate—were great rarities in the region. Her holdings increased substantially in value and continue to do so to this day.

CHAPTER 3: OPEN SEASON ON THE RICH

1. There is another story told about Buck Duke, the truth of which cannot be determined. This is that he planned to give up his American citizenship following the creation of the income tax. He had long been in a business that required him to spend several months a year in England, so he was familiar with the country, the people, and the government's attitude toward business.

The British public knew that Duke had the money to buy himself a peerage if he so chose. He was also a friend of the royal family and an acquaintance of the American ambassador to the Court of St. James, Walter Hines Page. Upon his arrival in London, he immediately arranged for a lease with purchase option for a mansion in the Mayfair section. When England declared war on Germany, foreigners and many British fled the land. There was a chance that the Dukes would be stranded abroad for the duration of the war, something Buck avoided only with the ambassador's help.

2. Quote from interview with Mrs. William Few, Duke University, Durham, North Carolina, by Frank Rounds, September 14, 1963. Material provided by the Columbia University, City of New York, Oral History Research Office of the Butler Library.

CHAPTER 5: LEARNING TO BE INDEPENDENT

1. Interview with Mrs. E. C. Marshall of Charlotte, North Carolina, October 1, 1963, conducted by Frank Rounds with Marshall Pickens for the Duke Endowment. Material provided by the Columbia University, City of New York, Oral History Research Office of the Butler Library.

2. Pony Duke and Jason Thomas, *Too Rich: The Family Secrets of Doris Duke* (New York: HarperCollins, 1996), p. 63.

## CHAPTER 6: COMING OUT

1. Stephanie Mansfield, *The Richest Girl in the World* (New York: G. P. Putnam's Sons, 1992), p. 75.

## CHAPTER 7: FIRST MARRIAGE

1. Something somewhat similar occurred during World War II with service as PT boat captains. The navy men chosen to command PT boats were frequently rich youths with little in their backgrounds that would warrant such responsibility. However, they all had spent years operating their family yachts, and the PT boats were the size of and had the handling characteristics of the typical yacht. While sometimes the captains were effective, in the most famous example of the weakness in the system, John F. Kennedy was given the command of *PT-109*. Failing to take a mission seriously, he broke radio and direct observation contact with two other PT boats during a mission. While he and the men who should have been on alert were talking, his boat was struck by a Japanese carrier.

2. Stephanie Mansfield, *The Richest Girl in the World* (New York: G. P. Putnam's Sons, 1992), p. 85.

## CHAPTER 8: A FOOL AND HIS WIFE ARE SOON PARTED

1. Doris Duke, "My Honolulu House," *Town & Country* (August 1947), p. 73.
2. Ibid., p. 77.
3. Pony Duke and Jason Thomas, *Too Rich: The Family Secrets of Doris Duke* (New York: HarperCollins, 1996), p. 100. Duke's story is confusing. He says that the abortion was performed on his cousin in New York's Queen's Hospital in 1939. There was no Queen's Hospital in Manhattan, although there was one in the borough called Queen's—Queen's Borough Hospital. The problem with assuming she went to that hospital is that it not only took care of the poor, it specialized in highly communicable diseases. Doris Duke Cromwell might have had no qualms about using a hospital taking care of indigents, and certainly her hush money would be attractive to the staff. It is doubtful that she would have put herself in a place known to have highly contagious patients throughout. What is certain is that when her second pregnancy brought about the premature birth and death of her daughter a year later, the hospital *was* called Queen's, only that Queen's was located in Honolulu, Hawaii.
4. The Winchell item had far more impact in 1940 than it would today. Winchell felt that the private life of every important position could be mined for material for his column. He felt that politicians had to meet the moral standards the public expected from their own family situation. Since this was a time when divorce was not in favor by most Americans, Cromwell's plan to divorce following an election was important.

How extreme this view was, and how long it lasted, can be seen by what happened during the 1960 Democratic National Convention in Los Angeles, twenty years after the Cromwell fiasco. A young Massachusetts senator named John F. Kennedy, still considered a lightweight in New England, was spotted by Winchell and other reporters leaving the apartment of a girlfriend. Since Kennedy was being primed for the presidency, Winchell knew he had a good story. He immediately telephoned his editor in New York City and dictated the item.

The editor was shocked. Jack Kennedy was married. There was no way the newspapers of the nation would run the scandalous item about a married man. It would hurt his marriage, and that was something that was not done back then. Yet had his character been known, the outcome of the convention and the election would have been very different. The fact that Winchell was allowed to use the Cromwell item showed little respect people had for Jimmy.

## CHAPTER 9: PLAYGIRL, SPY, AND WRITER

1. The story of Doris Duke's loss of Captain Henderson is based on an evaluation of what was happening at the time. Different biographers have come to different conclusions. Some feel that she wanted to return to the United States. Her lover's death gave her the excuse she needed. Others feel that she was in immediate danger of being recalled to Washington for training, a more likely scenario. Certainly she needed to stay in Europe if she was to be able to travel wherever she desired. Thus the story being described is most likely the accurate one. The others are mentioned for clarity, should the reader be familiar with them.

## CHAPTER 11: DORIS DUKE IN TRANSITION

1. A common-law marriage is a legal marriage for tax, inheritance, and other purposes. There is no ceremony, no courthouse record. Generally government agencies follow the thinking of the Social Security Administration, whose policy then and later was that a couple was legally married if they met at least some of the following criteria: (a) The couple must have spent twenty-four hours together as man and wife. This can occur when vacationing and registering in this manner in a hotel; and (b) the couple considered themselves to be man and wife and presented themselves that way to others. Certainly the names in the cookbook, and many other indicators, show that Doris considered herself to be Mrs. Joey Castro.

2. There is some uncertainty as to whether Duke University officials or Duke family members more closely tied to the university than Doris were the ones who scoffed at her agricultural concepts. Pony Duke feels that she was swayed by family members who reinforced her feelings of intellectual inadequacy because she lacked a formal education. Certainly they would have had a strong influence on Doris and could have convinced her that she did not understand the mission of colleges and universities in general. However, she also felt as if she was not really a part of Duke University, that its officials were interested only in her money. Either way, the school failed to benefit.

3. As is so often the case with Doris Duke, there are questions as to what degree she was a believer in a quack cure and to what degree she wanted to be objective. Stephanie Mansfield in *The Richest Girl in the World* (see Chapter 6, note 1, above) quotes Peter Brooke telling of Doris having befriended a man who had a machine she believed cured her of skin cancer. She wanted Nat King Cole to use it since he was dying of cancer. And she wanted Brooke to write about the machine. According to the story, Brooke had it tested at UCLA and found it was fraudulent. He told Doris, who was livid and became angrier when she could not persuade Duke University to establish a lab for the inventor at their medical center.

4. A different story is given by Pony Duke and Jason Thomas in *The Family Se-*

*crets of Doris Duke* (New York: HarperCollins, 1996), pp. 178–179. They state: "The two had been drinking heavily for almost two days before she slid behind the wheel of the rental car. Eddie Tirella was staggering when he climbed from the passenger seat and struggled with the padlock at the gate. Doris was close to drunk when she joked to Tirella that his alcoholic condition was such that he could not open the lock. She laughed and pushed her heel into the accelerator to make the motor roar in an effort to startle Tirella, whose handsome face was caught in a sheepish and inebriated grin as he pretended to push away the car. The motor roared again. And he was dead."

The story is undoubtedly the one that Doris told her cousin, the one she wanted to live with. It may even be accurate. It does not answer the question about Doris's seeming failure to brake and the staff's removing all evidence. Admittedly, they might have been doing more than necessary to protect her, but the idea that the incident was nothing but drunken play between friends seems unlikely.

CHAPTER 12: THE TROUBLE WITH CHANDI

1. Bob Colacello, "Doris Duke's Final Mystery," *Vanity Fair* magazine (March 1994), p. 172.

CHAPTER 13: THE CHEF, THE BUTLER, AND THE GOLDEN GIRL

1. Bob Colacello, "Doris Duke's Final Mystery," *Vanity Fair* magazine (March 1994), p. 174.

2. Exhibit P to affidavit by Dr. Harry Demopoulos, p. RA 334; Surrogate Court identification RA 000334.

3. Ibid., Exhibit O; p. RA 330.

4. Ibid., Exhibit S; p. RA346–RA 347; identification RA 000346.

CHAPTER 14: BUTLER RISES

1. Cited in Pony Duke and Jason Thomas, *Too Rich: The Family Secrets of Doris Duke* (New York: HarperCollins, 1996), pp. 201–202.

2. Quotes from the Affidavit of Colin Shanley, State of New York Surrogate's Court: County of New York, Probate Proceeding, Will of DORIS DUKE, Deceased. File No. 4440–93, pp. 8–9, paragraphs 19–23.

3. Ibid., p. 9, paragraph 24.

4. Ibid., p. 12–13, paragraphs 33–34.

5. Ibid., p. 10, paragraphs 27–28.

6. Ibid., p. 30, paragraphs 37–42.

7. Ibid.

8. It is important to note two interesting points about the codicil to Doris Duke's November 4, 1991, Last Will and Testament. First, Bernard Lafferty's name is consistently misspelled. Although there have been many questions about the validity of the will and the ability of Doris Duke to reason at the time the codicil was prepared in April 1992, there is a chance that this is more a reflection of her wishes than many wish to believe. Pony Duke and others have talked about Doris constantly referring to Bernard Lafferty as "Rafferty," some feeling she wanted to demean him by calling him by something other than his correct name, others feeling she never remembered it. Whichever the case, it is doubtful that anyone other than Doris Duke would have done this deliberately.

The other points that are interesting are the fact that the designated bank is The Bank of New York and that she sets caps on the amount of compensation for both the co-executors ($250,000.00 each) and the bank handling the trust account ($7,000,000.00). In the earlier will from November 4, 1991, she named her accountant, Irwin Bloom, and Chemical Bank as co-executors. Chemical Bank had earlier been named for the July 28, 1987, will, although with the proviso that Chandi could name her own New York City bank or trust company within two months of Doris Duke's death. She authorized Irwin Bloom to receive "a maximum commission equal to Seven Million Five Hundred Thousand Dollars ($7,500,000.00) for the performance of his duties as an Executor hereunder." This is the same total she would later set aside to be divided among the co-executors and The Bank of New York. Thus the total is in line with her earlier desires.

CHAPTER 15: "DISORIENTED TO TIME AND PLACE"

1. April 11, 1995, letter from Nicholas T. Macris, M.D., to Richard H. Kuh, Esq., found in Section 2 of the Exhibits to Report of Richard H. Kuh, Limited Temporary Administrator, for the State of New York Surrogate's Court, County of New York, File No. 4440/93.

2. Quotes from the Affidavit of Colin Shanley, State of New York Surrogate's Court, County of New York, Probate Proceeding, Will of DORIS DUKE, Deceased. File No. 4440-93, pp. 25–26.

3. Probate Proceeding, Will of Doris Duke, Deceased. Volume I (pp. 1–208) 1404, Examination of CHARLES FREDERICK KIVOWITZ, M.D., taken on behalf of the Defendant JONES, at 711 South Hope, Room Malibu A, Los Angeles, California, commencing at 1:06 P.M., Wednesday, January 4, 1995, p. 91.

4. Ibid., p. 95.

5. Ibid., p. 98.

6. Colchicine, Vivactyl, Epogen, Premarin, Protropin, Dulcolax, Digoxin, Peri-Colace, Cardizem, multivitamins, folic acid, IV fluids, cefotetan, Haldol, Toradol, Restoril, Darvocet, and Halcion.

7. Ibid., plus TPN 85 cc/hour, Lipids, and Accucheck.

8. Colchicine, Vivactyl, Epogen, Premarin, Protropin, Dulcolax, TPN, Vitamin K, Lipids 20%, Valium, Meprobamate, Digoxin, Peri-Colace, multivitamins, folic acid, Zoloft, Durabolin, iron sulfate, Haldol, Halcion, Heparin, Restoril, Darvocet, Neosporin, Periactin, Reglan, hydrocortisone.

9. From general Daily Records of Doris Duke transcribed from original notes, pp. 11–13.

10. All quotes concerning William Doyle, Jr., are taken from his Affidavit of May 22, 1995, for the Probate Proceeding, Will of DORIS DUKE, Deceased. File No. 4440-93, State of New York Surrogate's Court, County of New York. (Herafter cited as Doyle Affidavit.)

11. Daily Records of Doris Duke, pp. 15–16.

12. Ibid., pp. 16–17.

13. Ibid., p. 19.

14. Ibid., p. 20.

15. *Consultation*—Infectious Disease dated 03/04/93. The Consultant was

Philip Zakowski, M.D., and the patient's name is listed as Norma Jane, the pseudonym of Doris Duke. A carbon copy of the report was sent to Charles Kivowitz, M.D.

16. Doyle Affidavit, pp. 12–14.

17. Daily Records of Doris Duke, pp. 23–24.

18. Ibid., pp. 24–25.

19. Ibid., p. 25. The list includes Colchicine, Periactin, Epogen, Premarin, Protropin, Dulcolax, Amoxicillin, iron sulfate, Digoxin, Peri-Colace, Cardizem, multivitamins, folic acid, Vitamin K, Zoloft, cefotetan, Neosporin, Prednisone, Ativan, Restoril, Darvocet, meprobamate, TPN 85, Lipids 20%, IV fluids.

20. Second Codicil to Last Will and Testament of Doris Duke, dated March 14, 1993, p. 8.

21. Daily Records of Doris Duke, p. 33.

22. Doyle Affidavit, pp. 20–21.

23. Affidavit of Ann Bostich in Probate Proceeding, Will of Doris Duke, Deceased, pp. 10–12.

24. Doyle Affidavit, p. 21.

25. Ibid., p. 24.

26. Daily Records of Doris Duke, pp. 63–65.

## CHAPTER 16: OH WHAT A TANGLED WEB WE WEAVE . . .

1. Daily records of Doris Duke, p. 20.

2. Deposition of Charles Kivowitz, M.D., Wednesday, April 19, 1995, pp. 1428–1429.

3. Probate Proceeding, Will of DORIS DUKE, Deceased, File No. 4440–93; Affidavit of Colin Shanley, given on January 13, 1995.

4. Statement of Dr. Harry A. Glassman dated May 4, 1995. This statement was found in the Surrogate Court records. However, it was never signed by Dr. Glassman. It was a typed, five-page statement that is not noted as an affidavit, deposition, or other court document. It is presumed to be authentic. It is also presumed to be a statement *not* made under oath.

5. A photocopy of the $500,000 check signed by George Reid presumably on behalf of Doris Duke, whose name is typed over the signature place, was #1002 of the United States Trust Company of New York. U.S. Trust, like many other banks, does not begin checks with #1. Instead, it starts with the number 1001. This means that whenever the account was opened, this was only the second check to be written. By contrast, on September 21, 1993, a check on the Doris Duke account of Chemical Bank on Broadway in New York was issued to Dr. Charles Kivowitz. That check was for $10,000 and the check number was 018344, indicating that many checks had been written on that account. Photocopies of both checks, front and back, were included as exhibits 35 (Glassman) and 38 (Kivowitz) in the volume Exhibits to Report of Richard H. Kuh, Limited Temporary Administrator. This was done for the Surrogate Court Judge Eve Preminger and is listed as File No. 4440/93 in the Probate Proceeding, Will of DORIS DUKE, Deceased.

6. Chronology taken from April 11, 1995, report of Nicholas T. Macris, M.D., 1430 Second Avenue, Suite 102, New York, New York 10021, made to Richard H.

Kuh, Esq., of the law firm Warshaw, Burstein, Cohen, Schlessinger & Kuh concerning the Estate of Doris Duke.

7. Ibid.

8. Ibid., p. 9.

9. Details both from "Chart Setting Forth Drugs Administered to Miss Duke from October 14, 1993 to October 28, 1993" and "Home Chart/Excerpts From Nurse's Notes September 20–October 28, 1993."

10. Report of Dr. Nicholas T. Macris, April 11, 1995, pp. 10–11.

11. Affidavit of Tammy Payette, January 13, 1995, File No. 440–93, State of New York Surrogate's Court, County of New York.

12. Deposition of Charles F. Kivowitz, M.D., Vol. 5, January 12, 1995, p. 911.

13. Tammy Payette would also come to the attention of law enforcement officers after she allegedly stole possessions from one or more of the people who employed her as a nurse. The accusations she made were not the result of a plea bargain to help the case against her, at least as far as can be determined when talking with the authorities. The statement by Dr. Kivowitz concerning his deliberately increasing the morphine in a way that was likely to cause death helps support her honesty in this instance.

14. These and subsequent quotes are from the Tammy Payette Affidavit of January 13, 1995.

15. Quotes from the Affidavit of Colin Shanley, State of New York Surrogate's Court, County of New York, Probate Proceeding, Will of DORIS DUKE, Deceased, File no. 4440–93, p. 41.

16. See note 14, pp. 10–11.

CHAPTER 17: DEAD TO RIGHTS

1. Quotes from *VERIFIED COMPLAINT* Supreme Court of the State of New York County of New York, ANN BOSTICH, MARIANO DE VELASCO and COLIN SHANLEY Plaintiffs, against WILLIAM DOYLE, LEE ANN WATSON, KATTEN MUCHIN & ZAVIS, a partnership and BERNARD (a.k.a. JOHN MASON a.k.a. PETER MALONE) LAFFERTY Defendants, p. 4. (Hereafter cited as Verified Complaint.)

2. Ibid., p. 5.

3. March 6, 1995, letter to Raymond J. Dowd, Esq., Attorney at Law, 277 Broadway, Suite 1010, New York, NY 10007, from Harry B. Demopoulos, M.D. Re: Doris Duke/Physical Therapy for Elizabeth Shanley.

4. Quotes from Verified Complaint, p. 6.

5. Ibid., p. 13.

6. Ibid., pp. 13–15.

7. U.S. Trust Memorandum concerning possible conflict of interest and U.S. Trust Memorandum indicating opinion from outside counsel. These were dated November 22 and November 23, 1993, respectively. Also U.S. Trust cover letters (variously dated) to Bernard Lafferty—November 26, 1993, April 11, 1994, September 16, 1994, October 31, 1994, and January 4, 1995.

8. Exhibits to Report of Richard H. Kuh, Limited Temporary Administrator, State of New York Surrogate's Court, County of New York, Probate Proceeding, Will of DORIS DUKE, Deceased, File no. 4440/93 (hereafter cited as Report of Kuh); E.

Preminger, Surrogate: Sections 15 and 16. Also copy of Exhibit K to Demopoulos Affidavit, pp. RA252–RA 254.

9. Report of Kuh; E. Preminger, Surrogate, p. 12.

10. Traffic Collision Report 194-04957.

11. All prescriptions from Mickey Fine Pharmacy, 433 N. Roxbury Drive, Beverly Hills, California 90210. They were all prescribed by Dr. Michael Horwitz, who felt that Lafferty's prognosis for recovery from the drug addiction was excellent.

12. Report of Kuh; E. Preminger, Surrogate; Section #3.

13. STATE OF NEW YORK SURROGATE'S COURT: COUNTY OF NEW YORK; In the Matter of the Application of the Preliminary Executors of the Estate of Doris Duke for Permission to Make Advance Distributions of Certain Legacies and for the Issuance of Limited Letters of Trusteeship with Respect to Certain Charitable Trusts, under the Will of DORIS DUKE deceased; File no. 4440/93; Affirmation of Raymond J. Dowd, Esq., on Behalf of Ann Bostich, Mariano de Velasco and Colin Shanley in Opposition to a Petition for Selected Advance Distributions by the Preliminary Co-Executors; dated January 12, 1994.

CHAPTER 18: DEATH AND SUSPICION

1. Deposition of Charles P. Kivowitz, M.D., Vol. 5, January 12, 1995, p. 911.

2. Probate Proceeding, Will of DORIS DUKE, Deceased, Vol. I (pp. 1–208); 1404, Examination of CHARLES FREDERICK KIVOWITZ, M.D., taken on behalf of the Defendant JONES, at 711 South Hope, Room Malibu A, Los Angeles, California, commencing at 1:06 P.M., Wednesday, January 4, 1995, pp. 83–84.

3. Ibid., p. 84.

4. Ibid.

5. Ibid., Vol. 2, January 5, 1995, pp. 241–242.

6. Ibid., p. 243.

7. Ibid., Part 5, January 12, 1995, p. 867.

8. Ibid., p. 868.

9. Ibid.

10. Ibid., p. 869.

11. Ibid., pp. 873–874.

12. Taped interviews with Dr. Mel Kirschner (10/11/95) and Vicki Michelle (10/11/95 and 10/12/96).

13. Report of Richard H. Kuh, Limited Temporary Administrator; State of New York Surrogate's Court, County of New York; Probate Proceeding, Will of DORIS DUKE, Deceased, File no. 4440/93 (hereafter cited as Report of Kuh); E. Preminger, Surrogate, p. Section 37 of the Exhibits.

14. Section 37 of the Exhibits to the Report of Kuh, pp. 29–30.

15. Affidavit of Ann Bostich in Probate Proceeding, Will of DORIS DUKE, Deceased, pp. 20–21.

16. Ibid., pp. 21–22.

17. Exhibits to Report of Kuh, Section 9.

18. Ibid., Section 11.

19. Ibid., Sections 26 and 27.

20. Ibid., Section 27.

# Index

Rodin, Odile, 178
Roland, Gilbert, 164
Roller derby, 16
Romania, 214–15
*Rome Daily American, The,* 156
Roosevelt, Eleanor, 131, 147
Roosevelt, Franklin D., 104, 107, 108,
    126, 127, 129, 131, 132–33, 133,
    134, 136, 140, 141
Roosevelt, Kermit, 144
Rosenstein, Pearl, 264, 266, 279, 286,
    287, 288, 315, 329
Rough Point, 51–52, 103
  debut of Doris at, 82
  described, 222–24
  lawsuit to gain control of, 74
  restoration of, 179–80
Rubinstein, Howard J., 290
Rubirosa, Porfirio, 151–61, 199
  as ambassador to Argentina,
    159–60
  as assassin, 151, 152
  death of, 178–79
  described, 151
  divorce from Doris Duke, 160–61
  Jews of Vichy France and, 153
  as lover, 151, 158, 159, 160, 161,
    178–79
  marriages:
    to Danielle Darrieux, 153–54,
      155
    to Doris Duke, 154–61, 170–71,
      324
    to Barbara Hutton, 169–70,
      171
    to Trujillo's daughter, 152, 153
  obituary, 170
Rush, George, 319
Rusk Institute for Rehabilitative Med-
    icine, 294
Russell, Bertrand, 48–49
Ryan, Ann, 302
Rybak, Tom, 41, 214, 231, 312
  Chandi's relationship with Doris
    Duke and, 202, 237
  as Doris Duke's chef, 222–26,
    228–29, 239
  extent of duties, 230–31
  hiring of, 219–22
  professional relationship, 225–26

  resigns, 232–34
  salary, 222
  Lafferty and, 227–34, 297

St. Regis Hotel, 38
Saks Fifth Avenue, 178
*Sandpiper, The,* 176
Sands, Nellie, 24–26
*San Jose Mercury News,* 208
Saretta, Phyllis "Phaedra," 198
Sargent, John Singer, 224
*Saturday Evening Post,* 169
Savoy Records, 184
Scribner's Sons, Charles, 107
Scripps-Howard newspaper chain,
    110
Seabra, Nelson, 298
Secondhand smoke, 55
Segregation, racial, 10–11, 66–67
Self-Realization Fellowship, 171, 172,
    179
Semens, Mary Duke Biddle Trent,
    174
Serling, Rod, 204
Severance, John L., 96–97
Severances, 96
Shainwald, Mrs. Ralph, 37
Shangri-La, 142, 198–99, 217, 225
  art used to furnish, 120–23, 176
  construction of, 121
  estate valuation of, 122
  last visits by Duke to, 278
  musicians hanging out at, 163
  naming of, 127
  planning of, 127
  property for, 127
  during World War II, 143
Shanley, Colin, 272–74, 278–79, 289,
    299, 312, 313–16
  as Doris Duke's chef, 238, 239,
    240–43, 315–16
  on Doris Duke's mental status,
    261–62
  employment agreement, action for
    breach of, 293–96, 298, 314–15,
    323
  on Lafferty's household role,
    240–43
  mother of, 294–95, 312, 315